The Political Appropriation of the Muslim Body

Susan S. M. Edwards

The Political Appropriation of the Muslim Body

Islamophobia, Counter-Terrorism Law and Gender

palgrave
macmillan

Susan S. M. Edwards
London, UK

ISBN 978-3-030-68895-0   ISBN 978-3-030-68896-7   (eBook)
https://doi.org/10.1007/978-3-030-68896-7

This Palgrave Macmillan imprint is published by the registered company Springer Nature Switzerland AG
The registered company address is: Gewerbestrasse 11, 6330 Cham, Switzerland

Dedicated to those who stand up, speak out and brave the tide to turn it

PREFACE

John Keating, the inspirational and unorthodox teacher of English literature, played by Robin Williams, in the film, *Dead Poets Society* 1989, jumps up on his desk and addressing his students explains:

> "Why do I stand up here? Anybody?
> I stand on my desk to remind myself that we must constantly look at things in a different way...".

Hannah Arendt, in *The Human Condition* (1958), spoke of the moral obligation and freedom to think otherwise. Looking, thinking and seeing otherwise, in this moment in time, is my purpose. There are number of influences that have directed this writing project, personal, political and scholarly which, contiguously and contrapuntally, intersect in making sense of the present problem I see and experience. I am mindful of Arendt's warning that the passions are no substitute for rational argument, but, at the same time, there is no politics that is completely devoid of emotion. This is the time to speak up, to act and to write. The anti-Muslim discourse and its real impact on the lives of men and women who are Muslim I see as a major ignominy of our time. This is the moment to speak out about the racialisation of Muslim men and women and Muslim communities. To be silent is to be complicit. It is true, that recognising the racialisation of the Muslim community, the acts perpetrated against them: torture in Guantánamo Bay, women's headscarf's being pulled from their heads in the streets, vile words spoken online and much more provides a trigger for my writing intervention. Empathy may drive my commitment, but it does not compromise my documentation of the evidence of the assault on the Muslim corporeal body. My disquiet is personal, arising from a commitment to challenging racism in all its forms and because of my connectedness, through marriage to the Middle East and to the Muslim faith and so I watch on and over more carefully, as over the years this racialisation has shifted its predominant marker from region, country, nationality, language, race, colour and now to faith. I have watched the Western forays into Arab Muslim countries in pursuit of nothing more than self-interest and the West's appropriation of the law, at every level, to fortify its assault. I bear witness to the racialisation of family, friends and those who identify with the Muslim faith. And so, the "personal is the political" and the political *is* very personal. I shrink at every attack by ISIS and Islamic terrorists or when a man or woman of Muslim faith attacks or kills others, not only do I consider the impact on the victims and their families but also because I know that there will be revengeance on every Muslim, everywhere. I contemplate the wider consequences of such revengeance for my daughters and their daughters and sons, tomorrow and after. Subject position imposes itself, of course, on what I see and perceive and what I say and write. As Edward Said wrote "…no production of knowledge in the human science can ever ignore or disclaim its author's involvement as a human subject in his own circumstances" (cited in Bayoumi and Rubin (ed) 2001:77). There is every reason to be suspect, of writers who write from the margins, and to be suspicious of their motive, purpose and vantage point. I will let the text speak for itself and the reader be the judge.

I do not agree that only those who are the subject of an injustice, prejudice and discrimination have the right to speak. Jacqueline Rose addresses this question when defending Sylvia Plath who was criticised for the way in which she made reference to the holocaust in her poetry. Rose says of Plath that she speaks figuratively and that she does not "[steal] the historical event" (2011:259) but was trying to find a way of connecting (2013). I understand too the concerns of those who regard the outsider's speech as a symbolic theft of the narrative from authentic voices. I make no claim to be the authentic voice, nor do I steal another's space.

But there is a very grave harm in silence, a grave harm in apathy and a grave harm in indifference. Cornel West in his 2018 lecture "Speaking Truth to Power" reflects on the words of Rabbi Abraham Joshua Heschel, who wrote: "Indifference to evil is more insidious than evil itself. It is a silent justification affording evil acceptability in society" (at 16.31-3 minutes). Hannah Arendt in *Between Past and Future* (2006) similarly warned of the danger of moral neutrality. This book is none of those things. It is a clarion call to reject apathy, to speak out, and to take a stand. Such responsibility has been urged by so many writers. Frantz Fanon, in *Black Skin, White Masks* (1952) pleads "Oh my body, *make of me a man* who always *questions!*"

The questioning that drives this book has been rising for several decades, emerging from segmented screenshots, past freeze frames: my field trip to the American University in Cairo, when as a Ph.D. student I set out to explore the gender politics of sexual abuse in Middle Eastern societies. My own marriage under UK law inducted me into the masculinism and discriminatory nature of UK citizenship law demonstrating that my biological sex would deny me rights that British men had as of right. I have watched, and witnessed in so many ways the subtleties, nuances and blatancies of discrimination on the grounds of sex, gender, class, race, colour, nation and now religion and being Muslim comes to the fore. The concerns set out in these pages that have preoccupied my thinking have also developed whilst teaching in lecture halls in the UK, US, the Caribbean, Australia, Europe, Asia, Africa, Japan and the Middle East, in workshops, conferences, with students, colleagues and with activists, as together we have charted, trailed, tracked and documented the politics of sex and gender, minorities, faith, representation, human rights, the rule of law, counter-terror law, racism, criminal justice, criminal law, representation and cultural discourse and their relevance to this defilement of the corporeal Muslim body.

During the period of writing Brexit and "Brexit extremism" and "Trumpism" has been a brooding omnipresence, with its stirring up of dangerous factions and divisions and celebration of "us" and "them". The outbreak of the deadly Coronavirus disease in 2019 (COVID-19) has changed our lives, exacerbating the existing divisions in health, economic and educational life chances and enforcing isolation, impacting domestic violence, mental health, poverty and survival. Covid is now being used as an excuse to legitimate and rush through highly questionable legislation that will impact detrimentally on freedom and challenge the Rule of Law. In February 2020, the extension of prison terms for those already serving prison sentences for "terrorist related offences" was hastily introduced (Terrorist Offenders (Restriction of Early Release) Act 2020). This was followed swiftly by the Counter-Terrorism and Sentencing Bill in May 2020 primed to introduce harsher measures which will disproportionately impact Muslim men and women, and in September 2020 the Covert Human Intelligence Sources (Criminal Conduct) Bill, when passed will remove vital oversight and accountability of undercover police officers and their operations affecting us all.

In October 2020 two Muslim women were stabbed under the Eiffel Tower "by white women shouting, 'dirty Arabs' 'Go home to your own country'". Two women wearing a headscarf were attacked on a London tube station, racially abused and physically assaulted. Such incidents although frequent are little reported. By contrast, the public anxiety over terrorism remains high and the random stabbings in June 2020 of six victims in Glasgow (all of whom survived) in a hotel housing 91 asylum seekers, was responded to as a terrorist incident, and received worldwide publicity. The attacker was shot dead. Few inquired about the mental health of asylum seekers during Covid lockdown. Attacks on Muslims in the physical and online world have continued to increase since 9/11 and peak whenever there is a terrorist incident anywhere in the world as if such acts of terrorism gives reprise permission to attack any Muslim. Covid's enforced isolation has demanded new ways of working and more time is spent online where algorithms creating echo bubbles foment hate speech, and ineffective regulation of the web leaves racism against all communities largely unchecked.

It is a time for conscience. Jack Shaheen, in the Foreword to Leans' second edition of *The Islamophobia Industry* (2017), heralds Lean's book as an example of "conscience driven leadership" which inspires "people of good will" to stand up and end divisive forces. There is, said the late Tony Benn (2005), an obligation to think for oneself no matter the consequences. It is a time, as Raymond Williams (1958:376) writes, for the "unlearning" of "the inherent dominative mode". Their pleadings are all apposite. It is a time too for empathy, though "We may not have enough courage to display it" (Maya Angelou). The real apology would be to do nothing. And in embracing the Rose linguistic turn in her interpretation of Plath, of whom and in her defence, Rose (2013) says: "Plath did not appropriate the sufferings of others, instead their sufferings appropriated her" (at 39.12 minutes) in that same linguistic and figurative turn, I say that the West's war on

Muslims at every level and their corporeal hurt has appropriated me. We have a choice. So, in returning to John Keating "I stand on my desk".

London, UK   Susan S. M. Edwards
December 2020

REFERENCES

Arendt, H. 1988/1958. *The Human Condition*. Chicago: The University of Chicago Press.
Arendt, H. 2006/1961. *Between Past and Future*. London: Penguin.
Bayoumi, M. and Rubin, A. [eds]. 2001/2000. *The Edward Said Reader*. London: Granta.
Benn, T. 2005. *Dare to be Daniel*. New York: Random House.
Dead Poets Society. 1989. Director: Peter Weir.
Fanon, F. 2008/1952. *Black Skin, White Masks*. New York: Grove Press Atlantic Monthly Press.
Lean N. 2017/2012. *The Islamophobia Industry*. London: Pluto.
Rose, J. 2011. *The Jaqueline Rose Reader*, ed. J. Clemens and B. Naparstek. Durham and London: Duke University Press.
Rose, J. 2013. Jacqueline Rose on Zionism, Freud, Sylvia Plath and more. Melbourne Writers Festival 2013 in a series of events from the London Review of Books. https://www.youtube.com/watch?v=D-qyuEBL0-o. Accessed 11 November 2020.
West, C. 2018. Cornel West "Speaking Truth to Power." https://www.you tube.com/watch?v=-Bc6TRjptKI at 16.31-3 minutes. Accessed 11 November 2020.
Williams, R. 1958. *Culture and Society*. London: Hogarth Press.

CONTENTS

CHAPTER 1

Introduction

Who Speaks? Who Can Be Heard?

Dale Spender in *Man Made Language* (1980) in speaking to the gendered exclusion of women sets out her thesis in which she argues that men control language and meaning and impose their view on the world. Catherine MacKinnon in *Only Words* (1993: 5) speaks of how the social and political worlds construct a woman's lack of place. "You learn that language does not belong to you, that you cannot use it to say what you know, that language is not what you learn from your life, that information is not made out of your own experience". Gilligan (2016 [1983]) talks of this "lack of place", because one speaks in a different voice.

There are other exclusions. Robert J.C. Young when speaking of the colonial erasure in *Postcolonialism* (2003: 1) asks this question of his audience:

> Have you ever felt that the moment you said 'I', that 'I' was someone else and not you? That is some small way, you were not the subject of your own sentence? Do you ever feel that whenever you speak, you have already in some sense been spoken for? Or that when you hear others speaking, that you are only ever going to be the object of their speech?... How can we find a way to talk about this?

Spivak (1988) identifies the problem of "being spoken for" as the experience of all women, and especially women of the "third world", and

© The Author(s), under exclusive license to Springer Nature Switzerland AG 2021
S. S. M. Edwards, *The Political Appropriation of the Muslim Body*, https://doi.org/10.1007/978-3-030-68896-7_1

migrant and diaspora women living in the West and women of colour, where their experience is a multiply layered exclusion. Crenshaw (2016, 2017 [1997]) uses the concept of intersectionality to understand the several configurations of women's experience. Understanding and challenging the structural and ideological forces which instantiate the "not you" and "not I" has been a preoccupation of "Third wave feminism" Spivak (1988, 2006), Saadawi (1997), Carby (1997). Carby (51) goes further and notes that Western discourses by eschewing non-Western voices "are acting within the relations of racism". Malia Bouattia laments that similar exclusion strategies are still played out in 2020, and speaking of the experience of Muslim women writes: "Muslim women, we are told, must be rescued, celebrated, and brought into the fold" but only "on the basis of our own voices remaining absent. We are not part of the conversation" (2020: 210). As I set out in the Preface, I will not take the space of other voices, what I will do as a woman on the margins of the Muslim experience, through marriage and family connections, is to document the ideological and political forces that have "Othered" and excluded the Muslim voice and document the material consequences for the lives of Muslim men and women.

How the West has essentialised, spoken for, decided and represented "the Muslim", through biased and self-serving racialisations, is a central consideration of this work. These tropes and denegations are not only "constative", that is to say, not merely descriptive narratives about Muslims but are "performative" in the impact they have on Muslim lives individually, collectively and militarily. Such duplicitous representations have precipitated, orchestrated and incited anti-Muslim racism on the streets and in the digital world, and provided the scripts that have in part assisted in justifying and condoning Western state lawlessness for example in the "War on Terror" (WOT) in the name of "securitisation" and on the domestic front in the introduction of counter-terror laws that have suspended human rights and directed their force particularly on Muslim communities. Racialised characterisations of "the Muslim" male have characterised justifications appropriated by US military excusing their brutality and torture of Muslim detainees held in Guantánamo Bay, Cuba and the sexual abuse of Iraqi prisoners in Abu Ghraib prison, Iraq. Western powers deftly appropriate such negative tropes to assist their territorial expansionism in the Middle East (Atwan 2015), and as the UN Special Rapporteur, Richard Falk (2014) has also pointed out, to support Israel's continuing occupation of the occupied territories. That is not to ignore the attacks on Western states by ISIS and Islamic terrorists since 9/11, most recently in Vienna 2020, and attacks across the world, including in Syria and parts of Iraq and elsewhere, but these terrorising events have been appropriated by Western powers to essentialise all Muslims and Arabs.

CONTESTED TERMS

I use the nomenclature "racism" to speak of the Western assault on Muslims. Stuart Hall in a lecture delivered in 1987 (1996: 443) had already identified how being "Muslim" had come to function as a racial category. In his theorisation of race as a "floating signifier" he articulates the emergence of "new ethnicities" and sets out how the binaries of black/white, us/them, have reconfigured to re-emerge through religious signifiers. I use the term "Islamophobia" throughout this book, to refer to a calcified denigration, at all levels and in all institutions and modes of thought, of Muslim men, women and their communities. I recognise that it is a contested term and I understand why. Lean remarking on the several protracted debates describes this as a "laborious and ceaseless pursuit" (Lean 2019: 11) since "Islamophobia" is generally understood to mean thought, practices, acts and conduct that is anti-Muslim. Certainly, as to the literal meaning of "phobia" psychoanalysis has clearly defined it within the family of neuroses. "Phobia is a neurosis characterized by the anxious fear of an object (in the broadest sense of anything outside the individual) or by extension of a situation" (cited in Fanon 2008 [1952]). Those on the right who reject the term fear that acceptance of it will limit anti-Muslim speech (discussed in Chapter 3). However, there are also some on the left who oppose the term and have campaigned against its usage and against the definition of "Islamophobia" agreed by the All-Party Parliamentary Group on British Muslims (APPGBM), "Islamophobia is rooted in racism and is a type of racism that targets expressions of Muslimness or perceived Muslimness", on the basis that to accept it might prohibit criticism of the more conservative elements within Muslim communities. I understand this concern especially voiced by those who have experienced the forces of religious conservatism, particularly in non-Western countries where religious theocracy dictates, and the fear that their critique of fundamentalist and conservative forces within these countries and within diasporic commentaries living in the West will be shut down. Maryam Namazie (2019) for example is concerned with those ultraconservative forces and says of the Muslim right that "Muslimness tends to exclude doubters and dissenters – anyone not 'authentically' regressive enough, not veiled enough, not segregated enough, not submissive enough, not pro-Sharia enough, not modest enough, not angry enough and not offended enough".

In rejection of the APPG definition, John Jenkins and Trevor Phillips (2018) in their response entitled *Defining Islamophobia* are not only critical of the definition but also scathing of those who have devised it. "Unfortunately, the APPG's confused report *Islamophobia Defined* demonstrate that its authors appear to understand neither the concept of racism nor the meaning of Islamophobia" (6). Jenkins and Phillips query, "...would the prohibition of the niqab become an example of 'anti-Muslim racism'?" (6). They also consider that since the "Home Secretary is of Pakistani Muslim heritage; [and] ... the winner of The Great British Bake Off, can be a hijab-wearing second generation Bangladeshi immigrant" then such examples are sufficient evidence to demonstrate that the UK is "open to Muslims". However, applying this same logic to Margaret Thatcher her elevation as the UK's first female Prime Minister did not alter the structural gender inequality, nor did it ensure that equality for all women would be protected. In a similar vein Israel's support for LBGTI in what has been described as "pink washing" cannot be taken as the barometer on its democracy. Others who oppose the proposed definition, and here I include some feminists on the left, have considered it would amount to "privileging of a certain kind of victimhood".

As my focus is primarily on Western discourse and representation of Muslims, I tend to agree with Lean that whatever the debates about its etymology they do not undercut the basic spirit of the word as it is most deployed. I will be using the terms "Islamophobia", and anti-Muslim prejudice interchangeably. However, I will not be shutting down critical debate on the problem of religious conservatism in non-Western countries which I address in Chapter 8. So, by "Islamophobia" I adopt the definition of the Runnymede Trust first devised in 1997 and developed in 2017 "Islamophobia is any distinction, exclusion, or restriction towards, or preference against, Muslims (or those perceived to be Muslims) that has the purpose or effect of nullifying or impairing the recognition, enjoyment, or exercise, on an equal footing of human rights and fundamental freedoms in the political, economic, social, cultural or any other field of public life" (1) (See also House of Commons debate 2019). The racialisation of Islam and being a Muslim is reflected in this self-scrutinising example from Ed Vulliamy, who when writing on the Bosnian genocide, asks a man: "Are you a Muslim or a Bosnian Croat?" to which the man replies: "No, I am a musician!". "Muslim" is insinuated into Western ways of seeing, thinking, perception and consciousness, it becomes the marker. No longer is the question "But where are you from?" with its pejorative undertone by those searching for an "us" or "them" clarification, instead: "What religion are you?" has come to dominate the us/them inquiry.

Such racism also insinuates itself in the level of the psyche of the racialised subject in how he/she perceives himself/herself in relation to the world. Identity is also grounded in a context of how others perceive and construct us. Fanon theorised that "negritude" is a product of the white man's gaze (2008 [1952]). James Baldwin said of black people, "...you believed you belong where white people have put you" (Baldwin "Cambridge Union Speech 1965": at 1.40 minutes). In much the same way Esposito observes: "Islamophobia dictates the prisms through which Muslims are viewed" (cited by Shaheen in Lean 2017: xv). Kazim Ali in *The Coloniser and the Colonised* describes being trapped in the identity of the suspect by the "violence in [his accuser's] heart" (cited in Breen-Smyth 2014: 234).

As for Muslim women rigid Western stereotypes are imposed upon her, and women who wear the headscarf/hijab and who wear makeup are often confronted for breaking the Western-imposed stereotype (Gani 2020: 140). Such fixity and demands of Muslim female appearance by Western others give them, so they think, permission to discipline. The female Muslim body and its visibility have made women a target for street vigilantes. Muslim women are spat at, have their headscarf's torn from their heads are verbally abused (Perry 2014) physically assaulted (Hussein 2019: 87) and even when pregnant then kicked in the head (see CNN News Australia 2019). In Canada, in November 2020, Bill 21, the religious symbols ban prohibiting headscarfs, is being contested in the courts, as such legislation has a disproportionate impact on Muslim communities. Meanwhile, crimes committed against Muslim women are underreported and hidden, whilst Muslim male criminal suspects are highly newsworthy feeding the unremittingly pathologisation of the Muslim male subject in public discourse (Hussein: 87). In documenting this preoccupation with her body I ask how has "this" particular body become positioned at the centre of the West/East binaries of civilised/uncivilised, secularism/fundamentalism, where "her" Muslim body is now no longer regarded as a symbol of religious piety, or passivity but an emblem of

Islamic extremism and resistance. To call all this malevolence against Muslims, to "tell it like it is", to condemn it and try to limit it by naming it "Islamophobia" is hardly "privileging of a certain kind of victimhood".

A MORAL RESPONSIBILITY

What is the responsibility of scholars, of academics and of political activists to this Muslim misrepresentation, discrimination and maltreatment? Noam Chomsky (1967) in answering this question says responsibility demands insisting on the truth, providing historical context and challenging distorted ideology.

> The responsibility of intellectuals [is] to speak the truth and to expose lies. This, at least, may seem enough of a truism to pass over without comment ...Intellectuals are in a position to expose the lies of governments, to analyse actions according to their causes and motives and often hidden intentions. In the Western world, at least, they have the power that comes from political liberty, from access to information and freedom of expression. For a privileged minority, Western democracy provides the leisure, the facilities, and the training to seek the truth lying hidden behind the veil of distortion and misrepresentation, ideology and class interest, through which the events of current history are presented to us. (cited in Smith and Smith 2019: 7)

Edward Said's 1993 Reith Lecture, *Representations of the Intellectual*, echoes Chomsky's conviction, for Said, intellectual responsibility lies in the importance of exposing those sources of power and authoritarianism that distort truth. As Spivak (1988: 280) recognises: "[W]hat Said emphasizes [is] the critic's institutional responsibility". Feminism, broadly speaking, has also been concerned with interrogating and challenging the so-called truth and especially destabilising the fallacy of the male claim that the male view of the world is an objective truth. Feminist legal scholarship, for example, has exposed the masculinism within structures of law and thinking about law and rights. Lahey demonstrates how legal theory and legal reasoning itself is masculinist (1991: 3) whilst Charlesworth and Chinkin (2002) show how the laws of the "international state" have failed to take account of women or to recognise violence against women both in times of peace and in times of war and argue that from all perspectives discrimination against women is deeply embedded in institutions, institutional practices and modes of thought as women are absent from participation in decision-making and governance.

PRIVILEGED DISCOURSES

But feminism is diverse in its politics, participation, activism and theorising. Some feminism(s), especially mainstream or "white feminism" as Carby (1997) and Bouattia (2020), amongst many others, point out, has also been part of the problem of privileging Western, white and class privileged discourse, whilst excluding and essentialising non-Western women and women of colour. Mariam Khan goes further and makes the point that since some feminism and some feminists "disapprove[s] of the hijab, the burqa, modest culture and other key aspects of the Muslim identity" then *Feminism Needs to die!* (2020: 105).

There is of course no uniform Muslim female or uniform Muslim identity. Muslim women in non-Western countries across the world have different histories and experiences. Western Muslim diaspora comprise different races, colour, sexuality, politics, ethnicity, class, communities, from the world over, Europe, Africa, the Middle East and other regions, and Muslims who are second-generation have parents and grandparents with these same diverse backgrounds. Crenshaw (2016, 2017 [1997]) insists on the importance of understanding and responding to the intersectionality of women's and men's experience locally, regionally, nationally and the multiple identities as they intersect with race, class, gender, sexuality and LGBTQI, and the myriad of other ways in which life is experienced and structured. This is important here too. Importantly Crenshaw (2016) identifies the structured nature of prior defined frameworks of thinking, which foreclose a particular recognition of the world whilst at the same time orientating as authentic a particular way of seeing and construction as legitimate. These prior defined frameworks and their role and responsibility in and for exclusion have been explored by many writers. Judith Butler in *Gender Trouble* (1999 [1990]: vii) examines the pervasive heterosexual assumptions which limit the meaning of gender to received notions of masculinity and femininity, privileging heteronormativity.

This work then is written from a counter-narrative position and refutes the essentialist imposition of a singular identity which Bernard Lewis in his thesis *The Roots of Muslim Rage* (1990) and Samuel Huntington in the

Clash of Civilisations (1993) are want to present with their monochromatic vision of Islam and Muslims. Instead, I document the fomented Western rage directed at "the Muslim" and at "the Arab" with its reductionist understanding of those of Islamic faith, of Arabs, and those with Muslim connections. In this undertaking I take as my lead Edward Said's reply to Huntington in his article "The Clash of Ignorance":

> Certainly neither Huntington nor Lewis has much time to spare for the internal dynamics and plurality of every civilization, or for the fact that the major contest in most modern cultures concerns the definition or interpretation of each culture, or for the unattractive possibility that a great deal of demagogy and downright ignorance is involved in presuming to speak for a whole religion or civilization. No, the West is the West, and Islam, Islam. (Said 2001: 12)

Such an examination demands an analysis of the interrelationship between power and what passes for "knowledge", and in this case requires an analysis of how Western power imposes its own preferred version of "arrogated knowledge" extolling it as an "objective world view" whilst at the same time silencing, marginalising and discrediting other viewpoints and perspectives. One such example is found in the UK government's counter-terrorism "Prevent" programme, which, until successfully challenged in the courts in 2019, defined "extremism" as "a vocal and active opposition to fundamental British values" (see Chapter 5). Meanwhile such alternative or critical viewpoints, those that Foucault calls "subjugated knowledge" (Foucault 1976, cited in Gordon 1980: 82, see also Jackson 2012) are branded insurrectionary. This "subjugated knowledge" is that knowledge which James Baldwin in describing the black experience said was "unspoken by the subjugated... never said to the master" (1965: at 0.40 minutes). The suppression of the counter-narrative is an all-pervasive, deliberate and political act. Vulliamy documents how the American *Observer* newspaper refused to run his stories in the lead-up to the invasion of, and during the war in Iraq, from 2002 onwards, in which his main storyline focused on the false intelligence and non-existence of weapons of mass destruction. John Simpson's (2012) efforts at truth-telling were also recalibrated and when reporting on the Bosnian war he recalls an American correspondent showing him an email from the foreign editor instructing him in the future to concentrate only on the "Serbs" and the "Muslims" and omit any reference to the "Croats". "The

Muslim" is continuously manufactured through Western eyes, fortified by negative representation which in turn manufacture and reproduce the conditions for, and justification of, "Islamophobia" or anti-Muslim racism which Lean (2017), Kundnani (2015), Zempi and Awan (eds) (2019), amongst many others, have documented. Call it what you will, but do not undercut the basic spirit of the words nor become so costive that those trying to expose what is happening, become estopped or derided.

ACADEMIC DISCIPLINES AND METHODOLOGY

A word on methodology. The "rules of the game" within the social sciences, philosophy, law and other subject areas have been built on schematisation and the development of disciplines, and sub disciplines, which like modern algorithmic echo bubbles have remained largely hermetically sealed, where boundaries are policed and controlled by experts within a specialism where interlopers are resented and excluded. Such boundary rules and presumptions are rejected here as limiting and an interdisciplinary cross-cutting perspective is required. This subject of study is complex and requires both an intersectional framework and an interdisciplinary approach. "Islamophobia" or anti-Muslim racism has now become a study and a sub-discipline, where intellectual, political and academic scholarship and activism meet, from the fields of law, international law, international relations, journalism, media, power and politics, criminology and sociology, psychology, gender studies, feminism and cultural representation. In an attempt to engage with this expansive landscape omissions are inevitable, but I trust that the reader will forgive the flaws in such a cross-cutting undertaking.

This work began as a concern with the Western all-consuming vilification of Muslim women and their body and appearance and the efforts by the law to press a particular "framing" of the Muslim female body, and in this sense I borrow Helena Kennedy's (1993) locution from the title of her study of gender, women and the law "Eve was Framed". The pathologisation of the Muslim male as offender and suspect terrorist became a concern after 9/11 as did the representation of all Muslim men following the Rochdale child abuse cases by British men of Pakistani origin in 2012. These concerns were also being paralleled since 9/11 with the merging counter-terror legislation and its erosion of human rights (Edwards 2008, 2010a, b). These several strands were brought together by my ongoing research work on gender and on counter-terrorism and also in the Middle

East including my visit to Iran in 2010 to present a paper at the International Conference on Multiculturalism and Global Community 24–27 on the hijab (Edwards 2010c). Together with my own personal experience as a woman with Muslim family connections I began to document the several ways in which this anti-Muslim racism manifested and operated and has come to determine the experience of Muslims living in the West especially since 9/11. It has become a subject about which I can no longer remain silent.

THE DOCUMENTATION

The documentation unfolds over eight chapters including this one which examine the cultural, social and legal forms and material consequences that underpin this anti-Muslim agenda. In Chapter 2, I set out the background and history of "Islamophobic" or anti-Muslim tropes and their contiguity in the present. Islamophobia and anti-Muslim sentiment existed long before 9/11, albeit that for some 9/11 precipitated an acceleration in Western military interference, the WOT and anti-Muslim sentiment. The origin of the cultural production of Arab and Muslim society and its peoples has a legacy rooted especially in British and French colonialism and in the manufacture and reproduction of a discourse which is embedded in culture and institutions about the people and societies of the East, of Arabs and Muslims. No one else has better identified and articulated this historic tendency and contemporary configurations than Edward Said, who, through analysis of cultural and institutional forms, described what he regarded as a Western mindset, which he named "Orientalism". This denoted a perceptual universe, in which the Muslim man was, and still is, perceived through Western linguistic descriptors and in all forms of cultural and political production as "savage" and "barbaric", and the Muslim woman essentialised as "passive", "suborned" and "sexualised". Reiterated and further exaggerated at this moment in time, these stereotypes have added to this catalogue a terrorist, extremist and radicalisation turn.

Whilst such images functioned as justifications for Western domination in erstwhile colonial times, they continue to function as ideological drivers in recent Western "civilising" missions in for example, Afghanistan and Iraq, this time underpinned by an ideological and messianic quest to "save Muslim women" from Muslim men. Since 9/11, the "barbaric"

Muslim male trope has become re-envisioned in Western cultural production and in policy, politics and law, and hardened in the Western mind. The barbaric depiction has made way for the appropriation of discourses of denial (see Cohen 2001) exonerating the US's use of torture against Muslim foreign nationals captured overseas and imprisoned in Guantánamo Bay, Cuba (Chapter 6). Such depictions have influenced new thinking on "securitisation" and positioned as necessary the suspension of human rights protections for foreign national terrorist suspects (Muslims) (Chapter 5) and in some circumstances suspended human rights for all. As for the trope of the passive Muslim woman, suborned without agency, since 9/11 this continues to act as a blueprint for understanding especially those women living under Taliban rule in Afghanistan, the House of Saud in Saudi Arabia and under the mullahs in Iran (Chapter 8). However Muslim women diaspora and second-generation Muslims or those of Muslim descent living in the West, who wear Islamic dress are now perceived rather differently, where covering with the headscarf (hijab) or face veil (niqab) once considered evidence of a backward and inferior culture, is now in some cases read as a statement of rejection of Western "host" culture and an indicator of suspect terrorist leanings (Hussein 2019).

Anti-Muslim tropes are continuously implanted into our social, political and neural networks, shaping cognitive thinking like cyborgs, and prejudice is "designed in" by the systems, signs, signatures and meaning of language which in turn condition our responses. The perpetual reinforcing of particular tropes, and so-called "knowledge" through repetition in closed echo chambers promulgates a Manichean world of "us" and "Muslims" where: "Violence is the primary lens through which Muslims and Arabs are portrayed" (Shaheen in Lean 2017: xxi). Chapter 2 then is not merely a debate with Said's "Orientalism" thesis, it is also a demonstration of its contemporary relevance, forming a backdrop for the political and material reality of anti-Muslim sentiment that it shapes and the West's continuing imperialism and quest for world domination. Said's gendered occlusion is infilled with my own detailing of the Orientalist tropes of Eastern women that are manifest in literature, anthropology and in cultural and artistic forms which continue to resonate with a contemporary relevance.

Chapter 3 examines the contemporary ideological production and reproduction of these Orientalist narratives in their "constative" configuration and their "performative" impacts within public and political discourse, redolent in the speech of politicians and public figures, journalists and commentators, recurrent in newspapers and on the streets and in the digital world. Prime Ministers and Presidents have engaged in leading, shaping and defining the parameters and shifting the limits of permissible speech about Muslims. Negative stereotypes, ridicule and, to a lesser extent, hate speech has been defended by the appropriation of human rights law and the banner of freedom of speech. The ubiquity of anti-Muslim speech in contemporary politics including Brexit and "Trump extremism" together with identity discourses driven by an "us and them" mentality has further emboldened far-right groups and led to an escalation in assaults on Muslims, a rise in online hate crime and a corresponding fear and sense of exclusion within Muslim communities. Such stereotypes "injure innocent people often permanently" (Shaheen in Lean 2017: xx).

Chapter 4 explores the West's claim to an unswerving deference to the "Rule of Law" (ROL) and its values of freedom, equality, good governance, democracy and basic human rights for all, which it proclaims it is eager to export. Yet, deliberation on the ROL reveals its malleability, capriciousness and adulteration by Western state power. Misappropriation of the ROL has led to its misuse to justify war, defend territorial ambitions especially in "War on Terror" (WOT) campaigns. So, for example, the international ROL was invoked when the UK invaded Iraq yet eschewed when Iraqi detainees were abused by US troops, and when Baha Mousa was unlawfully killed by British Army officers. The international ROL is simultaneously appropriated and eschewed when the legitimacy of the occupation of Palestine is considered. Mike Pompeo, in 2019, when rejecting the 2016 United Nations resolution stated: "After carefully studying all sides of the legal debate, this administration agrees with President Reagan [who, back in 1980, expressed a similar sentiment]. The establishment of Israeli civilian settlements in the West Bank is not per se inconsistent with international law" (Borger and Holmes 2019).

Chapter 5 considers the operation of the ROL in the UK and how its norms have been set aside by the need for enhanced securitisation where counter-terrorism law since 9/11, compromises justice and due process. The legislative response to 9/11 has authorised an inventory of new law aimed at enhanced prevention, detection and punishment of "terrorist related activity" albeit vaguely defined. The Counter-Terrorism and Sentencing Bill 2020 especially, as Cornford (2020) argues, has condoned "chilling" limitations on freedoms. Executive power has been vastly extended, wresting decision-making power from Parliament and from the judiciary, riding roughshod over human rights and civil liberties and where intrusive surveillance is sanctioned. Such measures are informed by so-called "intelligence" which draws on a dubious profiling based on Orientalist tropes, stereotypes and prejudices where Muslims are suspected and essentialised and read through a terror lens. Laws have been devised to criminalise thought, creating "mind crimes", limiting dissident challenges which are no longer voices considered essential to democracy but positioned as voices that threaten and undermine security and "our values". Judicial decision-making and judicial ad hominem and obiter commentary have revealed the deep chasm between the judiciary and the executive. Judges responding to demonstrations of executive power that have suspended rights for some criminal suspects, have described the secret trial, as "the stuff of nightmares" and struck down what they consider executive abuses where they are able. Lord Paddick in the House of Lords debate on the Counter-Terrorism and Sentencing Bill, 21 September 2020 (col 1621) reminded the House of the balance to be struck:

> We should not return to the days when the state could deprive someone of their liberties indefinitely without trial. We on these Benches have had enough of the Government's "talk tough" rhetoric and their low-cost or no-cost options that have no evidence to support their effectiveness. We will support every measure in the Bill where the evidence shows they are necessary and effective in keeping us safe from terrorism, but we will call out every measure where the evidence suggests they are unnecessary and ineffective.

The targeting by the "surveillance assemblage" has revealed a Muslim community under permanent siege, where policing and the law are a brooding omnipresence and an army in occupation. Lord Thomas of Gresford is not alone when speaking of the "Prevent" programme and in considering the duty of designated authorities to identify radicalisation, when he queries: "What are professionals—doctors, teachers and social workers—being asked to spot and report? What warning signs of radicalisation should they be aware of and look for? Who trains the professionals and what is the quality, clarity and helpfulness of such training?" (Counter-Terrorism and Sentencing Bill 21 September 2020 col 1645) (see also Saeed 2019).

Chapter 6 considers the exceptionalist response of the US to Islamic terrorism through an examination of the development of counter-terrorism measures and the degenerate use of torture. What makes the US "exceptional" is the authorisation of state (executive) sanctioned torture of foreign nationals. Sontag (2004) says "torture" has become us: "The photographs are us". This is what the US has become. Sands (2006) describes the US as "lawless" in its response to terrorism, a response which has, limited personal liberty, suspended rights, and freedoms, flaunted international human rights law with impunity, and treated terrorist suspects outside the criminal process. Operating outside the law the US has removed any protections for suspects including Geneva Convention safeguards, whilst empowering military commissions to meet out a summary injustice. Elaine Scary says of the adulterated ROL: "the prohibition of torture.... is not one important law among many important laws. Rather, it is the philosophical foundation on which all other laws are created and without which our confidence in all other laws waiverers" (cited by Shaheen in Lean xvi). The torture of "internees" in Guantánamo and in US-controlled territories, including Bagram and Abu Ghraib, has been legitimated through the manipulation of language enabling raising the threshold of permissible "interrogation"—à la torture. Photographs of abused Muslim men in Abu Ghraib, showing acts of cruelty committed by the US military upon their bodies live on forever in the www, affecting the sense of identity and self-esteem of all Muslims men and women, individually and as a group.

Muslim women, in answer to these several cultural productions of "the Muslim" (discussed in Chapters 2 and 3), and the appropriation of these tropes to justify and legitimate the WOT to "save Muslim women" (Chapter 4), the surveillance of Muslims and the development of UK counter-terror laws which particularly target Muslims (Chapter 5), and the violation, torture and humiliation of Arab and Muslim men (Chapter 6), speak up and speak out and respond in various ways. Chapter 7 then considers Muslim women's voice of resistance which takes on many forms documenting how women in asserting identity and demonstrating solidarity turn to the headscarf or in some cases a face veil in an expression of empathy. Some women wish to outwardly profess a visible Muslim/Islamic faithed identity through wearing the hijab (headscarf), or niqab (face covering) (Chapter 7). Some women wear a headscarf or face covering as a statement of solidarity, some as a statement of resistance to the West and to its values, some as a statement of political resistance against discrimination, or resistance to Western foreign policy in Muslim majority countries. Other Muslim women have taken a decision not to wear the headscarf or any identifiable items which in making them visible expose them to at risk of physical assault, insult and in some cases death (see Zempi and Chakraborti 2014; Zempi and Awan (eds) 2019, discussed further in Chapters 3 and 7). Some Western nations, especially France and other parts of Europe, in claiming to defend a version of secularism and of equality and freedom from state-imposed religion, have introduced legislation prohibiting headscarves in schools and permitted places of work to do likewise if they so choose, whilst face coverings are criminalised and banished from all public places. Their laws have been justified through state-imposed meanings of Islamic dress. This hegemony disenfranchises the meaning such dress holds for Muslim women and erases Muslim women physically, socially and metaphysically in an act of state-institutionalised discrimination and exclusion. That is not to ignore the power of some Muslim patriarchy in controlling Muslim women's bodies nor in forcing these dress styles upon women as part of a broader pattern of male coercion. Chapter 8 attempts to grapple with such questions of women's forced subornation through family and personal status and the imposed requirement in appearance, dress and head, face and body covering. In this context, I examine the appropriation of dress as a symbol of male authority over women, a mark of patriarchy's enduring presence, a statement of a revival of Islamic conservatism, and in some cases a demonstration of fundamentalism. The impact of how "double colonialism" continues to enforce patriarchy and eschew women's fundamental human rights, is relevant, and in this regard, I focus on fundamentalist forces in Afghanistan, Saudi Arabia and Iran, and women's resistance to these systems and structures. It is here I also take up a critique of mainstream or "white feminism " and the need for Muslim women to speak in their own voice, to wrest a platform, locally, nationally and globally and to take that space as of right. But what is of supreme significance in this last chapter is the reminder of Western power's appropriation of the Muslim female body to gain a military advantage in the region and to reassert Western superiority by using women's subornation in these countries to proclaim, yet again, as Said's Orientalist exegesis had identified the West's own self-congratulatory higher morality and civilisation. Mona Eltahawy (2016) states first and last "*My Body belongs to Me*" "My body is mine, it does not belong to the state, it does not belong to the mosque, it does not belong to the church, it does not belong to my family it belongs to me". In that same vein neither does her body belong to the West. In that same vein Nasrin Sotoudeh an Iranian lawyer currently imprisoned for representing women who resist the forces of religious fundamentalism says, "As long as it is in their hands, they can decide our lives" (film "Nasrin" 2020).

"The Political Appropriation of the Muslim Body: Islamophobia, Counter-terrorism Law and Gender" is a work that contributes to that public discourse and that voice and counter fire of resistance to bring about a transformation and to assist in pressing the "unlearning" of "the inherent dominative mode" (Williams 1958: 376) in Western orientalist thinking and conduct.

References

The All-Party Parliamentary Group (APPG). 2018. Islamophobia Defined: The Inquiry into a Working Definition of Islamophobia. https://appgbritishmuslims.org/ Accessed 2 December 2020.

Atwan, A.B. 2015. *Islamic State the Digital Caliphate*. London: Saqi Books.

Baldwin, J. 1965. Cambridge Union Speech 1965 "Pin Drop Speech." https://www.youtube.com/watch?v=NUBh9GqFU3A. Accessed 18 October 2020.

Borger, J., and O. Holmes. 2019. US Says Israeli Settlements No Longer Considered Illegal in Dramatic Shift, November 18. https://www.theguardian.com/world/2019/nov/18/us-israeli-settlements-no-longer-considered-illegal-palestinian-land-mike-pompeo. Accessed 18 October 2020.

Bouattia, M. 2020. Between Submission and Threat. In *It's Not About the Burqa*, ed. M. Khan, 209–222. London: Picador.

Breen-Smyth, M. 2014. Theorising the "Suspect Community": Counterterrorism, Security Practices and the Public Imagination. *Critical Studies on Terrorism* 7 (2): 223–240.

Butler, J. 1999 [1990]. *Gender Trouble*. London: Routledge.

Carby, H.V. 1997. White Woman Listen! Black Feminism and the Boundaries of Sisterhood. In *Black British Feminism: A Reader*, ed. H. Mirza, 45–53. London: Routledge.

Charlesworth, H., and C. Chinkin. 2002. Editorial Comment Sex, Gender, and September 11. *American Journal of International Law* 96 (3): 600–605.

Chomsky, H. 1967. A Special Supplement: The Responsibility of Intellectuals. *NYRB*, February 23.

CNN News. 2019. Pregnant Woman Wearing a Headscarf Kicked in the Head in Australia. https://edition.cnn.com/2019/11/23/australia/pregnant-woman-attacked-australia-intl-scli/index.html. Accessed 14 November 2020.

Cohen, S. 2001. *States of Denial*. London: Polity.

Cornford, A. 2020. Terrorist Precursor Offences: Evaluating the Law in Practice. *Criminal Law Review*, 8: 663–685.

Counter-Terrorism and Sentencing Bill 21 September 2020, Volume 805. https://hansard.parliament.uk/lords/2020-09-21/debates/A622E717-DE61-4496-A0DB-5EE2FF47A3FB/Counter-TerrorismAndSentencingBill. Accessed 10 November 2020.

Crenshaw, K. 2016. The Urgency of Intersectionality October TEDX. https://www.ted.com/talks/kimberle_crenshaw_the_urgency_of_intersectionality. Accessed 14 November 2020.

Crenshaw, K. 2017 [1997]. *Intersectionality*. New York: The New Press.

Edwards, S.S.M. 2008. Human Sacrifices at the Altar of Terrorist Control Secretary of State for the Home Department v MB; Secretary of State for the Home Department v AF. *Denning Law Journal* 20: 221–238.

Edwards, S.S.M. 2010a. The European Court of Human Rights—Universalist Aspirations of Protection in the Middle of the Edge of Occupation. *Denning Law Journal* 22: 145–171.

Edwards, S.S.M. 2010b. Defacing Muslim Women—Dialectical Meanings of Dress in the Body Politic. In *Rights in Context: Law and Justice in Late Modern Society*, ed. R. Banakar, 127–147. London: Ashgate.

Edwards, S.S.M. 2010c. Women 'Body and Soul'—The Right to Self-Authenticity Under the European Convention of Human Rights in UK and Europe. In *International Conference on Multiculturalism and Global Community Tehran*, Iran, 24–27 July 2010.

Eltahawy, M. (2016). *My Body Belongs to Me*. January 27. https://www.youtube.com/watch?v=PZmb30fsF54. Accessed 18 October 2020.

Falk, R. 2014. INTERVIEW Richard Falk on ISIS and Islamic "Essentialism "by Daniel Falcone, "Report of the Special Rapporteur on the situation of human rights in the Palestinian territories occupied since 1967. United Nations General Assembly Human Rights Council Twenty-Fifth Session. Agenda item 7. https://truthout.org/articles/richard-falk-on-isis-and-islamic-essentialism/. Accessed 17 October 2020.

Fanon, F. 2008 [1952]. *Black Skin White Masks*. New York: Grove Press.

Foucault, M. 1980 [1976]. TWO LECTURES Lecture One: 7 January 1976 (on *Power and Knowledge*). In *Power/Knowledge: Selected Interviews and Other Writings 1972–1977*, ed. C. Gordon, 1980, 78–92. New York: Pantheon Books.

Gani, A. 2020 [2018]. Representation as a Feminist Act. In *Can We All Be Feminists?* ed. J. Eric-Udorie, 133–145. London: Virago.

Gilligan, C. 2016 [1983]. *In a Different Voice*. Harvard: Harvard University Press.

Hall, S. 1996. New Ethnicities. In *Critical Dialogues in Cultural Studies*, ed. D. Morley and K.H. Chen, 441–450. New York: Routledge.

House of Commons. 2019. Debate on Islamophobia, May 16. https://hansard. parliament.uk/commons/2019-05-16/debates/CF834846-65CA-46CD-B955-CDEF42BAFB26/DefinitionOfIslamophobia. Accessed 14 November 2020.

Huntington, S. 1993. Clash of Civilisations. *Foreign Affairs* 72 (3): 22–47.

Hussein, S. 2019 [2016]. *From Victims to Suspects; Muslim Women Since 9/11*. Yale: Yale University Press.

Jackson, R. 2012. Unknown Knowns: The Subjugated Knowledge of Terrorism Studies. *Critical Studies on Terrorism* 5 (1): 11–29.

Jenkins, J., and T. Phillips. 2018. *Defining Islamophobia*. Policy Exchange London: A Policy Exchange Research Note.

Kennedy, H. 1993. *Eve Was Framed*. London: Vintage.

Khan, M. 2020. Feminism Needs to Die. In *It's Not about the Burqa*, ed. M. Khan, 105–115. London: Picador.

Kundnani, A. 2015 [2014]. *The Muslims Are Coming*. London: Verso.

Lahey, K. 1991. Reasonable Women and the Law. In *At the Boundaries of Law Feminism and Legal Theory*, ed. M. Fineman and N.S. Thomadsen, 3–21. London: Routledge.

Lean, N. 2017 [2012]. *The Islamophobia Industry*. London: Pluto Press.

Lean, N. 2019. The Debate over the Utility and Precision of the Term 'Islamophobia'. In *The Routledge International Handbook on Islamophobia*, ed. I. Zempi and I. Awan, 11–17. London: Routledge.

Lewis, B. 1990. The Roots of Muslim Rage. *The Atlantic*, September.

MacKinnon, C. 1993. *Only Words*. Harvard: Harvard University Press.

Namazie, M. 2019. The APPG's Definition of 'Islamophobia' Is a Triumph for Fundamentalists. https://onelawforall.org.uk/the-appgs-definition-of-islamophobia-is-a-triumph-for-fundamentalists/. Accessed 2 December 2020.

Nasrin. 2020. Director J. Kaufman.

Perry, B. 2014. Gendered Islamophobia: Hate Crime against Muslim Women. *Social Identities* 20 (1): 74–89.

Runnymede Trust. 2017 [1997]. *Islamophobia*. https://www.runnymedetrust. org/uploads/Islamophobia%20Report%202018%20FINAL.pdf. Accessed 2 December 2020.

Saadawi, N. 1997. *The Nawal Saadawi Reader*. London: Zed Books.

Saeed, T. 2019. Islamophobia and the Muslim Student: Disciplining the Intellect. In *The Routledge International Handbook on Islamophobia*, ed. I. Zempi and I. Awan, Ch. 14, 172–185. London: Routledge.

Said, E. 2001, October 22. The Clash of Ignorance. *The Nation*.

Sands, P. 2006. *Lawless World*. London: Penguin.

Simpson, J. 2012. The War Is Dead, Long Live the War: Bosnia—The Reckoning by Ed Vulliamy—Review. *The Observer*, April 22. https://www.thegua rdian.com/books/2012/apr/22/vulliamy-war-dead-bosnia-review. Accessed 18 October 2020.

Smith, N., and A. Smith. 2019. Reflections on Chomsky's 'The Responsibility of Intellectuals'. In *The Responsibility of Intellectuals: Reflections by Noam Chomsky and Others after 50 Years*, ed. N. Smith et al., 7–25. London: UCL Press.

Sontag, S. 2004. Regarding the Torture of Others. *New York Times*, May 23.

Spender, D. 1980. *Man Made Language*. London: Routledge.

Spivak, G. 1988. Can the Subaltern Speak Can the Subaltern Speak? Originally published in *Marxism and the Interpretation of Culture*, ed. C. Cary Nelson and L. Grossberg, 271–313. Urbana, IL: University of Illinois Press.

Spivak, G. 2006 [1998]. *In Other Worlds*. London: Routledge.

Williams, R. 1958. *Culture and Society*. London: Hogarth Press.

Young, R.J.C. 2003. *Postcolonialism A Very Short Introduction*. Oxford: Oxford University Press.

Zempi, I., and I. Awan (eds.). 2019. *The Routledge International Handbook on Islamophobia*. London: Routledge.

Zempi, I., and N. Chakraborti. 2014. *Islamophobia, Victimisation, and the Veil*. London: Palgrave Macmillan.

CHAPTER 2

Muslim Racialised Tropes: "Orientalism", Past and Present

INTRODUCTION

Noam Chomsky makes a plea to intellectuals, to "lift the veil of ideology" (sic) and insist on truth, emphasising the importance of historical context (1967). The historical context is necessary to establish a framework for understanding the contemporary racialisation of Muslims in the Middle East and in the West and its origins in what Edward Said and others have identified as "Orientalism", some preferring to describe this as a "Eurocentric" ideology (Varisco 2008; Amin 2010 [1988]). This body of knowledge which professed to be the "truth" about the East and what is now called the Middle East and its people was reinvigorated after 9/11 and egregious stereotypes of the East and Middle East, of Muslims and Muslim diaspora and of Islam, were promulgated by Western statesmen and politicians, Western media, commentators and writers, whilst dissenting voices of resistance speaking to alternate narratives and truths were distorted, denigrated and silenced. This episteme of so-called "knowledge" about Muslims has been challenged by dissenting voices described as "Islamophobia" and identified as a racialised discourse (Meer and Modood 2019). Both as a term and as a phenomenon Islamophobia has been vigorously contested. Melanie Phillips, writing in the *Jewish Chronicle* (11 April 2019), in an article-entitled "We must call out the Muslims who hate Jews", retorts: "Islamophobia ...was coined to suppress rational, legitimate and necessary acknowledgment of the dangers within the Islamic world". President Marie van der Zyl, of the Board of Deputies of British Jews, disagrees with Phillips: "You can count on me as a committed ally of the Muslim community". Phillips continues, and in the *Jewish Chronicle* (16 December 2019) in an article entitled "Don't fall for bogus claims of 'Islamophobia'", ratchets up her riposte, this time professing that the entire concept of "Islamophobia" is not only a ruse to silence criticism of Islam but, she also claims that it is "anti-Jew". The Board of Deputies of British Jews responding to Phillips, doesn't seem to follow Phillip's logic either: "Anti-Muslim prejudice is very real, and it is on the rise. Our community must stand as allies to all facing racism" (*The Guardian*, 17 December 2019).

Race prejudice, based on colour, race and nationality, now characterise prejudice against Muslims where race, colour and nationality, are all collectively racialised under the marker of faith. Stuart Hall in "New Ethnicities" (1996: 443) recognised that features of marginalisation and "otherness" could also be applied in the Muslim context, this he develops in his paper written at that time "Race-the sliding signifier" (2017: 31) where he explains how race is a cultural, historical and discursive construct and not a biological fact, where racial signifiers are subsumed in discourses of cultural difference and where race operates as a language, its signifiers referencing the system of meaning fixed in a culture (2017: 45–46). Hall recognised that religion, in this instance, Islam, had come to function as if a racial signifier, essentialising, homogenising, reifying, objectifying and attributing to Muslims racial markers and tropes in assuming a collective and monolithic Muslim consciousness and identity. Hall was also concerned that such conditions of existence have "real effects, outside the scope of the discursive" (1996: 443). Such "real effects" can be seen in their material realisation in the international context where for example US and UK support for the "War on Terror" (WOT), is sanctioned, and where US Presidential executive orders authorised the unlawful detention and torture of Muslim men in Guantánamo Bay. Such "real effects" are also particularly conspicuous in police surveillance and in the treatment of Muslim communities as "suspect communities" (Pantazis and Pemberton 2009). Such "real effects" also materialise in a "gendered Islamophobia" directed at Muslim women identified because of their dress and its conspicuity, and where European states, Canada, Australia and the US, whilst claiming a secularist and equality purpose, manage out Muslim identity through regulating and erasing "her" body.

In exploring the historical relevance and force of essentialised representations of Muslims in the West and in Muslim-majority societies I review first, the contribution of Edward Said (1978, 1994) to this discourse, especially his thesis on "Orientalism" and its enduring relevance for an understanding of the contemporary construction of Muslims. Second, I consider Said's critics, those who oppose his Orientalism thesis, those who consider it has limitations, and those who recognise the importance of his thesis but are critical of its gender omissions. Here, I am particularly interested in postcolonial feminist scholarship which, whilst critical of Said's neglect of women and of gender, nonetheless recognise the importance of his framework for an analysis of Orientalism's gendered representation (see Spivak 1988; Yeğenoğlu 1998; Lewis 1996). In attempting to infill Said's neglect of the woman and gender question, and in recognition of the supreme importance of gendered orientalism to understanding the "real effects" of this discourse for Muslim women in the past and in the present time, I document through three case examples the pervasiveness of gendered orientalism in cultural discourse. In this exercise, I consider briefly first "feminist" literature of the eighteenth century, second anthropology of the nineteenth century and third orientalist art and photography of the nineteenth and early twentieth centuries. Said's emphasis on a "contrapuntal reading" (1994: 49, 59) of the past and its importance in drawing on its elision in the present, is especially relevant to exploring contemporary representations of Muslim men and women.

Post 9/11, the female Muslim subject is no longer considered solely as the passive, "Other" to be saved, as portrayed in Wollstonecraft's "feminist" writings (below) or the sexualised "Other" as discovered by Reina Lewis (1996) in her study of orientalist artistic representations (below), but also as a terrorist suspect to be damned and punished (Hussein 2019) especially exemplified in the case of the London schoolgirl Shamima Begum, who left the UK when 15 years of age to join ISIS, then to be banished by the UK government. Shamima Begum, vulnerable, failed by police inaction, exploited by the popular press, used by right-wing politicians to garner support for harsher counter-terror measures, became and remains the bête noire and modern Muslim muse of female terrorism. I conclude this chapter by considering the enduring impact of these several tropes, for Muslim identity, life chances and experiences in the material world, those "conditions of existence and real effects, outside the scope of the discursive" (Hall 1996: 443). It is evident that within the contemporary discursive there is a renewed enthusiasm for Orientalist dehumanising dogma, now the staple "speak" of leaders of nations, of governments, political parties, security agencies, the media entourage and found in public institutions and places of free thinking and learning, as schools and Universities are compelled to implement the government's toxic "Prevent" strategy (Saeed 2019). The impact and "real effects" that such a perceptual mind-set has on the West's international relations, foreign policy, and so-called "diplomacy", in other words, its territorial and military ambitions are discussed in later chapters.

Constructing the Orient

The Muslim "Other" is an imagined phantasm of long-standing historical misrepresentation, conceived within the Western imperialist mind, where the East and its people are represented as "barbaric" and people of the West, "civilised". Such Oriental tropes, to a greater or lesser extent, with local configurations, is created by Western thinking about all Muslims, whether born outside or in the West. This body of belief, about "the Orient" and its people has been the subject of study of post-colonialist writers, including Frantz Fanon (1965, 1967), Edward Said (1978), Gayatri Spivak (1988, 1998), and Homi Bhaba (2004). Whilst Edward Said best theorises and articulates "Orientalism" as an ideology, Anouar Abdel-Malek (1963), in his article "Orientalism in Crisis", had already embarked on a project of investigating the Orientalist's motivation. Abdel-Malek placed "Orientalists" into two groups, "ethnists" those who set out, as they saw it, to objectively document the Orient (and here Ken Jacobsen (2007: 86) agrees with Abdel-Malek that many Western traveller writers did not regard themselves as superior) and those whose purpose of study and writing was undertaken with a view to occupy and dominate a region and its peoples whom were regarded as inferior. At the same time, a formidable body of postcolonial scholarship was already emerging, most notably the work of Fanon (1965), who was documenting the subornation of the colonised, the creation of "Otherness", and rise of counter liberation nationalist struggles within the African, and specifically, Algerian context.

Edward Said—Grand Master

In "Orientalism", Said, identified a way of thinking, and a perceptual universe of representation about Arab and Muslim people from the

Middle and Near East which was captured in all forms of cultural production including art, literature, public and political commentary, which in turn shaped ways of seeing, understanding and responding to men and women of the so-called Orient, whether individually, nationally or militarily. (It is here that the "real effects" of Hall's discursive, that is the way in which meaning, representation and culture, considered to be constitutive, materialise). It was, declared Said, a racist ideology where manifestations of the power of the West and its cultural, political and legal institutions defined, and reproduced narratives in their own interest. Influenced by Michel Foucault's writings on "Power and Knowledge" (1980 [1976a, b]) Said explores how these assertions masquerade as real "knowledge" and function as "regimes of truth." (These articulations of Muslims and Muslim majority societies find contemporary repetition especially in and through the media and in digital form and are representations endorsed by politicians and in state practices see Chapter 3). This "knowledge" and "regime of representation" does violence by perpetrating and perpetuating injustice against all Muslims in the international and domestic WOT (see Chapters 4–6), and in the proliferation of "dress laws" which as a vehicle of control of Muslim women's identity, regulate her body, proscribe her appearance, and effect the wider attempt to destroy Muslim group identity, (see Chapter 7).

Said's thesis, presented in *Orientalism* (1978), is considered the most influential, though contested, exegesis on how the West has constructed the Near East, which as Varisco (2008: 4) concedes: "changed our way of thinking forever" and gave birth to postcolonial theory (9) (see also Macfie 2008 [2002]). Since 9/11 these scripts, narratives and representations have been enthusiastically reappropriated to justify counter-terrorism strategies, from the "Prevent" programme in the UK and its counterpart in the US, to the WOT and US and UK military ambitions in the Middle East region. Said writing later in *Culture and Imperialism* (1994: 59) offers what he calls a "contrapuntal" reading of civilisation and culture, observing the interconnections between past, present and future understandings of nationhood, civilisation and culture, crucial to an understanding of contemporary constructions of Islam and Muslims, Muslim diaspora and Muslim majority societies, which he explains depend on "reading back" to the stereotypology and myth of earlier representation. "As we look back at the cultural archive, we begin to re-read it not univocally but contrapuntally" (59) (see also Chowdhry 2007).

In his seminal essay "Arabs, Islam and Dogmas of the West" (1976) Said documents how the West has constructed the Arab and Oriental psyche as "backward", "savage", "exotic", "inferior", "evil", based on "the Orient's special place in European Western Experience" (1978: 1, 2) and the "ontological and epistemological distinctions made between the Orient and (most of the time) the Occident" (5). This dogma he demonstrates is redolent in all cultural representations, including the writings of poets, novelists, travel writers, anthropologists, philosophers, political theorists, economists, and found in the decisions and actions of imperial administrators, all of whom: "have accepted the basic distinction between East and West as the starting point for elaborate accounts concerning the Orient, its people, customs, mind, destiny, and so on..." (1978: 5). Such fantasy, myth, and distortion are repeated, reinvented, reconfigured in Western studies of Arabs and Islam (104), and serve as essential tools of imperialism enabling colonial ambitions (132). In both *Orientalism* (1978) and in *Culture and Imperialism* (1994), he elaborates on the four dogmas he outlined in this 1976 article.

First, Orientalism is characterised by a binary representation of the Orient and the Occident, where people of the Orient are depicted as incapable of creating democratic, civilised, or egalitarian societies. Exploring the enduring force of this trope for the modern era, in *Covering Islam* (1997: x, [1981]) he demonstrates how such exaggerated stereotyping and belligerent hostility towards Muslims, is iterated through media propaganda, rhetoric and language (see Chapter 3). The occident West, by contrast, occupies the moral, cultural, ethical, political and economic high ground, and is represented as advanced, developed, its people humane, educated and cultured, its political institutions democratic and egalitarian, and its values fair, just and bound by the Rule of Law (ROL). (The speciousness of the Western claim to the ROL is examined in Chapters 4–6). Second, Said argues that an aspect of this dogma is the tendency to represent the Orient through "classical observation" (he means fixed, constructed cultural tropes) rather than "modern oriental realities". Such modern realities demonstrate how Western foreign policy has engaged in territorial ambitions of occupation. In "The Arab Portrayed" (1968), (Said 1970: 4–5) the Arab is represented as a pariah:

> In the mind's syntax, then, the Arab, if thought of singly, is a creature without dimension.... If the Arab occupies space enough for attention, it is a negative value. He is seen as a disrupter of Israel's and the West's

existence, or ... as a surmountable obstacle to Israel's creation in 1948. Palestine was imagined as an empty desert waiting to burst into bloom, its inhabitant's inconsequential nomads possessing no stable claim to the land and therefore no cultural permanence.

Third, in developing further his thesis on the East/West binarism he identifies the tendency to represent the Arab/Eastern/Muslim viewpoint as subjective and irrational, whilst the Western viewpoint is always objective and rational (Macfie 2009: 2). This, parallels, and mirrors male/female gendered binarism, where male opinion, theories and reflections are always considered to be rational and objective, whereas the female voice is always considered to be subjective and irrelevant (Spender 1980). Operating at the level of language, discourse, and power, Orientalism places "the other" in a subordinated position in institutional practices and in fixing ways of thinking. As Fanon recognised in the Algerian colonial context: "The oppressor, through the inclusive and frightening character of his authority, manages to impose on the native new ways of seeing, and in particular, a pejorative judgement with respect to his original forms of existing" (1967: 38). Fourth, Said demonstrates how the Orient has been historically feared and demonised, depicted as devoid of redeeming features or qualities, such that domination and occupation by the civilised West, and by force, is both justified and necessary. Such tropes are repeated in the West's contemporary justifications for WOT strategies. This representation of the Orient is expressed through hostility and specifically hostility to Islam.

POWER—WHO SPEAKS—WHO REPRESENTS?

Said asks himself this question: "How did philology, lexicology, history, biology, political and economic theory, novel writing, and lyric poetry come to the service of Orientalism's broadly imperialist view of the world?" (Bayoumi and Rubin 2001: 81). Postcolonial writers including Spivak, have been concerned with how such representations are projected as naturalised and pass for objective "truth" and "knowledge". What we know about Muslims, Arabs and the Middle East unfolds not from the mouths of the Muslim Arab or Middle Eastern inhabitant or the Muslim diaspora but from what (Western) thinkers have said and written, as if the West holds the oracle on truth. Knowledge, crafted by the West about the East, is legitimated through the power of ideology: "...the movement towards the winning of a universal validity and legitimacy for accounts of the world which are partial and particular, and towards the grounding of these particular constructions in the taken-for-grantedness of 'the real'" (Hall cited Lopez 2007: 261). Said in *Orientalism* asks himself the "How did...?" question and in considering "who speaks", draws on the work of Foucault's *Archaeology of Knowledge* first published in (2002 [1969]), *Discipline and Punish* first published in (1991 [1975]) and his lectures on "Power and Knowledge" first published in 1976 (in Gordon 1980). Said is also influenced by Louis Althusser (1971) who developed a theorisation of the relationships of power. Said relies on Gramsci's concept of "hegemon" in approaching how: "European ideas about the orient, themselves iterating European superiority over Oriental backwardness become instantiated as truth in cultural and political institutions and in fixing the ways of thinking about Muslims" (1978). Said is influenced by Foucault and discourse (Said 1978: 3) and especially Foucault's "Lecture One" (1976a) delivered on 7 January 1976 on the subject of "Power and Knowledge", where he identifies two types of knowledge, "arrogated knowledge" (that body of knowledge which claims to speak to truth) and "subjugated knowledge" which is the dissident voice. Foucault says of "subjugated knowledge":

".... one should understand something else...namely a whole set of knowledges that have been disqualified as inadequate to the task or insufficiently elaborated; naive knowledges, located low down on the hierarchy, beneath the required level of cognition or scientificity" (cited in Gordon 1980: 82). In an interview on the question of "Truth and Power" Foucault explains further. "Truth isn't outside power.... each society has its regime of truth... the types of discourse which it accepts and makes function as true" (cited in Faubion 2000: 131). This framework and understanding of "arrogated" and "subjugated" knowledge are fundamental to Said's work and importantly to an understanding of how representations of Muslims, were imagined and how they are now imagined, and the political and material force of such ideas emboldening the WOT and counter-terror strategies.

In answering Said's question, "How did ...."?, and in considering Foucault's construct of "arrogated knowledge" (see Chapters 3 and 4) Althusser's (1971) identification of the role of ideology and state apparatuses is also relevant to understanding the role of public and private institutions including the government, the executive, and the state, in the production of these two "knowledges". Althusser writes: ".... the school (but also other State institutions like the Church, or other apparatuses like the Army) teaches 'know-how', but in forms which ensure subjection to the ruling ideology or the mastery of its 'practice'". Knowledge or ideas that do not serve the state apparatus, or in Marxist terms, knowledge that does not serve the ruling economic, intellectual and political force, in society are ideas that are consciously suppressed (Foucault's "subjugated knowledge").

Both Foucault and Althusser identify the centrality of the legal apparatus in this wider episteme of subjugation. "...the domain of the law, [are] permanent agents of these relations of domination, these polymorphous techniques of subjugation" (Foucault 1976b, cited in Gordon 1980: 96). (I consider further the legal apparatus in Chapters 4–7). "Subjugated knowledge" then is that dissident voice, the critical counternarrative, and also in this instance the Muslim voice which is silenced through strategies of marginalisation and distortion (see Chapter 3). For Spivak, it is specifically the voices of "Third World" women - the subaltern, for Saadawi, the voices of Arab women, for Said, the Arab/Muslim male voices, that are disregarded and suppressed. In the contemporary Western context, counter-knowledge is subjugated through silencing, misrepresentation of dissent, through distortion and accusation. For example, those who challenge the dominant orthodoxy of US foreign policy in the Middle East are officially discredited. Noam Chomsky has long been labelled as an "apologist for terrorism" and more recently following his criticism of former President Trump's racist treatment of Congresswoman, Ilhan Omar, who, when she challenged Trump was told by him "she can go back home"! (22 July 2019). "Arrogated knowledge" on the other hand masquerades as truth. Said writes, "the will to exercise dominant control has discovered a way to clothe, disguise, rarefy, and wrap itself systematically in the language of truth, discipline, rationality, utilitarian value and knowledge" (1983: 216).

Debating Said

Said's Orientalism thesis is not without its critic's—the "neo-orientalists," largely Middle Eastern scholars, who consider their subject position and Eastern or Middle Eastern connections insulate their work from any Orientalist bias and lends authority to the truth of their findings. There are also some European scholars who repudiate his Orientalism thesis altogether, considering it exaggerated and a slur on their scholarship, and like the "neo-orientalists" also regard their work bleached of Euro-centric or Orientalist bias. Said is criticised too, for neglecting the way in which "the Oriental woman" was spoken for, exploited, and repre-sented. This omission is both curious and disappointing particularly as gendered orientalism was so blatantly evident in historical constructions of the Orient, and is especially centrifugal in the present where the West's "saving Muslim women" mission has served as one of the key justifications for the Western invasion of Afghanistan and Iraq.

Those critics who repudiate Said's work are particularly angered by his claim that their studies in anthropology, history, ethnography and elsewhere have also contributed to the derogatory tropes about which he protests. Said says "it would be Panglossian to call irrelevant" (1994 [1993]: 342).

Gabrieli (1965) in "an Apology for Orientalism" (in Macfie 2008: 79), admits that some Orientalists may have colluded with Western thinking. Bernard Lewis (1990) refutes the possibility of even a scintilla of bias in his own scholarship and accuses Said of politicising and polluting what was "innocent" (see also Adib-Moghaddam 2011). It does seem rather implausible that these writers were ignorant of Foucault's theorisations on "Power and Knowledge" (1980 [1976a]) which were so influential within the social sciences in understanding the inevitable bias in cultural theory and the critiques within philosophy, jurisprudence and the social sciences which deem the nirvana state of "value freedom" in scholarship, unattainable. Max Weber (1946), C. Wright Mills (1943), Fred Blum (1944), Peter Berger and Thomas Luckmann (1966), Howard Becker (1967) and Hilary Putnam (2012), as but a few writers amongst many, all attest that the very act of choosing an object of study is a political act immersed in values of the scholar. As Arthur Brittan writes: "It has become increasingly obvious that the sociologist's self-image enters into his sociological work as a constitutive element of the process" (1972: 323). As Bertens (2013: 177) puts it in the context of Orientalist study:

> For Said, Western representations of the Orient, no matter how well inten-tioned, have always been part of this damaging discourse. Even those Orientalists who are clearly in sympathy with Oriental peoples and their cultures – and Said finds a substantial number of them – cannot over-come their Eurocentric perspective and have unintentionally contributed to Western domination. So instead of the disinterested objectivity in the service of the higher goal of true knowledge that Western scholarship

has traditionally claimed for itself, we find invariably false representations that have effectively paved the way for military domination, cultural displacement, and economic exploitation.

Whether Said himself over essentialised Orientalist scholarship continues to be debated. His critics claim that he was overly selective and himself reductionist by excluding those academic scholars who presented Islam in a positive light, Al Azm (1981: 13) cites as evidence the writings of the French orientalist Massignon. In this example below, they may well have a point. Massignon's in "The Arab Miracle" writes:

> It is true that the Arabs at present are discouraged by the evil that is said of them. So it is up to their hosts, like Vintejoux, and myself, to shout to our Arab friends to hold out, to resist all this enslaving propaganda which proposes to them to renounce their honor, their tradition, their ancestors, to capitulate before the colonialist force and the capital of the banks to conform their way of thinking and acting to this false civilization of robots that no longer believes in itself, nor in God, and aspires to subdue Universe to a climate of American 'digests' imbeciles, written in 'basic' (or in 'pigeon') English. All this fabrication of fake ersatz will fall shortly. Let them hold on? The world needs them.

Al Azm (1981: 6), Little (1979: 129), Ibn Warraq (2007), Gellner 199, (cited in Irwin 2006: 299) are his harshest critics, however, Said's thesis cannot be that easily destabilised.

By 1996 in an interview with *The New York Times,* Said remarked that the negative tropes of Arab and Muslim had worsened, and that the West's view of the Arab world had contracted. Orientalism was then as it is now an ideological production, produced and directed (although not exclusively) by the West as objective knowledge in a discursive formulation and "regime of truth" about Muslim people and people of the Middle East, what Howard Becker (1967: 241) might have called: "the subordinate narrative partisan in the hierarchy of credibility". This so-called knowledge and "regime of truth" continues to shape the West's perception of the Muslim "other," functioning in the same way as racist ideology (Varisco: 365 nb 247) or what Samir Amin (Varisco: 134) has described as "modern, cultural Eurocentricity".

Contesting Said's Male Narrative

At the time Said was writing there was a vibrant women's movement characterised by vociferous debates between mainstream feminism, "white feminism", "black feminism" and an emerging body of feminist scholarship on Eastern, "Third World" women (Spivak 1988) and Muslim women (El Guindi 2003 [1977] and Nawal Saadawi 1980). However, in Said's writings women appear only as a wisping ephemeral and passing thought, and even then, Said himself seems to Orientalise them. Varisco identifies the problem: "A ...sin of gender omission by Said is the reduction of the fantasized femme oriental to the preeminent symbol of oppression" (2008: 159). *Orientalism* (1978) and *Culture and Imperialism* (1994) are texts in which Said dealt with the masculinist nature of Oriental discourse, a universe written largely by men about men, which Said himself seems to replicate (Macfie: 113). Varisco (2008: 155) observes: "*Orientalism* is a man's book". It is certainly about a man's world.

Said's shortcomings on the woman and gender question, are found in his silences and fragmented and cursory literary documentation, which include Flaubert's characterisation of the Egyptian courtesan, Kuchuck Hanem, whom Said describes as: "...the widely influential model of the Orient woman; she never spoke of herself, she never represented her emotions, presence, or history" (*Orientalism* 1978: 6). Flaubert's gender characterisations which eroticise the Oriental woman also seem to incite only a limited response from Said.

> Woven through all of Flaubert's Oriental experiences, exciting or disappointing, is an almost uniform association between the Orient and sex. In making this association Flaubert was neither the first nor the most exaggerated instance of a remarkably persistent motif in Western attitudes to the Orient . . . Why the Orient seems still to suggest not only fecundity but sexual promise (and threat), untiring sensuality, unlimited desire, deep generative energies, is something on which one could speculate... Nevertheless, one must acknowledge its importance as something eliciting complex responses, sometimes even a frightening self-discovery, in the Orientalists, and Flaubert was an interesting case in point. (1978: 188)

Feminist scholarship, not surprisingly, has taken Said to task. Yeğenoğlu (1998: 10, 25), says that Said relegates gender and sexuality to a sub-domain of Orientalism in a reductionist treatment and uniform representation of the Orient and sex (see also Cannadine 2002: 88–89 and Macfie: 335). Rana Kabbani (1986) is particularly critical of his dismissal of women travel writers and their accounts of the Orient, Said, describing them as merely "token travellers". Judith Mabro (2009) and Reina Lewis (1996) by contrast recognise women travel writers as supremely significant since it was only women who were permitted to visit the harems and document first-hand (Lewis: 157, Andrea 2009). However, Yeğenoğlu, and Mabro also recognised that some women travel writers (who were white and privileged) also played a role in the creation of the Oriental female stereotype.

In 1989, in an interview, with Raymond Williams, Said makes a meek attempt to defend his neglect of women and gender. "I really do feel that in that situation (Imperialism and Orientalism) in the relationships between the ruler and the ruled in the imperial or the colonial or racial sense, race takes precedence over both class and gender" (Williams 1989: 196). This stance was typical of male scholars at the time. Said attempts further to exonerate himself by disavowing any intentional omission of gender. "As for the issue of gender, well, I think the way people see suppression is always important, because I have never been conscious of suppressing gender" (194). In *Culture and Imperialism* (1994: 262) and in consideration of more recent contemporary struggles, again, only a cursory reference is made to the role of feminism and women in Arab nationalism, yet women were at the very epicentre in the 1950/1960s struggle for Algerian independence (Go 2013) and constituted the centrepiece of Fanon's postcolonial essay on the political dynamism of the face veil ("Algeria Unveiled" 1965). Said's *Culture and Imperialism* contains several references to Fanon but there is no real engagement with his work. It is surprising too, that the question of patriarchy is similarly absent from both *Orientalism* and *Culture and Imperialism*, not even appearing as an index entry. Said had the opportunity in revisions to these texts, and in forewords and afterwards to address these omissions, but he does not do so. An interview later with Peter Osborne and Anne Beezer (1996: 74) provides a further opportunity for him to reflect, however any serious thinking on women and gender, remains absent.

What I was doing in *Orientalism*, twenty years ago when I was writing it, was pointing out two things: the extraordinary degree to which the orient had become feminized by male writers in Europe: and the way in which the women's movement in the West was hand in glove with the imperialist movement.....It's only very recently – I would say in the last four or five years – that the question of race and gender have been joined, in a historical and theoretical way– as opposed to just gender.

Given these omissions Said's criticism of the celebrated Egyptian feminist writer and activist, Nawal Saadawi, whom he says is "overexposed" and "over cited" (1990: 280) (see also Amireh 2000) is curious.

Her success in the West generates much scepticism. The western interest in her is not innocent, some critics believe. They argue that she is acclaimed not so much because she champions women's rights, but because she tells western readers what they want to hear. In this view, the West welcomes her feminist critique of Arab culture because it confirms the existing stereotypes of Arabs and Muslims as backward, misogynist and violently oppressive. (1990: 280)

Saadawi, in turn makes no reference to Said's work either (perhaps not altogether surprising), although Western imperialism and Orientalism is central to her critique.

In Said's defence, many scholarly writings certainly prior to 1970s, systematically eschewed the gender question or considered it less important or perhaps thought their work would be considered less relevant if they addressed gender. Attempts to address the question of women's exclusion and unequal treatment were trivialised, and marginalised though some feminist writers writing on the experience of American and Western women and equality were fearsome (Freidan 1963; Millet 1970; Mitchell 1975). An interrogation of the gender question was also absent or minimalised by even the more radical thinkers, especially pre-1970. To note, Hannah Arendt, the celebrated political theorist, writing in the 1950s–1960s and who died in 1975, provoked much feminist controversy especially within feminist political theory for subsuming the woman question, for her treatment of the public private domain, and her criticism of the Black Power movement (Young-Bruehl 1997: 311). In her work, which focused on the search for an understanding of totalitarianism, especially in her writings on the Nazi state and the holocaust and on the question of evil and its banality (*Eichmann in Jerusalem* 1963) she did not see herself as a feminist but "as a historian of European Jewry" (313) who was concerned with the need to understand how this genocide occurred, which she considered most urgent (see Benhabib 1996; Maslin 2013). For an academic interrogation of the Orientalisation of women in colonialism, imperialism and postcolonialism and its resonance in the present moment we must look elsewhere to what has loosely been called transnational or "third world" feminism. Mohanty (1984), Spivak (1988), Bhaba (2004) and Saadawi (1997), for example, have focused on the specificity of women's "Othered" representation and material experience throughout the Middle East, in the "Third world" and in Western diasporic communities. Spivak is concerned with the cultural construction of "Otherness" and focuses on the construction of "Third world women" and non-European women, and their marginalisation and appropriation by institutions of capitalism and imperialism and by the sexual economy of the West. She uses the concept of the "subaltern", originally coined by Gramsci, to describe the displacement and exclusion of particular groups.

...subaltern is not just a classy word for "oppressed", for the Other, for somebody who's not getting a piece of the pie. [...] In postcolonial terms, everything that has limited or no access to the cultural imperialism is subaltern—a space of difference. Now, who would say that's just the oppressed? The working class is oppressed. It's not subaltern. [...] Many people want to claim subalternity. They are the least interesting and the most dangerous. I mean, just by being a discriminated-against minority on the university campus; they don't need the word "subaltern" [...] They should see what the mechanics of the discrimination are. They're within the hegemonic discourse, wanting a piece of the pie, and not being allowed, so let them speak, use the hegemonic discourse. They should not call themselves subaltern. (1988: xx)

For Spivak, the Western occidental vantage point eroticised, sexualised, marginalised, excluded, erased and destroyed the woman of the subaltern. An erasure reminiscent of Fanon's postcolonial observations in his account of the destruction of the black man made non-existent in the white man's gaze, and through the mental attitude of denial by the master: "I don't see you" (see *Fanon: Black skin, White masks*, film, Julien, 1996). In the Algerian colonial context Fanon explains that it is through the construction of "Otherness" that the black man begins to see himself. "The oppressor, through the inclusive and frightening character of his authority, manages to impose on the native new ways of seeing, and in particular, a pejorative judgment with respect to his original forms of existing" (1967: 38). For Spivak, if a woman was acknowledged, then she was maligned and mischaracterised in a way that served the dominant orthodoxy of the occidental imagination of Western patriarchal supremacy. Her thesis "Can the Subaltern Speak?" explores the subordinate place of the "subaltern" woman in dominant Western discursive practice and super-structural institutions. Spivak details how the subaltern was "spoken for" (1988: 90). This being "spoken for" where you learn that language does not belong to you (MacKinnon 1993: 5) continues and is challenged by contemporary feminist writers and activists (see Bouattia 2020). Spivak, draws on the work of Foucault ([1976b]), in exploring the construction of power and knowledge, arguing that non-Western ways of being, living and culture are not merely marginalised, but actually decimated and destroyed, and women, in particular, are at the mercy of this erasure and violence. The resonances between Spivak's theorisation and the contemporary representations of the Muslim woman, her body and her dress are obvious.

The power of the "Orientalist" discourse to construct non-Western women as the "Other" also resonates throughout Saadawi's academic (1997) and fictional writings. But like some of the Western women travel writers criticised by Lewis and Mabro (above), Saadawi (1980) also accuses in this case Western feminism for its complicity within Orientalist presumptions. (Jacoby 2015: 532 also points to the enduring resonance of this view within some feminism(s) where "Third World" women are perceived as passive others, victimised by the aggression of their own men and "primitive" cultural practices).

> Influential circles, particularly in the Western imperialist world, depict the problems of Arab women as stemming from the substance and values of Islam, and simultaneously depict the retarded development of Arab countries in many important areas as largely the result of religious and cultural factors, or even inherent characteristics in the mental and psychic constitution of the Arab peoples. ... They tend to depict our life as a continual submission to medieval systems and point vehemently to some of the rituals and traditional practices such as female circumcision.... I am against female circumcision. But I disagree with those women in America and Europe who concentrate on issues such as female circumcision and depict them as proof of the unusual and barbaric oppression to which women is exposed only in African or Arab countries. (Saadawi 1980: i, xv)

There is also the complicity of the feminist scholar. Saadawi in her critique of Orientalism in academia (1997: 125, 147) points out, how women academics from the Middle East are treated as an intellectual sub-species by white American feminist "sisters" (see Chapter 8).

"Orientalist" Tropes of Women: Past Contiguities

Notwithstanding criticism of Said on the woman, it is generally agreed within postcolonial feminism that his thesis on Orientalism provides a framework important to the development of feminist scholarship (McClintock 1995; Yeğenoğlu 1998; Reina Lewis 1996) and remains of ambient relevance for understanding the contemporary representations of Arab/Muslim women and men, and for an interrogation of the treatment of Muslims in the post 9/11 period (which I discuss later). Spivak, and more recently Yeğenoğlu, together with a substantial body of scholarship by women on women's personal status in the Middle East and in diasporic communities in the West, collectively demonstrate the breadth of postcolonial feminist analysis of the tropes of Oriental women within colonial discourses, and the perpetuation of these tropes in contemporary narrations, all of which are understandings inspired by Said's framework and interlocutions (see also Weber 2001). Whilst Said focused on the effects of Orientalist ideology made by men in their representation of "Othered" men, post-colonial feminism focuses on the Orientalisation of gender produced by men in the construction of "Othered" women. Whatever the cultural form, whether in the written word, pseudo-science, art and photography, etc., historical Western imagery presented Muslim and Eastern women as the voiceless docile subjugates of men, submissive, "covered" and veiled, whilst at the same time turning them into pornographic tropes, sexualised and eroticised for the Western male gaze. These past tropes have contiguity in the present in constituting the female Muslim subject. If Said's omitted women from his observations on Orientalism, his strength lay in his method since "After *Orientalism* scholars in the humanities and social sciences could no longer ignore questions of differences and the politics of representation" (Bayoumi and Rubin 67). Recognising the importance of "writing back" I note by way of example the deep-seatedness of gendered Orientalism in three cultural forms. First, in early feminist literature notably, the writing of Mary Wollstonecraft, second in pseudo-scientific anthropology notably, the writing of Ploss, Bartels and Bartels and third, in the paintings and photography of the nineteenth and early twentieth-century drawing on Reina Lewis's critique of orientalist paintings and Malek Alloula's (1986) study of the 1930s "Algerian" photographic post card. These representations are not fixed in history, by any means, but continue to carry a contemporary, contiguous and contrapuntal resonance.

The "Mahometan" "Backward" Woman in Early Feminist Tracts

The Muslim female trope of docility, subjugation and backwardness resonates throughout Orientalist cultural forms of the period from eighteenth to twentieth century, propagated in cultural texts, written largely by men, however the texts of the acclaimed feminist and advocate of women's rights, Mary Wollstonecraft, epitomised imperial feminism, and Orientalism. Said in *Culture and Imperialism* had noted Wollstonecraft's feminist role in influencing Ram Mohan Roy's struggles for female emancipation in India (1994: 218), "Wollstonecraft, mobilized the early campaign for Indian women's rights, a common pattern in the colonized world" (263) however no mention is made of her deep disdain for the Orient. In *A Vindication of the Rights of Women* (1792), considered the seminal text of Western feminism, in challenging the abject slavedom of English middle-class women (Chapter 2: 92) she chooses Islam, and what she imagines women's position within it to be, as the comparator and the benchmark of female oppression to send out a warning on the consequences of female enslavement, holding up the Muslim woman under Islam as the binary opposite of Western woman's liberated strivings. With repeated references to "in the true style of Mahometanism", she writes:

> In a treatise, therefore, on female rights and manners, the works which have been particularly written for their improvement must not be overlooked; especially when it is asserted, in direct terms, that the minds of women are enfeebled by false refinement; that the books of instruction, written by men of genius, have had the same tendency as more frivolous productions; and that, in the true style of Mahometanism, they are treated as a kind of subordinate beings, and not as a part of the human species, when improvable reason is allowed to be the dignified distinction which raises men above the brute creation, and puts a natural sceptre in a feeble hand. (Introduction: 6)
> Thus Milton describes our first frail mother; though when he tells us that women are formed for softness and sweet attractive grace, I cannot comprehend his meaning, unless, in the true Mahometan strain, he meant

to deprive us of souls, and insinuate that we were beings only designed by sweet attractive grace, and docile blind obedience, to gratify the senses of man when he can no longer soar on the wing of contemplation. (Chapter 2: 19)

Bernadette Andrea (2009) in her critique of Western feminist responses to the "Orient" and their complicity with wider Orientalist and imperialist discourses cites Hunt (2003) who concludes that Wollstonecraft: "...turned the claim that Western European Christian women were the most fortunate women in the world, and Muslim women the most oppressed, into an unassailable truth" (Andrea 2009: 274). Andrea finds in Wollstonecraft the tendency to displace patriarchal oppression onto Oriental society (284). She calls for a decoupling of the terms "women" and "Islam" from this monolithic conceptualisation (275) and in challenging the effacement of women's agency provides evidence of a counter-discourse from less publicised feminist travel writers. In this alternative narrative, which demonstrates female agency, through the diaries of Lady Mary Wortley Montague, who accompanied her husband Lord Montague as ambassadors wife to the Ottoman empire from 1716–1718 and had first-hand experience of the oriental woman, Andrea uncovers striking evidence of a counter-discourse (2007: 10) presenting a very different reality from the Western male representation of the oppressed Muslim woman. Muslim women unlike English women had their own property (2007: 82) as Lady Montague pointed out. On women's private and social status and polygamy Lady Montague wrote: "'Tis true that, that their law permits them four wives, but there is no instance of a man of quality that makes use of this liberty, or of a woman of rank that would suffer it" (2007: 278). Andrea recognises the contrapuntal and modern resonances of these tropes, concluding that such early modern cultural productions have a relevance for the "global gender politics of our postcolonial age" (2007: 11). Interestingly, Susan Okin (1999), in her critique of contemporary multiculturalism (to which I return in Chapter 8) advocates "extinction" of Muslim culture, as did many early feminists, as the solution to what Western feminists perceived to be Muslim women's unequal and subjugated status.

In the case of a more patriarchal minority culture, no argument can be made based on self-respect or freedom that the female members of the culture have a clear interest in its preservation. Indeed, they might be much better off if the culture into which they were born were either to become extinct (so that its members would become integrated into the less sexist surrounding culture) or, preferably, to be encouraged to alter itself so as to reinforce the equality of women. (Okin 2–3)

Woman - East /West Binarism in Anthropology

Herbert S Lewis's claim that Said ignores anthropology, almost entirely (2007: 774), is perfectly true (see also Asad's critique of the orientalist bias in anthropology [1973]). So, by infilling this lacuna I turn to examine probably one of the most influential texts in the field of "pseudo-science" on "the woman question", Ploss, Bartels and Bartels, *Woman: An Historical and Gynaecological Compendium* (originally written in 1885, 1935 being the first English edition) provides further evidence for Spivak's thesis on the Orientalist representation of "Third World" and non-European women. Ploss, Bartels and Bartels, in a three-volume illustrated tome, depict women of the West as civilised, whilst non-Western women are "Othered," and described as "non-civilised", "less civilised", "savage", "less savage", "barbarous", "less barbarous" (Vol III: 124). Ploss et al's professed "scientific" account trades on the binarism of the race markers of the Aryan versus the non-Caucasian woman, where the non-Caucasian was recorded as being not quite as cultured, beautiful and dignified as the Western Aryan female type. So writes Ploss et al.: "The black and yellow races are generally repugnant to our European sense of smell" and anthropologists report on the "pathetic ugliness of aboriginal women," "Nubian women are conspicuously ugly in old age", and the women of Somalia "painfully ugly". Most shocking is the blatant disavowal of any respect for the dignity of women of "the Other" or "subaltern" whose genitalia are graphically, gratuitously and forcibly exposed and photographed, staged in scenarios aligned to contemporary pornographic genre. It was seemingly acceptable to photograph the vulva and hymen of women of the subaltern—mainly African women, purportedly to chart the clinical stages of female circumcision, child labour, birthing etc., whilst proclaiming deference to science and expanding knowledge of "customary practice". The absolute objectification of the woman of the "Other" was commanded by her forced submission, undressed, arranged and photographed, the doctor, anthropologist and photographer all fully in the knowledge of the importance of cultural systems of honour and shame, yet in the eyes of the Western medical anthropologist the women were treated as mere specimen body parts.

By contrast, Caucasian Aryan women, with tresses of hair flowing over clothed nubile bodies, are photographed in staged Grecian poses found in so-called "high art" to underscore the superiority of the European woman and the dominance of the Western ideal of beauty. The contrapuntality and contiguity of the past representations resonate into the present. Eddo-Lodge critiques Western beauty ideals and the focus on white flesh remarking somewhat tongue in cheek that: "some media didn't believe that black and brown women are beautiful enough to bother objectifying" (2018: 176). Contemporary pornography is built on racism, not only of the black male subject but Black and Asian women are especially violated. Alice Walker observes: "For centuries the back woman has served as the primary pornography 'outlet' for white men in Europe and America" (Walker 1981: 42, Collins 1993). In Ploss's compendium it is significant that references to, and photographs of, Arab and Middle Eastern women are conspicuously absent, although a passing reference is made to Islam and ancient civilisations. The photographs of women in this compendium are of the least powerful, the most subordinated of all women, who could not resist colonial power or the power of the taker, maker and orchestrator of the indecent photograph. Crenshaw's (2017 [1997]) thesis on powerlessness and of the intersectionality of class, race, colour, sexuality, nationality, etc., and how these dimensions determine a different experience for women all are demonstrated here. However, as Islam required women to be "covered", Muslim women were "saved" from such dehumanising pornographisation since it would not have been possible to photograph Muslim women clothed, even less their naked constituent body parts. As Jacobsen (2007: 57) observes, in another context: "Islamic propriety deterred Eastern sitters posing for the camera because it was forbidden in Islam" and considered blasphemy, noting that the Arabian Peninsula in any form was little photographed before 1880 (55).

But, whilst Ploss et al. (1885) were drawing together a spectacle of colonialist anthropology of the "lesser" "uncivilised" colonised woman, it seems that the Arab/Muslim woman was not "saved" at all since she too was also debased if not in the physical sense then in and by the sexualised Orientalist representations of art form where she became the imagined muse of so-called Western "artistic" representation of the late nineteenth and twentieth century. Here, paintings of the Oriental woman of the Middle and Near East projected a sexualised gendered trope onto the male consumer in what became an increasingly commercialised market trading on her body in erotic imagery.

Sexualised and "Orientalised" in the Western Male Psyche

In Orientalist art and photography of the nineteenth and twentieth century, the Near Eastern and Middle Eastern/Arab/Muslim female body was at the epicentre of a vista of the Orient, constructed by the Western voyeuristic psyche. A psyche looking on, eroticising and sexually objectifying, imagining, penetrating beyond the face veil and into the closed harem of the Sultan's palace. As Scott (2007: 54) writes: "women piqued the imagination of French colonialists". The "latent orientalism" that Said identified (but little developed) is demonstrated here, in the sphere of the unconscious where the subliminal desires, unconscious fantasies, and sexual longings of the Western male are laid bare in the field of vision, concretised in artistic representation of paintings and photography. This genre said nothing about the Orient but everything about the culture that produced such imaginings, where racism, sexual longing, and sexual objectification of "Othered" women metamorphosed into so-called art. Through the fantasy and imaginings of the painter, "she" was the woman uncovered, raped, and possessed. This desire is yet a replicated expression of Dworkin's (1989) analysis of contemporary pornographic representation where "the sex" lies in the power and domination.

This Orientalist mythical genre depicted the West's mysterisation of the East, through representations of the harem, women bathing in exotic dress, veiled and undressed. Jacobsen (2007: 57) notes: "The representation of an odalisque, or female slave, has been the cause of much mythology in the West ever since Ingres' painting". Of course, few Western painters had ever travelled to the East and those that had certainly did not have access to the scenes they painted. Jean Auguste Dominique Ingres "The Turkish Bath" (1863) depicts a group of women he had never seen, nude and bathing, in erotic poses, and sexually objectified. Jean-Léon Gérôme, similarly, created several paintings of unclothed women bathing, "Femmes Au Bain" (1898), "Harem Pool - A Bath" (1876), and "Women Bathing Her Feet - A Moorish Bath" (1901). Whilst Frederic Leighton had visited Egypt and Damascus he had never stepped inside the harems he painted. His "Odalisque" (1860) represents the Oriental woman exotically clothed, as sensual and longing. As

Malek Alloula (1986: 130) observes, the odalisque is: "metamorphosed by Orientalist painting into the sublimated image of the one enclosed in the harem". In some paintings the gaze is reversed where women are not merely to be looked at, but they do the looking in gazing out of the picture frame and enticing. It is here that they are cast as provocateurs who are then held responsible for the male desire that is elicited. Eugène Delacroix's subject in "The Odalisque" (1825), is a naked woman, reclining on a divan, open, yielding, looking out of the canvas into the eye of the Western male gaze, waiting and wanting "to be had". Mariano Fortuny's "Odalisque" (1861) repeats this phantasm and encourages the voyeurism of the gaze, his nude female subject is reclining and although looking away from the canvas she beckons to the Arab loot player in the background of the composition. But even where the Oriental woman is fully clothed and her head covered, her availability is promised and the allegory repeated, as in Jean Raymond Hippolyte Lazerges' "Rendezvous in Arab street" (1873). Here, the female subject completely veiled, reveals nothing but her eyes, and is in a street with a man whose arm is draped around her. Masculine desire and racism drive the recurrent trope of Oriental female sexual availability. Jacobsen (2007: 85) notes that for all this objectification and Orientalist genre Said, dedicates only a few sentences to Orientalist painting as a cultural form.

Reina Lewis in her incisive study on *Gendering Orientalism* (1996) forgives Said for such omissions and utilises his Orientalist framework to demonstrate how the Oriental woman becomes a metaphor for the Orient itself and contends that the Western desire to literally lift the face veil and to uncover is not a desire to liberate and to make free, but a desire to control and possess the Eastern body (12). However, she also maintains that it was not only the masculinist *oeuvre* that created the Eastern sexualised trope, since women painters also played their part in this cultural production. The artist Elisabeth Jerichau-Baumann plays on the iconography of Orientalised sexuality in her painting "An Egyptian Pottery Seller near Giza" (1876). Her subject wears a semi-transparent garment and her full pouting lips look out of the canvas. However, Henriette Browne, who painted two Harem interiors and a flute player, unlike men who had no access to the harem, had privileged access to this world. This access to palaces and the harem reveals an intimacy with the Orient in her work. Browne's women, are fully clothed, engaging with one another, and no baths to be seen anywhere. Lewis points out: "women's differential gendered access to the positionalities of imperial discourse produced a gaze on the Orient and the Orientalised 'other' that registered difference less pejoratively and less absolutely than men" (4).

The arrival of the photographic form, during this period, continued the phantasm and sexualisation of Oriental women, where photographic postcards served the commercialised European market and demand for pornography. Photographic representations of the harem, half-clad Arab and Turkish women, face veiled and semi-naked were produced from the end of the nineteenth century. The scenarios were all constructed and contrived in studios with female models (see for example "Woman revealing bare breast" Schier and Schefft c1860s; Claude-Joseph Portier "Odalisque"—lying on a coach c1870s; Jean Geiser's "Mauresque danseuse"—Woman with breast uncovered c1870: and "Jeune Bedouine" c1910—breasts uncovered; Mercelin Flandrin's "Moroccan singer"—nude c1870 and Auguste Rosalie Bisson "The Egyptian Pavilion"—completely nude c867). Jacobsen (2007: 65) points out that the photographs of purportedly Turkish and Eastern women, were compiled in photographic studios, in England and elsewhere. "The Arabian Peninsula being little photographed because of the blasphemous occupation of photography".

Malek Alloula's *Colonial Harem* (1986) documents the colonial photographic postcard of Algeria and the Algerian woman from 1900 to 1930, as El Guindi puts it: "staging the colonial fantasy of the French" (2003: 23). Half-naked, breasts uncovered, veiled, and unveiled, sexualised, and partly hidden El Guindi explains: "The colonial post cards staged Algerian woman to evoke images about women's quarters as prison (17–26), naked bodies, "sub-eroticism" (105–24) and "oriental sapphism" (95–104). In all these visual representations, as in the so-called Orientalist art, the veil (the face covering or niqab and the face, body and head covering of the burqa) assumes a highly eroticised sexual significance. Of the political significance, Harlow (1986: xv) says of Alloula's postcards: "Possession of Arab women came to serve as a surrogate for and means to the political and military conquest of the Arab world" (in El Guindi: 172) (see also Jacobsen (2007: 91). Joseph Massad (2007) in *Desiring Arabs* remarks: "The West's construction of her sexuality, double binds the Oriental woman, who suppressed by and in her own 'uncivilised culture', ugly and despised or to be desired, 'had,' consumed and discarded, is also trapped in her culture, from which only the revolting and violent chivalry of the Western male could save her".

Said, neglected the subject of face veiling, head covering and body covering and the sexualised Orientalist representations of women in cultural and art forms, although in general terms his work does contain references to the Orient as "feminine". Said's omissions may be several, but his contribution to understanding European racism of the Arab/Muslim and Near and Middle Eastern region peoples provides an enduring framework for analysis of contemporary anti-Muslim racism and Islamophobia which continues to reproduce these and other tropes of Muslim men and women, from Middle East, Arab and Muslim countries, and also of Arab and Muslim diasporic communities in the West. The Muslim man remains constructed as he was then, as dangerous, violent, albeit now as terrorist. We witness however a seismic shift in the representation of the Muslim women, who, whilst she remains subordinated under Muslim patriarchy and religious theocracy especially in Muslim majority countries, and remains a sexualised and alluring trope in the Western mind she now has another persona that of an active woman of agency, of resistance and with terrorist sympathies conveying in Western imagination a jihadist signature so incisively documented by Shakira Hussein in her thesis *From Victims to Suspects* (Hussein 2019).

Contemporary Tropes – Women to Be Saved and Terrorists to Be Damned

Polysemicity: Veiled Agency or Veiled Subornation

As Dabashi (2011) observes the response to the terror atrocities in New York 2001, Madrid 2004, London 2005 were "blown up into political outrage at Muslims in particular and Islam in general" (3). "The emergence of Islam as the nemesis of the West gave a new lease of life to old-fashioned Orientalism" (11). In the contemporary landscape especially post 9/11, the Muslim woman has been transformed from helpless passive victim to terrorist menace. This transformation lies at the heart of Shakira Hussein's thesis (2019: 3). Whilst a sign cannot be abstracted from its meaning, covering the face with a face veil or the head with headscarf, once essentialised as a signature of subservience, religious observance and sexualisation is now regarded, in some cases, as an emblem of terrorism, extremism, and radicalisation.

The polysemicity and ambivalence of meaning attaching to these garments can be observed in situations where both covering and uncovering takes on a precise political configuration as defined by others looking in and as defined by the subject herself. For example, in 1923, Hudā Shaʿrāwī, a nationalist and feminist, removed her headscarf and face veil as a sign of resistance to the oppression of women in Egypt. In Algeria, in the 1950s and 1960s, as an expression of political resistance to the colonial occupation by the French, and a mark of solidarity with the Maghreb, Algerian women refused to remove their face veil. Hall (2012) rightly said: "No sign is fixed in its meaning" (see also Julien 1996: at 40.00 minutes). Fanon, in *Algeria Unveiled* (1965) understood well the historic dynamism of the veil in women's fight for Algerian independence. The French presented their quest to unveil Algerian women as an evangelical mission to save them (El Guindi 2003: 169–170). Such women saving missions are found repeated in current justifications for the WOT.

> A woman was 'saved' ...Every veil that fell, everybody that became liberated from the traditional embrace of the haik, every face that offered itself to the bold and impatient glance of the occupier, was a negative expression of the fact that Algeria was beginning to deny herself and was accepting the rape of the coloniser. Algerian society with every abandoned veil seemed to express its willingness to attend the master's school and to decide to change its habits under the occupier's direct and patronage. (1965: 42)

As Fanon observed "Unveiling is breaking her resistance to colonial rule" (1965). The French considered the face veil a dangerous physical weapon of resistance as it could be used by women to hide and transport weapons to various parts of the city. Hall (see Julien 1996) in explaining its revolutionary potential explores Fanon's concept of "turn[ing] the veil against its meaning" (at 41.01 minutes) where the Algerian woman said Hall: "appropriated the veil to...deliver explosives because she could depend on the reactionary reading by the French" (at 40.44 min). In May 1958, an official unveiling ceremony forcibly unveiled women. Its purpose it was said was to modernise Algeria, but it was undertaken to undermine the cultural roots of the colonised Algerian (El Guindi: 176). At the psychical level, a face hidden from gaze carries its own power of strength and agency. "The Arabs elude us because they conceal their women from our gaze" (Scott 2007: 55, 63). Once physically and psychically stripped the unveiled faces of women were then photographed by the colonisers official photographer, Marc Garanger, the purpose to provide a living record, to humiliate women and Muslim society and break their resistance (discussed further in Chapter 7). The face veil, at least, in this context, signified resistance, defiance and agency against the French colonisers albeit that in a Maghreb context the face veil had always been a standard-bearer of patriarchy.

If Said had nothing to say about the culturally specific meaning of covering in its many forms, face veiling, head covering or body covering then consideration of its polysemicity and local articulation has been the preoccupation of Near Eastern and Middle Eastern feminist writings from the second half of the twentieth century to the present. Fadwa El Guindi *Veil Modesty and Resistance*, first published in 1977 (2003), Unni Wikan, *Behind the Veil in Arabia* first published in 1977 (1982), Carla Makhlouf, *Changing Veils: Women and Modernisation in North Yemen* (1979), represent just some of the emerging scholarship when Said was writing on the significance of dress and covering for Muslim women, and together with the headscarf's placement at the centre of the 1978 Islamic Revolution (Shirazi 2019) it seems incomprehensible that Said eschewed the political and local appropriation of these dress forms. Later texts including Leila Ahmed's 1982 essay and *Women and Gender in Islam* (1992). Anne McClintock *Imperial Leather* (1995), and Meyda Yeğenoğlu *Colonial Fantasies* (1998), continued exploring the local articulation and theorisation on covering, its meaning, its local presence, and its significance for those who wear it, as well as its continuing Orientalisation and representation by the West.

More recently Joan Wallach Scott, *The Politics of the Veil* (2007), Lila Abu-Lughod, *Do Muslim Women Need Saving?* (2013), Mona Eltahawy *Headscarves and Hymens: Why the Middle East Needs a Sexual Revolution* (2015), and Shakira Hussein's *From Victims to Suspects* (2019) are just some of the several texts that have focused on covering post 9/11, exploring its meaning for those who cover, and the West's representation of covering in the context of international relations and the WOT, examining especially the appropriation by the West of Muslim women's dress and its own self-declared missionary and humanitarian ruse of removing dress in "civilising" and "saving women" (Abu-Lughod's thesis 6–7, 62). In this, the Muslim woman's body is read at least through Western eyes as a barometer of civilisation, as it buttresses its self-professed altruism about which Spivak spoke earlier, that of "White men ...saving brown women from brown men" (Spivak 1988: 92). Such an appeal to gender equality ennobles anti-Muslim bigotry. The "saving Muslim women" rhetoric is based on fallacious presumptions which continue to endorse Orientalist and colonialist representations (Ahmed 1982 and 1992; Yeğenoğlu 1998) whereas Khalid (2011) observes "other" women are represented as the "voiceless victims of a barbaric (male)". As Hussein observes "The role of Muslim women is endlessly malleable to suit the political needs of the moment" (3). The West's moral and political crusading strategy continues, which Said had earlier identified. The centrality of the West's perception of women of the East, which it deploys to legitimise the West's wider political ambitions and justification for military intervention, cannot be overlooked.

Shifting Meaning—Terrorist Signatures: "Shamima Begum"
The presumption that Muslim women lack agency and therefore could not be engaged in terrorist related acts, was an image that was already, even prior to 9/11, shifting and is discussed by Hussein (2019) *From Victims to Suspects*. The precise moment when terrorist imagery and agency began to run alongside and compete with the passive subordinated image of Muslim women as victims of Muslim men is not easy to pinpoint. But as with this shifting image, her dress, face veil and to a lesser extent the headscarf/hijab, also came to represent not only subservience but also resistance and terrorist sympathies and the "clash of civilisations" of which Huntington spoke (Almila 2019). Popular media, in all its forms, began to promote this new reading of Muslim women's dress, as a sign of potential dangerousness (see Chapters 3, 7). At the same time, academic scholarship on the involvement of women in extremism was emerging. Khalid (2011: 18), Hamoon Khelghat-Doost (2016), Patel and Westermann (2018) and others, have considered the way in which this evolving representation of Muslim women's contemporary role has been depicted. Feminist criminology, notably the scholarship of Jacoby (2015), Laster and Erez (2015) and Zempi and Chakraborti (2014) amongst others, have also explored the female terrorist trope in official discourses and in public and media representation. Impressions of Muslim women, now to be feared, as undermining the "British" family values, are images influencing government discourse and institutional decision-making (discussed further in Chapter 3).

I conclude this chapter utilising Hall's framework for understanding the impact of such tropes on "conditions of existence and real effects, outside the scope of the discursive" (Hall 1996: 443) in examining two contemporary cases from the UK by way of my concluding evidence. The first, is the fake story of the child "AB", the second, the unjust saga and treatment of Shamima Begum.

The media story of child *AB* purportedly featured a "white" British child being "taken over" by an "alien" Muslim culture to serve a bigoted readership. Newspapers columnists presented what turned out very quickly indeed to be a fake story as a "clash of civilisations". The child "*AB*," who was five years old, had been removed from her mother's care in March 2017 and placed with foster parents. *The Times* newspaper report (28 August 2017) led with a sensationalist headline which was inaccurate: "Christian child forced into Muslim foster care - Concern for girl who had cross removed and was encouraged to learn Arabic". The story was embellished with a pixelated photograph (taken from behind the subject) of a young child with flowing blonde hair, her hand held by a woman dressed in a long black tunic (gelabaya), and a head covering/hijab, and face covering/niqab. The image was intended to create the impression that it was indeed a photograph of the child "*AB*" and her foster carer, which it was not, whether the newspaper at the time knew this was neither the foster carer or the child concerned I know not. It was however very shortly afterwards reported that the photograph, originally printed in the *Daily Mail*, had been digitally altered, and the woman's face being covered with a veil and that the photograph was not of the carer or the child. Relying on an Orientalised leitmotif, the child's blonde hair was juxtaposed with the carer's long black tunic and head covering, to underscore in visual form a "clash of civilisations" to feed an already burgeoning "moral panic" particularly following the disappearance of three schoolgirls, including Shamima Begum, from Bethnal Green Academy (discussed below).

When the case of *AB* came to court the presiding judge remarked on the media reports and the photograph. "[14.21] The court expresses its concern that photographs of the child and foster carer have been published in the press..." (Albeit at that time, a day after, the judge was unaware that the photograph was a fake). The Independent Press Standards Organisation (IPSO) soon after, received 200 complaints in connection with the press reportage of this story. Then the truth unfolded. The foster placement was discovered to be a short-term respite placement, so *AB* was "hardly forced into care", care which, in any event, ended on 29 August 2017, the day following the media flurry. The maternal grandparents of "the Christian child" *AB* turned out to be of the Muslim faith, and *AB* was also of dual nationality. *The Times* report of 3 October 2017, in a spectacular volte face, published this headline: "Muslim fosterers gave 'warm care' to Christian girl in Tower Hamlets". On 2 November 2017, the London Borough of Tower Hamlets was given permission to publish an alternative version rebutting the original inaccurate claims. Meanwhile, *The Guardian* reported (25 April 2018) that Katie Hopkins, had Tweeted shortly after the story first broke an image of the original inaccurate front page asking: "Which individual at Tower Hamlets was responsible for the abuse of this little girl?" The next day on 29 August 2017 it was clear there had been no story, just unadulterated bigotry. An investigation by the IPSO discovered inaccurate reporting and upheld the complaint by the local authority against *The Times*. The Muslim Council of Britain said that *The Times* had pushed an: "inaccurate, misleading, and bigoted narrative" (*The Guardian*, 25 April 2018). Clear evidence of women's Islamic clothing once a trope of subjugation became a metonym and emblem of radicalisation. The reporting on this family law case had hoped to capitalise on the omnipresent "moral panic" created by the disappearance of three schoolgirls from Bethnal Green Academy, who left the country in February 2015 and travelled to Syria to join ISIS. A story that has dominated the front pages ever since.

Shamima Begum is my second case who as a young schoolgirl of 15, along with Amira Abase 15 and Kadiza Sultana 16 years of age, left the UK on 17 February 2015, during the school half term to travel to Syria to join young men of ISIS who had groomed them over the internet and social media. Atwan (2015: 12) notes: "Islamic States recruitment machine is largely online....In Islamic countries, initial approaches were more often made via an intermediary or recruiter, but in the West, most said they had either direct messaged via Twitter or Facebook, or had been contacted by a friend, relative or acquaintance already inside Islamic State, to initiate their own migration, and received practical advice and logistical instructions" (12). The belief at that time that women and young girls were unlikely terrorist recruits (see *Women and Terrorist Radicalization: Final Report* concluded that women were: "often seen as passive, victims, helpless, subordinate and maternal.....as a result they are not considered to be potential terrorists, nor perceived to be as dangerous as their male counterparts" (Organization for Security and Co-operation in Europe 2013: 3), may have contributed to the under policing and failure of the authorities to act in locating the schoolgirls whom their families had immediately reported as missing when they failed to return home from school. Yet two days after their disappearance, CCTV showed the schoolgirls passing through a border control and waiting in a bus station in Turkey. These images became the iconography, not of vulnerable, coerced and trafficked schoolgirls groomed in cyberspace (as they undoubtedly were Edwards 2017b) but the faces, of Muslim female terrorists. No consideration was given to their age (two of the girls were 15, the oldest only 16) or to the local authority, school and police duty to safeguard minors (Children Act 1989s 17). The failings of these authorities were the subject of an investigation by the UK government Home Affairs Committee on 10 March 2015 (Edwards 2015). At this committee hearing, the Metropolitan Commissioner, Sir Bernard Hogan-Howe, apologised for the significant police errors. The British Police were aware of the schoolgirl's disappearance on 17 February, having been notified by the parents, but failed to notify the Turkish authorities of their departure from the UK for Istanbul until 19 February.

On 13 February 2019, in Al-Hawl refugee camp in Northern Syria, and due to give birth to her third child (her two other children, one son at eight months, one daughter at one year and nine months, both having died from malnutrition and disease) Shamima Begum now 19 in an interview with Andrew Loyd, reporter with *The Times* newspaper, said she wanted to return home. The "Bring me Home" Loyd/Begum interview occupied media reports for several weeks, where Begum was always represented across all media reports as extremely dangerous. The timing of the interview and media reporting coincided with the introduction of tougher anti-terror measures in The Counter-Terrorism and Border Security Act (2019) (CTBSA) (which received Royal Assent on 12 February 2019) and as it was met with much criticism from human rights organisations. The timing of *The Times* interview with Begum on 13 February, a day after the CTBSA became law, could not be said to be mere happenstance. On 14 February 2019, the Begum story occupied the front page of *The Times* and four further pages focusing on her remark: "When I saw my first severed head it didn't faze me at all". This then became the signature across all media reporting and became the strap line through which she was read thereafter as a "potentially dangerous fanatic" (*Daily Mail*, 15 February 2019). Anne Widdicombe (former MEP and member of the Brexit Party) said: "Britain should not raise a finger to help her" (*Daily Mail*, 20 February 2019). The British government, to date (March 2021) has remained resolute in its determination not to do so. Loyd revisited Begum (*The Times*, 2 April 2019) and in an interview, conducted shortly after the death of her third child and now held in the Al-Roj refugee camp, perhaps feeling safer there, she said she regretted joining ISIS, and that she was brainwashed, and at the al-Hawl camp, anyone speaking out against ISIS would be assaulted or possibly killed. Loyd's 2 April interview displays a shift in the narrative, acknowledging for the first time the possibility that Begum was groomed online and included her remarks that in her previous interview her comments were not made freely: "I was afraid of my life and my child's life... women being put in prison, husband's being executed. I was shocked". The media circus has continued and the dangerous trope imagery squeezed out a little further when on 17 February 2020, *The Guardian's* Dan Sabbagh interviewed Begum and although with very little evidence to corroborate his story reported that she was a member of al-Hisba (ISIS's morality police), that she carried a Kalashnikov and said Sabbagh "allegedly" "stitched suicide bombers into explosive vests".

Discipline, Control and Banish

The removal of citizenship to Shamima Begum and denial of her right to return, is a clear example of how power is used to discipline, control, punish and banish its subjects. Foucault's *Discipline and Punish* (1991 [1975]) explores how the punishments of physical control and the less visible discipline of the "soul" are utilised by the state. Certainly, punishment through banishment represents the ultimate form of physical and spiritual admonishment, an example of what Goldberg (2002: 109) calls "racial governmentality". In 1958, the US Supreme Court in *Trop v Dulles* denounced the stripping of citizenship, regarding it as "a form of punishment more primitive that torture" and in Roman law, "ex silium" denoted both voluntary exile and *banishment* as a capital *punishment* alternative to death. As Armstrong (1954) points out it constitutes the most fearful fate which primitive law could inflict (758). Kapoor and Narkowicz (2019) note the fragility of citizenship and how the UK government, through executive power, and legislation, has devised ways of using citizenship in an expansion of state securitisation in including citizenship deprivation (Counter-Terrorism and Security Act [CTSA] 2015, s 2–4.) Whilst the Home Secretary has the power under the Royal Prerogative, to withdraw citizenship, "for the public good" the exercise of this power is reviewed by the courts, in this case the Special Immigration

Appeals Commission (SIAC). And so, in a series of cases, the government's continual refusal of her return has been challenged by her lawyers in the course of several court hearings. On 22 October 2019, a four-day hearing was held on preliminary issues (*Shamima Begum v Secretary of State for the Home Department* 2019). In a separate application, by way of judicial review, which was turned down, her lawyers challenged the Home Secretary's refusal to grant her entry clearance (EWHC 2020) to argue her case. As Jacoby (2015: 538) writing about the general situation facing such outcasts said: "the major challenge is, these girls and women who already joined are now located in situations of armed conflict, outside the reach of international law, without diplomatic support and difficult, if not, impossible to rescue". On 7 February 2020 SIAC upheld the Home Secretary's decision. In July 2020, in a further appeal, her lawyers succeeded in persuading the court that she should be permitted to return to effectively put her case. On November 25, her case was considered once again and on February 26 2021 the UK Supreme Court rejected all grounds of her appeal to return.

The press preferred the epithet of the dangerous "Jihadi bride". Begum, had said in a Loyd interview that her only role in the caliphate was "to make babies". Katherine Brown's research however is also significant in its finding of Muslim women's sense of being an outsider: "The perceived failure of Western states to give young Muslims a sense of belonging, purpose and value as Muslims and citizens is striking in the online accounts of these women jihadis" (*BBC News*, 6 October 2014, "Analysis: Why are Western women joining Islamic State?"). Narratives that offer an explanation outside religiosity and outside a female passivity pathology or as in this case the new female terrorist trope suggesting that other political, social, and economic and colonialist influences may be a contributory factor are "subjugated narratives" that are shut down (see later for example the official criticism of Cheri Blair and Jenni Tonge cited in Chapter 3). Yet, the real influences are indeed undoubtedly complex, geopolitical, including the WOT, the invasion of Iraq, the treatment of Muslim men in Guantánamo and Abu Ghraib, and the hate crime and hate speech against Muslims, and in Begum's case victimisation and coercion through online trafficking of a young adolescent minor failed by responsible authorities who had a duty to protect.

CONCLUSION: WOMEN, MEN, ALL ARE RACIALISED

As for the Muslim male he continues to be characterised, as, he always was, dangerous, violent, demonised, as a violent man of rage (see Bernard Lewis above), to be feared, and "a threat to be contained" (Khalid 2011: 23), all the tropes that Said identified in *Covering Islam* (1997: xxx, 11) and in all of his texts and now, with the recent addition of a stereotype of sexual predator (at least in the UK context especially with reference to Muslim men of Pakistani origin). And as Kundnani (2007: 127) points out: "Those who were once abused as 'Pakis' are now abused as Muslims". Meer and Modood (2019: 22) recognise this contiguity with the past "How Muslims in Europe are perceived today is not unconnected to how they have been perceived and treated by European empires and their racial hierarchy in earlier centuries". Fuelled by media representation (see Chapter 3) these stereotypes have "real effects" outside the discursive, whether in increased surveillance (see Chapter 5), or suppression of dissent (see Chapter 3, Lynch 2013) or subject to hate crime. The criminal conduct of some men whose family heritage is originally from Pakistan and were convicted for sex trafficking of young girls now adds "sexual predator" and paedophile to the Muslim trope. Tufail's (2019) research identifies a "racialised panic" and demonstrates how the negative portrayal of the Muslim male, especially the Muslim male of the Pakistani and Asian community has resulted in holding the whole community to account (148). The Jay Report (2014) on Rotherham estimated that 14,000 children had been abused, but the report also recognised that the police bore some measure of responsibility as they treated the young girls with contempt (149). It is also relevant that historically this contempt is mirrored in the inadequate state response to child protection influenced by public, legal and official notions that young girls and adolescents are contributory negligent in their demise. My research into Prostitution in the 1990s revealed that young girls (minors) were being systematically groomed and exploited yet they were criminalised by police and by the courts in much the same way as adult women, and considered unworthy of protection. Today these now adult women who were prosecuted as children find that their criminal convictions remain on record. (In 2020, women who were prosecuted as young girls at that time have finally been recognised as having been victims not offenders (see R *(on the application of QSA) v Secretary of State for the Home Department* [2018] and

R (on the application of QSA) v Secretary of State for the Home Department [2020]. The retention of their convictions on police records was the subject of questions in parliament Parliamentary Questions 1 July 2020, a court has ruled that they should still remain on police files).

Jack Straw, MP framed the more prominent cases of trafficking of young girls by men of Pakistani origin as a "suspect community" problem. "But there is a specific problem which involves Pakistani heritage men ... who target vulnerable young white girls. ...We need to get the Pakistani community to think much more clearly about why this is going on and to be more open about the problems that are leading to a number of Pakistani heritage men thinking it is OK to target white girls in this way" (Prince: 2011). This narrative has been repeated and has come unjustly to define the whole male Pakistani community in the UK. Martin Amis in *The Second Plane: September 11, 2001–2007* (a collection of his journalism on 9/11) takes this pathologising further and identifies what he regards as sexual frustration and testosterone as characterising all Muslim men and communities. This racialisation of sex and sex offending has its origins in white supremacist racists characterisation of the black African male (Hernton 1969). Fanon (2008 [1952]) deals at length with this mythology the "Negro symbolizes the biological" (144) and "has been subjected to the image of the biological-sexual-genital..." (178). Angela Davis writes "In the history of the United States, the fraudulent rape charge stands out as one of the most formidable artifices invented by racism. The myth of the Black rapist has been methodically conjured up whenever recurrent waves of violence and terror against the Black community have required convincing justification" (Davis 1983: 73). This racialisation is extended to the Muslim male and is the subject of Raphael Patai's *The Arab Mind* (2003) a compendium of Orientalising. These racialised and Orientalist representations of Muslim women and Muslim men are constantly reiterated in the media and through public rhetoric (see Chapter 3) projected as truths that have a material impact outside the discursive with "real effects" fuelling hatred, division and exclusion.

The Orientalist stereotypes of which Said spoke have served bigotry and Islamophobia in a myriad of cultural forms, and on the global agenda have functioned to bolster justifications for the WOT on Muslim majority countries including the denigration of the Palestinian Arab, whilst legitimating counter-terror strategies at home, control of the Muslim community's family life and the decimation of the Muslim woman's body. As for Said "his commitments to his scholarship ... have made him arguably the most important intellectual of the latter half of the twentieth century" (Bayoumi and Rubin 2001: xii).

REFERENCES

Abdel-Malek, A. 1963. Orientalism in Crisis. *Diogenes* 11 (44): 103–140.
Adib-Moghaddam, A. 2011. *A Metahistory of the Clash of Civilization: Us and Them Beyond Orientalism*. Hurst: Columbia UP.
Ahmed, L. 1982. "Western Ethnocentrism and Perceptions of the Harem". *Feminist Studies* 8 (3): 521–534.
Ahmed, L. 1992. *Women and Gender in Islam: Historical Roots of a Modern Debate*. Yale: Yale University Press.
Abu Lughod, L. 2015 [2013]. *Do Muslim Women Need Saving?* Harvard: Harvard University Press.
Almila, A., and D. Inglis. 2019. *The Routledge International Handbook to Veils and Veiling Practices*. New York and London: Routledge.
Althusser, L. 1984 [1971]. Ideology and Ideological State Apparatuses. In *Lenin and Philosophy and Other Essays*, 121–176. New York: Monthly Review Press.
Al Azm, S. 1981. Orientalism and Orientalism in Reverse. *Khamsin* No 8. London: Ithaca Press.
Amin, S. 2010 [1988]. *Eurocentrism: Modernity, Religion, and Democracy: A Critique of Eurocentrism and Culturalism.*, 2nd UK ed. Edition. Nairobi, Capetown, Dakar and Oxford: Pambazuka Press.
Alloula, M. 1986. *The Colonial Harem*. Manchester: Manchester University Press.
Amireh, A. 2000. Arab-Feminism in a Transnational World. *Signs* 26 (11): 215–249.
Andrea, B. 2007. *Women and Islam in Early Modern English Literature*. Cambridge: Cambridge University Press.
Andrea, B. 2009. Islam, Women, and Western Responses: The Contemporary Relevance of Early Modern Investigation. *Women's Studies* 38: 273–292.
Arendt, H. 1963. *Eichmann in Jerusalem*. London: Viking Press.
Armstrong, M. 1954. Banishment: Cruel and Unusual Punishment. *University of Pennsylvania Law Review* 111: 758–786.
Asad, T. 1973. *Anthropology and the Colonial Encounter*. London: Ithaca Press.
Atwan, A.B. 2015. *Islamic State: The Digital Caliphate*. London: Saqi Books.
Bhabha, H. K. 2004 [1994]. *The Location of Culture*. London: Routledge.
Bayoumi, M., and A. Rubin. 2001. *The Edward Said Reader*. London: Granta.
Becker, H. 1967. Whose Side Are We On. *Social Problems* 14 (3): 239–247.
Begum (Shamima) v Secretary of State for the Home Department SC/163/2019 https://www.judiciary.uk/wp-content/uploads/2020/02/begum-v-home-secretary-siac-judgment-1.pdf. Accessed 10 November.

Benhabib, S. 1996. *The Reluctant Modernism of Hannah Arendt*. London: Sage.
Berger, P.L., and T. Luckmann. 1966. *The Social Construction of Reality*. London: Vintage.
Bertens, H. 2013. *Literary Theory: The Basics*. London: Routledge.
Blum, F.H. 1944. Max Weber's Postulate of "Freedom" from Value Judgments. *American Journal of Sociology* 50 (1): 46–52.
Bouattia, M. 2020. Between Submission and Threat. In *It's Not About the Burqa*, ed. M. Khan. London: Picador.
Brittan, A. 1972. Systems, Structures, and Consciousness: The Social Psychology of Meaning. In *The Rules of the Game*, ed. T. Shanin. London: Tavistock.
Cannadine, D. 2002. *Ornamentalism: How the British Saw Their Empire*. Oxford: Oxford University Press.
Chomsky. 1967. A Special Supplement: The Responsibility of Intellectuals. *NYRB*, February 23.
Chowdhry, G. 2007. Edward Said and Contrapuntal Reading: Implications for Critical Interventions in International Relations. *Millennium—Journal of International Studies* 36 (1): 101–116.
Collins, P.H. 1993. Pornography and Black Women's Bodies. In *Making Violence Sexy*, ed. D. Russell. Buckingham: Open University Press.
Crenshaw, K. 2017 [1997]. *On Intersectionality*. Columbia: Columbia University Press.
Dabashi, H. 2011. *Brown Skin, White Masks (The Islamic Mediterranean)*. London: Pluto.
Davis, A. 1983 [1981]. *Women Race and Class*. New York: Random House.
Dworkin, A. 1989. *Pornography Men Possessing Women*. London: The Women Press.
Eddo-Lodge, R. 2018. *Why I'm No Longer Talking About Race*. London: Bloomsbury Press.
Edwards, S.S.M. 2015. Protecting Schoolgirls from Terrorism Grooming. *International Journal of Family Law*. 3: 236–248.
Edwards, S.S.M. 2017a. Targeting Muslim Women Through Dress. In *Women, Law and Culture Conformity, Contradiction and Conflict*, ed. J. Scutt. Palgrave: Macmillan.
Edwards, S.S.M. 2017b. Cyber-Grooming Young Women for Terrorist Activity: Dominant and Subjugated Explanatory Narratives. In *Cybercrime, Organised Crime, and Societal Responses*, ed. E. Viano, 23–47. New York: Springer.
El Guindi, F. 2003 [1977]. *Veil Modesty and Resistance*. Berg 3PL.
El Saadawi, N. 1990. *The Nawal El Saadawi Reader*. London: Zed.
Eltahawy, M. 2015. *Headscarves and Hymens: Why the Middle East Needs a Sexual Revolution*. London: Weidenfeld and Nicolson.
Fanon, F. 2008 [1952]. *Black Skin, White Masks*. New York: Grove Press.

Fanon, F. 1965. *Studies in a Dying Colonialism.* New York: Monthly Review Press.

Fanon, F. 1967. *Towards the African Revolution.* New York: Monthly Review Press.

Faubion, J.D. (ed.). 2000. *Michel Foucault Power Essential Works of Foucault 1954–1984,* vol. 3. London: Penguin.

Foucault, M. 2002 [1969]. *Archaeology of Knowledge* (2002 ed). London: Penguin.

Foucault, M. 1991 [1975]. *Discipline and Punish.* London: Penguin.

Foucault, M. 1980 [1976a]. TWO LECTURES Lecture One: 7 January 1976 (on *Power and Knowledge*). In *Power/Knowledge: Selected interviews and other writings 1972–1977,* ed. C. Gordon, 78–92. New York: Harvester Press.

Foucault, M. 1980 [1976b]. TWO LECTURES Lecture Two: 14 January 1976 (on *Power and Knowledge*). In *Power/ Knowledge: Selected Interviews and Other Writings 1972–1977.* (1980), C. Gordon, 92–108. New York: Harvester Press.

Freidan, B. 1963. *The Feminine Mystique.* London: Penguin.

Gabrieli, F. 1965. Apology for Orientalism. In *Orientalism A Reader,* ed. A.l. Macfie (2009 [2000]), 79–85. Edinburgh: Edinburgh University Press.

Go, J. 2013. Decolonizing Bourdieu: Colonial and Postcolonial Theory in Pierre Bourdieu's Early Work. *Sociological Theory* 31(1): 49–74.

Goldberg, D.T. 2002. *The Racial State.* Oxford: Wiley Blackwell.

Hall, S. 1996. New Ethnicities. In *Critical Dialogues in Cultural Studies,* ed. D. Morley and K.H. Chen, 441–450. New York: Routledge.

Hall, S. (ed.). 2012. *Representation: Cultural Representations and Signifying Practices.* London: Sage.

Hall, S. 2017. *The Fateful Triangle: Race, Ethnicity, Nation* (The W. E. B. Du Bois Lectures) Harvard: Harvard University Press.

Hernton, C. 1969. *Sex and Racism in America.* London and New York: Harper Collins.

Hunt, M. 2003. Women in Ottoman and Western European Law Courts in the Early Modern Period or Were Western European Women Really the Luckiest in the World?! Conference paper, "Attending to Early Modern Women", University of Maryland at College Park.

Hussein, S. 2019 [2016]. *From Victims to Suspects.* Yale: Yale University Press.

Irwin, R. 2006. *For Lust of Knowing: The Orientalists and Their Enemies.* London: Penguin.

Jacobson, K. 2007. *Odalisques and Arabesques: Orientalist Photography 1839–1925.* London: Bernard Quaritch Ltd.

Jacoby, T. 2015. Jihadi Brides at the Intersections of Contemporary Feminism. *New Political Science* 37 (4): 526–542.

Jay, A. 2014. "The Jay Report". Independent Inquiry into Child Sexual Exploitation in Rotherham (1997–2013). https://www.rotherham.gov.uk/downloads/download/31/independent-inquiry-into-child-sexual-exploitation-in-rotherham-1997—2013. Accessed 15 November 2020.

Julien, I. 1996. *Fanon: Black Skin, White Masks*. Film directed by Isaac Julien, Video Pal Format. https://www.youtube.com/watch?v=tQhwK0QM1gA. Accessed 11 November 2020.

Kabbani, R. 2008 [1986]. *Europe's Myths of Orient: Devise and Rule*, New ed. London: Saqi Books.

Kapoor, N., and K. Narkowicz. 2019. Unmaking Citizens: Passport Removals, Pre-emptive Policing, and the Reimagining of Colonial Governmentalities. *Ethnic and Racial Studies* 42 (16): 45–62.

Khalid, M. 2011. Gender, Orientalism, and Representations of the "Other" in the War on Terror. *Global Change, Peace and Security* 23 (1): 15–29.

Khelghat-Doost, H. 2016. Women of the Islamic State: The Evolving Role of Women in Jihad. *Counter Terrorist Trends and Analyses* 8 (9): 21–26.

Kundnani, A. 2007. *The End of Tolerance*. London: Pluto Press.

Laster, K., and E. Erez. 2015. Sisters in Terrorism? Exploding Stereotypes. *Women and Criminal Justice*. 25 (1–2): 83–99.

Lewis, B. 1990. The Roots of Muslim Rage. *The Atlantic*. September 266, 3. http://pages.pomona.edu/~vis04747/h124/readings/Lewis_roots_of_muslim_rage.pdf. Accessed 9 August 2020.

Lewis, R. 1996. *Gendering Orientalism Race Femininity and Representation*. London: Routledge.

Little, D.P. 1979. Three Arab Critiques of Orientalism. *Muslim World* 69, 2 reprinted in Macfie A.l. (2008 [2002]). *Orientalism*, 110–131. London: Routledge.

Lopez, A. 2007. The Aesthetic Pleasures of War: Understanding Propaganda in an Age of Television. In *Media Literacy: A Reader*, ed. D. Macedo S. Steinberg 256–272. Peter Lang Inc: International Academic Publishers.

Lynch, O. 2013. British Muslim Youth: Radicalisation, Terrorism, and the Construction of the 'Other'. *Critical Studies in Terrorism* 6 (2): 241–261.

Mabro, J. 2009. *Veiled Half Truths: Western Travellers: Perceptions of Middle Eastern Women*. London: I. B. Tauris.

Macfie, A.l. 2008 [2002]. *Orientalism*, 2008 ed. London: Routledge.

MacKinnon, C. 1993. *Only Words*. London: HarperCollins.

Makhlouf, C. 1979. *Changing Veils: Women and Modernisation in North Yemen*. Austin: University of Texas Press.

Maslin, K. 2013. The Gender-Neutral Feminism of Hannah Arendt. *Hypatia* 28 (3): 585–601.

Massad, J. 2007. *Desiring Arabs*. Chicago, IL: University of Chicago Press.

McClintock, A. 1995. *Imperial Leather: Race, Gender, and Sexuality in the Colonial Contest*. London: Routledge.

Meer, N., and T. Modood. 2019. Islamophobia and the Racialisation of Muslims. In *The Routledge International Handbook on Islamophobia*, ed. I. Zempi and I. Awan, 18–31. London: Routledge.

Millet, K. 1970. *Sexual Politics*. London: Penguin.

Mitchell, J. 1975. *Psychoanalysis and Feminism*. London: Penguin.

Mohanty, C. 1984. Under Western Eyes: Feminist Scholarship and Colonial Discourses. *Boundary 2* 12 (3): 333–358. On Humanism and the University I: The Discourse of Humanism. (Spring–Autumn).

Mills, C., and Wright. 1943. The Professional Ideology of Social Pathologists. *American Journal of Sociology* 49(2): 165–180.

Okin, S. M. 1999. Is Multiculturalism Bad for Women? *PART 1* In *Is Multi Culturalism Bad for Women*, ed. J. Cohen, M. Howard, and M. Nussbaum. Princeton: Princeton University Press.

Organization for Security and Co-operation in Europe. 2013. *Women and Terrorist Radicalization: Final Report*, March 1.

Osborne, P., and A. Beezer. 1996. *A Critical Sense: Interviews with Intellectuals*. London: Routledge.

Pantazis, C., and S. Pemberton. 2009. From the 'Old' to the 'New' Suspect Community Examining the Impacts of Recent UK Counter-Terrorist Legislation. *British Journal of Criminology* 49 (5): 646–666.

Parliamentary Questions 1 July 2020 (Prostitution: Criminal Records). https://questions-statements.parliament.uk/written-questions/detail/2020-07-01/67586. Accessed 10 November 2020.

Patel, S., and J. Westermann. 2018. Women and Islamic-State Terrorism an Assessment of How Gender Perspectives are Integrated in Countering Violent Extremism Policy and Practices. *Security Challenges* 14 (2):53–83. Special Issue: Celebrating and Interrogating Women and National Security.

Ploss, H., P. Bartels, and P. Bartels (eds.). 1935 [1885]. *Woman: An historical and gynaecological Compendium* (first published in Germany in 1885) London: Heinemann Medical Books.

Putnam, H., and V. Walsh (eds.). 2012. *The End of Value Free Economics*. New York and London: Routledge.

R. *(on the application of QSA) v Secretary of State for the Home Department* [2018] EWHC 407 (Admin), https://www.casemine.com/judgement/uk/5b2897cd2c94e06b9e19b4ee. Accessed 10 November 2020.

R. *(on the application of QSA) v Secretary of State for the Home Department* [2020] EWCA Civ 130. https://www.bailii.org/ew/cases/EWCA/Civ/2020/130.html. Accessed 10 November 2020.

Saadawi, N. 1980. *The Hidden Face of Eve*. London: Zed Press.

Saadawi, N. 1997. *The Nawal Saadawi Reader*. London: Zed Books.

Saeed, T. 2019. Islamophobia and the Muslim Student: Disciplining the Intellect. In *The Routledge International Handbook on Islamophobia*, ed. I. Zempi and I. Awan. London: Routledge.

Said, E. 1970 [1968]. The Arab Portrayed. In *The Arab-Israeli Confrontation of June 1967*, ed. I. Abu-Lughod, 1–9. Evanston: Northwestern University Press.

Said, E. W. 1976. Arab Islam and Dogmas of the West. *New York Times*, Oct 31.

Said, E. 1983. *The World, the Text, and the Critic*. Harvard: Harvard University Press.

Said, E, W. 1990. Embargoed Literature. *Nation* 251(8, September 17): 278–80.

Said, E. W. 1994 [1993]. *Culture and Imperialism*. London: Vintage.

Said, E. W. 2001 [2000]. *The Edward Said Reader*. In M. Bayoumi and A. Rubin (ed.). London: Granta.

Said, E. W. 2007 [1997]. *Covering Islam*. London: Vintage.

Said, E. W. 2019 [1978]. *Orientalism*, edition. London: Vintage.

Scott, J. 2007. *The Politics of the Veil*. Princeton: Princeton University Press.

Shirazi, F. 2019. Iran's Compulsory Hijab: From Politics and Religious Authority to Fashion Shows. In *The Routledge International Handbook to Veils and Veiling Practices*, ed. A. Almila and D. Inglis. New York and London: Routledge.

Spender, D. 1980. *Man Made Language*. London: Routledge.

Spivak, G. 1988. Can the Subaltern Speak Can the Subaltern Speak? originally published in *Marxism and the Interpretation of Culture*, ed. C. Nelson and L. Grossberg, 271–313. Urbana, IL: University of Illinois Press.

Spivak, G. 2006 [1998]. *In Other Worlds*. London: Routledge.

Trop v Dulles, 356 U.S. 86. 1958. https://supreme.justia.com/cases/federal/us/356/86/. Accessed 10 November 2020.

Tufail, W. 2019. The Racialised and Islamophobic Framing of the Rotherham and Rochdale Child Sexual Abuse Scandal. In *The Routledge International Handbook on Islamophobia*, ed. I. Zempi and I. Awan, 147–160. London: Routledge.

Varisco, D.M. 2008. *Reading Orientalism: Said and the Unsaid*. Washington: Washington University Press.

Walker, A. 1981. *You Can't Keep a Good Woman Down*. Florid: Harcourt Books.

Warraq, I. 2007. *Defending the West: A Critique of Edward Said's Orientalism*. London: Prometheus Books.

Weber, C. 2001. Unveiling Scheherazade: Feminist Orientalism in the International Alliance of Women. *Feminist Studies* 27 (1): 125–157.

Weber, M. 1946. *From Max Weber: Essays in Sociology*. Oxford: Oxford University Press.

Wikan, U. 1991 [1982]. Behind *the Veil in Arabia: Women in Oman*. Chicago: University of Chicago Press.

Williams, R. 1989. *The Politics of Modernism*. London: Verso.

Wollstonecraft, M. 1792. A Vindication of the Rights of Women. http://www.earlymoderntexts.com/pdfs/wollstonecraft1792.pdf. Accessed 1 August 2020.

Yeğenoğlu, M. 1998. *Colonial Fantasies*. Cambridge: Cambridge University Press.

Young- Bruehl, E. 1997. Hannah Arendt Among Feminists. In *Hannah Arendt Twenty Years Later*, ed. L. May and J. Kohn, 307–324. Cambridge, MA: Massachusetts Institute of Technology.

Zempi, I., and N. Chakraborti. 2014. *Islamophobia, Victimisation, and the Veil*. London: Palgrave.

CHAPTER 3

Anti-Muslim Speech

INTRODUCTION

Freedom to speak and to write, freedom to think otherwise (Arendt 1958) and to express a view or an opinion, is a fundamental democratic right, and so is the freedom to dissent, to disagree and to contest. Freedom is this two-sided right, or it is nothing at all. John Milton, the English poet, in his essay *Areopagitica* (1644), in speaking to the second proposition wrote: "The State shall be my governours, but not my criticks". Milton, no doubt, would have supported the publication by Julian Assange's of "alleged" US war crimes, and the right without fear of punishment, to engage in "core political speech". John Pilger says: "The danger that Julian Assange faces can easily spread to the present and past editors of *The Guardian*, *The New York Times*, *Der Spiegel*, *El Pais*, the *Sydney Morning Herald* and many other newspapers and media outlets around the world that publish the Wikileaks revelations about the lies and crimes of our governments. Speak up now or wake up one morning to a new kind of tyranny" (Pilger 2019). Is freedom to speak an absolute or qualified right? And, if qualified, where is the line and who decides where it is to be drawn?

In this chapter, I explore both these questions and consider them in the context of anti-Muslim or "Islamophobic speech", documenting the misrepresentation of Muslims in political, public and everyday discourse,

S. S. M. Edwards, *The Political Appropriation of the Muslim
Body*, https://doi.org/10.1007/978-3-030-68896-7_3

in what (Hall 1996) identifies as the realm of the "discursive". Anti-Muslim speech in all its forms, in the spoken and written and digital word is an embedded feature of the democratic landscape which has an impact beyond an assault on individual dignity, and where the "performativity" of speech serves to garner public support and justification for the West's military ambitions in Muslim majority countries, the War on Terror (WOT), and the ill-treatment and torture of Muslim detainees held in the US military prisons (see Chapter 6). At the same time, this anti-Muslim discourse is underpinned by suppressing and discrediting "core political speech" which challenges foreign policy, the WOT and counter-terror measures at home, and challenges the normalisation of anti-Muslim speech.

For example, the UK government's *Counter Terrorism Policy for medical staff and teachers as part of the Prevent agenda* (2020) lists the Campaign Against the Arms Trade (CAAT), Greenpeace, Campaign for Nuclear Disarmament (CND), and the Palestine Solidarity Campaign alongside neo-Nazi Groups (CAAT News 2020, Issue 255: 14). Clare Collier, advocacy director at Liberty, responding, said: "We have long warned that the government's counter-terror agenda is one of the greatest threats to free speech in the UK. If you are passionate about anything from climate change to social justice or fighting racism in the UK today you risk being labelled extremist and your details being passed to the police" (Dodd and Grierson 2020). A further much contested example, reported in (*New Arab*, 23 September 2020) of speech prohibition is the de-platforming by Zoom of Leila Khaled (a Palestinian refugee who in 1969 was involved in the attempted hijacking of an El Al plane) who due to speak on 23 September 2020 at San Francisco State University and again on 23 October at the University of Hawaii Mānoa (UHM). Zoom had prohibited the hosts from using its software on the basis that Khaled's participation violated one or more of its policies (You Tube and Facebook is also reported as shutting down the event).

In exploring this two-sided coin of freedom of speech and suppression of "core political speech", I consider first, and in general terms Foucault's theorisation of the relationship between power and "who speaks" and what can be said (see also Chapter 2). Second, I review the role of law in balancing this freedom to speak against any potential harm (s) that its exercise may cause. Third, I examine the escalation in anti-Muslim speech and its normalisation, identifying the social and political catalysts,

including the impact of "Trumpism", Brexit, the rise of far-right nationalist movements, and the terrorist events of 9/11 and global Islamic
terrorism all of which provide the context for this inuring. Fourth, in
documenting the evidence of anti-Muslim speech I consider the representation of Muslim women and Muslim men within cyberspace, mainstream
media, film, cartoons and so-called satire. Fifth, I turn to the other side
of the freedom banner and consider the role of power in suppressing
"core political speech". In this endeavour, I am reminded of Cornel West,
who said: "In an age of mendacity ...Telling the truth is subversive...its
counter-cultural" (West 2017). Sixth, and finally, I document the "real
effects of the discursive" (Hall 1996: 451) and examine the impact and
effect of this totalising anti-Muslim discourse on Muslim lives.

POWER AND THE WORD: SPEECH AND DENIAL

Whilst the limits of speech are laid down in law, and subject to legal interpretation, the law does not decide who speaks, nor does it decide what
is deemed "knowledge" or "truth", as these are contested and ligated
discourses. I have considered the role of power in determining what
passes for knowledge (see Chapter 2) and referred to Foucault's writing
on "Power and Knowledge" (Lecture One, 7 January 1976, Gordon
1980: 81) and the "arrogated knowledge" or discourse, determined by
the powerful which is relevant here. James Baldwin explained how "arrogated knowledge" in the context of white America, worked. "When I was
growing up, I was taught in American history books, that Africa had no
history, and neither did I. That I was a savage about whom the less said,
the better, who had been saved by Europe and brought to America. And,
of course, I believed it. I didn't have much choice. Those were the only
books there were. Everyone else seemed to agree..." (Baldwin 1965a).
Louis Althusser's framework, also discussed in Chapter 2 is relevant here,
especially his essay "Ideology and Ideological State Apparatuses" (1971)
in identifying how state institutions serve the interests of the political and
economic elite promulgating and reproducing ideas and "knowledge"
through the "ideological state apparatuses" (ISAs), especially the press,
media, law, education, work and civic society. And here I continue with an
examination of "a mode of discourse with supporting institutions, vocab-
ulary, scholarship, imagery, doctrines" (Said 1978: 2) including, "the
web of racism, cultural stereotype, political imperialism, dehumanizing
ideology holding in the Arab or Muslim" (27). I consider too the use

to which these "ideological fictions" (349), are put in emboldening the West's territorial ambitions in the Middle East region and justifying what the West calls "necessity and self-defence" imperatives. Lean (2017) and Chomsky (2003), amongst many others, have identified this denigration and labelling of Muslim men as "terrorist" and Muslim women as "terrorist sympathisers" as part of a wider "industry" of Islamophobia which serves these political and foreign policy interests (see Chapter 4), pressing "ideological myths into service" (Lean: 63).

Anti-Muslim speech has seeped into the everyday lexicon of government speak, of officials, the executive and politicians, and has become institutionalised in public practice, habituated and normalised in popular media and rendered "banal" (in the sense that Arendt [1951] used the word). A public inuring, desensitisation, and apathy has resulted in the disappearance to vanishing point of the parameters of "satire" and "fair comment" giving way to a relentless stream of "unacceptable generalisations of the most irresponsible kind [about Muslims] that could never be used for any other religious cult, or demographic group" (Said 1997: xvi).

Of Foucault's "subjugated knowledge", this dissent or counter-speech or alterity, which Terry Eagleton (2015, 2018) calls going "against the grain", is the speech that governments and powerful others work to shut down politically, ideologically and financially, through silencing or discrediting. As Cornel West in his lecture "Speaking Truth to Power" (2018) recognises, "Frank speech will get you in trouble"! For publishing "core political speech" Julian Assange, publisher of WikiLeaks, has been detained in Belmarsh prison, London since September 2019, facing extradition to the US be tried, under the US Espionage Act (1917). Mark Curtis (historian and journalist) in his book *Secret Affairs* (2018a: xviii; see also 2018b), also remarks on the way in which "core political speech" is discredited. His writing is subversive in that he argues that the primary purpose of Western invasions of Arab and Muslim counties was to advance British geopolitical, commercial and capitalist interest, in pursuit of "political and military control over an oil rich region" (155–156) and also speaks of the UK government's collusion with radical Islam. In a public lecture, delivered in 2008, he said:

> You cannot and you will not get an article published if you talk about nonsensities like Britain might somehow be involved in terrorism …and the state sponsored terrorism we hear very little about (at 1.08 minutes).

Britain counts as one of the leading supporters of terrorism in the world today (at 1.23 minutes) assassinating foreign leaders is basically a British tradition. (Curtis 2008: at 3.24 minutes)

The UK government's counter-terror "Prevent" and "Channel" programme, which whilst officially aimed at preventing "radicalisation" (see Chapter 5), also undermines the right to "core political speech" by implying that criticism of British foreign policy, especially from Muslims, may be evidence of radicalisation and extremism. "Taji Mustafa, a media representative of Hizb-ut Tahrir (HUT) noted that: 'Prevent has rightly become a toxic brand – not because it has been wrongly executed or misunderstood, but because it is a fundamentally flawed and 'toxic' agenda...It has worked on a presumption that those with Islamic values or political views that dissent from the state's standpoint are to be considered suspect, so needing state-organised reprogramming through the Channel programme'" (Richards 2017: 145). State efforts to shut down "core political speech" are by no means new. Historian, E.P. Thompson (1979, 1980), writing on the state of the British nation in 1961, and the banishment of dissent from political life said:

> when any affirmative measure, such as Freedom of Information Act, is being drafted, the entire invisible establishment of 'public servants' is alerted, and immense pains will be taken to offer some innocuous consensus (to journalists, etc.) While at the same time strengthening hard core security provisions, which are then offered with a new legitimacy. (1980: 176–177)

Like George Orwell's *Nineteen Eighty-Four* (1949), Thompson delivers a chilling prophecy on the modern era, where the policing of dissent has taken on a renewed vigour post 9/11 directed especially at Muslim women and Muslim men, and anyone else critical of government policy. I now turn to examine the legal limits of speech.

SPEECH LAW—THE LEGAL GOVERNANCE OF SPEECH ACTS

The substantive norms protecting freedom of speech and codified in law developed from strivings to protect the right to "core political speech". This protection is subject to judicial interpretation, malleated by the social and political context. In 2010, the US Supreme Court in *Citizens United v Federal Elections Commission* (2010) held that political speech, being the most protected form of speech under the First Amendment, warrants the highest level of scrutiny against the laws that regulate it, and in the UK, the Court of Appeal, in the case of *R v Butt v Secretary of State for the Home Department* [2019] protected that speech, when it struck down paragraph 11 of the *Prevent duty guidance issued to higher education institutions*. The guidance had asserted that "extremist views", included views that "actively oppose fundamental British values". The court held that such guidance undermined, s 31 of the Counter-Terrorism and Security Act 2015 which defends freedom of speech.

Several important historical landmarks attest to these strivings. The British Bill of Rights (1689) granted the right to freedom of speech in Parliament, protecting political dissent and asserting the power of Parliamentary speech. The French Declaration of the Rights of Man (1789) included a provision for freedom of speech for all citizens, everywhere. The United States Constitution (1791), held: "Congress shall make no law respecting an establishment of religion, or prohibiting the free exercise thereof; or abridging the freedom of speech, or of the press; or the right of the people peaceably to assemble, and to petition the Government for a redress of grievances". International law, including the Universal Declaration of Human Rights (UDHR) (1948) Article 19, protects freedom of speech, which is guaranteed in two binding United Nations covenants, the International Covenant on Civil and Political Rights (ICCPR) Article 19, 1966/76, and the International Covenant on Economic, Social and Cultural Rights (ICESCR) 1966/76. In the UK and across Europe, the European Convention on Human Rights (ECHR) 1950, Article 10, provides that everyone has the right to freedom of speech and expression, limited by law: "as necessary in a democratic society …in the interests of national security, territorial integrity or public safety, for the prevention of disorder or crime, for the protection of health or morals, for the protection of the reputation or rights of others, for preventing the disclosure of information received in confidence, or for maintaining the authority and impartiality of the judiciary". Significantly, equality and non-discrimination Conventions, for example, the International Convention on the Elimination of All Forms of Racial Discrimination (ICERD) requires speech to be balanced against the right to equality and freedom from discrimination, and Article 20 (2) prohibits "[a]ny advocacy of national, racial, or religious hatred that constitutes incitement to discrimination, hostility or violence".

Words That Wound: UK, Race/Religious Speech Regulations and Freedoms

As to personal hurtful and harmful speech, UK domestic law balances the freedom to speak with the harm that speech might cause. This balance of freedom to speak and individual protection from harm is undertaken in the wider context of considering equality norm obligations and is subject to an unfolding interpretation. The Public Order Act (POA)1986 (s 5 (1) (a)), sets out the legal parameters and prohibits speech which includes words, visual displays and publications if the representations made are: "Threatening or abusive...where the intention or likelihood of the speaker is to stir up racial, hatred". The characteristics of religion and sexual orientation were later added following the Race and Religious Hatred Act 2006 (in 2007, s 29B-G). This Act was intended to close the loophole by which racial groups which included Jews and Sikhs were protected whilst excluding Christians and Muslims. Speech that merely "insults", once unlawful under the POA 1936 and 1986, was decriminalized in 2013 since it was considered to interfere with freedom of speech (Crime and Courts Act 2013 s 57(2)). This removal demonstrates the fluidity of the thresholds and the interpretation of what is harmful and the lawful limits of speech. There is however inconsistency as "insult" is retained exceptionally with regard to "racist" chanting at football matches, presumably because of the potential for public disorder (Football Offences Act (1991) s 3 (2)(b), as amended), however, there is no prohibition against "religious" chanting. As to the prohibition on speech against religious belief, the POA (s 29 J), speech which involves "discussion, criticism or expressions of antipathy, dislike, ridicule, insult or abuse of particular religions or the beliefs or practices of their adherents, or of any other belief system or the beliefs or speech, of its adherents, or proselytising or urging adherents of a different religion or belief system to cease practising their religion or belief system" is protected. Striking a balance between freedom to speak and the proception of harm is like trying to draw a line in desert sand just as the wind blows. This unsatisfactory situation is currently being addressed by the UK Law Commission in a consultation document on "Hate Crime" (2020) which sets out proposals for an all-inclusive legal framework where religious hate speech is placed on an equal footing with race hate speech. As Meer and Modood (2019: 23) observe Muslims have less protection because of an assumption that Muslim identities are chosen.

Outside the criminal law, there are further protections and those whose speech might incite racial and religious hatred and wish to come to the UK may be prevented from entry. The Secretary of State for the Home Department (SSHD) has the power to prevent the entry of those whose behaviour may be considered "unacceptable" including: "writing, producing, publishing or distributing material, public speaking including preaching, running a website, using a position of responsibility such as a teacher, community or youth leader" (Home Office guidance, *Exclusion from the UK* 2018). In 2009, Jacqui Smith MP (SSHD), prohibited Geert Wilders, Leader of the Dutch Party for Freedom (PVV), and a promulgater of anti-Muslim rhetoric, from entry into the UK. In a letter to Wilders she said: "Your presence in the UK would pose a genuine, present, and sufficiently serious threat to one of the fundamental interests of society... your statements about Muslims and their beliefs, as expressed in your film 'Fitna' and elsewhere, would threaten community harmony, and therefore public security in the UK" (*GW (EEA reg 21: "fundamental interests") Netherlands* [2009] [5]). In October 2009, Wilders appealed this decision to the Asylum and Immigration Tribunal (AIT) who found that:

[3] He expresses his views in a manner which any right-thinking person would regard as offensive to the religion of Islam and its founder. His aim as he declares it is to persuade others that the religion and culture of Islam is not one that should be tolerated or followed. He has made a film called 'Fitna' which interposes readings from the Koran, the holy book of Islam, with images of atrocities committed around the world, with the implication that the relevant suras of the Koran encourage or permit the acts portrayed.

However, in allowing his appeal the Tribunal said: "[48] ... the proposed exercise of freedom of expression was one to which the highest value ought to be given and it was substantive because the right to freedom of movement supports the right of freedom of expression which he sought to exercise". Wilders had taken advantage of the freedom of speech provision introduced by the Racial and Religious Hatred Act (2006) that inserted s 29 J, into the POA (see above) which permitted speech, if and only if it is deemed to amount to no more than "ridicule and insult". So, were Gilder's utterances merely "ridicule and insult"? The court deemed them to be so. In a further case in 2013, Jacqui Smith excluded

Pamela Geller and Robert Spencer from entry because of their reputation for anti-Muslim speech and inciting religious hatred (see Mondon and Winter 2019). Geller and Spencer challenged this decision by way of judicial review (*R (Geller and Anor) v Secretary of State for the Home Department* [2015]. Geller opposed extreme Islam and the introduction of Sharia law, and funded adverts on public transport in San Francisco and New York which read: "In any war between the civilized man and the savage, Support the civilized man. Support Israel. Defeat Jihad" and displayed a picture of the Prophet Muhammad with a pig's face superimposed on it on her blog. She said: "I don't know where it is in America that you can't make jokes or make fun". She described Barak Obama as "the jihad candidate", said he was: "using all branches of government to enforce the Shariah", said that "The State Department [is] essentially being run by Islamic supremacists" (Kundnani 2015: 250–251) and called for a boycott of Campbell's soup because halal versions were available (249). Spencer was responsible for the far-right "Jihad Watch" website, had published material including *The Politically Incorrect Guide to Islam (and the Crusades)*, and said that he could prove that: "traditional Islam contains violent and supremacist elements", and that "its various schools unanimously teach warfare against and the subjugation of unbelievers". As co-founders of the *Freedom Defense Initiative and Stop the Islamization of America* which is described as an extremist and far-right group, the purpose of their UK visit was to address an EDL (English Defence League—a far-right group) rally. Geller and Spencer challenged the lawfulness of the UK's interpretation of "unacceptable behaviour" in its exclusion policy. The Court of Appeal ruled that the government's policy was not unlawful and that the decision to exclude fell properly to the SSHD [12].

Former President Trump's visits in 2018 and 2019 were not stopped despite his record of anti-Muslim tirades on Twitter and in public commentary including his Executive order (s) banning Muslims from specific countries from entering the US (see Khan et al. 2019). Cornel West (2019) lamenting what he calls "the Trumpian moment" says, "There is a neo-fascist in the White House and a "normalization of racist discourses coming from above". The Speaker of the House, John Bercow MP, spoke out against Trump's proposed address to both Houses of Parliament during his UK visit. On 6 February 2017, Bercow said: "I am even more strongly opposed to an address by President Trump in Westminster Hall, we value our relationship with the US. However, as far as this place is concerned, I feel very strongly that our opposition to racism, and to sexism and our support for equality before the law and an independent judiciary are hugely important considerations in the House of Commons". Bercow was forced to apologise.

PRINCIPLES OF FREEDOM AND SPEECH

Two Philosophical Positions

With regard to the jurisprudence two positions on freedom have informed judicial decision-making. Whilst anti-Muslim speech, as indeed any racist speech, is damaging, there are some who argue that tolerating such speech is for the public good. Whether the law should impose limits on speech has been long debated. John Stuart Mill (the British philosopher and economist) argued that: "The only purpose for which power can be rightfully exercised over any member of a civilised community, against his will, is to prevent harm to others" (*On Liberty* 1869). The harm that Mill has in mind is physical harm. Isaiah Berlin (1965: 17) disagrees, it is, he says, a mistake to defend all speech since this would lead to a situation of "negative liberty". Berlin is particularly concerned with fanatical regimes and right-wing popularist movements:

> ...there has, perhaps, been no time in modern history when so large a number of human beings, both in the East and West, have had their notions, and indeed their lives, so deeply altered, and in some cases violently upset, by fanatically held social and political doctrines. Dangerous, because when ideas are neglected by those who ought to attend to them– that is to say, those who have been trained to think critically about ideas–they sometimes acquire an unchecked momentum and an irresistible power over multitudes of men that may grow too violent to be affected by rational criticism. (1965: 17)

Concerned with the material consequences of harmful "speech", Berlin cites the German poet Christian Heine and the political activist Benjamin Constant who both warned that unlimited ideas can destroy civilisations (1965: 26). Joel Feinberg (1987: 187) and Anthony Waldron (2012: 126), agree and consider that Mill sets the bar of harm too high and in limiting an understanding of harm to the physical realm ignores the social harms of loss of dignity and inequality. Berlin, Feinberg and Waldron are concerned with speech's "performativity", that is, not just with what speech says "constative" (see Austin 1962) but with what speech does, that is, its power to perform actions in the world. This is developed further in Searle's (1999 [1969]), discussion of "illocutionary speech" and the power of speech to command. *Brandenburg* (see below) provides such an example.

In addition to the "performative" and "illocutionary" power of speech, there is also harm in the way in which the subject is constituted in, and through, language. Baldwin for example, wrote about how the black subject is constated, insisting that the "American Negro" exists only by construction in the United States. Recognising the "performativity" of assaultive speech in *Words That Wound* (1993) and speech's power in constructing the subject, Matsuda et al. (1993) cite Kendall Thomas who writes: "'We are raced.' We are acted upon and constructed by racist speech. The meaning of 'Black' or 'white' is derived through a history of acted-upon ideology". Said similarly observed: "The Orient was Oriental-ized not only because it was discovered to be 'Oriental' in all those ways considered commonplace by an average nineteenth century European but also because it *could be* - that is, submitted to being – *made* Oriental" (in Bayoumi and Rubin: 72). The performativity of speech and its impact on the subject is explored further by Delgado and Stefancic (2012 [2001]) and Crenshaw (2019) in examining the layering of speech especially where class, race, colour and gender intersect. Similarly, the construction of the female/feminine and the gendered subject in language has been explored in pornography hate speech by Andrea Dworkin (1989) *Pornography: men possessing women,* and Catharine MacKinnon in *Only Words* (1993). Whilst Judith Butler in *Gender Trouble* (1990) and *Excitable Speech: A Politics of the Performative* (1997) sets out to explore the linguistic construction of gender and heteronormativity. Butler argues that speech can function as a form of "linguistic injury" in that speech interpellates the subject. Returning then to Berlin:

> Since the law recognizes equality rights, then freedom of speech must also be weighed against other claims, [and] The extent of a man's, or a people's, liberty to choose to live as they desire must be weighed against the claims of many other values, of which equality, or justice, or happiness, or security, or public order are perhaps the most obvious examples. For this reason, it cannot be unlimited. (1965: 29)

If, anti-Muslim hate speech functions as a communicative act (Waldron: 368) where the subject is controlled and dehumanised (Waldron: 364, Awan and Zempi 2015a) and dignity destroyed (Zempi and Awan (eds) 2019; Mason-Bish and Zempi 2018), then, as MacKinnon (1993: 16) maintains the attempt to balance these competing speech rights, sets equality and freedom of speech "on a collision course" where there is: "a submerged tension between equality rights as they have long been recognized, in which discrimination expression is without question a discriminatory act, and a current direction in First Amendment interpretation" (54).

Tolerating Hate Speech to Protect Speech Freedom

In turning now to the court's appropriation of these two philosophical positions in balancing these competing rights, legal opinion and judgments have straddled these two positions. Justice Brandeis in *Brandenburg v Ohio* [1969] recognised that "to make men free", here he means to protect "core political speech", it was necessary, as Justice Roberts had put it in *Snyder v Phelps* [2011]) "not to stifle public debate". Of course, the *Brandenburg* case was not about protecting public debate but about regulating race hatred. Clarence Brandenburg had invited a news network to film a Ku Klux Klan (KKK) rally in June 1964 during which a leader said that unless something is done about the race situation in this country white people are going to have to take "revengeance" against certain ethnicities. Brandenburg was charged (on August 4 the mutilated and tortured bodies of three civil rights activists, James Earl Chaney, Andrew Goodman and Michael Schwerner were found). The US Supreme Court however quashed Brandenburg's conviction and held that hate speech was protected so long as it did not "intend to and [was] likely to provoke imminent violence" (notwithstanding the murders of the civil rights activists). This decision was a significant departure from the earlier legal position held in *Beauharnais v Illinois* [1952] where Justice Frankfurter found for libel against the writer of a leaflet which was intended to rally people who read it, with these words to "protect the white race from being mongrelized....and terrorized" by "the rapes, robberies, guns, knives and marijuana of the negro" (Waldron 2012: 27).

Strossen (2018: 28) whilst abhorring hate speech, is concerned that shutting down such speech may lead to prohibiting "core political speech" and this position led in the 1990s to contests between Strossen and

Andrea Dworkin the anti-pornographer (see Duberman 2020: 259). She provides examples where in defining "core political speech" as hate speech debate has been shut down, citing the French case of *Baldassi*. Here, twelve pro-Palestinian activists who went into supermarkets wearing T-shirts with the message "Long live Palestine, boycott Israel", and handed out leaflets that said: "You can oblige Israel to respect human rights. Boycott Israeli imports. Buying imported Israeli products amounts to legitimising the crimes in Gaza and endorsing Israeli government policy", were convicted of a criminal offence and their convictions upheld. Baldassi and others appealed their convictions to the European Court of Human Rights (ECt.HR) (*Baldassi and Others v France* [2020]), the ECt.HR held that the French law criminalising BDS, violated the right to freedom of expression. The UK's Supreme Court also reversed an earlier government ban on the exercise of "core political speech" and in *R (on the application of Palestine Solidarity Campaign Ltd.) v Secretary of State for Housing, Communities and Local Government* [2020]) held that the Secretary of State guidance of 2016 that effectively banned engagement in boycotts, divestment and sanctions against foreign nations and UK defence industries, was inappropriate.

The other position is found in the Supreme Court judgment in the Canadian case of *R v Keegstra* [1991]. Here, a high school teacher, communicated anti-Semitic statements to his students, and convicted of unlawfully promoting hatred against Jews. He appealed that decision and the appeal court held that whilst he had: "[1] …attributed various evil quantities to Jews…described Jews to his pupils as 'treacherous', 'subversive', 'sadistic', 'money-loving', 'power hungry' and 'child killers' … that Jewish people seek to destroy Christianity and are responsible for depressions, anarchy, chaos, wars and revolution and created the Holocaust to gain sympathy" his conduct was not unlawful. This decision of the lower courts was overturned by the Supreme Court.

Both Waldron and Strossen make persuasive arguments. Should we heed Berlin's case for limiting hate speech given its "performativity", influence, and impact, and especially its more recent wider digital reach and permanence? (O'Regan 2018). Should we be mindful of the more extreme consequences of hate speech alluded to by Berlin, providing, as it does, one of the conditions necessary, as Glover (2002) observes, which "makes killing possible". Arendt (2017 [1951]) in *The Origins of Totalitarianism*, demonstrated how speech that defiled Jews in Germany and

Nazi-occupied territories ended in mass murder and genocide (Wendel 2004) and Delgado and Stefancic (2009: 363) warn:

> Practically every instance of genocide came on the heels of a wave of hate speech depicting the victims in belittling terms. For example, before launching their wave of deadly attacks on the Tutsis in Rwanda, Hutus in government and the media disseminated a drumbeat of messages casting their ethnic rivals as despicable. The Third Reich did much the same with the Jews during the period leading up to the Holocaust.

On the other hand, Arendt in *The Human Condition* ([1958]), was also insistent on the necessity of defending a public space in which ideas are tolerated in building the plurality of a political community (see also Greene and Simpson 2017). These countervailing arguments provide the ongoing contested framework for consideration of anti-Muslim speech and its harms. So, what then is the evidence of anti-Muslim speech which is harmful and may incite others to harm them?

Anti-Muslim Speech

Anti-Muslim speech has been ingrained in the cultural fabric for some time. Said begins his 1968 essay, "The Arab Portrayed", reflecting on one such example, and describes Princeton University's tenth reunion, where a fancy-dress costume comprising of an Arab robe, headdress and sandals was chosen for the celebratory event. Then, after the June "Arab–Israeli" war, there was a change in the programme, where, in addition to the proposed costume, the class were to process with their hands above their head "in a gesture of abject defeat". Said explains: "…the American consciousness of the Arab, permitted this tasteless demotion of a people into a stupid and offensive caricature" (1968: 1). Whilst tropes of this kind are reiterated, "the Arab"/Muslim is not merely derided, as in the Princeton example, but demonised. Islamic terrorism, Al Qaeda, ISIS/ISIL worldwide has provided the justification and played into the hands of those who promote negative and essentialised imagery of all Muslim men and women, everywhere. Western rage, Atwan (2015: 213) notes, is: "…rampant, particularly in the aftermath of the recent attacks on Europeans in Paris, Copenhagen and Sousse …. Little mention is made, either, of the hundreds of attacks on Muslims and Islamic locations in the West or the growing sense of insecurity that Europe's

Muslims experience as a result". 9/11 and other terror attacks across the world, in the UK (Manchester, London Bridge), US (Orlando), France (Paris—Bastille Day and outside Charlie Hebdo in September 2020 and the murder of a schoolteacher in October in Paris), Germany (Berlin), Australia (Lindt Café Sydney, and Melbourne) and Vienna, have fuelled the increase in, and sense of justification for, anti-Muslim speech and cyberhate on Twitter and the social media network (Williams and Burnap 2016). Legewie (2013), King and Sutton (2014) and Hanes and Machin (2014) chart the impact terror incidents have on galvanising tensions. Together with the divisiveness of Brexit, and what Cornel West, with specific reference to the White House, describes as "the normalisation of racist discourses coming from above" is a spiraling assemblage of securitisation, counter-terror legislation, including the "Prevent" programme (Richards 2017: 10).

Brexit, "Trumpism" and "New Nationalism"

Brexit, the UK's departure from the European Union, leading up to, and since, the referendum on 23 June 2016, forged new alliances, deepened existing divisions, fomented racism in general and Islamophobia in particular. "In August 2016, ... the Equality and Human Rights Commission in the UK issued a report which, the commission's chairman noted, revealed a picture of a 'very worrying combination of a post-Brexit rise in hate crime and long-term systemic unfairness and race inequality'" (Richards 2017: 68). The Brexiteer's anti-European personality, unintentionally endorsed anti-diversity and anti-inclusion tendencies, emboldening a new fake identity and "imagined community" of Brexiteers, as people like "us", and anti-Brexiteers, as people like "them" (Anderson 2016 [1983]). This "out of Europe" programme was hijacked by right-wing popularist, anti-asylum and anti-immigration movements whose purpose was to press for further exclusion of "the other" and defeat multiculturalism (Cole and Cole 2009, Cockburn 2015) (see Chapter 5). Evidence from the *European Commission against Racism and Intolerance* (ECRIL see Bayrakli and Hafez (eds) 2017, 2019) found that Brexit fever was paralleled by increasing anti-Muslim hate crime on the streets and offensive tweets online. The leader of the Brexit party Catharine Blaiklock resigned in 2019 after it was discovered that she had posted, via Twitter, grossly offensive anti-Muslim posts.

Anti-Islam and anti-Muslim, has been and still is vociferously promoted by former President Trump who, on 29 November 2017, *The Guardian* reported as re-tweeting anti-Muslim videos which had been posted by the deputy leader of the British far-right extremist group "Britain First". Unsurprising therefore that Cornel West (2019) in an interview with Medhi Hasan talked of his concern with what he described as "white nationalists in the White House". "Britain First" was later banned in 2018. It was also a member of this group, Thomas Mair, who shot dead Jo Cox MP before the EU referendum in 2016, shouting "Britain First" as he murdered her. CDU politician Walter Lübcke who campaigned for the admission of refugees in Germany was also murdered by a right-wing extremist (cited in Bayrakli and Hafez 2019: 39). During the 2016 election, Trump said of former President Obama: "He doesn't have a birth certificate, or if he does, there's something on that certificate that is very bad for him. Now, somebody told me – and I have no idea if this is bad for him or not, but perhaps it would be - that where it says religion, it might have 'Muslim'. And if you're a Muslim, you don't change your religion, by the way!"

Trump's Executive orders provide evidence of anti-Muslim discrimination but also of a US movement, "Trumpism" gathering popular support that will remain notwithstanding his departure from Presidential politics. Order 13769 (2017) "Protecting the Nation from Foreign Terrorist Entry into the United States" banned the entry of persons from seven Muslim majority countries, including Syria—(the very country that President Trump's military machine had just bombed!) Sudan, Iran and Iraq, Yemen, Somalia and Libya. Trump's Executive Order 13780 (2017) endorsed the racialisation of all Muslims as potential terrorists. A further Order, 13798 (2017) said to be designed to protect free speech and religious liberty, only served to protect and empower right-wing conservatives and religious organisations and individuals who opposed same-sex marriage, transgender identity, and pre-marital sex. Rhetoric of nationhood, patriotism, identity and exceptionalism were gilded onto a manifesto of hate, replete with derogatory comments about Mexicans, Hispanics and Muslims. "We cannot allow all of these people to invade our Country.... This sustained influx of illegal aliens has profound consequences on every aspect of our national life — overwhelming our schools, overcrowding our hospitals, draining our welfare system, and causing untold amounts of crime,...It must end NOW!" (Trump's Tweets, June 2018).

Muslims were singled out for his special invective. "There is a Muslim problem in the world…. Islam hates us". When asked by the CNN reporter interviewing him, "Do you mean all 1.6 billion Muslims?" he replied, "I mean a lot of 'em. I want surveillance of certain mosques and we have to look at the Muslims and do something. This is war and we have to stop them" (Trump 2019). In this way, Trump gilded an anti-immigrant agenda onto a patriotism rhetoric.

Liberal Islamophobes

Whilst Islamophobia, anti-Muslim prejudice and discrimination are contiguous with right-wing interests, including neo-fascism and right-wing nationalism, the *European Islamophobia Report* (Bayrakli and Hafez (2017) found that anti-Muslim propaganda and discourse, is also promoted by social democrats, liberals, leftists, as well as conservatives. Matthew Parris's article in *The Times*, 27 August 2005 "Never mind what the woman thinks, wearing a veil is offensive to me" is such an example. Lean (2017 [2012]) in his book *The Islamophobia Industry*, identifies the following groups "liberal Islamophobes", the influence of the Christian right (102) the pro-Israel right (140) as having prominence in the "monster making" of the Muslim community (21,165). Lean identifies the counter-terrorism Quilliam Foundation, London (set up by Majeed Nawaz and Ed Hussain) citing as evidence the appearance of Quilliam leaders alongside Israeli politicians (who oppose a Palestinian state) and Quilliam's receipt of funding from right-wing interests, referring here to Tommy Robinson (of the EDL) whom he says Robinson has said that Nawaz's group had paid him thousands of pounds (175–176). Lean points to the liberal support for military intervention in Muslim majority countries and to domestic policies revolving around "securitization" which target the Muslim community (167) and the liberal tendency that challenges what it sees as the status of women under Islam. UK "Liberal" and neo-liberal voices, including former Prime Minister, David Cameron, called for a new doctrine of "muscular liberalism" (Richards 2017: 138) by which "British values" could be exerted with security lying at the heart. In 2011, he said: "Frankly, we need a lot less of the passive tolerance of recent years and a much more active, muscular liberalism. A passively tolerant society says to its citizens, as long as you obey the law, we will just leave you alone. It stands neutral between different values".

British statesmen have also led from the front in promulgating anti-Muslim sentiment and setting a plimsol line of what is publically acceptable. David Cameron when Prime Minister, spoke of "draining the swamps" of Muslim extremism. Such descriptors have spilled into the generic refugee rhetoric where immigration is described in terms of the need to "limit the swarm of migrants". Together with a rejection of multiculturalism, nationalism takes a pride in denigrating Muslims. Bikhu Parekh (2000) who championed multiculturalism, and respect for minority cultures, intra-cultural dialogue, and "building of common bonds and the resolution of difference" (Parekh 2019: 166) calls this contempt for multiculturalism, the "ethnocentric tendency" citing David Cameron who said: "multiculturalism leads to terrorism" (Parekh 2019: 166). Baroness Caroline Cox, in adding her personal loathing said: "Cultural relativism is the greatest disease we face in Europe today" (*The Guardian*, 5 March 2010, "Geert Wilders anti-Islam film gets House of Lords screening").

Europe: Far-Right Anti-Muslim Nationalism

Far-right nationalism in the UK and Europe is also a key driver in emboldening anti-Muslim speech and discrimination where anti-immigration strategies and sentiments have, in some countries, become state-sponsored praxis (Lean 2017: 228). As Bayrakli and Hafez observe: "… the far-right political camp has moved from the periphery to the center and become integral to the political landscape in Europe" (2017: 11). Richards (2017: 85) identifies "xenophobic identity" as the core value emerging in several so-called freedom parties and movements, whose point of unification is what they regard as an attack on the supremacy of the majority community. Whilst counter-terrorism continues to focus on Islamic extremism it is in fact far-right groups who are increasingly taking to acts of terrorism, and Europol, in 2019, found that right-wing extremists "enjoy much greater freedom to act on major social media platforms" (*The Independent*, 23 June 2020). Whilst it is true that during the Covid-19 pandemic public support for Europe's leading political parties has waned (Macshane 2020), the banalisation of far-right and white supremacist ideologies in Europe is ever-present (Bayrakli and Hafez 2019: 9). In Austria, the "Freedom Party of Austria" (FPÖ) and far-right Interior Minister, Herbert Kickl, says he is fighting against what he calls "population replacement". The party's anti-Islam leaflet:

"Tradition beats immigration", was said by its critics to echo the visual tropes of Nazi propaganda (*The Guardian*, 29 April 2019, "Austrian Deputy leader endorses far-right term 'population r eplacement'"). In Bulgaria, the nationalist United Patriots union in the GERB-led coalition government, led by Prime Minister Boyko Borissov, actively encourages anti-Muslim attitudes. Evidence of pro-Nazi groups was witnessed on 14 October 2019, at the Bulgaria/England football match where some Bulgarian fans engaged in racist chanting, making monkey noises and brandishing the Nazi salute (*The Guardian*, 14 October 2019, "England crush Bulgaria 6-0 but racist chants force stoppages in qualifier"). In Finland, the right-wing popularist "Finns party" leader, Jussi Halla-aho, was fined by Finland's Supreme Court six years ago for comments linking Islam to paedophilia. One of the party's deputy leaders, in 2017, Laura Huhtasaari, was fined for a Facebook post calling for a Muslim-free Finland, which a court said amounted to discrimination against an ethnic group. In Italy, the Northern League's candidate, Attilio Fontana, warned of the risk that the: "white race disappears and is replaced by migrants", and in August 2019, Deputy Prime Minister Salvini said Europe would become an "Islamic caliphate" unless nationalist parties made gains in the European elections and introduced tougher anti-immigration policies (*The Guardian*, 2 May 2019, "Matteo Salvini: vote for nationalists to stop European caliphate"). He is currently facing charges for refusing to let migrants disembark from a boat at sea (October 2020). In Slovenia, the television company "24TV" broadcast, these words: "Obviously, we do not have enough terrorists, rapists and other criminals in Europe. It seems that leading politicians want to bring even more. Only this can explain their desire for the ever-increasing inclusion of migrants and Muslims in European countries" (Bayrakli and Hafez 2017: 20). In Latvia, the slogan of the "Action Party of Eurosceptics" (Eiroskeptiķu Rīcības partija) reads: "We are not against Muslims, we are against the Islamization of Latvia and Europe" (Bayrakli and Hafez 2017: 21). The Latvian National Alliance (Nacionālā apvienīb) stated that it would not let into Liepāja "illegal immigrants called 'refugees' – potential criminals, terrorists and idlers! There will be no mosques here!" (Bayrakli and Hafez 2017: 22). In Hungary, Prime Minister Orbán promotes nationalism with his anti-Muslim "Fidesz" party (Chapter 4). In Germany, the AfD party warns of the danger of Islam and the need to resist the "invasion" of foreigners. Roger Boyes (*The Times*, 12 February 2020) points out that the AfD, is represented in all the country's 16 state parliaments and is the largest opposition party in the Bundestag with its sinister wing led by Bjorn Hocke who talks of the coming death of the nation through population replacement and deplores Germany's public remorse for the Holocaust. In Switzerland, mosques have been banned since 2009 (Lean: 228). In Holland, Geert Wilders (PVV) threatened the mass deportation of Muslims. In France, Bayrakli and Hafez (2019: 318) write: "Islamophobia in France is a systemic racism – or even a state racism" including Right-wing members of Parliament "Les Republicains" and "National Rally", and the government itself including Macron, Blanquer and Castaner (see Faytre in Bayrakli and Hafez 2019). In Belgium, Amina Easat-Daas (2019) notes the growth in the far-right presence which "paved the way for increased legislated limitations on visible Muslim appearance in education and employment" (in Bayrakli and Hafez 2019: 122) (discussed further in Chapter 7). She provides an example of the freedom to ridicule and insult noting:

> in February 2019 students at the Pater Jozefieten school in Melle came to school dressed as stereotypical Arabs/Muslims. The students wore Gulf Arab-style thobes, veils, and headscarves, accompanied by explosive belts. The school students proceeded to mock Islamic prayer in the school corridors. (cited in Bayrakli and Hafez 2019: 126)

Resonances of Edward Said's account of Princeton's reunion! Gendered Islamophobia is demonstrated across Europe in the legal restrictions placed on Muslim women and girls wearing the headscarf/hijab in schools and workplaces and the face covering/niqab in public places (discussed in Chapter 7). In the UK, the United Kingdom independence party (UKIP) election manifesto of 2017 promised a public ban on "face coverings", proscription of shariah courts and further immigration restrictions. Nigel Farage, when its leader, warned of rising public concern about immigration, partly because he said people believe there are some Muslims: "who want to form a fifth column and kill us" (*The Guardian*, 12 March 2015).

In 2016, the Secretary of State, Amber Rudd, responded to the rise in neo-Nazi groups by proscribing "National Action", for its incitement to violence. In its portfolio it stated: "In regard to violence, all violence has been of self-defence by patriots against mobs of state backed anarchists who are free to organise and attack all legal right-wing demonstrations. If [we] were in the United States it would have been our full legal right to shoot them all dead" (cited in Allen 2019: 7). Proscription is discussed further in Chapter 5. Cleland et al. (2018) in analysing 845 posts across 78 threads on an EDL message board from 20 September 2013 to 4 October 2013 examined how online activists construct and foment racial prejudice. "Whites" were presented as blameless victims, and hostility towards Islam and Muslims and racist commentary, redolent. The UK rupture from the rest of Europe (Brexit) emboldened by "we" and "us" imagines some supreme community sharing common features of right-wing identity discourse stoking fears that the "white" race and its culture are being replaced by immigrants reiterating the rhetoric of "Identitarian" ethno-nationalist movements across Europe. This then, is part of the wider context and evidence across Europe of the rise of far-right anti-Muslim groups where "Islamophobia" has become a unifying feature of nationalist fervor and patriotism.

Some Thoughts on Nationalism and Identity

The ideology that underpins the more extreme instances of hatred of Muslims requires unravelling and more detail than I can offer here. Arendt (2017 [1951]), Cohen (2001) and Glover (2002) argue that hate is not reducible to individual pathology or to childhood upbringing or episodic individualism, since social, economic, cultural disadvantage which breeds hostility and the power to preach hate and socialisation are all relevant. Narratives of hate and the justifications for hate, racial and religious, are learned and socially and politically endorsed and are found within nationalist movements. Bieber's (2018: 519) constructs of, "latent nationalism" and "exclusionary nationalism" (521), for examining right-wing nationalism in Europe, are relevant. Latent nationalism is characterised by a jingoistic belief, in country, the kind of exceptionalism that President Trump celebrates. "Exclusionary nationalism" emerges in response to indigenous or exogenous shocks to the system which may be ideological, economic, institutional or social, or for example, the rise in terrorism which may cause mass violence, pogroms, "deadly ethnic riots", hate crimes, and physical attacks (Bieber: 534). Far-right groups in Europe can be characterised by their identification a self-invented idea of "nationalism", with its claims to a messianic appeal of nationhood, to ideologies and traits of a "warrior race", of "whiteness", of purity, and hypermasculinity. Whilst Anderson ([1983], 2016: 7) and Sand (2009, 2014: 13) debunk any romantic notion of nationhood and identity "Nationalism arouses deep attachments: ...because the members of even the smallest nation will never know most of their fellow members, meet them, or even hear of them, yet in the minds of each lives the image of their communion" ([1983]: 6) there is, the darker side of nationalism with its roots in fear and hatred of the "other", and affinities with racism ([1983]: 149).

Anti-Muslim Women Speech

Muslim women are a particular target for anti-Muslim speech. In this Farris, in *In the Name of Women's Rights: The Rise of Femonationalism* (2017) identifies the neo-liberal tendency to appropriate the equality and women's rights rhetoric to promote an otherwise xenophobic and anti-Islam agenda around matters, including the Shariah law. (One wonders from where this knowledge with regard to Islamic family law and personal status derives, for it is certainly a most specialist area well beyond the ken of an undergraduate law student, yet Wilders, Marie Le Pen and Salvini and far-right nationalists, neo-liberals, the right-wing media seem clinically obsessed with it). Edward Said (cited in Bayoumi and Rubin 2001: 175) recognised this tendency more generally when he wrote, "To speak of 'Islam' in the West today... 'Islam' is unlikely to mean anything one knows either directly or objectively". Badinter referring to face veiled women "I think we are dealing with some very sick women" (1). Boris Johnson, prior to becoming Prime Minister, and perhaps with a self-ingrained sense of entitlement to say what he thinks even if it insults Muslim women verbally, said that wearers of the veil:

> look like letterboxes, resemble bank robbers, and that the garment is absolutely ridiculous", adding, "If a constituent came to my MP's surgery with her face obscured, I should feel fully entitled — like Jack Straw — to ask her to remove it so that I could talk to her properly". (*The Independent*, August 8, 2018)

Entitled?! I am reminded of Berlin and Waldron's observations on the consequentialist impact of such speech, and Hall's concern with the "effects outside the scope of the discursive" (1996: 443) in that Johnson's remarks give tacit permission to others to insult. His remarks were said to have resulted in a 375% spike in anti-Muslim hate incidents (Read 2019). Whilst the Conservative party called for an investigation into whether Johnson had breached the party's code of conduct an independent panel concluded, that whilst the language used was arguably "provocative", it would nevertheless be "unwise to censor excessively the language of party representatives or the use of satire to emphasise a viewpoint, particularly a viewpoint that is not subject to criticism". So, here we find, as is so often the case, and as MacKinnon pointed out in relation to pornography, whether speech is deemed "ideas" or as here, a "viewpoint", or whether it is deemed "inequality" determines the limits which can then be placed upon it (1994: 21). Writing in *The Guardian* (8 August 2018) Baroness Warsi expressed a quite different view.

> In his *Telegraph* piece, Johnson was making a liberal argument. He was saying that we shouldn't ban the burqa, as Denmark has done. But his words signalled something else. He said – not only to those Muslim women who veil, but to many more who associate with a faith in which some women do – that you don't belong here, he refused to accept that these phrases were some kind of mistake, and the offence inadvertent - Johnson is too intelligent and too calculating for that. No, this was all quite deliberate. His refusal to apologise supports that.

Muslim mothers also have been at the receiving end of disapprobation and regarded as the primary transmitters of culture have been held responsible, at least by David Cameron, for not preventing the recruitment of their offspring into terrorist organisations. Cameron said:

> If you're not able to speak English, you're not able to integrate, you may find, therefore, that you have challenges understanding what your identity is and you could be more susceptible to the extremist message that comes from Daesh. (Edwards 2017)

As Bouattia writes such: "statements aimed to demonize our apparent inability to integrate and act within British society ..." (2020: 211).

Muslim women provide the visible Muslim target for far-right animosity. In Belgium, the Vlaams Belang (right-wing extremist Flemish nationalist party), in its 2013 campaign video ("La vidéo du Vlaams Belang contre l'immigration et l'islamisation'") used Muslim women wearing Muslim dress to instill fear and intensify hatred. Originally posted on YouTube (now removed), this video ends with a caption and call to action "Stop Immigratie – Stop Islamerising" and so its illocutionary force and performativity should bring it within any law that prohibits incitement. The scene begins with white children riding a merry-go-round trying to catch a tassel which hangs above their head, playful fairground music from a Wurlitzer can be heard. Abruptly, the Wurlitzer stops and the music changes, diminishing and augmenting chords create a mood of fear, and menace at which point two face veiled fully robed Muslim women come into screen and sit on the merry-go-round and the children are replaced until only Muslim women ride. The music changes again and chords of c and d flat replicate the irregular minor chords, the camera zooms into a close screenshot of a woman's henna patterned hand and she catches the tassel with ease (Edwards 2014: 288). Is this speech the kind that Justice Brandeis in *Brandenburg v Ohio*, Justice Roberts in *Snyder v Phelps*, and Nadine Strossen have urged must be tolerated so all speech can be free?

Anti-Muslim Tropes Online, in Media, Film and "Satire"

Direct acts of anti-Muslim hatred discrimination speech and assaults are fuelled by this anti-Muslim rhetoric whether in newspapers, film, cartoon images and satire in hard copy, or celluloid and on digital platforms, web sites, the internet, YouTube channels and in social media, Facebook, and Twitter (Littler and Kondor 2019), now the main channels of communicating hatred and fake news.

The Rise in Cyber-Islamophobia

Gheorghiu (2018) reports that the Centre for the Analysis of Social Media (CASM) at Demos, conducted research on hateful, xenophobic, anti-disability, anti-Semitic and anti-Islamic expressions on Twitter and found in one month alone, 215,247 hateful messages. The UK Law Commission in its *Hate Crime* Consultation paper (2020) cited the House of Commons Home Affairs Committee (2017) which reported:

> YouTube was awash with videos that promoted far-right racist tropes, such as antisemitic conspiracy theories... On Twitter, there were numerous examples of incendiary content found using Twitter hashtags that are used by the far-right... A search for those hashtags identified significant numbers of racist and dehumanising tweets that were plainly intended to stir up hatred... On Facebook we found community pages devoted to stirring up hatred, particularly against Jews and Muslims, although much of the

content that is posted on Facebook is done so within "closed groups" and is not as openly available as similar content is on Twitter. (Law Commission 2020: 459)

The Oxford Internet Institute underlined that news reposted by unaccountable websites is more viral than news diffused by online newspapers (cited in Bayrakli and Hafez 2019: 446). The UNCHR reports the problem of increasing polarisation created by echo chambers and algorithms that confirm particular views by reinforcement. Del Vicario et al. (2015) found that the www was "fruitful environment for the massive diffusion of unverified rumors" and generating "homogeneous and polarized communities". Lean agrees that algorithms have shut down diversity of opinion and debate through echo chambers (84) which have served to confirm to Islamophobes their self-belief. This has become particularly dangerous especially where during Covid-19 lockdowns and exacerbated by isolation where the greater public use of the web and exposure to its echo chambers provides the breeding ground for far-right xenophobia.

Fake News: The Birmingham 'Trojan Horse' Affair

As for mainstream news and media reportage and Islamophobia, already in 1997, the Runnymede Trust called upon the Press Complaints Commission to modify its terms of practice regarding the distorted and negative reporting of Muslims, particularly as anti-Muslim propaganda was accompanied by an increase in violent attacks upon them. Oborne and Jones' report, "Muslims under Siege" (2008) found an all-pervasiveness of negative and racist commentary in mainstream media. Christopher Balls (cited in Lean 2017: 98), in his study of 1084 press releases, using plagiarism software to compare stories, detected similarities between the press releases and the story content, and found a reproduction of an identical racist narrative. Katie Hopkins in *The Sun*, likened refugees to "cockroaches". The same newspaper ran a headline "1 in 5 Brit Muslims' sympathy for jihadis".

Stories are distorted and some invented. Richard Peppiatt, a *Daily Star* news reporter, resigned following the newspaper's propaganda and boosting of the EDL's incitement of racism and Islamophobia. In giving evidence to the Leveson Inquiry (2011) he described a top-down pressure to unearth stories that fitted certain narratives of "immigrants are taking over" and the Muslim security threat. Peppiatt told the inquiry how he invented a story about a non-existent Muslim bomb plot. Why would he do such a thing? He explained that as EDL stories attracted a lot of phone callers to the paper, generating much interest, his superiors said: "Right, we need to have more of these stories ...This will sell us more papers if we keep sort of banging this drum" (Leveson: 708). Such willingness to feed and invent such stories confirms Herman and Chomsky's core thesis in *Manufacturing Consent: The Political Economy of the Mass Media*, concerning the profit orientation of the mass media (1988: 3). It is difficult to disagree with Baroness Warsi, who when delivering the 2017 Fifth annual Leveson lecture, said: "In sections of our press, [Islamophobia] is relentless and deliberate. Steadily and methodically using paper inches and columns to create, feed and ratchet up suspicions and hostilities in our society, driving communities apart and creating untold – and unnecessary – fear and distress".

Ratcheting up and trading on anti-Muslim antipathy was said to be the motive behind "The Birmingham Trojan Horse affair", a further example of a confected scandal. This "affair" spoke of a plot said to be orchestrated by teachers, school governors and parents, to radicalise pupils in fourteen Muslim schools in Birmingham in 2014 (Holmwood and O'Toole 2017, Miah 2017) and alleged gender inequality and bullying. One of the allegations referred to a jihadi video being recorded in the school media centre, an accusation that turned out to be entirely false. Instead, "the video" was related to a documentary being produced by a television company. *The Times* newspaper reported that 100 Islamicist teachers were involved yet none of the original charges against the teachers were of extremism or radicalisation, as the press had reported, but were charges of "undue religious influence", echoing the government's fear of a growing and creeping Islamification in publicly funded schools (Meer 2014). In 2014, this supposed plot was made the subject of two official investigations, one on behalf of Birmingham City Council (The "Kershaw Report" 2014) and the other on behalf of the Department of Education (the "Clarke Report"). The investigation went on for two years, eventually collapsing in May 2017, when it became known that the so-called prosecution witness statements had been created, not through direct oral statementing from the witnesses, but, from statements given to the Clarke investigation, and furthermore, the materials had not been disclosed to the defence. This evidence debacle was covered up, the press instead attributing the inquiry's collapse to a "technicality". The Clarke report conceded that the way evidence had been gathered in the withholding of witness statements was "an abuse of process", and that the Educational Trust itself disputed the allegations required disciplinary proceedings to be discontinued (Miah 2017: 3). The debacle attracted the attention of writers and the play "Trojan Horse", was developed with Leeds Playhouse, LUNG theatre. Andrew Gilligan's report (*The Times*, 2 September 2018) however continued to milk the discredited story with a strapline: "A new play distorts the truth of how Muslim hardliners took over schools in Birmingham". On 1 September 2017, Samira Shackle, writing in *The Guardian* with the strapline "the fake plot", finally printed the truth. "Yes", there were bigoted teachers, and "Yes" there was a preference in the school for the teaching of English and Maths, over drama, and "Yes", in a school with predominantly Muslim pupils, there was a Muslim morning assembly, and "Yes" in accordance with the equality objective there were prayer rooms. How was this, she asks, a plot to radicalise pupils? The timing of the Trojan horse fiction was significant as it surfaced at the same time as the introduction into legislation of the government's "Prevent" agenda which set out a duty to "promote fundamental British values" with which Muslim schools were considered be less reflective.

Deliberately Complicit: The Film Industry

Beyond cyber space and press misrepresentation, Muslim characterisations are fixed in film. Said, in *Covering Islam* (1997: xxxii) details how large-scale feature films and television, feature the classic Muslim villain with "glinty eyes and a passionate desire to kill" (1978: 26, 325) and where: "...electronic and print media have been awash with demeaning stereotypes that lump together Islam and terrorism, or Arabs and violence, or the Orient and tyranny" (347). In 1972, Marlon Brando refused to receive an Oscar for "best actor", using the awards' ceremony as an opportunity to make a statement about imperialism and racism against the American Indian in the US film industry. "The motion picture community has been as responsible as any, for degrading the Indian and making a mockery of his character, describing him as savage, hostile and evil. It's hard enough for children to grow up in this world. When Indian children watch television, and they watch films, and when they see their race depicted as they are in films, their minds become injured in ways we can never know" (Marlon Brando, "The Unfinished Oscar Speech" *New York*

Times, 30 March 1973). No one has yet made a speech at the Oscar ceremony condemning the representation of Arabs or Muslims. Although all credit to Meryl Streep's critique of Trump at the Golden Globe Awards ceremony.

Alford (2018) applies Chomsky's propaganda model to an analysis of contemporary screen representations drawing on Jack Shaheen's (2003) analysis of US media, citing Fox TV's 24, Showtime's *Homeland* and HBO's *Sleeper cell* as three examples of television series that "stripped communities of their identities only to assign them a threatening character – the American/Arab Muslim neighbour as terrorist – that reinforced prevailing political positions" (Lean 2017: xxi). Shaheen in "Reel Bad Arabs" (2003), a review of more than 1000 films made since 1896, uncovers a constant negative demeaning and shallow imagery of the Muslim/Arab as terrorist and extremist where Muslim characters in American cinema have been "locked into the Arab cycle of identification", marginalised in plots focusing on white American protagonists with Muslims characterisation relying on stylised tropes of notorious sheikhs, maidens, Egyptians, and Palestinians. Bayraktaroğlu's research is but further evidence of the iterated tropes and one-dimensional figurative characterisation. In the *Muslim Male Character Typology in American Cinema Post-9/11* (2014, 2018) he documents the representations of the Arab/Muslim flying on carpets to terrorist recruitment, characterised by violence, terror, and rage, citing films like Hildago (2004) and *Rendition* (2007). He concludes that these "movies [have] reduced the diversity of Muslims and their multiple cultural experiences into a two-dimensional Arab stereotype which can only be explained as America's fixation with Arabs and Islam" (2014: 358). The recent transmission of *Bodyguard* (2018) a BBC drama, again reinforces the binarism of the female stereotype where the only female Muslim role in the drama is that of terrorist. All this provokes Riz Ahmed who, addressing the UK Parliament, calls for diversity in film and drama representation, setting up what he calls the "Riz test" to measure this racist typecasting.

Cartoons and Satire—Your Laughter—My Insult

The so-called "political cartoon" is yet another vehicle for promulgating anti-Muslim speech, yet here insult is so frequently positioned as "core political speech" (Gottschalk and Greenberg 2008). The 2005 Danish cartoons set a plimsol line, of "free speech". Penned by Kurt Wester-gaard, the most offensive cartoon represented an image of the prophet. The Arabic script on his turban arranged in the shape of a bomb and a fuse wire, already lit, and visibly protruding reads: "No God, but God and Mohammed is the Messenger of God". The newspaper, Jylands Posten (*The Morning Post*) which printed the image styles itself as "indepen-dent, liberal and center right", giving to what was a frontal attack on Muslims some political respectability. The publication instigated protests across the world (Müller and Özcan 2007) of the twelve Westergaard cartoons some were used for other purposes. Geert Wilders, the Dutch leader, of the right-wing party (PVV), intended to use the Westergaard cartoons in his so-called film, "Fitna". Westergaard objected to this use and claimed that his cartoons were intended to be directed at fanatical Muslims not at all Muslims and together with the Danish Association of Journalists took legal action, filing for an injunction to force Wilders to remove the cartoon of the Prophet Mohammed from his film. The action failed. Despite Jacqui Smith's, attempt to ban Wilders entry into the UK (see above), in 2010 he was invited to the House of Lords by UKIP leader Lord Pearson and crossbencher Baroness Cox. It is signif-icant that only half a dozen people were reported to have attended the event! at which Wilders showed his "film". Meanwhile, the Dutch Parlia-ment turned down his request for an exhibition of cartoons in Parliament, and Dutch TV prevented him from showing them although he exploited a loophole that permits such images to be shown in parliamentary elec-tion films. In his election campaign of 2017, he continued with his vitriol: "There is a lot of Moroccan scum in Holland who make the streets unsafe. If you want to regain your country, make the Netherlands for the people of the Netherlands again, then you can only vote for one party" (*BBC News*, 18 February 2017). Wilders was convicted, in a Dutch court in 2016 for incitement over the "scum" remark, though the court did not sentence him. He replied on social media to the judges that convicted him. "You will never be able to stop me" (*BBC News*, 9 December 2016, "Netherlands trial: Geert Wilders guilty of incitement").

Then there was the "Charlie Hebdo" cartoon images of insult including a cartoon depicting the Prophet as a naked baby and being pushed in a wheelchair. The magazine defended its position by saying that along with publishing demeaning images of Muslims and Islam, it also published demeaning images of other religions. So, one might ask, as indeed many did, what is the problem? Juss (2015) in his paper "Burqa-bashing and the Charlie Hebdo Cartoons" explains that "Both the Danish Cartoons and the Charlie Hebdo cartoons were defended by the shield of Article 10 'freedom of speech'. Proponents of freedom of speech contend there is an equal playing field". Juss asks whether the ridicule of a minority, disadvantaged and discriminated against can ever be equated to the ridicule of a majority in whom power is vested? The answer, says Juss, is that it cannot!. Enraged by the magazine's cartoons of the prophet, Muhammad Chérif and Saïd Kouachi went on to kill 12 people including cartoonists and employees of the magazine. Outraged reaction to their deaths acted as a catalyst giving rise to an exponential rise in anti-Muslim propaganda and hate crime. At the PEN America gala in Texas in 2015, an award was presented to the "Charlie Hebdo" magazine. Twenty-six writers joined six others—Peter Carey, Michael Ondaatje, Francine Prose, Teju Cole, Rachel Kushner and Taiye Selasi—and withdrew from the gala. Peter Carey said: "A hideous crime was committed, but was it a freedom-of-speech for PEN America to be self-righteous about?.... All this is complicated by PEN's seeming blindness to the cultural arrogance of the French nation, which does not recognize its moral obligation to a large and disempowered segment of their population" (cited in Edwards 2017). At the Gala, Geert Wilders delivered a keynote speech and together with other groups fomented further provocation by organising "Draw the Prophet Mohammed" cartoon contest. As Lean observes, the first Annual Mohammed Art Exhibition Contest took "a swing at Muslims under the banner of free speech" (2017: 52). In September 2020 as the trial in France for the 2015 massacre at "Charlie Hebdo" was underway the cartoons were republished leading to assaults on two "Charlie Hebdo" employees and on 17 October 2020, a schoolteacher who had shown the cartoons to his class of thirteen years olds, was murdered.

Satire is another cloak behind which anti-Muslim bigotry hides. Just fun! said Geller (above). Rod Liddle, *The Spectators'* columnist, writes commentaries that are considered by some to be offensive and anti-Muslim. *The Guardian* newspaper reported that a piece written by Liddle: "appeared to call for elections to be held on days when Muslims are forbidden by their religion to vote". Mike Katz, the national chairman of the Jewish Labour Movement (JLM), said Liddle promoted: "rancid views and racism.... We need to stand up to all racism - Islamophobia on the right and antisemitism from the left. Liddle's *Spectator* article is truly vile, casual in its deployment, but no less hateful and hurtful". Fraser

Nelson, the magazine's editor, is reported to have told *The Guardian* that the article should not have been published in the form that it was, though defending Liddle's right to "satirise" UK politics. Naming speech "satire" provides an almost bulletproof fence which protects racism neutralising any racist intention on the part of the author by connivingly situating it within the realm of permissible ideas.

CRUSHING THE COUNTER-NARRATIVE

So, what then of Foucault's "subjugated knowledge", of freedom of information about government activities, and matters inimical to state interests, and the freedom to dissent and Strossen's defence of "core political speech"? Chomsky is sceptical. He writes "dissidence carries personal costs that may be severe, even in society that lacks such means of control as death squads, psychiatric prisons, or extermination camps" (Chomsky 2008 in *Necessary Illusions*) and E.P. Thompson's (1980: 163) counterpoint on the secret state is chillingly prophetic.

> The national crisis, the state of emergency the deployment of armed forces the attempts to induce panic on the national media the identification of some out groups as a 'threat to security' ... these are becoming part of the normal repertoire of power.

In the UK, the Freedom of Information Act (2000) makes a claim to granting individuals the right of access to some information held by public authorities creating the illusion of a free state. However, state secrets are protected, and "harm-based exemptions" created, where information involves the security services (s 23) where such exemptions are subject to the "public interest test". We are told that requests for disclosures that could lead to embarrassment are simply blocked by a FOI unit of Orwellian proportions (https://www.opendemocracy.net/en/save-our-foi/, 24 November 2020). At the same time, the right of the state to private telecommunication authorised under the Investigatory Powers Act (2016), facilitates the burgeoning presence of CCTV on our streets and in public places, the introduction of secret courts, whilst the Covert Human Intelligence Sources (Criminal Conduct) Bill 2020 will eschew openness and accountability of state agents.

The denigration of dissent is another tactic of silencing. In the UK, its counter-radicalisation "Prevent" programme dubs any speech that is critical of the British state and its foreign policy, as potential evidence of radicalisation and extremism (see above). In the UK, as Kundnani explains, such a presumption may be applied to those who support Palestinians (131). In the US, when criticising the role of the US government in the WOT, Chomsky was "dismissed …as an apologist for Palestinian terrorism" (Edwards 2016; Chomsky 2003). Susan Sontag has been described as an "American hater", "moral idiot" and "traitor" (Joseph and Sharma 2003: xvii), for her comments published on 24 September 2001 in *The New Yorker*, when she said: "Where is the acknowledgement that this was not a 'cowardly' attack on 'civilization' or 'liberty' or 'humanity' or 'the free world' but an attack on the world's self-proclaimed super-power, undertaken as a consequence of specific American alliances and actions?" In an interview with David Talbot she said: "I just don't understand why debate equals dissent, and dissent equals lack of patriotism" (Sontag 2003: 107). Barbara and Rosa Ehrenreich-Brooks were also branded "traitors" for writing passages such as this:

> But imagine growing up, even in a middle-class household, surrounded by suffering, hopelessness, poverty and pain, in the ruins of Kabul, in the Gaza strip, in Alegrias ransacked towns, or in the bleak streets of Baghdad: imagine being brought up to believe that the suffering you see around you is caused by the hypocrisy and greed, obtuseness and injustice of the arrogant and licentious American superpower. (Ehrenreich and Ehrenreich-Brooks 2003: 139)

Madeleine Bunting the UK *Guardian* columnist, following an article in which she said: "What we have to fear from September 11 is not just Islamist fanaticism, but the US response to it" received vile hate mail and misogynist abuse "get laid" "shut your fat legs", etc. (Bunting 2003: 112).

FROM ANTI-MUSLIM BANTER TO HATE CRIME

These scripts, which ridicule, denigrate and stigmatise Muslims provide the ideological conditions and justificatory rationales for hate crime in the real world, on the streets and globally, and in this way the material conditions of the discursive, the "real effects", as Stuart Hall (1996) theorises, are manifested. Negative scripts some say, must be defended so that "core political speech" is free. Yet, the evidence shows that even in allowing anti-Muslim hate speech, Justice Brandeis' aspiration that all men will be free has not been realised and "core political speech" is silenced, and whistle-blowers punished.

The "real effects" of anti-Muslim hate speech are threefold. First, on an international scale, anti-Muslim scripts and derogatory stereotyping embolden foreign policy, justify territorial ambitions in other regions and provides the justifications and permissions for the inhumane treatment of "other" subjects, in for example, Guantánamo, Iraq and elsewhere (the subject of Chapters 4–6). Second, such stereotyping gives permission for the hate speech and aggravated crimes committed against Muslim women and men. Muslim women are particularly targeted, being identifiable through their appearance in wearing the headscarf/hijab, face veil/niqab or long dress/jilbab/gelabaya. Muslims as a group are also vulnerable, congregating in or outside their places of worship, as in the Finsbury Park Mosque attack in London (19 June 2017), and the attack on a mosque in Christchurch New Zealand on 15 March 2019 (Akay 2019). Third, this anti-Muslim speech in all its forms, text, online, visual imagery and gesture, and in physical and verbal attacks creates the harm to Muslims that Waldron spoke of in loss of dignity and equality, alienation, exclusion and harm to mental health. In addition, such imagery constitutes the Muslim subject in the field of vision of others and also in his and her own self-identification in the paradox of identity. This problem lay at the core of Fanon's thesis in *Black Skin, White Masks* (2008 [1952]) in his study of the colonised, and upon which Baldwin (1965b) reflected in the context of the African-American "that you belong where white people put you!"

On the first point then, in emboldening US and UK foreign policy Juss (2015) in his excoriating critique argues that free speech, liberal rights language, secular atheism, and parody are all used as pretexts by western elites to exercise power (27) and on the anti-Muslim discourse point cites Greenwald who writes: "the West has spent years bombing, invading and occupying Muslim countries and killing, torturing and lawlessly imprisoning innocent Muslims, and anti-Muslim speech has been a vital driver in sustaining support for those policies" (39–40). Chomsky and others point out, that the popular media in all its forms creates illusions of freedom of speech and of democracy whilst perpetuating distortions and misrepresentations of Muslims, whilst elevating themselves as guardians of civilisation, democracy and free speech. This I discuss in later chapters.

On the second point, Trump's rhetoric, Cameron's rhetoric, and Johnson's rhetoric, together with the right-wing and neo-liberal press, the far-right, cyber-Islamophobia and the industries of film, satire, and commercial fiction, have created the necessary conditions for hate crimes in the physical world, which lead to attacks on Muslims as individuals, on their places of worship, street crimes, assaults on women and men and assaults on children. Fear of attacks, bullying, and harassment impacts on the daily lives of Muslims and those with Muslim connections. My daughter (and because her father is of the Muslim faith), when 10 years of age, experienced this "banter" from a school classmate, who said "Your dad's a terrorist!". It was, intended as a joke. Jokes and anti-Muslim banter by a boy to a girl in the school playground! It bothered her enough to tell me and me enough to write to the school. The child's police officer father made his son apologise. This speech starts somewhere. Learning the rhetoric of racism starts long before the reunion at Harvard! The techniques to neutralise such scripts and offences are also learnt early on. Banter! Jokes! Satire! In 2018, the schoolboy Jamal Hijazi, a refugee, was pushed to the ground and had water poured on his face. He had suffered two years of abuse at school (*The Guardian*, 5 December 2018, "Syrian schoolboy suffered years of abuse"). But a Facebook page which read "Lots of Muslim gangs are beating up white English kids in Britain" and had more than 1 million followers, was the fake story that was spread. In 2018, I gave a presentation to sixth formers in a school where the form teacher warned me before I spoke that there were some "Tommy Robinson" (aka EDL) supporters in the classroom. Indeed, there were! as I discovered by the questions put to me by five of the pupils, as the only female headscarfed girl who sat at the front of the classroom cowered.

The criminal law in the UK and its implementation needs to do more to address anti-Muslim hate crime. The Law Commission published its Consultation document on "Hate Crime" in September 2020 outlining a series of proposals. Currently, the law identifies three kinds of hate conduct, (i) Threatening or abusive words (dealt with above), (ii) racial incitement, and (iii) racially aggravated or religiously "aggravated offences" including assault. The Crime and Disorder Act (CDA) (1998) s 28–32, recognises that criminal assault and acts of harassment may be of themselves "racially aggravated" (s 28(4)), such hatred includes "hostility" towards a racial group by reference to "race, colour, nationality (including citizenship) or ethnic or national origins". Hostility towards a "religious group", is defined in s 28(5) "as a group of persons with reference to religious belief or lack of religious belief". Yet there are few prosecutions. Where the offender is motivated by any one of five protected characteristics including disability, transgender status, race, religion, or sexual orientation, or demonstrates hostility, then enhanced sentencing is provided under s 145 and 146 of the Criminal Justice Act 2003. Further, s 125(1) of the Coroners and Justice Act 2009, requires the judge in sentencing to consider whether the offence was motivated by racial or religious hostility, age, sex, gender identity (or presumed gender identity), disability (or presumed disability) or sexual orientation.

However, as John Grieve Independent Chair of the Government's Hate Crime Advisory Group, recognised, "One of the greatest challenges is to reduce the under-reporting of hate crime". The European Islamophobia Report (Bayrakli and Hafez 2017) reported that Islamophobia in Europe shows only the tip of the iceberg. Home Office figures hate crime annual report (2017–2018) show 94,098 hate crime offences recorded by police (these are not prosecutions) but trying to disaggregate these figures and identify hate crimes against Muslims is not possible. However, of, 8336 "religious" hate crimes recorded in 2017–2018 it is generally agreed that Muslim adults were the most likely victims (again these are not prosecution figures). Other studies have gathered data on anti-Muslim hate crime prevalence, and for the period January to June 2018, the organisation "Tell Mama'" documented the instances of race hatred on the street reported to them. Of 685 incidents 608 were verified as being anti-Muslim or Islamophobic in nature. Two-thirds of incidents occurred offline or on the street (65.9%, $n = 401$), including 'abusive behaviour' (45.3%, $n = 182$), 'physical attack' (15.5%, $n = 62$) and discrimination (under 10%, $n = 40$). Over a third of incidents (34%, $n = 207$) occurred on social media platforms. On the street, women were the targets, due to the visibility of their Islamic dress constituting 58% ($n = 233$) of victims. "Tell Mama" also reports that about 700 Mosques in the UK have been attacked in some way since 9/11. Both the Leicester Hate Crime Project 2012–2014 (Chakraborti et al. 2014) and the Sussex Hate Crime Project (Paterson et al. 2018) found multiple discrimination experienced by Muslim women because of their faith, gender and race and expressed a concern that ethno-religious groups such as Sikhs and Jews were better protected by the category of "race" than groups that are legally considered to be "religious" groups only, for example, Christians and Muslims (cited by the Law Comm 2020: 159). The Law Commission's own hate crime review in 2014 found no reason why out of the five protected characteristics any should be treated differently (Law Comm 2020, para 8.25).

Muslim Women, an Easy Target

Hate crime includes verbal assaults, racially aggravated assaults, and murder where Muslim women were more likely because of their visibility to experience violence in the public sphere than Muslim men (see Alimahomed-Wilson 2017; Cainkar 2009; Naber 2008, 2012; Zempi and Chakraborti 2016; Law Comm 2020 12.53: 242). Mason-Bish and Zempi's research (2018) reported gendered and Islamophobic insults such as "Muslim bitch", and "Muslim whore" (cited in Law Comm 2020: 246) and women wearing the face veil experienced ridicule being called "ninja", "Darth Vader" and "letter box" (29, 53). Hussein (2015; 2019: 82) reports similar incidents in Australia. Women are subject to violent assaults. In the case of *R v Eyles* [2014] the male defendant pleaded guilty to an offence of "racially or religiously aggravated assault". The victim was shopping in Plymouth. She was wearing a hijab and carrying her 16-month old son. Eyles ran towards her shouting and swearing: "I don't want to fucking scare you, but I will.' 'It's all your fault.' 'Don't think I won't smash your baby's head in because I will". He punched her several times, took hold of the baby, and knocked the baby's head against a wall.

Physical violence is also prevalent against Muslim men. On 17 June 2017, Darren Osborne rammed a van into worshippers outside Finsbury Park mosque during Ramadan killing one man and injuring nine others. On 29 April 2013, Mohammed Salim was killed simply because he wore a Muslim dress. His killer, Ukrainian Pavlo Lapshyn, pleaded guilty to murdering Salim because he was not white and pleaded to plotting to cause explosions near mosques in Walsall, Tipton and Wolverhampton (*The Independent*, 29 April 2019). Zack Davies on 25 June 2015 was convicted of attempted murder of Dr. Bhambra (a Sikh dentist) in a racially motivated machete and hammer attack. Davies explained he just wanted to kill an Asian. He attempted decapitation. Bhambra's brother, said in a statement: "Sarandev was singled out because of the colour of his skin. We are in no doubt that had the racial disposition of this case been reversed this would be reported as an act of terror with a wider media coverage" (*The Guardian*, 25 June 2015). Michael O'Leary (*R v (Michael Patrick) O'Leary* [2015] was convicted of three offences, on separate victims, who were shopkeepers, whom he threatened with a knife and stabbed. O'Leary approached Mr Islam, a shopkeeper, brandishing one of the knives and told Mr Islam that he wanted to kill a Muslim. In 13 January 2018, Marek Zakrocki drove his car into a restaurant after telling his wife he wanted to "kill a Muslim" and was "doing this for Britain" and "Wanted to help his country".

Online Offences

There has been a rise, too, in online hate on Facebook, Twitter and other social media platforms directed at specific victims. The Protection from Harassment Act 1997s 4, provides for the prosecution of cyberbullying where a person is put in fear of violence, "Trolling" and "Virtual mobbing" intended to cause alarm and harm to the intended victim, is covered by the Malicious Communications Act 1988s 1, s 127 of the Communications Act 2003 makes it an offence to send a message of a "grossly offensive or of an indecent, obscene or menacing character" and the Public Order Act s 19 makes it an offence to publish or distribute written material which is "threatening, abusive or insulting is guilty of an offence if—(a)he intends thereby to stir up racial hatred, or (b)having regard to all the circumstances racial hatred is likely to be stirred up thereby". In *R v Bitton* [2019] the defendant was convicted under s 19 (1) and s 29c (1) of the Public Order Act 1986 for this post on his Twitter account:

> 12th May: "Kill a c**n, kill a c**n, kill, kill, and kill a c**n." 14th May: "'Kill the black bastards.' 'Negro c***s need bombing.' 'Time for these c**ns to get killed.'" 15th May: "'Burn every single mosque in England.' 'Kill the lot of these Muslims.'" 16th May: 'These Muslims need a full mosque at a time taking out." 17th May: "'Kill c**ns.' 'Jews need to die with the Muslims'.

The Recorder described the content of the tweets as "xenophobic", "nationalistic" and "vitriolic". In the case of *R v Ruth* [2014] the defendant pleaded guilty to two offences of conspiracy to cause criminal damage and conspiracy to send malicious communications. The malicious communication was sent to the Torquay Islamic Centre. It stated, "[12] Leave this town today or there will be hell to pay". The defendant in this case published online "Kill a Muslim day: punish a Muslim day" (3rd April

2018) and, pleaded guilty to 15 offences, including soliciting to murder and staging a bomb hoax. He sent letters to mosques, Muslim parliamentarians, including Lord Ahmed of Wimbledon, the Queen, David Cameron and Theresa May, and in a letter sent to the University of Sheffield, he offered £100.00 donation to charity for each killing and offered awards for each attack of throwing acid. The letters were titled "P**i filth", and in one was written you will be "slaughtered very soon". Cases of hate crime directed at a specific victim are also rife. John Nimmo sent Tweets to Luciana Berger MP, "watch your back Jewish scum", "regards your friend the Nazi" (27 July 2016, see also *R v Bonehill-Paine* [2016]). He was sentenced to 27 months in jail after pleading guilty to nine charges: four of sending a communication conveying a grossly offensive message, three of conveying a threatening message and two of sending a communication conveying false information.

Defamation is a further but limited remedy. In *Mughal v Telegraph Media Group Ltd* [2014], Mughal failed in his claim of defamation against *The Daily Telegraph* which had published this:

> [6] Much more important – from the point of view of the general public – you frequently find that Muslim groups like Tell Mama get taxpayers' money (though, in its case, this is now coming to an end). You discover that leading figures of respectable officialdom share conference platforms with dubious groups. You learn that Muslim charities with blatantly political aims and Islamist links have been let off lightly by the Charity Commission. And you notice that many bigwigs in Muslim groups are decorated with public honours. Fiyaz Mughal, for example, who runs Tell Mama, has an OBE. Obviously, it would be half-laughable, half-disgusting, if activists of the EDL were indulged in this way; yet they are, in fact, less extreme than some of those Muslims who are.

The case of *Monir v Wood* [2018] involved UKIP's campaign for the UK's general election in 2015 and its use of a Twitter account on which it published a defamatory libel about Mr. Monir, labelling him falsely as a paedophile, and publishing his name and photograph. The court finding in Monir's favour, said: "[236] Had this libel been published in a national newspaper, an award of £250,000 or more could easily have been justified. Taking all these matters into account, I consider that the appropriate award is one of £40,000". The UKIP campaign had also Tweeted: "Labour to dress bus in Burka to attract Muslim vote".

Anti-Muslim speech and hate crime and the threat of hate crime is causing Muslims, women, and men, their children, and wider families psychological and emotional harm. The All-Party Parliamentary Group (APPG) on Hate Crime (2018) discovered that the fear of victimisation was a very real problem (see also Zempi and Awan 2017) finding that some victims and putative victims took to evasive action to protect themselves from abuse by changing their journeys to and from work, leaving their jobs, not taking public transport, altering their appearance and removing religious clothing to hide their Muslim identity. Psychological and emotional impacts included depression, anxiety and fear of visibility. Awan and Zempi's (2015b) study reported on such harms and avoidances. In some cases, Muslims who had converted to Islam explained that they kept their English name to avoid being identified and risking anti-Muslim hostility. Some participants who were born into Islam had adopted western names to hide their Muslim identity, especially in a cyber context. Mental health problems were also noted (Paterson et al. 2018). The Royal College of Psychiatrists and the Muslim Council of Britain were also concerned that the UK government's "Prevent" programme may be a barrier to mental health services for Muslims (Bazian 2010; Allen 2014) (*The Independent*, 5 February 2019, "Hate crime victims left suicidal and afraid to leave home because of attacks 'unleashed after Brexit referendum'").

Conclusion: Impacts and Consequences

What does all this mean for identity? For belonging? For the impact and life of Muslims. Should this simply be tolerated? Does tolerating any of this hatred serve the public good? Such words and speech acts have real consequences on individuals, communities, and at the global level. For Waldron, the harm resonates long after the spoken word (37). He seeks to establish a rival public good (94) underscoring how hate speech causes real harms undermining the dignity, not only of those towards whom the hate is directed but of society as a whole and the public good of inclusiveness to which we are committed (4). Hate speech and its symbolic violence sends a message, a sign, condoning and inciting other members of society encouraging bigoted invective which defiles our public environment (3, 89). Waldron proposes an offence of group libel (34) and in this refers to the Penal Code in Germany and Sweden (40). Speech against Muslims does not occur on an equal playing field but in a cultural milieu where there is a brooding omnipresence of hate and permitted denigration, where Muslims are essentialised and suspected of terrorist leanings and/or offences, where a virulent public and media machine manipulates and trades in popularity and profit, creating insecurities and where nationalism and identity is exploited to feign some rallying cohesion and where anti-Muslim speech is orchestrated to serve wider state and political interests of the West, in its global agenda, including its WOT (the subject of the next chapter) (Herman and Chomsky 1988: 22; Curtis 2018b; Chomsky 2008, 2013). And, as Kundnani (2007: 128) points out in the UK context: "Every Muslim in Britain has come to be perceived as a potential terrorist and has had to explain themselves to the rest of the country as if what happened on 9/11 was somehow their doing".

All of this, suggests Richards (2017: 76), leads to a sense of aggrievement: "…a cognitive dissonance over living in the West but feeling very aggrieved about Western foreign policy, coupled with an experience of general Islamophobia, frequently emerge as the very indicators that cause some young people to feel more radical about their relationship with secular, Western democratic society".

References

Akay, L. 2019. Why Was I Asked to Condemn Islamist Violence Days After Christchurch? *The Guardian*, March 18.

Alford, M. 2018. A Screen Entertainment Propaganda Model. In *The Propaganda Model Today: Filtering Perception and Awareness*, ed. J. Pedro-Carañana, D. Broudy, and J. Klaehn, 145–158. London: University of Westminster Press.

Allen, C. 2014. Exploring the Impact and 'Message' of Street-Level Islamophobia on Visible Muslim Women Victims: A British Case Study. *Journal of Muslims in Europe* 3 (2): 137–159.

Allen, C. 2019. National Action: Links Between the Far Right, Extremism, and Terrorism. Commission for Countering Extremism. https://assets.publishing.service.gov.uk/government/uploads/system/uploads/attachment_data/file/834342/Chris_Allen_-_National_Action_Post_Publication_Revisions.pdf. Accessed 9 August 2020.

Alimahomed-Wilson, S. 2017. Invisible Violence: Gender, Islamophobia, and the Hidden Assault on U.S. Muslim Women. In *Women, Gender, and Families of Color*, vol. 5, no. 1, 73–97. Champaign: University of Illinois Press.

Anderson, B. 2016 [1983]. *Imagined Communities: Reflections on the Origin and Spread of Nationalism*. London: Verso.

Atwan, A.B. 2015. *Islamic State the Digital Caliphate*. London: Saqi Books.
Austin, J. 1962. Performative Utterances. In *How to Do Things with Words*. Oxford: Oxford University Press.
Althusser, L. 1984 [1971]. Ideology and Ideological State Apparatuses. In *Lenin and Philosophy and Other Essays*, 121–176. New York: Monthly Review Press.
Arendt, H. 2017 [1951]. *The Origins of Totalitarianism*. London: Penguin.
Arendt, A. 2018 [1958]. *The Human Condition*. Chicago: University of Chicago Press.
Awan, I., and I. Zempi. 2015a. *We Fear for Our Lives: Offline and Online Experiences of Anti-Muslim Hostility*. London: Tell MAMA.
Awan, I., and I. Zempi. 2015b. 'I Will Blow Your Face Off'—Virtual and Physical World Anti-Muslim Hate Crime. *British Journal of Criminology* 57: 362–380.
Baldassi and Others v France application no. 15271/16, 11 June, 2020. https://hudoc.echr.coe.int/fre#{%22itemid%22:[%22001-202756%22]}. Accessed 10 November 2020.
Baldwin, J. 1965a. Cambridge University Debate Transcript: James Baldwin Debates William F. Buckley (1965). BLOG#42. https://www.rimaregas.com/2015/06/07/transcript-james-baldwin-debates-william-f-buckley-1965-blog42/. Accessed 20 October 2020.
Baldwin, J. 1965b. Pin Drop Speech. Cambridge University Debate. https://www.youtube.com/watch?v=NUBh9GqFU3A. Accessed 20 October 2020.
Bayrakli, E., and F. Hafez (eds.). 2017. *The European Islamophobia Report*. http://www.islamophobiaeurope.com/wp-content/uploads/2018/04/EIR_2017.pdf. Accessed 9 August 2020.
Bayrakli, E., and F. Hafez (eds.). 2019. *The European Islamophobia Report*. https://www.islamophobiaeurope.com/wp-content/uploads/2020/06/EIR_2019.pdf. Accessed 21 October 2020.
Bayraktaroğlu, K. 2014. The Muslim Male Character Typology in American Cinema Post-9/11. *Digest of Middle East Studies* 23 (2): 345–359.
Bayraktaroğlu, K. 2018. *Muslim Male Character Typology in American Cinema Post-9/11*. Jefferson: McFarland.
Bayoumi, M., and A. Rubin (eds.). 2001 [2000]. *The Edward Said Reader*. London: Granta.
Bazian, H. 2019 [2010]. Islamophobia: An Introduction to the Academic Field, Methods, and Approaches. In *Islamophobia and Psychiatry*, ed. H. Steven Moffic, John Peteet, Ahmed Zakaria Hankir, and Rania Awaad, 19–31. New York: Springer.
Beauharnais v Illinois 343 U.S. 250. 1952. https://supreme.justia.com/cases/federal/us/343/250/. Accessed 10 November 2020.
Bercow, J. 2017. Address on President Trumps Visit. https://www.youtube.com/watch?v=QP0c6smM_NM.

Berlin, I. 1965. *Two Concepts of Liberty*. Chicago: Henry Regnery Co.

Bieber, F. 2018. Is Nationalism on the Rise? Assessing Global Trends. *Ethnopolitics. Formerly Global Review of Ethnopolitics* 17 (5): 519–540.

Bouattia, M. 2020. Between Submission and Threat. In *It's Not About the Burqa*, ed. M. Khan. London: Picador.

Bunting, M. 2003. Intolerance of Debate. In *Terror Counter-Terror Women Speak Out*, ed. A. Joseph and K. Sharma, 111–114. Zed: London and New York.

Butler, J. 1990. *Gender Trouble*. London: Routledge.

Butler, J. 1997. *Excitable Speech: A Politics of the Performative*. Routledge: New York and London.

Brandenburg v Ohio 395 U.S. 444. 1969. https://supreme.justia.com/cases/federal/us/395/444/ Accessed 10 November 2020.

CAAT News. 2020. The Quarterly Magazine for Campaign Against Arms Trade. Issue 255.

Cainkar, L. 2009. *Homeland Insecurity: The Arab American and Muslim American Experience After 9/11*. New York: Russell Sage Foundation.

Chakraborti, N., J. Garland, and S. Hardy. 2014. *The Leicester Hate Crime Project*. Leicester: The University of Leicester.

Chomsky, N. 2003. *Power and Terror: Post 9–11 Talks and Interviews*. New York: Seven Stories Press.

Chomsky, N. 2008. *Media Control: The Spectacular Achievements of Propaganda*. New York: Seven Stories Press.

Chomsky N. 2013 [1989]. *Necessary Illusions: Thought Control in Democratic Societies* (CBC Massey Lecture). Toronto: Anansi Press.

Citizens United v Federal Elections Commission 558 U.S. 310. 2010. https://supreme.justia.com/cases/federal/us/558/310/. Accessed 10 November 2020.

Cleland, J., C. Anderson, and J. Aldridge-Deacon. 2018. Islamophobia, War, and Non-Muslims as Victims: An Analysis of Online Discourse on an English Defence League Message Board. *Journal Ethnic and Racial Studies* 41 (9): 1541–1557.

Clarke Report. 2014. *Report into Allegations Concerning Birmingham Schools Arising from the 'Trojan Horse' Letter*, July 2014. https://assets.publishing.service.gov.uk/government/uploads/system/uploads/attachment_data/file/340526/HC_576_accessible_-.pdf. Accessed 20 September.

Cockburn, P. 2015. *The Rise of Islamic State: Isis and the New Sunni Revolution*. London and New York: Verso.

Cohen, S. 2001. *States of Denial*. London: Polity.

Cole, J., and B. Cole. 2009. *Martydom: Radicalisation and Terrorist Violence Among British Muslims*. Hove: Pennant Books.

Crenshaw, K. (ed.). 2019. *Seeing Race Again*. Berkeley: University of California Press.

Curtis, M. 2008. Lecture at the University of Salford Mark Curtis—International Conference Against Terrorism. https://www.youtube.com/watch?v=Ic_S2aydhjA. Accessed 9 August 2020.

Curtis, M. 2018a. *Secret Affairs*. London: Serpent's Tail.

Curtis, M. 2018b. Going Underground with Afshin Rattansi. https://www.youtube.com/watch?v=QM9EYrE3wqA. Accessed 9 August 2020.

Delgado, R., and J. Stefancic. 2012 [2001]. *Critical Race Theory: An Introduction*. New York and London: NYU Press.

Delgado, R., and J. Stefancic. 2009. Four Observations About Hate Speech. *Wake Forest Law Review* 44: 353–370.

Del Vicario, M., A. Bessi, F. Zollo, and F. Petroni. 2015. The Spreading of Misinformation Online. www.pnas.org/cgi/doi/10.1073/pnas.1517441113. Accessed 30 September 2020.

Dodd, V., and J. Grierson. 2020. Greenpeace Included with Neo-Nazis on UK Counter-Terror List. *The Guardian*, January 17.

Duberman, M. 2020. *Andrea Dworkin: The Feminist as Revolutionary*. New York: New Press.

Dworkin, A. 1989. *Pornography: Men Possessing Women*. New York: E.P. Dutton.

Eagleton, T. 2015. *Culture and the Death of God*, Reprint edition. New Haven: Yale University Press.

Edwards, S.S.M. (2014). "Proscribing Unveiling—Law; A Chimera and An Instrument in the Political Agenda. In *The Experience of Face Veils Wearers in Europe*, ed. E. Brems, 278–296. Cambridge: CUP.

Edwards, P. 2016. Closure Through Resilience: The Case of Prevent. *Journal Studies in Conflict and Terrorism* 39 (4): 292–307.

Edwards, S.S.M. 2017. Cyber-Grooming Young Women for Terrorist Activity: Dominant and Subjugated Explanatory Narratives. In *Cybercrime, Organised Crime, and Societal Responses*, ed. E. Viano, 23–47. New York: Springer.

Ehrenreich, B., and R. Ehrenreich-Brooks. 2003. A Twisted Sense of Duty and Love. In *Terror Counter-Terror Women Speak Out*, ed. A. Joseph and K. Sharma, 138–149. London and New York: Zed.

Europol. 2019. *EU Terrorism Situation & Trend Report* (TE-SAT). https://www.europol.euroa.eu/tesat-report. Accessed 21 October 2020.

Farris, S. 2017. *In the Name of Women's Rights: The Rise of Femonationalism*. Durham: Duke University Press.

Easat-Daas, A. (2019). The Gendered Dimension of Islamophobia in Belgium. In *The Routledge International Handbook on Islamophobia*, ed. I. Zempi and I. Awan. London: Routledge.

Fanon, F. 2008 [1952]. *Black Skin, White Masks*. Grove: Atlantic Monthly (2007).

Feinberg, J. 1987. *The Moral Limits of the Criminal Law: Harm to Others: Harm to Others*, vol. 1. Oxford: Oxford University Press.

Foucault, M. 1980 [1976]. TWO LECTURES Lecture One: 7 January 1976 (on *Power and Knowledge*). In *Power/Knowledge: Selected Interviews and Other Writings, 1972–1977*, ed. C. Gordon, 78–92. New York: Harvester Press.

Gheorghiu, Oana-Celia. 2018. *British and American Representations of 9/11*. New York: Springer.

Glover, J. 2002 [2012]. *Humanity a Moral History of the Twentieth Century*. New Haven: Yale University Press.

Gottschalk, P., and G. Greenberg. 2008. *Islamophobia and Anti-Muslim Sentiment Picturing the Enemy*. Lanham: Rowman and Littlefield.

Greene, A.R., and R.M. Simpson. 2017. Tolerating Hate in the Name of Democracy. *Modern Law Review* 80 (4): 746–765.

GW (EEA reg 21: "fundamental interests") Netherlands. 2009. UKIAT 00050. https://www.casemine.com/judgement/uk/5a8ff76a60d03e7f57eac496. Accessed 10 November 2020.

Hall, S. 1996. New Ethnicities. In *Critical Dialogues in Cultural Studies*, ed. D. Morley and K.H. Chen, 441–450. New York: Routledge.

Hanes, E., and S. Machin. 2014. Hate Crime in the Wake of Terror Attacks: Evidence from 7/7 and 9/11. *Journal of Contemporary Criminal Justice* 30: 247–267.

Herman, E., and N. Chomsky. 1988. *Manufacturing Consent: The Political Economy of the Mass Media*. London: Vintage.

Holmwood, J., and T. O'Toole. 2017. *Countering Extremism in British School? The Truth About the Birmingham Trojan Horse Affair*. Bristol: Policy Press.

Home Office. (2018). *Exclusion from the UK*. Published for Home Office staff 11 September 2018 https://assets.publishing.service.gov.uk/government/uploads/system/uploads/attachment_data/file/741420/exclusion-from-the-uk-v2.0ext.pdf Accessed 9 August 2020.

House of Commons Home Affairs Committee. 2017. *Hate Crime: Abuse, Hate and Extremism Online*, 2016/17: HC 609.

Hussein, S. 2015. The Myth of the Lying Muslim: 'Taqiyya' and the Racialization of Muslim Identity. ABC Radio, Religion and Ethics. https://www.abc.net.au/religion/the-myth-of-the-lying-muslim-taqiyya-and-the-racialization-of-mu/10098252. Accessed 9 August 2020.

Hussein, S. 2019 [2016]. *From Victims to Suspects*. New Haven: Yale University Press.

Joseph, A., and K. Sharma (eds.). 2003. *Terror Counter-Terror, Women Speak Out*. London and New York: Zed.

Juss, S. 2015. Burqa-Bashing and the Charlie Hebdo Cartoons. *King's Law Journal* 26 (1): 27–43.

Kershaw Report. 2014. *Investigation Report: Trojan Horse Letter*. https://www.birmingham.gov.uk/downloads/file/1579/investigation_report_trojan_horse_letter_the_kershaw_report. Accessed 20 October.

Khan, M.H., H.M. Adnan, S. Kaur, R.A. Khuhro, R. Asghar, and S. Jabeen. 2019. Muslims' Representation in Donald Trump's Anti-Muslim-Islam Statement: A Critical Discourse Analysis. *Religions* 10: 115.

King, R.D., and G.M. Sutton. 2014. High Times for Hate Crimes: Explaining the Temporal Clustering of Hate Motivated Offending'. *Criminology* 51: 871–894.

Kundnani, A. 2007. *The End of Tolerance*. London: Pluto.

Kundnani, A. 2015. *The Muslims Are Coming*. London: Verso.

Law Commission. 2020. *Hate Crime*. Consultation Paper No. 250 Crown Copyright.

Lean, N. 2017. *The Islamophobia Industry*, 2nd ed. London: Pluto Press.

Legewie, J. 2013. Terrorist Events and Attitudes Toward Immigrants: A Natural Experiment. *American Journal of Sociology* 118: 1199–1245.

Lord Justice Leveson Report. 2011. *An Inquiry into the Culture, Practices and Ethics of the Press* https://webarchive.nationalarchives.gov.uk/201401 22201759/. Accessed 9 August 2020.

Littler, M., and K. Kondor. 2019. Terrorism, Hate Speech and Cumulative Extremism on Facebook: A Case Study. In *The Routledge International Handbook on Islamophobia*, ed. I. Zempi and I. Awan. London: Routledge.

MacKinnon, C. 1993. *Only Words*. Harvard: Harvard University Press.

MacKinnon, C. 1994. *Only Words*. Harvard: Harvard University Press.

Macshane, D. 2020. The Onward March of the Nationalist Far-Right Across Europe Is Over. *The Independent*, October 15.

Mason-Bish, H., and I. Zempi. 2018. Misogyny, Racism, and Islamophobia: Street Harassment at the Intersections. *Feminist Criminology* 14: 540–559.

Matsuda, M.J., C.R. Lawrence, R. Delgado, and K. Crenshaw. 1993. *Words That Wound: Critical Race Theory, Assaultive Speech, and the First Amendment*. Westview: Westview Press.

Meer, N. 2014. *Racialization and Religion: Race, Culture and Difference in the Study of Anti-Semitism and Islamophobia*. London: Routledge.

Meer, N., and T. Modood. 2019. Islamophobia and the Racialisation of Muslims. In *The Routledge International Handbook on Islamophobia*, ed. I. Zempi and I. Awan, 18–31. London: Routledge.

Miah, S. 2017. *Muslims, Schooling and Security: Trojan Horse, Prevent and Racial Politics*. London: Palgrave.

Mill, J.S. 2012 [1869]. *On Liberty*. Cambridge: Cambridge University Press.

Milton, J. 1644. *Areopagitica*: A Speech for the Liberty of Unlicensed Printing to the Parliament of England. https://manybooks.net/titles/miltonjo608608. html. Accessed 1 November 2020.

Mondon, A., and A. Winter. 2019. Mapping and Mainstreaming Islamophobia: Between the Illiberal and Liberal. In *The Routledge International Handbook on Islamophobia*, ed. I. Zempi and I. Awan, 58–70. London: Routledge.

Monir v Wood [2018] EWHC 3525 https://www.bailii.org/ew/cases/EWHC/QB/2018/3525.html. Accessed 10 November 2020.

Mughal v Telegraph Media Group Ltd. 2014. EWHC 1371. https://www.bailii.org/ew/cases/EWHC/QB/2014/1371.html. Accessed 10 November 2020.

Müller, M.G., and E. Özcan. 2007. The Political Iconography of Muhammad Cartoons: Understanding Cultural Conflict and Political Action. *Political Science and Politics* 40 (2): 287–291.

Naber, N. 2008. Introduction: Arab Americans and US Racial Formations. In *Race and Arab Americans Before and After 9/11: From Invisible Citizens to Visible Subjects*, eds. A. Jamal & N. Naber, 1–44. Syracuse, NY: Syracuse University Press.

Naber, N. 2012. *Arab America: Gender, Cultural Politics, and Activism.* New York: NYU Press.

The New Arab. 2020. September 23. https://english.alaraby.co.uk/english/news/2020/9/23/zoom-blocks-leila-khaled-webinar-after-protests. Accessed 6 November 2020.

Oborne, P., and J. Jones. 2008. *Muslims Under Siege.* London: Democratic Audit.

O'Regan, C. 2018. Hate Speech Online: An (Intractable) Contemporary Challenge? *Current Legal Problems* 71 (1): 403.

Orwell, G. 1949. *Nineteen Eighty-Four.* London: Penguin.

Parekh, B. 2000. *Rethinking Multiculturalism: Cultural Diversity and Political Theory.* Harvard: Harvard University Press.

Parekh, B. 2019. *Ethnocentric Political Theory.* London and New York: Palgrave.

Parris, M. 2005. Never Mind What the Woman Thinks, Wearing a Veil Is Offensive to Me. *The Times*, August 27. https://www.thetimes.co.uk/article/never-mind-what-the-woman-thinks-wearing-a-veil-is-offensive-to-me-tdpgppvmmth. Accessed 1 November 2020.

Paterson, J., M.A. Walters, R. Brown, and H. Fearn. 2018. *The Sussex Hate Crime Project: Final Report.* Brighton: University of Sussex.

Pilger, K. 2019. UK: Journalist Pilger Slams London's 'Dictatorship' Over Treatment of Assange, September 3. https://www.youtube.com/watch?v=vMjFrFAukjw&feature=share. Accessed 9 August 2020.

R v Bitton. 2019. EWCA Crim 1372. https://fra.europa.eu/en/databases/anti-muslim-hatred/node/5148. Accessed 15 November 2020.

R v Bonehill-Paine. 2016. EWCA Crim 980. https://www.judiciary.uk/judgments/sentencing-remarks-of-mr-justice-spencer-r-v-joshua-bonehill-paine-harassment-of-luciana-berger-mp/. Accessed 10 November 2020.

R v Butt v Secretary of State for the Home Department. 2019. EWCA Civ 256. https://www.judiciary.uk/wp-content/uploads/2019/03/r-butt-v-sshd-judgment.pdf. Accessed 10 November 2020.

R v Eyles. 2014. EWCA Crim 322. Thompson Reuters Westlaw Edge UK.

R (Geller and Anor) v Secretary of State for the Home Department. 2015. EWCA Civ 45. https://www.casemine.com/judgement/uk/5a8ff71460d0 3e7f57ea73fc. Accessed 22 January 2020.

R v Keegstra. 1991. LRC (Const) 333. https://www.canlii.org/en/ca/scc/ doc/1990/1990canlii24/1990canlii24.html. Accessed 10 November 2020.

R v (Michael Patrick). 2015. EWCA Crim 1306. https://www.3tg.co.uk/cases/ 2015/08/20/r_v_oleary_michael_patrick.asp. Accessed 10 November 2020.

R (on the Application of Palestine Solidarity Campaign Ltd.) v Secretary of State for Housing, Communities and Local Government. 2020. UKSC 16. https:// www.supremecourt.uk/cases/uksc-2018-0133.html. Accessed 10 November 2020.

R v Ruth. 2014. EWCA Crim 546. https://www.casemine.com/judgement/ uk/5a8ff7a760d03e7f57eb0dc1. Accessed 10 November 2020.

Read, J. 2019. "Significant Spike" in Islamophobic Incidents After Boris Johnson's Letterbox Remarks. The New European, September 2. https:// www.theneweuropean.co.uk/brexit-news/boris-johnson-islamophobic-rem arks-about-muslim-veils-54034. Accessed 22 January 2020.

Richards, J. 2017. Extremism, Radicalization and Security: An Identity Theory Approach. London: Palgrave Macmillan.

Said, E. 1970 [1968]. The Arab Portrayed. In The Arab-Israeli Confrontation of June 1967, ed. L. Abu-Lughod, 1–9. Evanston: Northwestern University Press.

Said, E. 1978. Orientalism. London and New York: Penguin.

Said, E. 1997. Covering Islam. London and New York: Penguin.

Sand, S. 2009. The Invention of the Jewish People. London: Verso.

Sand, S. 2014. How I Stopped Being a Jew. London: Verso.

Searle, J. 1999 [1969]. Speech Acts: An Essay in the Philosophy of Language. Cambridge: Cambridge University Press.

Shaheen, J. 2003. Reel Bad Arabs: How Hollywood Vilifies a People. Annals of the Academy of Political and Social Science 588 (1): 171–193.

Sontag, S. 2001. The Talk of the Town New Yorker Writers Respond to 9/11. New Yorker, September 24.

Sontag, S. 2003. The Traitor Fires Back. In Terror Counter-Terror Women Speak Out, ed. A. Joseph and K. Sharma. Zed: London and New York.

Strossen, N. 2018. Hate: Why We Should Resist It with Free Speech, Not Censorship. Oxford: OUP.

Snyder v Phelps. 2011. (No. 09-751, 564 U.S. 786, 792, 2011). https://www. law.cornell.edu/supct/html/09-751.ZS.html. Accessed 10 November 2020.

Thompson, E.P. 1979. The Secret State. Race and Class 20 (3): 219–242.

Thompson, E.P. 1980. Writing by Candlelight. London: Merlin.

Trump, D. 2019. Comments About Muslims. CBS https://www.youtube.com/watch?v=Pijb9hz4eRg, https://www.youtube.com/watch?v=-G9G79oImG4. Accessed 9 August 2020.

Vlaams Belang. 2013. La vidéo du Vlaams Belang contre l'immigration et l'islamisation. http://vimeo.com/49146085. Accessed 9 August 2020.

Waldron, J. 2012. *The Harm in Hate Speech*. Harvard: Harvard University Press.

Wendel, B. 2004. The Banality of Evil and the First Amendment. *Michigan Law Review* 102: 1404–1422.

West, C. 2017. "Dr. Cornel West on the Unpopular James Baldwin". https://www.youtube.com/watch?v=X2kH6kSY6ps. Accessed 20 October 2020.

West, C. 2018. Cornel West: "Speaking Truth to Power", March 2, 2019. https://www.youtube.com/watch?v=-Bc6TRjptKI. Accessed 25 October 2020.

West, C. 2019. "There Is a Neo Fascist in the White House" with Mehdi Hasan. *Up Front*. https://www.youtube.com/watch?v=-Bc6TRjptKI. Accessed 19 October 2020.

Williams, M.L., and P. Burnap. 2016. Cyberhate on Social Media in the Aftermath of Woolwich: A Case Study in Computational Criminology and Big Data. *British Journal of Criminology* 56 (2): 211–238.

Zempi, I., and I. Awan. 2017. Doing 'Dangerous' Autoethnography on Islamophobic Victimisation. *Ethnography* 18 (3): 367–386.

Zempi, I., and N. Chakrobarti. 2016. *Islamophobia, Victimisation and the Veil*. London: Palgrave Macmillan.

Zempi, I., and I. Awan (eds.). 2019. *The Routledge International Handbook on Islamophobia*. London: Routledge.

CHAPTER 4

The "Rule of Law" and the "War on Terror"

Introduction

The terrorist attacks on the World Trade Towers and the Pentagon on 11 September 2001 (9/11), by nineteen hijackers from Saudi Arabia, Egypt and Yemen, resulting in just under 3000 deaths, was unprecedented. 9/11 provided the catalyst and pretext for a new era of "securitisation" which Joseph and Sharma (2003) call the "9/11 syndrome". It remains an enigma how three aircraft reached New York and Washington uninterrupted by US surveillance systems. Survivors, still without answers, on 11 September 2019, continued to wonder why no one had been officially investigated (Summers and Swan 2011). A legal case against *Saudi Arabia*, launched by victims' families and *survivors eventually persuaded the US government to release the names of* suspects. In 2012, a report by the Federal Bureau of Investigation (FBI) said its agency was investigating Saudi nationals, Fahad al-Thumairy and Omar Ahmed al-Bayoumi, who had allegedly helped the attackers (*BBC News*, 13 September 2019, "9/11 attacks: US to reveal key name in Saudi lawsuits"). On September 13, 2019, further disclosures were made. What is known is that 15 of the 19 hijackers were of Saudi Arabian nationality, the FBI having announced the names on September 27, 2001. However, as for explaining the lack of any prosecutions, the US said little, it was similarly mute about the Saudi assassins of Jamal Khashoggi.

© The Author(s), under exclusive license to Springer Nature Switzerland AG 2021
S. S. M. Edwards, *The Political Appropriation of the Muslim Body*, https://doi.org/10.1007/978-3-030-68896-7_4

Following 9/11, the UK and the US, introduced a "securitization" programme and "exceptionalist" legislation which led to the suspension of the Rule of law (ROL) and suspended checks on state and executive power and due process norms especially in its treatment of foreign nationals (Muslim men) about whom the US said were terrorist suspects. Breaches of international and domestic ROL followed where, for example, the invasion of Afghanistan and Iraq (Muslim countries) (the US's retribution for 9/11), was given the *nom de plume* of "Operation Enduring Freedom" (OEF). Rightly cynical, Robert Fisk (2013) noted:

> The War on terror is the West's new religion.... So why not stop spraying bombs and depleted uranium shells on the people of the Middle East? And stop sending our wretched armies to occupy Muslim lands – which is exactly what al-Qa'ida wants us to do – and stop bribing Arab leaders to crush their own people. Instead, can we not visit these sad lands with justice? Justice for the Palestinians, justice for the Kurds, justice for the Iraqi Sunnis, justice for the people of southern Lebanon, justice for the people of Kashmir.

Sands (2006: 21) described the US and UK "War on Terror" (WOT) and OEF campaigns, as an assault on legal rules. The promise that: "Never ever should anyone be sentenced without trial" (Judge 2015: 136) was cast aside as US Presidential executive measures and legislation eschewed human rights and the international ROL, whilst at home, authorised the imprisonment and detention, in military custody in Guantánamo Bay, Cuba, of foreign nationals (Muslim men) without charge or trial (see further Chapter 6). The UK, through its executive measures and legislation, also authorised the imprisonment of foreign nationals (Muslim men) from 2001 to 2004 in Belmarsh Prison, London and like the US, also without charge or trial (see further Chapter 5).

The US, contumaciously flouted international human rights norms, including the United Nations Convention Against Torture 1985 (UNCAT). Such disregard legitimated by executive and legislative measures was written into the jingoistically entitled "Patriot Act" 2001 and the Military Commissions Act 2006. Acts of torture perpetrated by military personnel on (Muslim) "detainees" held in US detention, of whom the US state claimed were suspected of "terrorism related offences" or otherwise "concerned in terrorism" (a catch-all threshold) (see further Chapters 5 and 6), was approved and evidence obtained from torture, was deemed legally admissible and used as evidence for imprisonment without trial (Sands 2008). Meanwhile, Lord Judge reminds us all, from some legal land long lost, that regardless of race, ethnicity, colour of skin, creed or religion, equality can never ever be subverted (Judge: 124) (which also includes foreign nationals and Muslim men) but as Lord Bingham (2011: 144) lamented differential treatment: "runs through the [US] Patriot Act, which reserves its most severe measures for non-citizens". Speaking of the UK's own record Bingham cited the Joint Parliamentary Committee on *Counter-terrorism powers* (2004: para 44) which concluded that [the UK government] "regards the liberty interests of foreign nationals as less worthy of protection than … UK nationals" (58).

Both the US and the UK from thereon embarked on a programme whilst casting the ROL aside exploited its rhetoric by justifying their actions. The US embarked on its WOT programme, invading Afghanistan on 7 October 2001 and Iraq on 19 March 2003, in offensives which it considered both a legitimate and proportionate response to 9/11, and an "inherent" right of self-defense under Article 51 of the UN Charter. This action was supported by the UK government. In a note from Prime Minister Blair to President Bush on 28 July 2002, Blair wrote: "I will be with you whatever". As for the UK's part in the invasion of Iraq, *The Report of the Iraq Inquiry* (2016) (a British Public Inquiry chaired by Sir John Chilcot), found that the UK had not upheld the ROL at all but had subverted international human rights norms in an illegal enterprise. The Inquiry concluded, that, in March 2003 there was no imminent threat from Iraq, that the claim that there were weapons of mass destruction in Iraq was based on flawed intelligence, and that the UK went to war before peaceful options had been exhausted and against UN Security Council findings and recommendations. The Inquiry found that, Prime Minister Blair and Foreign Secretary, Jack Straw MP, blamed France for the "impasse" in the UN, and when they claimed that the UK Government was acting on behalf of the international community "to uphold the authority of the Security Council", the Inquiry found the UK was in fact undermining the Security Council's authority. Blair unendingly exploited ROL rhetoric, in one breath imposing it upon Iraq and in another bequeathing it as a propitious gift to ensure their freedom: "No longer is our existence as States under threat … our actions are guided by a more subtle blend of mutual self-interest and moral purpose in defending the values we cherish. In the end values and interests merge. If we can establish and spread the values of liberty, the rule of law, human rights and an open society then that is in our national interest too" (*Iraq Inquiry*, Vol 1, para 792: 174). On regime change, Blair set as the goal: "a peaceful law-abiding Iraq, fully reintegrated into the international community, with its people free to live in a society based on the rule of law, respect for human rights and economic freedom, and without threat of repression, torture and arbitrary arrest" (Vol 1, para 236: 237). Setting out the new policy framework for Iraq, Jack Straw similarly appropriated ROL rhetoric stating that the "case against Iraq and in favour (if necessary) of military action" needed to be narrated "with reference to the international rule of law" (Vol 1, para 458: 468). Blair went on to say: "if we care about these values of freedom, the rule of law and democracy, we should not flinch from the fight in defending them" and that "Britain" would "defend them with courage and certainty" (Vol 111, para 109: 23). President Lagos of Chile, for one, held a quite different view on how the ROL applied.

> Chile would 'not concur with a resolution' that failed 'to exhaust all the means available to complete Iraqi disarmament and preserve world peace'. It was 'still possible to reach an understanding and strengthen international unity'; and that unity would be 'the only guarantee of a stable, fair peace'. Chile believed that Iraqi disarmament could 'still be done while preserving and strengthening the international institutional framework afforded by the United Nations and its Charter and seeking any other alternative for the rule of law to prevail over force'. (Vol 111, para 563: 496)

Jeremy Waldron (2002, 2016) has long contended that the ROL is a politically contested ideal frequently invoked to advance interests which are legitimated by its self-validating claims, and when chimed, he says alarm-bells ring in analytic circles. Paul Burgess (2017) and Judith Shklar (1998) share his scepticism, contending that the ROL is merely a vehicle for state power.

> It would not be very difficult to show that the phrase 'the Rule of Law' has become meaningless thanks to ideological abuse and general overuse. It may well have become just another one of those self-congratulatory rhetorical devices that grace the public utterances of Anglo-American politicians. No intellectual effort needs therefore be wasted on this bit of 'ruling-class chatter'. (Shklar 1998: 17)

My consideration in this chapter is to explore how all that sits under the ROL banner, has been exploited to press particular interests, internationally and domestically in the wider discipline and control of largely Muslim people. I begin on a high note with documenting the unedited version and momentous achievements of the ROL, its evolution, and its modern iterations, its virtues as a concept and aspiration, and its overriding purpose to harness state power and set a standard embodying fairness, justice, due process and protection of fundamental human rights. The ROL in restraining absolute power institutes a constitutional and governance framework characterised by: the clear separation of law from the adjudicatory governmental and executive function, an impartial judiciary and a system of governance where there is procedural and substantive constancy. Lord Judge (2015) hailed law as the "the safest shield" in this service. Second, I move on to examine the ROL's vulnerability to state power. Roberto Unger (1977), for example, speaks of the ROL as a shield behind which liberalism lurks, masking hierarchies and exploitation and subjugation to sinister groups (cited in Shklar 1998: 29). In the third part of this chapter, I explore in a little more detail, and through three examples the decimation of the ROL considering first the WOT, second the lawlessness of some of those in the British army in Iraq with particular regard to the "Battle of Danny Boy" and third the Palestinian humanitarian crisis and treatment of Palestinian Arabs in Gaza, 99% of whom are Muslim (Chomsky and Pappé 2015). Fourth, and turning to the UK, I choose two case study examples which demonstrate how the ROL is breached on the home front whether in international trade dealings (Gardner 2020) or in disavowing international obligations to refugees fleeing from countries devasted, although not exclusively, by Western invasions.

One cannot hide from the fact that the ROL is constantly compromised by state power. Shklar (1985: 12) reminds us to always ask the question: "who governs, who verifies, who decides?" Foucault's rhetorical answer is "whom does discourse serve?" (in Faubion 1980: 115).

THE UNCUT VERSION OF THE RULE OF LAW

I turn first then to the early strivings to establish the Rule of Law. The early limitations on power (monarchal) and the instantiation of the positive rights of freedom, liberty, equality and justice, are to be found in embryonic form in Magna Carta (1215). By 1991, Magna Carta had been cited in more than 900 decisions of US state and federal courts and was, says Judge, "bred into the bones of the US constitution" (Judge 2015: 212). From 2001, in the US, especially, and with regard to Muslim foreign nationals and immigrants, it had been "bred out", and individual and constitutional rights diluted or annulled, demonstrated by, as just one example, the maltreatment of Arab/Muslim "detainees" held at Guantánamo. Magna Carta, as a charter of English liberties, had championed the fundamental principles that, no one shall be put to death, that everyone shall be free and that justice shall not be delayed, denied or sold. These undertakings formed the basis of a constitutional framework which cleaved power from dictator's and kings, separated the power of the monarch from the legislature, the executive from the judges, established parliamentary democracy and the supremacy of the ROL and enshrined in law the positive rights of freedom, liberty and justice. The evolution of this desideratum is chartered by several important landmark cases.

The ruling in the case of *Prohibition del Roy* [1607] challenged the hegemony of the monarch establishing that judges should determine the law. Edward Coke, Chief Justice of the Court of Common Pleas, ruled that legal cases were "to be decided by ...judgment of law" declaring "the law is the safest helmet; under the shield of law no one is deceived". The decision in the case of *Entick v Carrington* [1765] limited the power of parliament and the executive. Carrington was authorised by Lord Halifax, the Secretary of State, to break in and trespass in Entick's home and search and remove documents and property. Entick sued Carrington. Carrington replied that he was acting under legal warrant. Lord Camden, the presiding judge, said: "If this is law it would be found in our books, but no such law ever existed in this country; our law holds the property of every man so sacred, that no man can set his foot upon his neighbour's house without his leave", declaring that the prerogative powers of the monarch and the government could only be authorised by some specific rule of law. On this question alone, the UK, and especially the US governments have delegated unto themselves vastly extended executive powers in the name of "security", including racialised surveillance, policing, detention and punishment, which compromise individual liberty (see further Chapters 5 and 6). Regarding the trial process, the common law provided safeguards against unlawful detention and torture. The power to review the lawfulness of detention, "habeas corpus" (produce or bring up the body) was established as early as 1300 (Bingham 2011: 13, 17, 22). In

1627, in the "Five Knights Case" (Darnel's case) [1627] this legal safeguard of review was invoked when 76 men who refused to pay taxes to the King Charles 1, objecting to his misuse of their money to fund his wars on other countries, were arrested and imprisoned. Five of them petitioned for a writ of "habeas corpus cum causa" asserting that, under Magna Carta: "no man should be imprisoned but by the legal judgment of his peers or by 'lex terrae'" (the law of the land). They were released in 1628, when Parliament passed the Petition of Rights Act (1628) which established several protections, including the prohibition against imprisonment without just cause strengthened by the Habeas Corpus Act (1679) which prohibited "banishment" and sending persons to countries beyond the reach of habeas corpus. In 1689, the Bill of Rights, limited the power of the monarch and included the freedom to petition the monarch, and ensured freedom from cruel and unusual punishment and from punishment without trial. (Such safeguards have been suspended in the US in their use of unlawful detention and cruel punishments against Muslim detainees, see further Chapter 6, whilst Shabina Begum has been banished).

In its more recent iterations, the ROL's desideratum has prized the positive human rights norms of "justice" and "liberty" as defining characteristics. Lord Acton, in his lecture on "Nationality" (1862) said: "...liberty occupies the final summit...it is almost, if not altogether, the sign, and the prize, and the motive in the onward and upward advance of the race... ...Liberty is not a means to a higher political end. It is itself the highest political end". The values of liberty and freedom are codified in international, regional and domestic human rights law. The United Nations, Universal Declaration of Human Rights (UDHR) 1948, sets a common standard for all nations. Eleanor Roosevelt, who led the American delegation, stated: "We wanted as many nations as possible to accept the fact that men, for one reason or another, were born free and equal in dignity and rights, that they were endowed with reason and conscience, and should act towards one another in a spirit of brotherhood. The way to do that was to find words that everyone would accept". The UDHR institutes the protection of the right to liberty and security, to life, to be free from slavery and torture, to be recognised as a person, to be free from discrimination and have the right to an effective remedy, to be free from arbitrary detention or exile, to a fair and public hearing, and the right to the presumption of innocence. Sands (2006: 11) hails this as the: "single most important international instrument ever negotiated".

However, this declaration was non-binding, and the UN Charter did not impose any legal duty on member states to comply (Robertson 2012: 38). Individual states conscious of the motes in their eyes, for example, France and the UK, who were not willing to grant democracy and independence to "their" colonies, were not overzealous to become signatories and be bound by its terms. The UK dispute over the Chagos Islands provides one such example, where the UK dismissed Chagos's claim to "independence" and evicted the Chagossians from the Island sending them to Mauritius to enable the UK to fulfil its own prior arrangement with the US to build a US Military base on the Island. The UN, on 25 February 2019, in its Advisory Opinion, held: "the process of decolonization of Mauritius was not lawfully completed when that country acceded to independence" concluding that the UK was under an obligation to bring its administration of the Chagos Islands to an end. In 1966, the International Covenant on Civil and Political Rights (ICCPR) and the International Covenant on Economic and Social Rights (ICESR), both of which were legally binding, embodied many of the principles the UNDHR had established. Further protections were agreed in other Conventions, notably the Convention on the Prevention and Punishment of the Crime of Genocide, 1948, and the United Nations Convention against Torture and Other Cruel, Inhuman or Degrading Treatment or Punishment (UNCAT) 1984. This international convention, which the US had signed, was contumaciously ignored, in the treatment of Guantánamo detainees. Guantánamo, said the US, was outside US soil and such binding conventions therefore did not apply (see further Chapter 6). The protection of these several rights is further secured in regional conventions. So, for example, across Europe, the European Convention on Human Rights (ECHR) 1951, Article 2, protects the right to life, and Article 3, protects against torture or inhuman or degrading treatment or punishment. Article 5 establishes the right to liberty and requires that detention, arrest and conviction must be lawful. Article 6 establishes the right to a fair trial, Article 8, establishes the right to respect for a private and family life and Article 14, prohibits discrimination in the exercise of these rights. Freedom of religion and speech, Articles 9 and 10, respectively are also protected. These positive freedoms of liberty, due process, fair trial, freedom from cruel punishment, are also incorporated in the US Constitution of 1787. Since nation states are required to be compliant with their own law, and with regional and international conventions, to which they are signatories, it is conspicuous that the US has refused to sign several international conventions demonstrating its unwillingness to be constrained by internationally agreed substantive rights norms and by the ROL, when it so chooses.

What then do we expect of the ROL? Kofi Annan, when Secretary General of the United Nations, identifies a ROL as: "...constraining the weak and the powerful alike...a principle of governance in which all persons, institutions and entities, public and private, including the State itself, are accountable to laws that are publicly promulgated, equally enforced and independently adjudicated" (2004). Shklar (1998) Bingham (2011) and Raz (2009 [1979]) in reviewing its common features identify these expectations to include: clear limits to the power of the state, accountability of government and the executive and mechanisms for review, clear and transparent rules with predictable and certain outcomes (Bingham: 37, 42), constraints on judicial discretion and "judge made law" (45), and protection of equality before the law to which: "all persons and authorities within the state, whether public or private, should be bound" (8). Importantly, the ROL embodies the fundamental principle that no one is above the law, no parliament, no executive, no monarch, no Prime Minister and no President: "the rule of law applies to both judges and ministers" (Hailsham 1983: 49).

But as Shklar, Bingham, Waldron and others point out, the ROL is politically malleated. Lon Fuller (1958) warns that the formal or procedural ROL is merely a "tinsel of legal form" where internal morality may be disregarded (Bennett 2011: 607). Shklar (1998: 22) agrees, acceding that a purely procedural ROL with its formal rationality may be stripped and devoid of any positive rights or limits on arbitrary power, which as she and others, notably Arendt (2017 [1951]) observed, may result in rule _by_ law, a perversion, witnessed in totalitarian and despotic regimes and under Nazi dictatorship where Shklar writes: "formal rationality of a civil law system can legitimise a persecutive war-state" (33). Arendt examined this contempt for law by those who drafted, applied and implemented Hitler's Nuremberg racial laws with their distinction between Reich citizens (full citizens) and nationals (second-class citizens without political rights) which: "paved the way for a development in which eventually all nationals of 'alien blood' could lose their nationality by official decree" (2017 [1951] ed: 376.) William Shirer (1960), the American war correspondent, documented in meticulous detail this Nazi tyranny and Steiner was to comment: "The events that were now to come to pass in Europe were quite literally beyond words, too inhuman for that defining act of human consciousness, which is speech" (Steiner 1984: 245, 247).

Elsewhere Waldron (2016: 9) cites a more a recent example of where procedural law is stripped of values, citing Arthur Chaskalson, former Chief Justice of South Africa at the World Justice Project in 2011, who said:

> [T]he apartheid government, its officers and agents were accountable in accordance with the laws; the laws were clear; publicized, and stable, and were upheld by law enforcement officials and judges. What was missing was the substantive component of the rule of law. The process by which the laws were made was not fair (only whites, a minority of the population, had the vote). And the laws themselves were not fair. They institutionalized discrimination, vested broad discretionary powers in the executive, and failed to protect fundamental rights. Without a substantive content there would be no answer to the criticism, sometimes voiced, that the rule of law is 'an empty vessel into which any law could be poured.'

Sydney Kentridge (2014) considering the ROL's antinomies, says

> Taken alone, it would cover the publicly made laws of slavery as enforced in the southern states of the USA before the civil war or the apartheid laws of South Africa before 1994 ... Detention without trial or legal process, internal exile of whole black communities, enforced racial discrimination - all these measures were authorised by law. (2014: 148)

We have every reason then to be sceptical when governments defend their actions by appealing to the ROL and we should always be on our guard and scrutinise their claims.

POWER—"RULING CLASS" AND "EXECUTIVE CHATTER"

"Ruling Class Chatter"

As Waldon forewarned the precise formation of the ROL is always subject to power (2002, 2016). For Shklar (1998: 17) it is a matter of state power and "ruling class chatter". Marx (1932 [1845–1846]), Foucault (in Faubion 1980), Althusser (1971), Collins (1982), Fine (1984) and Thompson (1980) regard law as an arm of the state, protecting powerful interests whether capitalist interest, foreign policy or global interest. The ruling interest has historically excluded other interests in protecting its own. Women's interests have been systematically excluded from governance, foreign policy, global affairs and from domestic and international law (Charlesworth and Chinkin 2002; Otto 2006) whilst ruling interest has always protected imperialist interest (Chomsky 2004). Law then, and the overarching ROL, is crafted and implemented in order to maintain existing power relations, protecting the powerful against the poor, the immigrant, the rough sleeper, women, etc., and now as I argue here, protecting the powerful against the Muslim man and woman. Louis Althusser in his theorisation on the relationship of law to state power (see Chapters 2 and 3) regarded law, along with institutions of government, the executive, the administration, the army, the police, the courts and the military, as having a centrifugal role in protecting state interest, by coercion and often by violence, if necessary, supported by discursive practices of propaganda and ideology to protect this hegemony (143). This theorisation regards the liberal and utilitarian view that the ROL is inherently just and equitable, as little more than "clap trap".

> There is no such abstract entity as the Rule of Law, if by this is meant some ideal presence aloof from the ruck of history, which it is the business of judges to 'administer' and of policemen to 'enforce'. That is all ideology. It used to be the ideology of kings and despots. It is now the ideology of the authoritarian state. (Thompson 1980: 230)

Hugh Collins, in *Marxism and the Rule of Law* (1982) and Bob Fine in *Democracy and the Rule of Law* (1984) similarly dismiss this liberal and utilitarian veneering.

"Executive Chatter"—Unbridled Power

Following 9/11, in the name of securitisation and in response to Chapter VII of the United Nations Charter, United Nations Security Council Resolution 1368 (2001), which required all States to take measures to prevent the commission of terrorist attacks, and deny a haven to those who finance, plan, support or commit terrorist attacks, the US and the UK executive interpreted widely what was a limited power to derogate from human rights norms (discussed further in Chapters 5 and 6). As Sands (2006: 228) laments, Prime Minister Blair and President Bush, used the events of 9/11 to "refashion the global legal order". In the

US, the President and the executive resisted international rules (Sands 2006: 14) and embarked on a programme of unwriting human rights, including denial of "habeas corpus" and abolishing the right of Guantánamo detainees to review their detention in Federal Courts. Significantly, on 24 June 2004, in *Rasul v Bush* [2004] (Rasul was a British citizen and one of the "Tipton Three") the Supreme Court supervened and held that the Patriot Act 2001, which declared that the Attorney General could detain any non-citizen whom he determined was engaging in terrorist activity or else a threat to national security without the right to review, was unlawful (see further Chapter 6). Justice Breyer (at [506]) for the majority, asserted: "It seems rather contrary to an idea of a constitution with three branches that the executive would be free to do whatever they want... without a check". Unbridled executive power in the US has condoned torture outsourcing it in other countries where it has involved the capture of persons in "extraordinary renditions" brought to the US for detention without trial. It has also developed its own brand of bespoked torture in detention centres under US military control. Further instances of the US's refusal to surrender to the ROL is demonstrated in its withdrawal from the Rome statute which established the International Criminal Court (ICC) and recognised the crime of genocide, crimes against humanity, war crimes and crimes of aggression (see further below). The US is one of several countries to have ratified the fewest number of international human rights treaties, ratifying only five of the 18 agreements passed by the UN. It has not signed the International Covenant on Economic Social and Cultural Rights (ICSCR) 1966, nor the Comprehensive Nuclear Treaty Ban (1996).

In the UK, the ROL, although to a lesser extent, has also been plundered by executive power, for example, human rights safeguards against unlawful detention for foreign nationals were rights deleted following the Anti-Terrorism, Crime and Security Act (ATCSA) 2001, Part IV. Significantly, this part of the Act was struck down three years later as unlawful, when in 2004 in *A and others v Secretary of State for the Home Department* [2004] (the "Belmarsh" case) the House of Lords declared this part of the Act incompatible with ECHR Article 5 right to liberty (see further Chapter 5). Unlike the US, the UK has not accepted information obtained from torture as a basis for detention. In *A and others v Secretary of State for the Home Department (No 2)* [2005] Lord Bingham reminded the court of the UK's erstwhile obligations: "[11] It is, I think, clear that from its very earliest days the common law of England set its face firmly against the use of torture". Interestingly, the human rights protections that former Prime Minister Theresa May was eager to tear down, and now Prime Minister Johnson's current bête noire, are the very same protections Theresa May (when Shadow Home Secretary during Prime Minister Blair's term of office) in 2005, defended, because she at that time considered that anti-terror legislation was giving the executive too much power! (see Jeremy Corbyn, Labour leader, BBC Election Debate, *BBC News*, 1 June 2017 "Reality Check: May and Corbyn's record on anti-terror legislation"). Her view in 2012, when Home Secretary under the coalition government, was somewhat different:

> When Strasbourg constantly moves the goalposts and prevents the deportation of dangerous men like Abu Qatada, we have to ask ourselves, to what end are we signatories to the Convention …. So, by 2015 we'll need a plan for dealing with the European Court of Human Rights. And yes, I want to be clear that all options – including leaving the Convention altogether – should be on the table. (*The Telegraph*, 12 November 2012, "Theresa May blames Europe for Qatada debacle")

Challenging the very governance edifice of the ROL and parliament itself, in August 2019, Boris Johnson requested the Queen to prorogue Parliament, and in effect, halt and suspend it. The Supreme Court in *R (on the application of Miller) v Prime Minister; Cherry and others v Advocate General for Scotland* [2019] declared this flexing of executive muscle unconstitutional, holding that parliamentary sovereignty was supreme, and the power to prorogue, limited (para [41]). A further example of the ever-present threat of executive power to fashion the ROL in its choosing and to interfere with "core political speech" was demonstrated on 19 December 2019 when, in the *Queen's speech*, Prime Minster Johnson proposed dismantling the Human Rights Act 1998, introducing new treason legislation, enhancing executive and political power over civil liberties, clamping down on counter-speech and dissent, including a proposal to make it illegal for public institutions to take part in Boycott, Divestment or Sanctions (BDS) campaigns against foreign countries and those who trade with them. Johnson's proposal was aimed at universities which introduced BDS policies against Israel in response to Israel's abrogation of its obligations under the international ROL regarding the rights of Palestinians including, its dismissive stance regarding the UN Human Rights Council resolutions to withdraw from occupied territories, to remove the separation of Gaza, to ensure equality for Arab-Palestinian citizens and, to ensure the right of return for Palestinians. A more draconian outlawing of the BDS campaign is evident in the US where former President Trump signed an executive order designating Jews as an ethnic group rather than an exclusively religious group, thus making any boycott an act of racial discrimination (Gerrard 2020). These attempts to silence "core political speech" (see Chapter 3) underscore Strossen's (2018) warning that closing down offensive and hate speech leads to closing down "core political speech" such as this. Rabbi Jill Jacobs, director of T'ruah: The Rabbinic Call for Human Rights, holds a different view on BDS:

> Those of us who are committed both to the future of Israel and to free speech must oppose this wrong-headed and dangerous federal and state legislation, which penalizes Americans for nonviolent political action and speech. (*The New York Jewish Week*, 26 December 2018 "How the Split Over BDS Laws Has Come to Test the Limits of Free Speech")

Since the European Court of Human Rights (ECtHR) in the case of *Baldassi and Others v France*, 11 June 2020, held that French legislation criminalising BDS, violated the right to freedom of expression (Article 10) perhaps the UK will reconsider its own position (see Chapter 3).

Trump when President interfered with US Supreme Court appointments in order to secure a compliant court and fixed judicial decision-making in the appointment of Brett Kavanaugh, notably contested because of his right-wing political leanings and his alleged sexism (which emerged following the testimony of Christine Blasey Ford regarding his past conduct and alleged attempted rape of her when a student), lurches the Court even further to the Right. The appointment of Amy Coney Barrett to the Supreme Court following the death of Ruth Bader Ginsburg immediately prior to the US election in 2020 guarantees Trump's ideological legacy. Prime Minister Johnson said he too would consider granting powers to the executive to elect the UK Supreme Court judiciary (*The Guardian*, 19 December 2019, "Queen's speech: PM points to harder Brexit and 10-year rule"). Lady Hale, Former President of the UK Supreme Court, warned against any attempt to politicise the appointment of judges (*The Independent*, 27 December 2019).

The International Rule of Law—Illegal War, Retribution and Occupation

The WOT, otherwise euphemistically called "Operation Enduring Freedom" (OEF) has with swagger appropriated the ROL rhetoric to support what many regard as unlawful. Whilst 9/11 may have provided the West with the justification for setting aside human rights protections, the Council of Europe 2002, "Guidelines on Human Rights and the Fight against terrorism" (adopted by the Committee of Ministers, 11 July 2002 at the 804th meeting of the Ministers' Deputies) offered a salutary warning:

> The temptation for government and parliaments in countries suffering from terrorist action is to fight fire with fire, setting aside the legal safeguards that exist in a democratic state. But let us be clear about this: while the State has the right to employ to the full its arsenal of legal weapons to repress and prevent terrorist activities, it may not use indiscriminate measures which would only undermine the fundamental values they seek to protect. For a State to react in such a way would be to fall into the trap set by terrorism and the rule of law. (5)

Western Lawlessness Using the ROL and Its "Broad Humanitarian Purpose"

The US's disregard for global rules and international and national norms, Sands (2006) describes as "lawless". "With the election of George W Bush in November 2000, a US Administration took office that was outspoken in its determination to challenge global rules. Soon it turned into a full-scale assault, a war on law" (xii). Kentridge (2014) agrees:

> Even in the modern era of democracy and human rights, governments have not found it easy to live up to the ideal of the rule of law. In the United States after the terrorist outrages of September 11, 2001, the Bush administration reacted with measures such as indefinite detention of suspects without trial, interrogations under torture and stringent limitations on access to the courts. The truth is that at no time and in no country can we take the rule of law for granted. (151)

Islamist global terrorism was used as a mandate for US occupation and war on other countries, the introduction of repressive counter-terror legislation at home and dismantling human rights protections for suspects and non-US citizens. The US WOT depended for its success on the production and reproduction of a supporting ideology and narrative—Foucault's "arrogated knowledge"—and on shutting down any dissent,—Foucault's "subjugated knowledge" (discussed in Chapters 2 and 3). In harnessing popular support Bush's rallying mantra: "You are either with us or with the terrorist" demonised dissent and "core political speech" and essentialised all Muslims as potential terrorists. Anti-Muslim propaganda, in the media mobilised Orientalist tropes where Muslim men and Muslim countries were described as "dangerous", "evil", "barbaric" and "uncivilised" and Muslim women who wore Islamic dress as potential "suspects".

By March 2006, an ABC News Poll, found that one-third of respondents considered that Islam "encourages violence" with 58% stating that within Islam there were more "violent extremists" than in other religions, and where all Muslims were described as "fundamentalist", "militant", "terrorist", "radical" or "extremist" in more than half of the media accounts analysed by Sides and Gross (2013: 586). Orchestrating a climate of fear was a vital part of the strategy in manufacturing consent and obtaining mass popular support (Chomsky 2011 [2003]: 18). Chomsky in his lecture on "The Unipolar Moment and the Obama Era" (2009), reported that in a matter of weeks, 60% of Americans were whipped up into a state of anxiety and fear considering Saddam Hussein such an immediate threat to the US that he must be removed. The US "Imperial Grand Strategy" secured popular consent with messianic claims and piety, claiming that troops were sent into Afghanistan in 2001, to "save" and "redeem" (Chomsky 2003: 11). Such lofty altruism is found repeated in the UK's support of US "intervention" especially in the invasion of Iraq in 2003, where the UK claimed, that delivering the ROL was its "broad humanitarian purpose". As the Iraq Inquiry (above) reported, Prime Minister Blair in an act of "humanitarian imperialism" (Bricmont 2007) used the persecution of the Iraqi people to validate his moral case for war (Kundnani 2007: 109), and to challenge Saddam Hussein's human rights record (Poole 2006: 3, 5). This moral high ground was set aside when Iraqi asylum seekers needed refuge, fleeing their war-torn country which UK foreign policy had in part created. George Orwell noted similar obfuscations in history. In "Politics and the

English Language" written in 1946, remarking on the inflated style as a kind of euphemism, he said:

> In our time, political speech and writing are largely the defence of the inde-fensible. Things like the continuance of British rule in India, the Russian purges and deportations, the dropping of the atom bombs on Japan, can indeed be defended, but only by arguments which are too brutal for most people to face, and which do not square with the professed aims of polit-ical parties. Thus, political language has to consist largely of euphemism, question-begging and sheer cloudy vagueness.... When there is a gap between one's real and one's declared aims, one turns as it were instinc-tively to log words and exhausted idioms.... Political language – and with variations this is true of all political parties, from Conservatives to Anar-chists – is designed to make lies sound truthful and murder respectable and to give an appearance of solidity to pure wind. (2000: 356, 359)

"Saving Muslim Women"

As for Muslim women, the West proclaimed itself as the great white saviour and where the US and UK invasion of Iraq was aided by an evangelical zeal to save Muslim women from Muslim men (Abu-Lughod 2013). As Al-Ali and Pratt (2009: 82) note, this resonated with what Spivak had described as "white men saving brown women from brown men" (see Chapter 2). Such claims were also made to support the inva-sion of Afghanistan (Charlesworth and Chinkin 2002: 600–605). Bush, the great white male feminist liberator, gave a speech to 250 women at the White House claiming: "The advance of women's rights and the advance of liberty are ultimately inseparable". Al-Ali and Pratt point out, as had Fanon (1965), that the "saving women" rhetoric is also a demonstration of hypermasculinity and the "superpowers" male power over other men, noting too that attempts to restructure gender rela-tions had other goals in sight notably the long-term protection of the US national security interest (84). This nauseating pretence of "saving women" demonstrated the willingness of Western powers to use Muslim women in this propaganda offensive. It is to be noted that no similar responsibility or high-mindedness has been so chivalrously extended to Saudi women in protection of their human rights, or to Yemeni women and children killed by US and British arms sold to Saudi Arabia used by Saudi in its war with Yemen, or to Palestinians killed by Israeli mili-tary "Operation Lead" in 2014. Significant too that for all this "saving women", the US refuses to sign the Convention on Elimination of all forms of Discrimination against Women (1979) (CEDAW), and the Convention on the Rights of the Child (1989) (UNCRC) and aligns itself with the Northern Alliance when countries in that alliance have not been respecters of women's rights. The close relationship with Saudi Arabia (see further Chapter 8) underscores the US and UK's double dealings in pleading for saving women, as Hensman (2003: 35) observes in Saudi Arabia "women are treated scarcely any better than under the Taliban".

President Bush has made no secret of his contempt for a reading of the ROL that interferes with his purpose. In an interview for *Newsweek*, at a "photo op" after a cabinet meeting, a reporter asked Bush if such punitive steps squared with international law. "'International law?' Bush answered, with an edge of sarcasm. 'I better call my lawyer. He didn't bring that up to me'" (*Newsweek*, 23 December 2003). Such contempt is demonstrated by the US's refusal to sign up to the International Criminal Court (ICC) in the Hague, and the International Criminal Court Rome Statute of 1998 which has jurisdiction over genocide and crimes against humanity and the fact that "the Bush administration...has been running an aggressive, mendacious and ill-informed campaign to undermine the ICC" (Sands 2006: 48). This includes accusations from Donald Rumsfeld (Secretary of Defence 2001–2006) of "The lack of adequate checks and balances on powers of the ICC prosecutor and judges; the dilution of the UN Security Council's authority over international criminal prosecutions; and the lack of an effective mechanism to prevent politicized prosecutions of American service members and officials" (Sands 2006: 49). In 2002 the American Service Members Protection Act (2002) was passed which authorised the US President to release any American national who was detained on behalf, or at the request, of the ICC. Disregard for the ROL and human rights norms that restrict state power is demonstrated by US treatment of Iraqi internees in Iraq, and the mistreatment of prisoners in Guantánamo and Abu Ghraib (see further Chapter 6). As for the UK, in addition to its support for the US its own treatment of Iraqi internees under British control during the Western invasion of Iraq is still under legal scrutiny in UK courts.

The UK's own appropriation of the ROL in justifying its role in the Iraq offensive relied on a mix of falsehood, fiction and weak evidence. Blair took the UK into war despite Sir Michael Boyce, UK's chief of defence staff, requiring substantiated evidence on the threat Iraq posed to the UK. Hans von Sponek (*The Guardian*, 22 July 2002) stated that the US Department of Defense and the CIA knew perfectly well that Iraq: "poses no threat to anyone in the region let alone to the United States, to argue otherwise is dishonest" (cited in Chomsky 2003: 41). The Butler Inquiry on *Intelligence on Weapons of Mass Destruction in Iraq* (2004), had already found that the key intelligence used to justify the war with Iraq was unreliable. (All this spilt out very publicly at the Chilcot Inquiry in 2016 (above)). Sands (2006: 183) remained baffled: "Why Blair joined in remains a mystery" in supporting US military action to bring about regime change. International law academics and lawyers regarded the use of force in Iraq as entirely illegitimate, and the humanitarian bleating in the name of the ROL, fatuous. Curtis (249) offered what was perhaps the real motive: "Britain under Tony Blair happily stood 'shoulder to shoulder' .... for reasons of pure self-interest: that terrorism would provide a rationale for a new phase in Britain's own military intervention around the world". To achieve this end game, the weapons of mass destruction (fiction) (and truth which cost David Kelly his life), was, "sexed up" (Sands 2006: 259). The BBC "Today" programme (29 May 2003), following Lord Hutton's findings reported that: "the Government probably knew before it decided to put it in its dossier ... that the statement was wrong that the Iraqi military were able to deploy weapons of mass destruction within 45 minutes of a decision to do so"; [and that No.10 had] "ordered the dossier to be sexed up". Meanwhile Prime Minster Blair and President Bush appealed to "Our values" for popular support. Blair, self-assured and talking as if President Bush's understudy said after the 7 July 2005 coordinated bombings in London which killed 56 people: "Let no one be in any doubt the rules of the game are changing...Should legal obstacles arise, we will legislate further, including, if necessary, amending the Human Rights Act in respect of the interpretation of the ECHR". Assured of his popular support, he said: "I want a law which says the Home Secretary, supervised by the courts, has got to balance the rights of the individual deportee against the risk to national security. This may involve an act which says this is the correct interpretation of the European [human rights] convention" (Sands 2006: 276–267). As to the US's maltreatment and systematic torture of Muslim men in military detention in Guantánamo and Iraq, the UK colluded in its silence. That particular chapter of devastating dystopia deserves a separate and detailed consideration and is documented in Chapter 6.

Incidents of Lawlessness and the British Army in Iraq

My second example of the decimation of the ROL concerns the incidents of maltreatment of Iraqi internees by some members of the British Troops in Iraq demonstrating breaches of the international ROL. The Al-Sweady Inquiry (*Report of the Public Inquiry into Allegations of Unlawful Killing and Ill Treatment of Iraqi Nationals by British Troops in Iraq in 2004*) a government ordered public inquiry, investigated the allegations of unlawful killing and ill treatment of Iraqi nationals by British troops at Camp Abu Naji, in Iraq in 2004. The killing of Baha Mousa in Basra, Iraq in 2003, by officers of the Queen's Lancashire Regiment was also the subject of a public inquiry (*The Baha Mousa Public Inquiry report*, 2011). The Al-Sweady Inquiry followed a high court writ from Khudar Al-Sweady, the uncle of Hamid Al-Sweady, who said that his nephew had been unlawfully killed by British officers. The remit of the Inquiry was to investigate the allegations of abuse brought by Iraqi internees. Sir Thayne Forbes, the chairman of the Inquiry found that most of the allegations were "without foundation and entirely the product of deliberate lies, reckless speculation and ingrained hostility" (at 5.201) but he did find that nine Iraqi detainees had been ill-treated. The Solicitor's Regulation Authority tribunal (*Solicitors Regulation Authority v Day and others* [2018]) who conducted an investigation into the professional conduct of solicitors acting for the many alleged Iraqi victims and their families, said "[27] Serious mistreatment and misconduct on the part of elements of the British forces was in due course in some respects established: sometimes in circumstances where the prior military investigations had been found to be inadequate altogether". Forbes in the *Al-Sweady Inquiry* said:

> I have come to the conclusion that the conduct of various individual soldiers and some of the procedures being followed by the British military in 2004 fell below the high standards normally to be expected of the British Army. In addition, on a number of other occasions, my findings went further. ... I have come to the conclusion that certain aspects of the way in which the nine Iraqi detainees, with whom this Inquiry is primarily concerned, were treated by the British military, during the time they were in British custody during 2004, amounted to actual or possible ill-treatment. (at 5.196)

So, in some respects, then, some members of the armed forces fell below the standards expected. The UK press focussed on the unproven cases and on the accusations of fabrication and Phil Shiner (Public Interest Lawyers PIL), the solicitor who led the investigations became "the" story. Following the *Al-Sweady Inquiry* findings Shiner was struck off the solicitors roll by the Solicitor's Disciplinary Tribunal (SDT) on 2 February 2017, for professional misconduct for what they held were false claims over the treatment of some Iraqi detainees. Notwithstanding, the Inquiry findings that there were limited cases of breaches by army officers, abuse may have been more widespread. Lucy Bowen, a military police special investigations officer, at the Inquiry, added some substance to that concern when she described how commanders of 1 Battalion, Princess of Wales, Royal Regiment (1PWRR) prevented her from questioning soldiers after the "Battle of Danny Boy", in 2004. (Police expose flaws in army's torture inquiry | Military | The Guardian, https://www.theguardian.com/uk/2009/jul/26/iraq-conflict-army-torture-inquiry). The Inquiry concluded that the conduct of some soldiers towards detainees breached the Geneva Convention, breaches which included, direct and indirect physical abuse, "tactical questioning", lack of food, reduced sight and sleep deprivation. Certainly, no one looking at photographs published in *The Guardian* (17 March 2014, Richard Norton-Taylor) of a British Army soldier standing over Iraqi detainees who were lying face down on the floor, blindfolded, hands tied in a plastic cuff behind their backs, with an army officer poking the end of a gun into the back of one of the detainees, can doubt their fear and terror. The Inquiry made a series of recommendations regarding interrogations. On the stripping of detainees, the Inquiry was concerned with: "The likely emotional impact that requiring an Iraqi Muslim man to strip naked in front of strangers... some of those personnel were women...", and that "forcible strip searching" was used far too readily during Processing at Camp Abu Naji on 14 May 2004 (at Vol 2, 5.169, p. 966). The need for interpreters was also highlighted, since there was evidence that requests "for medical attention, to use the lavatory or for the provision of drinking water" were met with being told to "be quiet" (at Vol 2, 5.176, p. 968). For example: "Ibrahim Gattan Hasan Al-Ismaeeli (detainee number 774), had been given medication forcibly and without his consent having been obtained beforehand or at all" (at Vol 2, 5.177, p. 969). A further recommendation stressed the need for a medical examiner to examine detainees to determine fitness prior to interrogation. Graphic uncorroborated evidence allegedly provided by the Iraqis who were interviewed by Phil Shiner and Martyn Day in connection with the incident at the British army base at Abu Naji, is more chilling, where the execution of up to 20 Iraqi civilians was reported and allegations of the torture of many of these men before death was said to involve horrific bodily mutilations. Phil Shiner in his evidence which he presented at a press conference in 2008 and was also reported in the House of Commons 17 December 2014 said:

> I have to say that killings, executions, torture, and abuse, sexual and religious humiliation of civilians became all too common during the British occupation of Iraq....5 survivors have witnessed seemingly in three separate venues at close hand: The execution of up to 15 men. Between 4 and 5 of these executions involving shots at close range and the remainder some sort of strangulation or throat cutting. Some of these executions preceded by torture or mutilations that are so horrific that our clients could not describe the prolonged screaming without breaking down. (col 1408)

Shiner also produced death certificates provided by the hospital doctors of the bodies of dead men which alleged that men had been taken to the local hospital, and recorded cases where two men, had their eyes gouged out, one man who was said to have had his penis cut off, one of the men died from a single shot to the head or from a bullet administered very close to the body and another man had signs of evidence of torture to the right side of his body. The truth of these cases is not proven as the allegations cannot be tested so whether they were fabrications we will never know. However, Anthony Williams (2012) a highly respected writer and author of a detailed account of the killing of Baha Mousa (below), has much respect for Shiner: "he challenged convention and indifference". Further cases have been brought in UK courts where Iraqi internees allege racist and homophobic language, and sexual, cultural, and religious abuse by British army officers (Duffy 2016). These matters are not closed.

In September 2003 in Basra, Iraq, Baha Mousa was abused and tortured to death whilst in the custody of British army officers. The *Baha Mousa Public Inquiry report* (2011) chairman, Sir William Gage, concluded "Cpl Donald Payne had violently assaulted Mr. Mousa in the minutes before he died, punching, and possibly kicking him, and using a dangerous restraint method, the inquiry found. While this was a 'contributory cause' in the death, Mr. Mousa had already been weakened by factors including lack of food and water, heat, exhaustion, fear, previous injuries and the hooding and stress positions used by British troops". The

Inquiry recorded that Baha Mousa had suffered appalling and gratuitous injuries and that Payne was a "violent bully" who inflicted a "dreadful catalogue of unjustified and brutal violence" (*R (Mousa) v Secretary of State for Defence* [2010]). *Payne served 12 months in military detention for the killing of Mousa* (Duffy 2016: nb 75). The Inquiry reported that: "Three other soldiers confirmed that Payne had demonstrated the 'choir' or 'chorus,' which involved arranging the detainees in a row and kicking each one in succession so that he would 'sing'" (Vol 1, 2.681). Dr Hill, the pathologist, reported that Baha Mousa had 93 separate external and internal injuries, including fractured ribs, a broken nose, marks around the throat describing "ligature", "asphyxia "and "restraint". The inquiry chairman queried why interrogation methods that had been banned by the UK more than 30 years earlier were being used during the Iraq campaign. SSgt Davies, in giving evidence, simply referred to "the training manual" and said that both the manual and a training course on "tactical questioning and prisoner handling", had justified tactics involving humiliation, stripping, threatening, depriving prisoners of their sight, use of blindfolds and hooding (Vol 1, 1159). These other methods, were in breach of the Geneva Conventions and these illegal methods were also used on detainees who were the subject of the *Al-Sweady Inquiry* (above). One officer and three NCO's were involved in the "tactical questioning" of the detainees. This included Peebles (the battle group internment review officer—BGIRO), the two tactical questioners, SSgt Davies and Smulski and Livesey (Vol 1, 2.850). Prisoners were hooded, placed next to a generator which was noisy and hot (the temperature in Iraq could rise to 58 degrees centigrade) and some detainees had been kept there for up to three hours (at 2.888), deprived of sleep (Vol 1, 2.885) kept in stress positions hooded and made to experience "white noise" which made some men exhausted and drop to the floor (at 2.891). Mousa's family and the nine other detainees who survived (see *Al Skeini and others v Secretary of State for Defence and another* [2007]) received 2.83 million in compensation in 2008 (very little in compensation). Litigation brought by Iraqi detainees and/or their families continues with other cases against the Ministry of Defence. The "Iraqi civilian litigation" including Alseran *and others v Ministry of Defence* [2018] which represents the four lead cases filing for compensation, and other remaining claims (Shackle 2018), allege inhuman treatment including being stripped naked, intrusive physical inspection involving sexual humiliation, hooding and physical assaults. Evidential issues have complicated the hearings including, whether the perpetrators were American or British, whether the detainees should have been treated as civilians and not prisoners of war, and whether the statute of limitations applies. The court in the *Alseran* case accepted that the MOD was responsible, that in some cases the prisoners should not have been treated as prisoners of war, and that the circumstances demanded that the limitation period for bringing a claim be suspended [855]. Damages awarded were assessed in accordance with the Judicial College Guidelines, which are hopelessly inappropriate for these kinds of cases. The amounts awarded are derisory, for example, the rate for unlawful detention is 100 pounds per day [957]. Alseran claimed that he was a civilian, unlawfully captured and whose body was used quite literally as a steppingstone [203] by British troops to walk over. This act was also photographed [163]. The court found a breach of Article 3 ECHR [233] as Alseran was not a prisoner of war and there was no lawful basis for his internment [313][330]. As for "MRE" and "KSU" who were also detained, they were forced to strip naked [343] their penis and buttocks inspected and photographed. KSU [345] was especially humiliated as he was "pulled by his penis and made him turn to the right. The 'doctor' then pulled KSU's penis down to make him crouch down before pulling his penis up to force KSU to stand back up. KSU said that, while this was happening, a group of soldiers were standing very close behind him, only around a metre away, and laughing at him" [365]. (This sexual abuse a demonstration of the hypermasculinity was entrenched in the power of the military. Accad (1990) explores this connection between sexual abuse and violence, which is considered further in Chapter 6 in the discussion on Abu Ghraib.)

The court found the allegations made by the four men credible and held their detention had been unlawful [537]. MRE was awarded damages for inhuman and degrading treatment of £16,440, in respect of a blow to his head which left some permanent disability, for being hooded with a sandbag he was awarded £11,000 and his unlawful detention for six days amounted to £600 [970]. As for Al-Waheed [556, 668] he was subjected to "tactical questioning" which involved "harsh" interrogation methods, permitted by the MoD at the time. For bruising and injury [561, 673] and harsh questioning [933 v] and beating he was awarded £15,000, £15,000 in respect of harsh interrogation and being deprived of sleep and of sight and hearing; and £3300 in respect of unlawful detention for 33 days. It is significant that in respect of the matter of the harsh interrogation, which was used by the MOD at that time, the *Baha Mousa Inquiry* found:

> The teaching of the "harsh" permitted insults not just of the performance of the captured prisoner but personal and abusive insults including racist and homophobic language. The "harsh" was designed to show anger on the part of the questioner. It ran the risk of being a form of intimidation to coerce answers from prisoners. It involved forms of threats which, while in some senses indirect, were designed to instil in prisoners a fear of what might happen to them, including physically'. (*The Baha Mousa Public Inquiry* Vol II, part VI, para [6.346])

Williams (2012) says Iraq has been forgotten. He has not done so and writes of:

> a culture of contempt and indifference permeating the army and government hierarchies. Protestations that Britain respects and promotes human rights and the laws of war have been accompanied by civilian and military commanders who do everything that they can to look the other way or even bury cases of abuse. Systems of criminal investigation have been established to pursue those responsible, but they are not impartial, independent, or effective.

This is all underpinned as Bob Connell in his writing on "Masculinity Violence and War" (1985) demonstrates by how masculinity is associated with aggressiveness and the capacity for violence (discussed further in Chapter 6). So, what then of the UK's adherence to the international ROL? Sands (2006) says the WOT was an invasion and an occupation of "lawlessness". Judges in the European Court of Human Rights in *Al-Saadoon and Mufdhi v The United Kingdom* [2010] (para 10–11) reached a similar conclusion. What impact do these instances of brutality have on the Iraqi people, on their attitude to the US and the British forces, and on their righteous sense of injustice? And what impact does knowledge of this maltreatment of Muslim men have on any Muslim man or woman, indeed on anyone, anywhere, who are right thinking?

Lawless Occupation of Palestinian Land

Outside the WOT (or perhaps not so), the US and the UK also profess to observe the ROL elsewhere in the international order and given this claim it is impossible to overlook the West's contumacious silence over the humanitarian crisis in Gaza (see Said 1978 [2001] "The Question of Palestine"). It is strikingly significant that "this" desperate situation, almost exceptionally, has become a suffering about which no one must talk, unless to condemn the Palestinians already condemned as refugees and prisoners in their own country (see the mainstream political response to the comments of Cheri Blair and Carol Tonge in Chapter 5). Pappé (2017a: 13) explains that he has spent much of his academic life trying to come to terms with this situation as he considers his own position as "part of the privileged oppressive majority". Jacqueline Rose, literary critic, intellectual and feminist writer has spent a large part of her academic life coming to terms with what she considers "the complex relationship of Jews to this land and to their identity" (Rose 2011, 2014) and what she describes as "the brutal policies towards Palestinians" (2013 at 5.35 minutes). She cites Jewish writers and thinkers concerned about the treatment of Palestinians, for example, Israel Shahak who said in 1975; "...if you say the word Palestinian in Israel you were "already half a rebel" (135) and cites Martin Buber who in 1948 objected "to the injustice being perpetrated on the Arabs" (189).

What then does the international ROL do to protect their rights? In 2018, the Israeli Knesset, by 62–55 voted, with 2 abstentions, to pass a nation-state law, specifying the Jewish nature of Israel, asserting: "the right to exercise national self-determination [in Israel is] unique to the Jewish people", establishing Hebrew as Israel's official language and downgrading Arabic, a language widely spoken by Arab Israelis, to a "special status." Such "national values" are further concretised in Jewish settlements which the state "will labor to encourage and promote", underscoring that only Jews in Israel have the right to self-determination. Benjamin Netanyahu announces on social media his vision, "[Israel is] ... not a state of all its citizens. ..., Israel is the nation-state of the Jewish People - and them alone" (11 March 2019). Pappé (2017a) has said that the new law introduces elements of apartheid into Israel's legislation. The Head of the Israel Democracy Institute, Yohanan Plesner, agrees and calls Netanyahu's law "jingoistic" and "divisive". Criticism from Jewish intellectuals is fierce. Gideon Levy laments: "Now there will be a law that tells the truth. Israel is for Jews only, on the books. The nation-state of the Jewish people, not of its residents. Its Arabs are second-class citizens, and its Palestinian subjects are hollow, nonexistent. Their fate is determined in Jerusalem, but they aren't part of the state" (*Haaretz*, 12 July

2018). Mordechai Kremnitzer, former dean of the Law Faculty at the Hebrew University of Jerusalem writing, in *Haaretz* (July 11, 2018), says Netanyahu's policy will: "foment a revolution, no less. It will spell the end of Israel as a Jewish and democratic state and make Israel a leader among nationalist countries like Poland and Hungary". Hannah Arendt beratingly said in 1961 (2006 [1961]: 7) that it was ironical, that rabbinical laws were no protectors of equality and inclusiveness: "with the result that no Jew can marry a non-Jew; marriages concluded abroad are recognized, but children of mixed marriages are legally bastards (children of Jewish parentage born out of wedlock are legitimate), and if one happens to have a non-Jewish mother, he can neither be married or buried". Schlomo Sand (2014) Israeli Emeritus Professor of History at Tel Aviv is concerned that "'Zionists' have rejected the principle of civil Israeli nationality where citizens of Israel have stamped on their passport 'Jew' or 'Arab,'" and queries how such labelling might be regarded, if, for example, it were to be applied in the UK. Sand regards the exclusion of non-Jews in Israel a dangerous anachronism, which, is, he says anti-democratic and anti-republican, and rejecting the biologistic and deterministic straitjacket, he criticises a categorisation that deems Jews a race which he regards as an "ethnocentric, racist or quasi racist position" (Sand 2014: 7).

What part has the international order, the international ROL and other nation states played, and what of their complicity? The UN, and the International Court of Justice (ICJ) consider Israel's continued construction of settlements illegal and which Chomsky and Pappé (2015: 155) regard as part of a strategic plan for removing Palestinians. Chomsky calls the occupation "criminal" and a gross violation of international law and Security Council resolutions (146). "Israelis", Chomsky says, have developed a very clear narrative that the Palestinians have brought it upon themselves resulting from unprovoked missiles attacks on the Jewish state by Hamas to which the state in self-defense must respond. For Rose, Hammas may be "wicked" but she says "that is not sufficient an excuse". Levy (2010) says that the occupation of Gaza is: "... more cruel, criminal and inhuman today than ever before" (2010: vii), citing "Operation Case Lead" (a three-week armed conflict between Palestinians in the Gaza Strip and Israel that began on 27 December 2008 and ended on 18 January 2009 in a unilateral ceasefire as an example of that cruelty. The conflict resulted in between 1166 and 1417 Palestinian and 13 Israeli deaths (4 from friendly fire). Levy described it as: "a horrific ratio rarely paralleled" (ix) which led, as Zachary Davies Boren reported, to Holocaust survivors and their descendants accusing Israel of "genocide" (*The Independent*, 24 August 2014 "Holocaust survivors and their descendants accuse Israel of 'genocide'"). Pappé has gone further describing Israel's policy towards the Gaza strip as "incremental genocide" (2007 [2006]: 147), where he traces the historical origins of the current illegal occupation and the history of Zionism as it emerged in the 1880s in central and eastern Europe documenting how operations against the Palestinians including the drive for a Jewish state, supported in the UN Resolution 181 (II) of 29 November 1947, was a "crime against humanity" in violation of the basic rights of the Palestinian people (31) (see also Palumbo 1987: 52).

Pappé (2017b) in "The Occupation is not Democratic" (*Jacobin*, 5 May 2017) acerbically says: "what we must challenge here, therefore, is not only Israel's claim to be maintaining an enlightened occupation but also its pretense to be a democracy. Such behavior towards millions of people under its rule gives the lie to such political chicanery". As Pappé points out such voices are forced to utilise the relative freedom of speech in the cyber world to call out and name this action a war crime, demanding that Washington observe its own laws and international ROL and end military aid to Israel. On the question of military aid, Chomsky accuses the US of hypocrisy, since US law states: "…no security assistance may be provided to any country the government of which engaged in a consistent pattern of gross violations of internationally recognized human rights" (Chomsky and Pappé 2015: 164–165). Chomsky and Pappé ask the question, what has happened to the ROL and especially why is it that with regard to the Palestinian Arabs, who are largely Muslim, the West is silent?

Those who go against the grain and engage in "core political speech" are discredited. Jewish voices or those with Jewish connections who criticise the Israel's policy towards Palestinians are also said to be full of self-loathing. Rose struggles to free a critical narrative from what she says are accusations of anti-Semitism, or if a Jew critical of the government of Israel then from charges of self-hatred (Rose "On the Myth of Self-Hatred" (2008). Sand, for his criticism of Israel's government policy towards the Palestinians has been banned from speaking, such was the case at the University of Nice in 2014. Professor Norman Finklestein, author of *Gaza an Inquest into Its Martyrdom* (2018) has been denied academic tenure in the US since 2007. Omar Baghouti (a Palestinian Arab and without Jewish connections) founder of the BDS movement (which states as its aim to work to end international support for Israel's oppression of Palestinians and pressures Israel into complying with international law) has been banned from lecturing in the US (*The Guardian*, 16 April 2019, "I co-founded the BDS movement. Why was I denied entry to the US?"). Pappé (2013: 12) describes the fierce opposition he has experienced. As Pappé and other Israeli's, and non-Israeli Jews, critical of Israel's governments' treatment of the Palestinians, and of the West's implacable support and complicity try to make clear, is that this counternarrative as Rose repeatedly points out has absolutely nothing to do with anti-Jewishness and everything to do with opposing a right-wing government (Rose 2011). Jacqueline Rose in grappling with what she sees says: "I hope you would probably recognize that there is something intractable about this conflict... that has a resilience.... an investment ...in its version of itself as victims of history and that is a form of licensing of what I would certainly describe as occupation and what is justifiable given that history" (2014 at 5.39 minutes).

I am aware that I have not answered my own question of why the West has contumaciously ignored the ROL when it comes to this question. What I can say is that the suffering of Palestinians is a suffering of a predominantly Muslim minority within Israel in which the West, the UK and the US are complicit and where a culture of denial is built into the social fabric (Cohen 2001: 157). There are consequences. Rose recounts the retired Israeli army colonel who said at a meeting of Israeli and European Jews: "An unjust Israel harms you" (2011: 324). She concludes: "Let me stress again. We are not talking about turning back history. Israel has a right to exist. .... the Jewish people did not survive attempted genocide to become the brutal oppressors of another people" (325). The late Sir Gerald Kaufman MP speaking in the House of Commons on "Gaza" (15 January 2009 col 407) is of the same view and again making a plea for the ROL (Volume 575, "Gaza Humanitarian Situation" 5 February 2014) says: "Impose sanctions, press the European community the UN, the US, our own country".

LAWLESS AT HOME

Further evidence of the West, and specifically the UK's abrogation of the ROL and its substantive norms in order to further its own interests (see Curtis 2018: xvii, 370), is demonstrated in its complicity in arms trade agreements with Saudi Arabia. Saudi Arabia, ranking top of the list for human rights abuses, is supplied with arms manufactured in the UK which have been used against Yemen since 2015. Currently, the Gulf States and Saudi Arabia account for half of all Britain's arms sales on so-called "defence" and "security technology" amounting to 100 billion dollars. On 20 June 2019, the Campaign against the Arms Trade (CAAT) challenged the UK government over its sale of arms to Saudi Arabia (*R* (*on the application of Campaign against Arms Trade*) *v Secretary of State for International Trade and others* [2019] Amnesty International, Human Rights Watch, Rights Watch UK and Oxfam International intervening. The Court of Appeal held UK sales unlawful, and in breach of international law and considered the position adopted by the Member States of the European Union in December 2008, which stipulated under Article 2 that Member States: "[15] shall ... deny an export licence if there is a clear risk that the ... equipment might be used in the commission of serious violations of international humanitarian law", applied (Council Common Position 2008/944/CFSP of 8 December 2008). The government responded and said it would seek to appeal this decision to the Supreme Court. Contumacious disregard characterised the Secretary of State for International Trade, Liz Truss's response, who on 26 September 2019, confirmed that further licensing of equipment to Saudi for use in Yemen would continue. On 25 April 2020, *The Guardian* reported that arms sales in 2019 increased by 1 billion over 2018 and in July 2020, the UK renewed its arms sales saying that any concerns were merely "isolated incidents". Lord Grimstone of Boscobel said: "We indeed have assessed that there were a small number of incidents that have been treated, for the purposes of the analysis, as violations of IHL [International Humanitarian Law]. However, these were isolated incidents that did not display any particular pattern, and our analysis shows that Saudi Arabia has a genuine intent and the capacity to comply with IHL in the specific commitments that it has made" (Hansard, *Saudi Arabia: Arms Sales*, 10 July 2020, Volume 804, col 1348). The very countries the Foreign and Commonwealth Office (FCO) "watch list" have flagged up as committing the worst human rights abuses are those same countries on the Department of Trade and Industry's (DTI) core arms trade markets for 2017–2018. International Trade Secretary, at the time, Liam Fox's, response was: "if regimes could not acquire the weapons, they needed legally there would be an eruption of unregulated sales" (*Daily Mail*, 12 September 2017).

Then there is the problem of unethical investments where some local authority pension funds unbeknown to its members have invested in arms manufacturing companies including BAE Systems, Airbus, Lockheed Martin, Raytheon and Northrop Grumman. In 2018, 43 pension funds were reported as directly holding shares worth £566 m in the five companies which earned £18.5 m in dividends (*The Guardian*, 10 January 2019). Council pension funds in Scotland *The Guardian* reported at the time had investments worth nearly £130 million in arms firms linked to Yemen's conflict, and shareholdings in five arms companies supplying to Saudi Arabia. The Universities Superannuation Scheme, USS has also been complicit at the time of *The Guardian* report in investing its funds in companies selling arms, including the multinational Textron which has been involved in the sale of cluster bombs. Whilst Universities have policies on socially responsible investment, some policies do not explicitly consider the arms question. Glasgow University was one such example, where, in 2019, three million pounds was invested in arms manufacturing companies, although CAAT (July–September 2020 is 257) reports Glasgow University's continued investment. The University of Cambridge colleges had 6.5 million in 2018, similarly invested. Significantly, in April 2020, in the case of *R (on the application of Palestine Solidarity Campaign Ltd and another) v Secretary of State for Housing, Communities and Local Government* [2020] the Supreme Court held that guidance issued by the Secretary of State for Housing, Communities and Local Government ("the Secretary of State") with regard to the local government pension scheme ("the scheme"), a statutory occupational pension scheme, was unlawful. The guidance issued and introduced in 2016, had banned the funds from disinvesting in companies or countries on ethical grounds, except where the government has imposed official sanctions.

This is how the ROL with its substantive norms of peace, and ethical values is working on the home front.

The treatment of refugees and migrants in the UK provides a further example which demonstrates the malleability of the ROL. OEF commenced in October 2001 with operations in Afghanistan, followed in 2003 by the invasion of Iraq. The outbreak of civil war in Syria 2011, the scourge of ISIS and the prolongation of the war by the West led to an unprecedented Syrian refugee crisis. From 2013 to 2017 Syrians constituted the main country of asylum seekers in the EU Member States. Whilst in 2018, Syrian first-time asylum applicants in the "EU 28" countries decreased from 102 thousand in 2017, to 81 thousand in 2018, "Syrian" was still the main citizenship of asylum seekers in eight EU Member States, Afghani's accounted for 7.1% of the total number of first-time asylum applicants and Iraqis 6.8% (*Eurostats*, 16 May 2020). The US and UK intervention in the WOT, or OEF as it preferred, professed a humanitarian purpose whilst creating thousands of displaced refugees. The UK has an obligation under the Convention Relating to the Status of Refugees (1951) and an overriding moral obligation to displaced persons. In 2018, of asylum seekers entering the EU, Migration observatory reports that the UK received (37,730, 6%) of applicants (Eurostat 2019). That is 0.6 asylum applications for every 1000 residents, compared to 1.2 across the EU-28, such that the UK ranks 17th in the EU for receiving refugees. The figures are complex and difficult to interpret. However, Amnesty International reports: that since January 2014 the UK has resettled 216 Syrian refugees ... a small proportion of the near 4 million Syrians in Turkey, Lebanon and Jordan. Hardly what the government pledged when setting up the scheme and when Prime Minister David Cameron announced the figure of 20,000 (and even then, a far lower target than other European countries).

Contrary to the spirit of the Convention, many EU countries have responded with increasing antinomy developing deterrence strategies including the introduction of anti-refugee laws and policies which deprive asylum seekers of material support, subject them to harsh conditions including, long processing periods for applications, confinement in detention centres, where the conditions in some amounting to cruel and inhumane treatment, and create a high bar required of evidence of "fear of persecution" in tribunal hearings. Lacey (2019: 19) calls this "crimmigration". In 2001, 78% of Iraqi victims were refused asylum. Anti-immigration is rampant across Europe. Hungary embarked on "exceptionalist" emergency measures by building a razor-wire fence of 170 km length across its border with Serbia, followed in 2016 by deterrent legislation, then punishment measures (Ormsby 2017: 1209). The UN High Commissioner for Human Rights, Zeid Ra'ad Al Hussein, denounced the law as "shameful" and "blatantly xenophobic" (*The Times*, 15 May 2020). In the UK, the Immigration Act (2016) s.66 schedule 12, creates classes of "ineligible people" and although there are some exemptions, the system for accessing support is complex. The Home Affairs Committee on "Immigration and Detention" (March 2019) found conditions were inhumane. In 2018, 24,729 people were effectively criminalised detained in conditions of high security, where families were segregated. Some are detained unlawfully. Then there are the deportations. In 2016, 785 people were returned from the UK to Afghanistan.

Between 2007–2015, 2018 adults who sought refuge, during this period when children, were deported, when they reached adulthood. In the year ending March 2018, the number of all asylum applicants in the UK was 2654, compared with Germany, for example, at 179,000 (*The Guardian*, 1 March 2017, "Britain one of the worst places in western Europe for asylum-seekers"). The UK media carried reports of "the swarm on our streets" (*Daily Mail*, 31 July 2015) and in fomenting moral panics, news strap lines asked; "How many more can we take?" (*The Independent*, 27 August 2015). Yet, when it suited, governments and politicians used the refugee crisis as a lever to gain support for continuing military intervention. This was especially so in the case of Syria, where following the drowning of 3-year-old Aylan, on 2 September 2015, linguistic descriptions of refugees changed from "swarm", "outsiders", "enemies" and "criminals", to "victims". Aylan was described as a "tiny victim of human catastrophe" of Assad's regime and used to justify continuing Western intervention in Syria. Curtis writes, "Britain went to great lengths to keep the war going helping to sabotage international talks that could have led to a negotiated outcome" (2018: 411). David Cameron, when Prime Minister, sympathised but only so far, remarking that resettlement would not solve the crisis. "We have taken a number of genuine asylum seekers from Syrian refugee camps and we keep that under review, but we think the most important thing is to try to bring peace and stability to that part of the world....I don't think there is an answer that can be achieved simply by taking more and more refugees" (*The Guardian*, 2 September 2015, "Britain should not take more Middle East refugees, says David Cameron"). Rania Khalek, who reported that it was US support for Syrian rebels that drove the refugee crisis that Trump capitalised on in March 2017, has now been silenced by being blacklisted.

Conclusion—The Rule of Law, Whose Shield?

The ROL is a banner held high, and self-satisfiedly immunises the West from criticism. At the same time, the West when it so chooses casts out some of the ROL's substantive norms rejecting what it regards as an unwarranted restraint on state power. In its decimation there is an "assault on the Muslim body", since it will not have escaped notice that Muslim communities and Muslim people, Muslim diaspora and Muslim women, the Muslim displaced seeking refuge are the subjects so affected.

This collective victimisation impacts on Muslim men and women on their lives, and on their sense of self and identity. It is impossible to refute Chomsky's (2004) repeated claim that a general sense of Muslim grievance is rooted in US foreign policy and is part of the problem of Islamic terrorism. "By October 2010 it was becoming hard to ignore the fact that the world was more concerned about the unbridled use of American power than.... about the threat posed by Saddam Hussein" (3). But it is not only critics of the US and left of centre commentators that are making these arguments. The UK's *Financial Times* also recognised political oppression and economic marginalisation as the root cause of Islamic extremism (Chomsky 2004: 210). Added to this provocation is the UK's complicity. The Inquiry Report into the UK's invasion of Iraq heard devastating evidence from within the establishment itself when Eliza Manningham-Buller, head of MI5, said that the UK invasion of Iraq made Britain more vulnerable to terrorism.

To my mind Iraq, Saddam Hussein had nothing to do with 9/11, our involvement in Iraq radicalised, for want of a better word, a whole generation of young people. Some British citizens saw our involvement in Iraq as being an attack on Islam.... The report was highly critical of what it called an 'ingrained belief' that Saddam Hussein's regime retained chemical and biological warfare capabilities (*Iraq Inquiry* 806), and that Iraq was a threat that had to be dealt with. Damningly no evidence had been identified that Iraq possessed weapons of mass destruction, with which it might threaten its neighbours and the international community more widely. (796)

'the US and Britain who, by invading Iraq, gave Osama bin Laden the Iraqi jihad'. (*The Guardian*, 20 July 2010, "Iraq inquiry: Eliza Manningham-Buller's devastating testimony")

In responding to the *Report of the Iraq Inquiry* on 6 July 2016, Angus Robertson MP (*Iraq Inquiry*, Hansard, Volume 612, col 894) accused the British Government of deception. Tim Farron MP (col 893) asked for an apology from the British Government for the British forces and the people of Iraq and reminded the House of the prophetic words of Charles Kennedy: "In 2003, the much-missed Charles Kennedy said in this House: 'The big fear that many of us have is that the action will simply breed further generations of suicide bombers'" (Official Report, 18 March 2003; Vol. 401, c. 786). But Michael Gove (2007), Warraq

(2017), former Prime Minister Tony Blair and others have scoffed at the conclusions of the Iraq Inquiry and Manningham-Buller's conclusions, that there may be a broader context to Islamic extremism for which the West must bear some responsibility, and reject those who: "attribute Islamist violence to specific, discrete grievances such as the presence of American troops on Saudi soil, the failure to establish an Arab Palestine state, or the material poverty of the Arab peoples" (11) preferring instead the explanation that religious theocratic ideology drives terrorism. Michael Gove (2007) says that the suggestion that the Western offensive (as I have detailed in this chapter, in its various expressions) has constituted the single greatest cause of anger across the Middle East "is a ludicrously reductionist argument" (54). The ROL as it has been appropriated by the West against Muslim people is not the safest shield of which Lord Judge spoke, at least, not for all!

REFERENCES

A and others v Secretary of State for the Home Department [2004] UKHL 56. https://iilj.org/wp-content/uploads/2016/08/A-v.-Secretary-of-State-for-the-Home-Department.pdf. Accessed 11 November 2020.

A and others v Secretary of State for the Home Department (No 2) [2005] https://www.bailii.org/uk/cases/UKHL/2005/71.html. Accessed 11 November 2020.

Abu-Lughod, L. 2015 [2013] *Do Muslim Women Need Saving?* Harvard: Harvard University Press.

Accad, E. 1990. *Sexuality and War Literary Masks of the Middle East.* New York: New York University Press.

Acton, Lord. 1862. *Nationality.* https://oll.libertyfund.org/titles/acton-the-history-of-freedom-and-other-essays. Accessed 11 November 2020.

Ahmad, E. 2006. *The Selected Writings of Eqbal Ahmad.* Columbia: Columbia University Press.

Al-Ali, N., and N. Pratt. 2009. *What Kind of Liberation? Women and the Occupation of Iraq.* Berkeley, Los Angeles, London: University of California Press.

Al-Saadoon and Mufdhi v The United Kingdom. 2010. Application no. 61498/08. https://www.bailii.org/eu/cases/ECHR/2009/409.html. Accessed 11 November 2020.

Alseran and others v Ministry of Defence. 2018. 3 WLR 95. https://www.judiciary.uk/wp-content/uploads/2017/12/alseran-ministry-of-defence-20171214.pdf. Accessed 11 November 2020.

Al Skeini and others v Secretary of State for Defence and another [2007] UKHL 26. https://publications.parliament.uk/pa/ld200607/ldjudgmt/jd070613/skeini-1.htm. Accessed 11 November 2020.

Al-Sweady inquiry report. 2014. *Report of the Public Inquiry into Allegations of Unlawful Killing and Ill Treatment of Iraqi Nationals by British Troops in Iraq in 2004.* https://www.gov.uk/government/publications/al-sweady-inq uiry-report. Accessed 6 August 2020.

Al-Sweady Inquiry Report. Wednesday 17 December 2014. Hansard - UK Parliament. https://hansard.parliament.uk/Commons/2014-12-17/debates/141 21731000002/Al-SweadyInquiryReport%20col%201408.

Althusser, L. 1971 [1984]. Ideology and Ideological state Apparatuses. In *Lenin and Philosophy and Other Essays*, 121–176. New York: Monthly Review Press.

Annan, K. 2004. Report of the Secretary-General. *The Rule of Law and Transitional Justice in Conflict and Post-Conflict Society's* S/2004/616. https://dig itallibrary.un.org/record/527647. Accessed 11 November 2020.

Arendt, H. 2017 [1951]. *The Origins of Totalitarianism.* London: Penguin.

Arendt, H. 2006 [1961]. *Eichmann in Jerusalem.* London: Penguin Classics Paperback.

Baldassi and Others v France application no. 15271/16, 11 June 2020. https://hudoc.echr.coe.int/fre#{%22itemid%22:[%22001-202756%22]}. Accessed 10 November 2020.

Bennett, M. 2011. Hart and Raz On the Non-Instrumental Moral Value of the Rule of Law: A Reconsideration. *Law and Philosophy* 30 (5): 603–635.

Bingham, T. 2011. *The Rule of Law.* London: Allen Lane.

Bricmont, J. 2007. *Humanitarian Imperialism: Using Human Rights to Sell War.* New York: Monthly Review Press.

Burgess, P. 2017. The Rule of Law: Beyond Contestedness. *Jurisprudence An International Journal of Legal and Political Thought* 8 (3): 480–500.

Butler Inquiry. *Review of Intelligence on Weapons of Mass Destruction: Implementation of Its Conclusions* (2004), Cm 6492 (2005).

Charlesworth, H., and C. Chinkin. 2002. Sex, Gender, and September 11. *American Journal of International Law* 96 (3): 600–605.

Chilcot, J. 2016. *The Report of the Iraq Inquiry*: Report of a Committee of Privy Counsellors, executive summary (House of Commons Papers) HC 708. https://www.gov.uk/government/publications/the-report-of-the-iraq-inquiry. Accessed 6 August 2020.

Chomsky, N. 2004. *Hegemony or Survival: America's Quest for Global Dominance.* London: Penguin.

Chomsky, N. 2011 [2003]. *Power and Terror, Talks and Interviews.* USA: Seven Stories Press.

Chomsky, N., and I. Pappé. 2015. *On Palestine.* London: Penguin.

Cohen, S. 2001. *States of Denial.* London: Polity.

Collins, H. 1982. *Marxism and the Rule of Law*. Oxford: Oxford University Press.

Connell, B. 1985. Masculinity, Violence and War. In *War/Masculinity*, ed. P. Patton and R. Poole. Sydney: Intervention.

Curtis, M. 2018. *Secret Affairs Britain's Collusion with Radical Islam*. London: Serpent's Tail.

Data Protection Bill 09 May 2018 Volume 640. https://hansard.parliament. uk/commons/2018-05-09/debates/CE43B0ED-87D3-4F63-B8A4-2A6 6964790C2/DataProtectionBill(Lords). Accessed 11 November 2020.

Duffy, A. 2016. Searching for Accountability: British-Controlled Detention in Southeast Iraq, 2003–2008. *International Journal of Transitional Justice IJTJ* 10 (3): 410–431.

Entick v Carrington [1765] 19 St Tr 1030, [1765] EWHC KB J98. https://www.bailii.org/ew/cases/EWHC/KB/1765/J98.html. Accessed 11 November 2020.

Eursotats Asylum Statistics. https://ec.europa.eu/eurostat/statistics-explained/index.php/Asylum_statistics. Accessed 9 August 2020.

Fanon, F. 1965. *A Dying Colonialism*. London: Penguin.

Fine, B. 1984. *Democracy and the Rule of Law: Liberal Ideals and Marxist Critiques*. London: Pluto.

Finklestein, N. 2018. *Gaza an Inquest into Its Martyrdom*. Berkeley, CA: University of California Press.

Fisk, R. (2013). "War on Terror Is the West's New Religion." *The Independent*, February 24.

Five Knights Case [1627] 3 How St Tr 1. https://www.britannica.com/event/Darnels-case. Accessed 11 November 2020.

Foucault, M. 1980. *Power and Knowledge: Selected Interviews and Other Writings 1972–1977*, ed. C. Gordon. New York: Pantheon.

Fuller, L. 1958. "Positivism and Fidelity to Law—A Reply to Professor Hart". *Harv Law Rev*, 71.

Gage, W. 2011. *The Report of the Baha Mousa Inquiry*, HC 1452–I. https://www.gov.uk/government/publications/the-baha-mousa-public-inquiry-report. Accessed 1 March 2020.

Gardner, F. 2020. Saudi Arabia: Just How Deep Are Its Troubles? *BBC News*, May 12. https://www.bbc.com/news/amp/world-middle-east-525 88971. Accessed 1 November 2020.

Gerrard, D. 2020. Boris Johnson's BDS Bill Brings Britain Closer to America and Israel Further from Peace. *The Independent*, January 3.

Hailsham, Lord. 1983. *Hamlyn Revisited: The British Legal System Today*. London: Stevens.

Hensman, R. 2003. The only alternative to global terror. In *Terror Counter-Terror Women Speak Out*, ed. A. Joseph and K. Sharma, 23–41. Zed: London and New York.

House of Commons. 2019. Home Affairs Committee *Immigration Detention* Fourteenth Report of Session 2017–19, 12 March 2019.

Joint Parliamentary Committee. 2004. *Counter-terrorism Powers: Reconciling Security and Liberty in an Open Society.* A Discussion Paper. HL paper 158, HC 713, CM 6147.

Joseph, A., and K. Sharma (eds.). 2003. *Terror, Counter-terror Women Speak Out.* London: Zed.

Judge, I. 2015. *The Safest Shield, Lectures, Speeches and Essays.* London: Hart.

Kentridge, S. 2014. *Free Country.* London: Hart.

Kundnani, A. 2007. *The End of Tolerance.* London: Pluto.

Lacey, N. 2019. Popularism and the Rule of Law. Working paper, 28 January 2019, LSE International Inequalities Institute. London.

Levy, G. 2010. *The Punishment of Gaza.* London: Verso.

Marx, K. 1932 [1845–1846]. *The German Ideology.* London: Lawrence and Wishart.

Ormsby, E. 2017. The Refugee Crisis as Civil Liberties Crisis. *Columbia Law Review* 117 (5): 1191–1229.

Orwell, G. 2000 [1946]. Politics and the English Language. In *George Orwell: Essays*, 348–360. London: Penguin.

Otto, D. 2006. Lost in Translation: Re-scripting the Sexed Subjects of International Human Rights Law. In *International Law and Its Others*, ed. A. Orford, 313–356. Cambridge: Cambridge University Press.

Palumbo, M. 1987. *The Palestinian Catastrophe.* London New York: Quartet.

Pappé, I. 2007. Genocide in Gaza. *The Electronic Intifada*, 2 September 2006. https://electronicintifada.net/content/genocide-gaza/6397. Accessed 11 November 2020.

Pappé, I. 2013 [2011]. *The Forgotten Palestinians.* Yale: Yale University Press.

Pappé, I. 2017a. *The Biggest Prison on Earth: A History of the Occupied Territories.* London: Oneworld Publications.

Pappé, I. 2017b. *No, Israel Is Not a Democracy.* Jacobin, May 5. https://www.jacobinmag.com/2017/05/israel-palestine-democracy-apartheid-discrimination-settler-colonialism. Accessed 1 November 2020.

Poole, P. 2006. *Unspeak.* London: Little Brown.

Prohibition del Roy [1607] EWHC KB J23; 77 ER 1342; 12 Co.Rep. 64. https://www.bailii.org/ew/cases/EWHC/KB/1607/J23.html. Accessed 11 November 2020.

R (on the application of Campaign against Arms Trade) v Secretary of State for International Trade and others [2019] EWCA Civ 1020. https://www.bailii.org/ew/cases/EWCA/Civ/2019/1020.html. Accessed 11 November 2020.

R (on the application of Miller) v Prime Minister; Cherry and others v Advocate General for Scotland [2019] 5 LRC 490. https://www.supremecourt.uk/cases/docs/uksc-2019-0192-judgment.pdf?fbclid=IwAR1K4DLbZLVDiplx 9rwgEwQm1F6bwBpC3WxROKvhv0tto0DZmov7tiGShDI. Accessed 11 November 2020.

R (on the application of Palestine Solidarity Campaign Ltd and another) v Secretary of State for Housing, Communities and Local Government [2020] UKSC 16. https://www.supremecourt.uk/cases/uksc-2018-0133.html. Accessed 11 November 2020.

R (Mousa) v Secretary of State for Defence [2010] EWHC 3304. https://www.bailii.org/ew/cases/EWCA/Civ/2011/1334.html. Accessed 11 November 2020.

Rasul v Bush. 2004. 542 U.S. 466; (2004) 321 F.3d 1134. https://supreme.justia.com/cases/federal/us/542/466/. Accessed 11 November 2020.

Raz, J. 2009 [1979]. The Rule of Law and Its Virtue. In *The Authority of Law: Essays on Law and Morality.* Oxford: Clarendon Press.

Robertson, G. 2012 [2002]. *Crimes Against Humanity,* 4th ed. London: Penguin Books.

Rose, J. 2008. On the Myth of Self-Hatred. In *A Time to Speak Out: Independent Jewish Voices on Israel, Zionism and Jewish identity.* ed. A. Karpf, B. Klug, J. Rose, and B. Rosenbaum, 84–96. London: Verso.

Rose, J. 2011. Why Zionism Today Is the Real Enemy of the Jews. In *The Jacqueline Rose Reader,* ed. J. Clemens and B. Naparstek, 322–325. Durham and London: Duke University Press.

Rose, J. 2014. *Interview—Jacqueline Rose on Zionism, Freud, Sylvia Plath and More.* London Review of Books (LRB) Melbourne Writer's Festival. https://www.bing.com/videos/search?q=you+tube+jacqueline+rose&docid=608015 215655586429&mid=DBD2CDE33B45C2BB6512DBD2CDE33B45C2BB 6512&view=detail&FORM=VIRE. Accessed 9 August 2020.

Said, E. 1978 [2001]. The Question of Palestine. In *The Edward Said Reader,* ed. M. Bayoumi and A. Rubin. London: Granta.

Sand, S. 2014. *How I Stopped Being a Jew.* London: Verso.

Sands, P. 2006. *Lawless World.* London: Penguin.

Sands, P. 2008. *Torture Team.* London: Penguin.

Shackle, S. 2018. The Iraq Historic Allegations Team Was Set Up by the Government to Investigate Claims of the Abuse of Civilians. After Its Collapse, Some Fear the Truth Will Never Come Out. *The Guardian,* June 7.

Shirer, W. 1960. *The Rise and Fall of the Third Reich.* New York: Book Club edition.

Shklar, J.N. 1985. Nineteen Eighty-Four: Should Political Theory Care? *Political Theory* 13 (1): 5–18.

Shklar, J.N. 1998. *Political Thought and Political Thinkers*, ed. S. Kaufmann. Chicago: University of Chicago Press.

Sides, J., and K. Gross. 2013. Stereotypes of Muslims and Support for the War on Terror. *The Journal of Politics* 75 (3): 583–598.

Solicitors Regulation Authority v Day and others [2018] EWHC 2726. https://www.bailii.org/ew/cases/EWHC/Admin/2018/2726.html. Accessed 11 November 2020.

Steiner, G. 1984. *A Reader*, 245, 247. Oxford: Oxford University Press.

Strossen, N. 2018. *Hate: Why We Should Resist It with Free Speech, Not Censorship*. Oxford: Oxford University Press.

Summers, A., and R. Swan. 2011. *The Eleventh Day*. New York: Doubleday.

Thompson, E.P. 1980. *Writing by Candlelight*. London: ASIN.

Unger, R. 1977. *Law in Modern Society: Toward a Criticism of Social Theory*. New York: The Free Press.

Waldron, J. 2002. Is the Rule of Law an Essentially Contested Concept (In Florida)? In the Wake of Bush v. Gore: Law, Legitimacy and Judicial Ethics. *Law and Philosophy* 21 (2, March): 137–164.

Waldron, J. 2016. *The Rule of Law*. Stanford Encyclopedia of Philosophy. https://plato.stanford.edu/entries/rule-of-law/. Accessed 6 August 2020.

Warraq, I. 2017. *The Islam in Islamic Terrorism*. World Encounter Institute: New English Review Press.

Williams, A.T. 2012. *A Very British Killing*. London: Jonathan Cape.

CHAPTER 5

UK Counter-Terror Law, Surveillance and the "Muslim Menace"

INTRODUCTION

In this chapter, I focus on the UK's response to 9/11 and the development of pre-emptive counter-terrorism measures and enhanced surveillance in the context of "securitisation", and document the "slippage of emergency law into domestic UK governance" (Cochrane 2013: 30). The expansion of UK counter-terror law has created new precursor offences based on "indicators of suspicion" founded largely on racialised presumptions and esoteric "knowledges" about likely Muslim suspects. Many commentators argue that "Simply being a Muslim", or "looking like a Muslim" (Hage 2017) "or being a national of countries in the Middle East, is sufficient in most instances to qualify you as a suspect" (Breen-Smyth 2014: 232). In reviewing UK counter-terror measures and the "surveillance assemblage" I consider first, the increasing power of the government and the executive, who following 9/11 appropriated the future threat of Islamic terrorism in crafting new measures which eschewed the ROL and human rights, for all and for Muslims in particular.

In considering the burgeoning of counter-terror law, Foucault's theorisation on the hegemonic power of what he calls "governmentality" is relevant to understanding how executive power has become omnipotent and sovereign, whilst his theorisation on the "surveillance assemblage" is

© The Author(s), under exclusive license to Springer Nature Switzerland AG 2021
S. S. M. Edwards, *The Political Appropriation of the Muslim Body*, https://doi.org/10.1007/978-3-030-68896-7_5

useful in identifying the increasing role of surveillance in expanding the reach of state power over its subjects. Second, I review the tranche of pre-cursor offences which criminalise conduct (action and thought) considered an indicator of extremism, or a prelude to the planning of a terrorism offence. The 2020 Counter-Terrorism and Sentencing Bill (CTSB) takes that prelude moment back even further and criminalises accessing and looking at certain material in cyberspace considered "useful" to terrorism and introduces further measures to "monitor" and "disrupt" convicted terrorists and those "who are of terrorist concern" (see CTSB 2020). These proposed offences add to an existing regime of offences which include, crimes of association, membership of organisations proscribed by the executive, possession of articles and the even more fanciful offences of "thought crimes" all described by Cornford (2020: 664) as a "preventive turn in contemporary criminal law". These post 9/11 legal creations subsist within a framework of inconstancy where there is no agreed definition of terrorism, and no certainty regarding the parameters of individual offences where, for example, determination of the offence of "possession" of documents considered "useful" to terrorism, is left to be decided by an apprehensive and fearing jury, well-indoctrinated by public media hysteria and fake news about Muslims which may make, not for justice, but, for bigoted verdicts. Third, I focus on the decimation of due process norms and the Rule of Law in the trial process itself. It is here that we witness how counter-terrorism processes have legitimated the secret trial, an anathema to transparency, and openness, which has become an institutionalised feature of "justice" under the command of counter-terror law. Not surprisingly, judicial voices spurn such assaults on the edifice of justice. Lord Scott describes secret trials and secret evidence as "the stuff of nightmares" whilst some judges yield albeit reluctantly to executive crafted law (*PWR and others v Director of Public Prosecutions* [2020] see below). Fourth, I consider the enveloping and brooding omnipresence of "surveillance creep", where state power operates at the generic level authorising an ever-increasing mass surveillance, and at the specific level targets Muslim communities and their families. In this regard, Haggerty and Ericson's (2000) incisive appropriation of Foucault's theorisation of the "surveillance assemblage" is relevant, in examining for example, the perniciousness of the "Prevent" programme, described by some as a "toxic" brand since it is based on stereotyping and sophistry with its objective of detecting potential "extremism" and "radicalisation" and its project of reprogramming, whilst directing its reach into the Muslim community. I conclude with a consideration of the disproportionate impact of these measures on Muslim men and women and their communities.

"Governmentality"—Executive Creep and Securitisation

In a series of lectures, originally entitled "Security, Territory and Population" delivered in 1978 (Faubion 2000: 200), Foucault develops his thesis on "governmentality" in which he describes a process whereby the state and the government exercise power over its citizens though securitisation measures buttressed by justificatory ideologies promulgated through "arrogated knowledge" whilst suppressing counter-narratives of "subjugated knowledge". In Lecture One "Power and Knowledge", 1976, he identifies "arrogated knowledge" as that body of knowledge which claims to speak to truth and "subjugated knowledge", otherwise the dissident and silenced voice. In explaining "governmentality" Foucault says this:

> By this word I mean three things: 1. The ensemble formed by institutions procedures, analyses, and reflections, the exercise of this very specific albeit complex form of power, which has as its target population, as its principal form of knowledge, and as its essential technical means apparatuses of security... 2. The pre-eminence ...of this type of power-which may be termed 'government'-resulting,... in.... a series of governmental apparatuses... 3. The process ...through which the state of justice .... [becomes] transformed into the administrative state and... becomes 'governmentalised'. (Faubion: 219–220)

For Foucault, law has a privileged place in "governmentality" as an extension of the sovereign body.

Public compliance with, and support for, counter-terrorism strategy and law require nuancing such legal measures as necessary and proportionate. Necessity arguments are aided by maintaining a public state of fear and panic and a heightened public perception of risk about the likelihood of terrorist incidents and offences. In this propaganda the racialisation of likely suspects focuses on the threat from within the Muslim community (Mythen and Walklate 2006; Debrix and Barder 2009; Zempi and Awan (eds) 2019). Gheorghiu (2018) in British *and American Representations of 9/11* uses the term "Extreme Otherness:

The Muslim Menace", borrowed from Said (2003: xvi) in his preface to the third edition of *Orientalism*, to describe the representation of the Muslim subject. It is here, in what Hall, Chomsky, Said and others have referred to as the realm of the "discursive" that consent is anchored. Popular support for counter-terror measures can only be secured where the public, through rhetoric and propaganda (Chapters 2 and 3) is so persuaded.

In understanding the structure of this intensification of counter-terror law, Ericson (2007: 27) utilises Foucault's concept of "counter law" developed in *Discipline and Punish* (1977: 222). Ericson identifies within current legislative expansion two aspects of "counter-law". In what he calls "Counter-law 1" he identifies the emergence of new laws and procedures which derogate from human rights norms and erode the existing legal framework of safeguards for suspects, defendants and those convicted. Already we have seen how the human rights protections for those already convicted has been eroded. The Terrorist Offenders (Restriction of Early Release) Act 2020, (an act which extended the period of imprisonment for prisoners already serving terms for "terrorist offences") singled out for exceptionalist treatment all those serving sentences for terrorist offences, however minor. This was followed by the Counter-Terrorism and Sentencing Bill (CTSB) 2020 which extends prison terms for serious terrorism-related offences. In "Counter-law II", Ericson identifies the intensification of security measures, including surveillance, the use of biometric data, enhanced policing and the targeting of new "suspect" (Muslim) communities (2007: 27; Haggerty and Ericson 2000: 605). This twofold characterisation of "Counter law" provides the framework for analysis in this chapter of the decimation of law, lamented by Judge (2015: 129) who in referring to the UK, said that the "Rule of Law" (ROL) is now an outcast, by Gearty (2017) who said, "the era of human rights law has ended" and by Strawson who said that 9/11 had "turned law to ground zero" (cited in Banakar 2010: 211).

Derogating from Human Rights Protections

Foucault's concept of "governmentality" aptly describes the activities of the government executive (see Chapter 4), the Prime Minister, the Secretary of State for the Home Department (SSHD) and the Foreign Secretary, who, through delegated powers, wrest control justifying their unilateral decisions by deeming such "exceptionalist measures" necessary for national security. Lord Walker warning against the unbridled use of executive power said:

> ... [the] non-specific appeal to the interests of national security can be used as a cloak for arbitrary and oppressive action on the part of government. Whether or not patriotism is the last refuge of the scoundrel, national security can be the last refuge of the tyrant [193]. (*Secretary of State for the Home Department v LG and others* [2017])

In December 2019, Boris Johnson, in his *Queen's Speech*, took advantage of public security anxieties by proposing chilling changes to the constitution demonstrating this "executive creep", including, making senior judges more accountable to Parliament and the executive by removing their independence, introducing further exemptions to access private data for the security services, and by proposing further limits on the right to judicial review, which would of course prevent lawful challenges to state/executive power.

Following 9/11, the UK government on 14 December introduced the Anti-terrorism, Crime and Security Act 2001 (ATCSA) which authorised the Human Rights Act 1998 (Designated Derogation) Order 2001 (SI 2001/3644), otherwise known as "the Derogation Order". This was the first step in the domestic War on Terror (WOT) and the erosion of the ROL and human rights, that both Judge and Gearty feared. The derogation order permitted dispensing with human rights protections under the European Convention on Human Rights (ECHR) where there was a "public emergency threatening the life of the nation" or in "time of war". This power (Article 15(1)) to "derogate", can only be enforced if "strictly required by the exigencies of the situation" and is only permitted regarding certain specified convention rights. States cannot derogate from "non-derogable" rights. Non-derogable rights include freedom from torture (Article 3), forced labour (Article 4 (1)), punishment without legal process (Article 7) and the right to life (Article 2) "except in respect of deaths resulting from lawful acts of war". Of course, in the UK there was no public emergency threatening the life of the nation, nor was the country at war. The UK government executive did not agree, and on 13 November 2001, in a statutory instrument, set out its position:

> There exists a terrorist threat to the United Kingdom from persons suspected of involvement in international terrorism. In particular, there

are foreign nationals present in the United Kingdom who are suspected of being concerned in the commission, preparation, or instigation of acts of international terrorism, of being members of organisations or groups which are so concerned or of having links with members of such organisations or groups, and who are a threat to the national security of the United Kingdom. (cited in *A and others v Secretary of State for the Home Department* [2004] [11])

This decimation of long established and cherished human rights was fiercely contested. Human Rights Watch, in a Briefing Paper (2004) said that it doubted that the threat to the United Kingdom since 9/11 had met the high threshold for "a public emergency" required by Article 15. This contested decimation was the subject of judicial comment in an appeal to the House of Lords, in the case of *A and others v Secretary of State for the Home Department* [2004] (the "Belmarsh" case) which involved Muslim foreign nationals who had been imprisoned from 2001 without charge, without trial and without any prospect of release. This exceptional and extraordinary detention had been authorised under s 23 of the ATCSA, which provided: "(1) A suspected international terrorist may be detained under a provision specified in subsection (2) [liable to examination or removal] despite the fact that his removal or departure from the United Kingdom is prevented (whether temporarily or indefinitely) by (a) a point of law which wholly or partly relates to an international agreement, or (b) a practical consideration". Imprisoned (already for four years) the "Belmarsh detainees" contended that there was no emergency threatening the life of the nation, nor war and therefore suspension of their due process rights, and subsequent detention was not justified. The House of Lords ruled that s 23 was incompatible with their human rights to liberty| (Article 5) and fair trial (Article 6) and struck down this part of the Act effecting their immediate release. Lord Scott, had this to say on executive power:

It is certainly true that the judiciary must in general defer to the executive's assessment of what constitutes a threat to national security or to the life of the nation. But judicial memories are no shorter than those of the public and the public have not forgotten the faulty intelligence assessments on the basis of which United Kingdom forces were sent to take part, and are still taking part, in the hostilities in Iraq. But I do have very great doubts whether the 'public emergency' is one that justifies the description of 'threatening the life of the nation'. Nonetheless, I would, for my part, be prepared to allow the Secretary of State the benefit of the doubt on this point and accept that the threshold criterion of article 15 is satisfied. 'To the extent strictly required by the exigencies of the situation'. [154]

Lord Rodger said: "... judges must be intended to do more than simply rubber-stamp the decisions taken by ministers and Parliament [164] .... The legitimacy of the courts' scrutiny role cannot be in doubt [176]". Lord Hoffman went much further in remonstrating this use of executive power.

> The real threat to the life of the nation, in the sense of a people living in accordance with its traditional laws and political values, comes not from terrorism but from laws such as these. [97]

Winston Churchill, when Prime Minister (1940–1945) said: "The power of the executive to cast a man into prison without formulating any charge known to the law, and particularly to deny him the judgment of his peers, is in the highest degree odious, and the foundation of all totalitarian government whether Nazi or Communist" (quoted in Césaire 1955: 36).

Elliott (2006) in reviewing this and other decisions berates what he regards as a highly deferential approach of the courts to the executive when matters of national security are said to be at stake and mindful of the danger of executive power, he calls for the urgent need to constitutionally secure the judiciary's role as guardian of fundamental rights lest judges be subject to "the whims of a sovereign legislature". This fear is even more prescient given Boris Johnson's wish list changes in his *Queen's Speech* (above).

Counter-Terror Law's Offences

Terrorism an Ill-Defined Muslim Assumed Crime

Following 9/11, the UN Security Council Resolution 1373, of 28 September 2001, required States to ensure that: "terrorist acts are established as serious criminal offences in domestic laws and regulations and that the punishment duly reflects the seriousness of such terrorist acts". Whilst the UN resolution stated that, "any act" of international terrorism constitutes a threat to international peace and security and requires member states to combat terrorism by "all means" no agreed definition of "international terrorism" or "terrorism" was provided. Dame

Rosalyn Higgins, former judge at the International Court of Justice (ICJ), expressed concern: "Terrorism is a term without any legal significance. It is merely a convenient way of alluding to activities, which States, or individuals widely disapproved of" (Higgins 1997: 14, 28). Gilbert Guillame, former ICJ President remarking on its nebulousness said: "What is perhaps most revealing about this global fight is that despite the plethora of domestic anti-terror legislation passed by member states since Resolution 1373, the international community is still nowhere further in agreeing a definition of 'terrorism'" (cited in Muller 2008: 113). This situation remains.

Such imprecision undermines one of ROL's overriding tenets which requires, as Bingham (2011) has constantly reminded, that a legal rule should be certain (38) and transparent (111, 171). Such uncertainty regarding the meaning of "terrorism" has permitted a wide application of law, police powers, investigatory processes, surveillance and disproportionate targeting of Muslim communities (Hargreaves 2018) and facilitated capricious and racialised (Muslim) indicators of extremism as evidence of criminality. Gearty (2017) has warned that the definition of "terrorism" in s 1(1) of the Terrorism Act 2000 is far wider than is popularly assumed.

Loosely drafted legislation has extended the reach of criminalisation to those with doubtful or tenuous links to terrorism defined activity by including, those "associated with terrorism"—the nomenclature used in the Terrorism Act (TA) 2000, and then later, persons "concerned in" terrorism—the language of ATCSA 2001 s 21 (2), and later again, those with a "connection with terrorism"—the language of the Counter-Terrorism Act (CTA) 2008 s 30. By 2019, the Counter-Terrorism and Border Security Act (CTBSA) used the terminology of "concerned with terrorism". As D'Souza-Lodhi in observing how the "suspect community" is identified writes: "'Terrorist'. Prior to 9/11 it was a descriptor for someone's activities; a person who terrorizes. Post 9/11, the word terrorist only meant Muslim; it had become a racialized term" (in Khan 2020: 117).

Then there is the much-used word "extremism" although not found, nor defined within government policy, nor in the so-called "deradicalisation" programmes, nor in the original "Prevent" strategy guidance. Vague, nebulous, lacking in definition and application, by 2019, when the revised "Prevent guidance" (Revised Prevent Duty Guidance for England and Wales, originally issued in 2015 revised on 16 July 2015 and April

2019) the meaning of "extremism" had simply spilt over and become elided with "opposition". The guidance defined it as:

> ... vocal or active opposition to fundamental British values, including democracy, the rule of law, individual liberty and mutual respect and tolerance of different faiths and beliefs. We also include in our definition of extremism calls for the death of members of our armed forces." 'Radicalisation' is another overused term and without statutory definition. In the revised Prevent strategy guidance it is described as 'the process by which a person comes to support terrorism and extremist ideologies associated with terrorist groups'. (para 7 2019)

Kundnani had already expressed his fears that the test of "extremism" involves: those who are critical of foreign policy (166), or resisted Israel's blockade of Gaza (167), or questioned troops in Afghanistan (as did Salma Yaqoob) which has the effect of "denying legitimacy of democratic opposition to government foreign policy from Muslims" (cited in Kundnani 2015: 167). The latest addition to this battery of criminal pre-cursor offences found in the CTSB 2020 will only further encourage already existent racist stereotyping and criminalising of Muslim communities (see also Pantazis and Pemberton 2009). This new trajectory in crime prevention is what Ericson (2007: 25) has identified as "criminalization based on precautionary logic" which has led to flawed intelligence, and conclusions based on Predictive Analytics programmes.

There is also a further problem in the expansion in executive discretion, already charted above, which in this counter-terrorism strategy spills over into determining new offences and those who are the likely offenders. In this regard creeping governmentalisation has conferred on government officials, especially the executive, arbitrary discretionary decision-making powers in respect of several offences including, for example, the proscription of organisations, widened police surveillance and charging discretion, and also authorised a wider discretion for prosecutors. Richard Jackson (2004) considers such ill-defined language and widening of power deliberate and politically orchestrated to enable the broadest reach of counter-terrorism law. This widening of criminalisation is furthered in the CTSB 2020 which lowers the criminal standard of proof for some offences including "Terrorism prevention and investigation measures" (TPIMS) where the standard of proof "on the balance of probabilities" is replaced with the lower threshold of "reasonable grounds for suspecting" which is vulnerable to a wide construction. The enveloping intrusion of counter-terror law creates new offences and undermines procedural safeguards (see Greer 2018; Lennon et al. 2018; Walker 2018). As Pantazis and Pemberton (2009: 653) noted "The fixing of Muslim communities rather than individual suspects within the gaze of counter-terrorist policing is underpinned by the discretionary nature of the powers contained in the Terrorism Act".

Indicators of Suspicion

Counter-terrorism law in a preventive turn determines what activities are likely preludes to terrorism and turns these proems into criminal offences (see McCulloch and Pickering 2009). In the absence of clear definitions and certainty and in circumstances of heightened anxiety of the fear of Islamic terrorist attack, the Muslim community en masse is under constant suspicion. Presumptions about who is likely to engage in terrorist activity are founded on what police call "intelligence" and there is a justifiable concern as experience has shown that such intelligence about crime in general has in the past drawn on racialised criminalising of minority ethnic communities. The MacPherson Report of the *Stephen Lawrence Inquiry* (1999) found that racism against black people was institutionalised throughout the criminal justice system. The *Lammy Review* (2017) reported that the disproportionate representation of BAME's in the criminal justice process, continued. The government's *Tackling Racial Disparity in the Criminal Justice System: 2020* response to the Lammy Review, intended to update progress into the treatment of, and outcomes for, BAME's in the criminal justice system, notably lacked any appreciation or critique of the racial profiling of the Muslim community in respect of counter-terror legislation and surveillance. Pantazis and Pemberton (2009) and others have identified Muslims as the new suspect community. Hall (1992) had already identified Muslims as a racialised group, where, following 9/11 especially, their racialisation had become a habituated reality. This was reflected in their treatment through all social, cultural and legal institutions, whether in the treatment of foreign nationals, or over-surveillance of Muslims in their places of worship, their streets, and communities, or the denigration of Muslim women by politicians. In this regard the application for judicial review brought by Mohammed Zahir Khan (*R (Khan) v Secretary of State for Justice* [2020]) on the grounds that the Terrorist Offenders (Restriction of Early Release) Act 2020 is discriminating against Muslims (although refused by the court) provides further evidence of the extent of discrimination.

Fear around the Covert Human Intelligence Sources (Criminal Conduct) Bill 2020 has revealed a world of undercover covert activity not only by M15 and M16 but police infiltration of particular interest groups especially those exercising their right to "core political speech" including Stop the War Coalition, Greenpeace, Black lives matter, Climate rebellion, trade unions, asylum charities, political activists, student activists, supporters of Palestine. James Brokenshire, the Minister for Security in moving the Bill said, "This legislation is being introduced to keep our country safe and to ensure that our operational agencies and public authorities have access to the tools and intelligence that they need to keep us safe—safe from terrorists, safe from serious organised crime groups, and safe from others who wish to cause harm to our country and our citizens". The concerns of those who fear that there will be no judicial oversight and that without these essential checks and balances such law and surveillance will disproportionally affect BAME and especially Muslim communities is very real.

The Crime of Membership of an Organisation and Executive Discretion

The Terrorism Act (TA) 2000 had already commenced the "creative" tendency to criminalise what was considered potential activity that may be a pre-cursor to later terror offences and criminalised what the government deemed to be an indicator of "extremism" including, limiting particular association, and membership of particular organisations. Under the act the executive has the wide discretionary power to impose a "proscription order" where "it" considers an organisation is "inimical to national interest" (s 3). Whilst Parliamentary assent must be sought by the Home Secretary before any such order is made, since the information on which the Home Secretary proposes to make the order cannot be disclosed, assent is given and in effect rubber stamped. No one would doubt that ISIS, Al-Qaeda, Daesh, al Muhajiroun, are rightly banned, but the lack of transparency regarding how these decisions are made, and the fact that the shadow foreign secretary and the Opposition do not have access to the same intelligence as the Home Secretary and the Minister undermines the ability to make any effective legal challenge and is therefore of concern. In July 2020, there were 76 international terrorist organisations proscribed by the UK government, controversially this list included organisations that resist tyrannical regimes, those that represent different sides locked in civil war, and those who have political Parliamentary representation in other countries. For this reason, Muller (2008), Bowring (2010) and Walsh (2018: 37), have argued that the proscription decision is a political act which has been extended beyond banning armed terrorist organisations to include political groups and dissenters. Lord Avebury in a House of Lords debate, on the introduction of the proscription order, when originally proposed, said, such a law would mean that:

> any armed opposition group or anybody who supports an armed opposition group in whatever country.... including repressive regimes... is ipso facto a terrorist and that under the Terrorism Act Nelson Mandela and the Zimbabwean (post-1980) and East Timorese (post-1975) resistance movements would have been considered 'terrorist'. (Lord Avebury Terrorism Act 2000, Home Office press statement 28.3.01)

Whilst this executive power to proscribe is subject to review by the courts, Jarvis and Legrand (2020) point out that by 2020 only four organisations had been successful in challenging the ban following appeal to the Proscribed Organisation Appeal Committee (POAC). This included Mujaheddin e Khalq in 2008, International Sikh Federation (ISYF) in 2016, and Hezb-e-Islami Gulbuddin (HIG) an Afghan political party in 2017 and in 2019 the Libyan Islamic Fighting Group (LIFG). Mujaheddin e Khalq (MeK) aka Peoples' Mujaheddin of Iran (PMOI) was successfully removed from the list in June 2008 following a decision of the Court of Appeal to uphold the decision of the POAC that had found the proscription of the (PMOI) unlawful, and the decision of the Home Secretary legally "perverse". The impact of proscription is wide, it suspends the right of association (ECHR Article 11) and the right of freedom of speech (Article 10). Lord Corbett, chairman of the British Parliamentary Committee for Iran Freedom, after the ruling said: "I now invite the former home secretary and foreign secretary, Jack Straw, to apologise for the hurt and harm he has done to the Iranian resistance by his supine agreement to the demands of the mullahs. Today's decision signals that the Iranian resistance—demonised, vilified, unjustly labelled terrorist—wants no more than to help the people of Iran to rid themselves of the misrule of the mullahs" (*The Guardian*, 1 December 2007 "Government ordered to end 'perverse' terror listing of Iran opposition"). There was no apology.

In February 2019, the political wing of Hezbollah was added to the list. Sajid Javid, Secretary of State, said "'Hezbollah' [is] continuing in its attempts to destabilise the fragile situation in the Middle East". This description is "echo chambered" by the UK media, and Google adds that Hezbollah's aim is to "destroy Israel". Hezbollah, which currently holds twelve seats in the Lebanese Parliament assert that their only purpose is to reclaim occupied Lebanese territory and restore it to the Lebanese people. That these lists of proscribed organisations are politically constructed is further illustrated by a recent UN Security Council and EU Court of Justice dispute over the PKK. The case of the PKK (Kurdistan Workers' Party) (2018) demonstrates Bowring and Muller's thesis that proscription is politically motivated (Bowring 2010: 249). In 2017–2018, the EU Court of Justice in the case of *Kurdistan Workers' Party (PKK) v Council of the European Union*, and the Belgium Court of Cassation/Appeals Court in the case of *Kurdistan Workers' Party PKK* (2019) deproscribed the PKK. Jarvis and Legrand (2018: 206) unravel the political motivation behind the original proscription. "In Turkey, for example, membership offences have been used as a means of suppressing domestic dissent and support for Kurdish separatism in which Kurds are ... 'routinely' prosecuted for crimes connected to the PKK or membership of the PKK on often spurious evidence". Since the PKK is not merely an organisation in opposition to the government, but one of the factions in a civil war, the Court found that counter-terrorism legislation was not applicable and held that the law of war and international humanitarian law applied in interpreting article 141 bis Criminal Code, which asserts that stipulations of terrorist crimes do not apply to "actions of armed forces during an armed conflict as defined and subject to international humanitarian law". The Court held that the PKK was a party in a non-international armed conflict with the Turkish State and the terrorism provisions of the Belgian Criminal Code did not apply. However, the Belgium government's foreign minister, Philippe Goffin, continues to rebut its own court and has said that the PKK is a terrorist organisation.

By 2019, the CTBSA further extended the pre-emptive power of the proscription regime, making it a crime for a person who "(1)(a) is supportive of a proscribed organisation, and (b) in doing so is reckless as to whether a person to whom the expression is directed will be encouraged to support a proscribed organisation". This expansion makes no mention of membership, instead the trigger for legal intervention is much lower and merely "supportive of" is sufficient to criminalise a person who may be named by the defendant in a defence statement, for example, "my lecturer encouraged me to consider the political aspect of proscription orders". Whilst the decision in R *v Choudary (Anjem) and another (No 2)* [2016], held that: "[15] the criminality lies in inviting support and the invitation must be made knowingly" [46, 70], the court in *PWR and others v Director of Public Prosecutions* [2020], held that such an act need not be intentional. In this case, in interpreting s 13 TA (as amended) the court held that the act of holding a flag and supporting the PKK creates the risk that others might be encouraged to support a UK proscribed organisation, and "whether or not he intends to do so or knows that he is doing so, is guilty of the offence [61]". The court, made no attempt to limit the wide reach of the legislation, stating: "I am satisfied that Parliament clearly intended by section 13 to create an offence which does not require mens rea, and it is not open to the court to interpret the section as if it had been drafted in different terms". This dictum suggests—that's the law and that's that! Walsh (2018: 39) and others, have expressed a concern that this decision will have a constraining effect on freedom of expression and association. Such constraints on expression are indeed the very problem Strossen (2018) (see Chapter 3) feared, when she critiqued the power of law to ban "core political speech".

The Crime of Possession and "Glorification"

Possession of articles which give rise to a "reasonable suspicion" that possession is for a purpose connected with the commission, preparation or instigation of an act of terrorism (s 57 (1) TA), or possessing a document or record containing information of that kind (s 58(1)) are part of this new panoply where purpose is read in and assumed by the act of possession. In the case of *R v F* [2007] the defendant, who had fled from Libya, was granted asylum in United Kingdom. He was found to have in his possession a copy of an Al-Qaeda training manual, a text about Jihad movements, and a text about the duty of a Muslim to work for Islamic state. He was convicted of offences under s 58. Whilst his appeal was dismissed, Lord Judge, in delivering the judgment of the court, expressed concern over the potential ambit of this section.

(9) ... as a matter of historical knowledge, many of those whose violent activities in support of national independence or freedom from oppression, who were once described as terrorists, are now honoured as 'freedom fighters'. Others, who continued to use violence to maintain resistance to national enslavement by invading forces, after the official surrender by their own governments, are regarded as heroes and heroines. Those who died in these causes were 'martyrs' for them. Indeed, we can look about the world today and identify former 'terrorists' who are treated as respected, and in one case at least, an internationally revered statesman. In many countries statues have been erected to celebrate the memory of those who have died in the course of, or have been executed as a result of, their violent activities, but who in time have come to be identified as men and women who died for the freedom and liberty of their countries or their consciences!

Suspect Muslims Who "Glorify"

By 2006, criminalising pre-emptive conduct under the broad rubric of "encouragement" (TA 2006 s1 (1) (2)), resulted in the government, designing a new bespoke offence which it called "glorification of terrorist activity" (s 1 (3) (a) 2006). This took the imagination of offence construction to new heights. "Glorification" like the word "terrorism" or "terrorist activity" was not defined, although it has certain theological resonances. Contested debates about its meaning, not surprisingly prolonged the passage of the bill (15 February 2006 col 1427 "Terrorism Bill (Programme) (No. 3)"). The object of the provision was to criminalise conduct and thoughts inclined to support terrorism. Hugely subjective, it might include tapping the "like" button on a Twitter feed regarding the action of a particular group or an innocent remark made. Since the Council of Europe Convention on the Prevention of Terrorism (2005) required member states to consider laws to deal with public provocation of acts of terrorism which must be "intentional", this provision contumaciously departed by introducing a lower threshold of strict liability.

Would "glorification" for example include Cheri Blair's speech, when in June 2002 (18 June *BBC News*) at the launch of a charity appeal for Medical Aid for Palestinians, she said of the suicide bomber who killed himself, 19 others, and injured 72 in an attack on a bus in Jerusalem: "As long as young people feel they have got no hope but to blow themselves up you are never going to make progress". Would "glorification" include the words of Carol Tonge? (Member of the European

Parliament) who, following her visit to Gaza in 2003, and distressed by what she saw, said: "You are almost getting a situation like the Warsaw ghetto. People can't get in or out. They can't work, they can't sell anything. There is this gradual squeeze.... It was an apartheid system". She recommended economic sanctions be applied against Israel and for the European Union or United Nations troops to be sent to Gaza. At a pro-Palestinian parliamentary meeting, she said of Palestinian suicide bombers: "If I had to live in that situation – and I say that advisedly – I might just consider becoming one myself...I do not condone suicide bombers, nobody can condone them" (*The Guardian*, 19 June 2003). Would it include the remarks made by ultra-Orthodox Yehuda Shaul, who said "No one returns from the territories [Gaza] without messing up his head" (cited in Rose 2011: 209). Would it include Susan Sontag's essay responding to 9/11, published in *The New Yorker* (24 September 2001) where she wrote "Where is the acknowledgement that this was not a 'cowardly' attack on 'civilization' or 'liberty 'or 'humanity' or 'the free world' but an attack on the world's self-proclaimed super-power, undertaken as a consequence of specific American alliances and actions?"

The danger of this broad discretion allows for governmentality's power to exact its prosecutorial might on "suspect communities" and on any opinion considered inimical to state interests, whatever that may be considered to amount to. Samina Malik was the first woman to be charged under terrorism legislation considered to have engaged in glorification.

Suspect Muslim Women

Samina Malik, bored with her job as a sales assistant at Smith's Heathrow Airport, posted material on the internet and scribbled notes on the back of till receipts, such jottings included: "The desire within me increases every day to go for martyrdom, the need to go increases second by second .... Kafir's your time will come soon.... no one will save you from your doom.... Raising Mujahideen [holy fighter] children.... Show the children videos and pictures of mujahideen and tell them to become strong like them". The police found in her bedroom material downloaded from the internet on how to make bombs and an encyclopaedia on Jihad. She styled herself, as "the lyrical terrorist" because she said she thought it "cool". Acquitted of a charge under s 57 (1) in that it could not be established that her possession of these articles was for the purpose of "the commission, preparation or instigation of an act of terrorism" she was convicted an offence under s 58 with its lower threshold of "likely to be useful" of "possession of material likely to be useful to committing or preparing an act of terrorism". It is not difficult to envisage how a jury fed by anti-Muslim propaganda and especially the publicity around female terrorist suspects (who were considered not only unusual and having deviated from conventional gender and cultural norms but doubly deviant and doubly dangerous), would, in a heightened state of panic and fear, believe that this kind of web surfing posed a threat. (It is to be noted that the CTSB 2020 proposes to criminalise the mere looking at such material which no doubt state surveillance capability authorised under the Regulation of Investigatory Powers Act 2000 (RIPA) will facilitate.) The judge handed down a suspended prison sentence although Malik had already spent five months in prison on remand, bail having been refused. Again, the heightened concerns over Muslim women's involvement in terrorist-related offences may have exercised a harsher discretion. On 17 June 2008, the Court of Appeal quashed her conviction (*R v Malik* [2008]) following the earlier decision in *R v K* [2008], where the court ruled that propagandist or theological material, no matter how extreme could not be considered of practical use to terrorists. The problem, said Lord Phillips, was that a decision about whether the material was of practical utility had been left to the jury [34]. Whether documents are "likely to be useful" is certainly a bafflingly question for the jury. How do they know? and how can they judge? Samina Malik was certainly not lyrical, nor a terrorist, in fact she was so very banally ordinary. When interviewed by police she made "no comment" but in her handwritten notes, written whilst in custody, she explained that she wanted to move on with her life and become a housewife. Subsequent case law in trying to more clearly define "glorification" have merely extended its scope. In *R v Faraz* [2013], "glorification" was defined to "include[s] any form of praise or celebration" adding "and cognate expressions are to be construed accordingly".

In 2014, Runa Khan's (*R v Khan* [2015]) sentence of five years imprisonment was upheld on appeal, in respect of four charges of dissemination of terrorist publications. She had posted four messages on Facebook including those of her children and a picture of a suicide vest. One post read: "Dear sisters if you love your sons, your husbands and your brothers prove it by sending them to fight for the sake of Allah", another post contained a route to Syria, and in another she re-posted an article: "Sisters role in Jihad off the battlefield" and another read "Raising

Mujahid Children" which said that mothers should show their children military books, CDs and videos to children "as young as a couple of years or even younger". These posts were circulated to 241 Facebook contacts. In her defence, it was said that none of those who received what she had posted had been "encouraged". Like Malik, women's involvement in such activity resulted in extremely wide and sensationalist media reporting feeding the panic about terrorism and about women's potential involvement.

SECRET EVIDENCE AND SECRET TRIALS

In addition to these new offences the counter-terror strategy introduced, for some suspects/defendants, a parallel system of "justice" of secret evidence and secret trials suspending due process norms of transparency and openness and, under some circumstances, the right to hear, test and challenge prosecution evidence. Kafka's (1994 [1925]) parable of the trial process and secrecy in a totalitarian society, is presented in a nightmare sequence and serves as a chilling parallel. Josef K, the central character is an ordinary citizen, perhaps even too ordinary, a bank cashier, who finds himself unexpectedly arrested for an unspecified crime that he knows nothing about and did not commit. There are resonances with the experience of Patrick Conlon of the Guildford Four, convicted for the IRA pub bombing in Guildford in 1974 (following extracted confessions and flawed forensic evidence) who, upon his release in 1989 after his conviction and that of the three others was quashed, came out of the Central Criminal Court to a crowd of supporters, uttering as his very first words: "I was convicted for something I did not do, for something I knew nothing about". As for Josef K, those who arrested him are unidentified agents from an unspecified agency. He is put on trial, but the evidence against him is never disclosed. Joseph is finally murdered, butchered in a gruesome way by his accusers and whilst they kill him, he is aware that he was expected to kill himself. Lord Archer of Sandwell in the House of Lords debate, 27 March 2001, on the TA 2000 (Proscribed Organisations) (Amendment) Order 2001, said: "there is something distasteful about a process which begins by convicting someone and then proceeds to inquire whether there is a case against them" (col 151).

As Ní Aoláin (2018: 117) notes, the empty abstraction and fear of terrorism flouts due process norms especially where derogation measures (discussed above) include the admissibility of closed material contrary to

ECHR Article 5, right to liberty and Article 6, right to fair trial. Such closed procedures derogate from open justice, where special advocates do not act for the parties they represent, nor owe them a duty of care (Jackson 2018: 100). Such procedures were hitherto unknown within the criminal law.

Secrets and Trials: "The Stuff of Nightmares"

The Special Immigration Appeals Commission (SIAC) created under the Special Immigration Appeals Commission Act 1997 (amended ATCSA 2001) introduced the role of Special Advocates, "security cleared lawyers" for cases involving "security classified materials". Of these secret hearings there was much criticism (see SIAC Report 2004–2005). Gareth Peirce, solicitor and human rights activist, said: "I am baffled as to why it was ever considered necessary [...] it has been a disaster... for our whole system of criminal justice" (SIAC Report 2004–2005: 15). Nine of the 13 Special Advocates in 2004–2005 disapproved of the system albeit they participated in it (17). One former Special Advocate, Ian MacDonald, felt his participation gave a "fig-leaf of respectability and legitimacy to a process which [he] found odious" and following the House of Lords judgment of December 2004 in "the Belmarsh case" he resigned (17). In response to the unlawful detention of the Belmarsh detainees, on 16 December 2004, in *A and others v Secretary of State for the Home Department* [2004] Lord Scott said of this secrecy:

> The grounds can be made known to a special advocate appointed to represent him, but the special advocate may not inform him of the grounds and, therefore, cannot take instructions from him in refutation of the allegations made against him. Indefinite imprisonment in consequence of a denunciation on grounds that are not disclosed and made by a person whose identity cannot be disclosed is the stuff of nightmares, associated whether accurately or inaccurately with France before and during the Revolution, with Soviet Russia in the Stalinist era and now associated, as a result of section 23 of the 2001 Act, with the United Kingdom. ([155])

The Punishment of Internal Curfew and External Exile

After the release of the Belmarsh detainees, the executive on 11 March 2005, introduced yet another addition to the dysfunctional family of counter-terror law in the Prevention of Terrorism Act 2005 (PTA), with its pre-emptive weapon of the "the control order" à la imprisonment in one's home without trial, extending the reach of "governmentality" through management and surveillance outside the public system into the private domain. (This order is currently being restyled under the CTSO Bill 2020.) Sydney Kentridge described the control order as "house arrest" (Kentridge 2014: 157), and as the lawyer, in 1975, acting for Steve Biko in South Africa (Biko was on trial for sedition!) Kentridge knows well what house arrest is, and what it means. This offence turns on the ill-defined phrase "terrorist related activity". These orders are virtually impossible to challenge as the "controlee" is not to know the evidence against him and therefore is unable to rebut it. Such orders originally operative for six months could be renewed "on as many occasions as the court thinks fit" sanctioned house arrest/home lockdown for a period of eighteen hours each day, reduced later to fourteen hours (see *Secretary of State for the Home Department v MB: Secretary of State for the Home Department v AF* [2007]). In 2011, following unremitting litigation in the courts, control orders were replaced by "TPims orders" (Terrorism Prevention and Investigatory Measures Act, TPIMA 2011) which require a higher evidential threshold of suspicion before being imposed. Bespoke conditions include tagging, an overnight residence requirement, restrictions on whom the subject can meet and where they can go, including foreign travel bans and relocation. Those under TPIMs orders are often separated from their families and children. The TPIMs order is now limited to two years and the conditions imposed are reviewable. The plea of those placed under such orders has been to charge them so the evidence can be seen, heard and tested. On this point s 10 requires the Secretary of State to consult with police as to whether there is evidence which could lead to a successful prosecution. It must be concluded then that for those under a TPIM order there is no such evidence.

Further pre-emptive counter-terrorism measures restrict movement where passport and travel documents can be seized, and travel bans to other countries imposed, extending the web of control in managing risk. For those who have left the country and wish to return (the Shakil case) and the Shamima Begum case (see Chapter 2) the 2015 Act introduced "temporary exclusion orders" (ss 2–4), permitting return only by authorisation of the Secretary of State (ss 5–8). The Secretary of State has used this power in preventing Shamima Begum's return. On 16 July 2020, the Court of Appeal overturned this decision and has permitted Begum's return but solely for the purpose of exercising her right to appeal the Home Secretary's original order of permanent exclusion. Lord Justice Flaux said:

> With due respect to SIAC (the Special Immigration Appeals Commission), it is unthinkable that, having concluded that Ms Begum could not take any meaningful part in her appeal so that it could not be fair and effective, she should have to continue with her appeal nonetheless... It is difficult to conceive of any case where a court or tribunal has said we cannot hold a fair trial, but we are going to go on anyway.

The approach to the legality of exile is divided. Max Hill QC currently DPP (when the Independent Reviewer of Terrorism Legislation), insisted we should be looking towards reintegration of those who joined ISIS and wish to return. Former Attorney General, Dominic Grieve QC MP, said:

> it is a fundamental principle of the common law in this country than an individual, unconvicted – the presumption of innocence applies – should be free to reside in his own land. The principle of exile, as a judicial or even administrative tool, has not been tolerated in this country since the late 17th century...what is proposed, even if exclusion is on a temporary basis, is a draconian and unusual power being taken by the State. The point has been made that the proposal could be in breach of our international legal obligations by rendering a person stateless. (Hansard, 2 December 2014: Col 228)

Shamima Begum, following the Supreme Court decision of February 26 2021, has not been allowed to return. Do these counter-terror measures improve securitisation? since that was, after all, their avowed intention, or do they merely discipline and punish? Cornford (2020: 685) considers that the pre-cursor offences contribute little or nothing to the threat of terrorist attack and in fact risk catching conduct that is innocent, concluding that judges have failed to limit the ambit of this unruly horse of counter-terrorism law. Meanwhile these laws, policies and procedural measures have impacted disproportionately on the "suspect" Muslim community.

"SURVEILLANT ASSEMBLAGE", "SUSPECT COMMUNITIES" AND "PREVENT CREEP"

Haggerty and Ericson's (2000) construct of "Counter-terror II" is useful to describe the expansion of surveillance in the wider counter-terror programme, characterised by a burgeoning technology of state surveillance systems, increased police and border security and local authority powers, in what Foucault called the "surveillant assemblage". The "surveillant assemblage" said to be intended to manage risk, and here the risk of terrorism, engages on the one hand in generic mass surveillance of public streets, cities, places, people and countries, whilst at the same time targets "suspect communities" who are marked out for a higher degree of monitoring and differential surveillance, for example in the proposed "Project Champion" in 2010 (a CCTV project to spy on Birmingham, Sparkbrook's community) and in the "Prevent" programme (with its suspecting Muslim overtones) which devolved surveillance responsibilities across all public and private institutions. Increased surveillance on the streets, on the internet and in the home, together with setting parameters and boundaries of permissible speech and ideas are all part of the government's preventive measures. There are two aspects to consider in this "surveillance assemblage", the first is the generic surveillance of us all, the second is the specific targeting and surveillance of Muslims who have been racialised as "suspect communities".

General Surveillance

The official justification for increased overt and covert surveillance is to protect the public against the terrorist threat, "Politically and rhetorically, securing against threat is the primary rationale for state surveillance" (Richardson 2016). By June 2020, former President Trump's aim was to make further amendments to the US Patriot Act 2006 to permit the National Security Agency (NSA) not merely to spy on its citizens but to watch what they were doing and have access to everyone's browsing history. Edward Snowden's revelations (2019) exposed the extent of US state intrusion. A former employee of the NSA, turned whistle-blower, he publicised the extent of government snooping, documenting routine disclosures where telephone companies provided the NSA with private records and where the "Prism" programme had access to private individuals use of Google, Facebook and Microsoft. This also turned out to be the paradigm of UK surveillance. Snowden's disclosures revealed that the UK, Government Communications Headquarters (GCHQ) was working closely with the US in a programme called "Tempora" where the programme "Xkeyscore" could search everything anyone does on internet, and the "Dishfire" programme could intercept text messages. The UK "Parliamentary Intelligence and Security Committee" (2015), in its review of the range of intrusive capabilities available to the UK intelligence agencies (*Privacy and Security: A modern and transparent legal framework*) confirmed that security agencies were indeed trawling bulk metadata. David Anderson, the Independent Reviewer of Terrorism Legislation in his *Report of the Bulk Powers Review* (2016: 1, 95) commenting on the extent of political involvement, considered the expansion of executive power and increased surveillance justified and necessary to protect national security. In 2016, the Investigatory Powers Act, said to have been introduced with the intended aim of providing transparency on the extent of state surveillance, was said by its critics to make legal the very illegalities that Snowden had exposed. In *Big Brother Watch & Ors v United Kingdom* [2018], 14 non-governmental organisations and other individuals brought an action in the ECtHR following the Snowden disclosures. The court found that the UK's legislative regime for external surveillance under the Regulation of Investigatory Powers Act 2000 (RIPA) was incompatible with Article 8, right to privacy and Article 10, right to freedom of speech. Further challenges were brought against the UK government in *R (on the application of National Council for Civil Liberties (Liberty) v Secretary of State for the Home Department and another (National Union of Journalists intervening)* [2019]), when Liberty brought an application in judicial review contending that the minimum safeguards for secret surveillance and bulk hacking had not been met. The court was not persuaded by Liberty's case and refused leave for judicial review. Exceptionalist justifications and the threat of terrorism constituted the arguments made on behalf of the government, in line with Anderson's conclusions. This decision is currently being appealed to the ECtHR. In October 2020, the ECJ, following a case brought by *Privacy Internationale*, imposed restrictions on state snooping especially the retention of phone and internet data, currently companies can retain such data for up to 12 months and also access where surfers have been on the web (Internet Connection Record) without authorisation. E.P. Thompson (1980), writing on state secrecy, identified the heightened level of surveillance to which dissent groups particularly were subjected then, and has a prophetic contemporary ring.

> ...the operators of the British security services are 'some of the most secret and arrogant' to be found in modern bureaucratic states.... I am insisting upon a peculiar combination of invisibility, lack of accountability, and the consequent composure of an antique ruling group which has been bred to govern from behind a wall of silence' (151)... It would amaze many British citizens to learn that these and other organiations are only at the end of a long historical line of ruling—class institutions, with agents or informants in trade unions, educational institutes, and political organisations (especially of the Left), and with direct access to the postal and telephone systems of the country; that they are larger and more powerful, and less subject to ministerial or parliamentary control than they have ever been; and that a large part of their function has always been to invigilate the British people themselves. (1980: 150)

How these restrictions will be interpreted is unclear especially as Brexit has weakened the power of EU regulations for the UK. Tony Porter, the Surveillance Camera Commissioner has spoken of his concerns regarding camera technology across Great Britain where 80,000 cameras across 183 councils representing only half of the UK's 343 local authorities in an unregulated regime (November 2020). Securitisation arguments and presumptions about risk continue to be the key that opens the door to more state surveillance. Such arguments depend upon securing popular consent achieved through the mobilisation of fear pandemics through media and political rhetoric (Ericson (2007) and Haggerty and Ericson (2000)). George Orwell, in his epic novel *Nineteen Eighty-Four*, in the fictional nation of "Oceana", envisaged a surveillance assemblage which includes routinised state spying. His writings are an ominous warning. The central protagonist, Winston Smith, is constantly watched in his home. "Any sound that Winston made, above the level of a low whisper would be picked up by it; moreover, so long as he remained within the field of vision which the metal plaque commanded, he could be seen as well as heard. How often the thought police plugged in on any individual wire was guesswork... every sound overheard every movement scrutinised" (1989 [1949]: 4).

Surveillance and Suspect Muslim Families

State surveillance targets "suspect communities" in watching particular individuals, families, communities and localities. Muslim communities are especially surveilled. Their greater likelihood of terrorist activity is premised on presumptions about what conduct constitutes "radicalisation" and "extremism", and who are likely to be radicalised. The lynchpin of this preventive project is the "Prevent" programme instituted in 2006. By 2015, it had become consolidated in the Counter-Terrorism and Security Act (CTSA) 2015 where s 26 places "Specified authorities" under a duty to: "have due regard to the need to prevent people from being drawn into terrorism". Specified authorities include education, health, local authorities and all public and private organisations, "Prevent" requires employers, schools, Universities, local authority social services, for example, to police their institutions and organisations and individuals within. So, student populations, school pupils and teachers, for example, are surveilled (Saeed 2019; Ghani and Nagdee 2019) and local authority social workers are required to watch and assess families for whom they have a responsibility for signs of "radicalisation" or "extremism". Its opponents allege that: "the Prevent strategy constitutes a thinly disguised strategy for spying and intelligence gathering, driven by official Islamophobia and racism; that it legitimises Islamophobia in society at large, criminalises harmless, law-abiding Muslim communities, violates their rights to privacy, freedom of expression and non-discrimination and has a chilling effect on public debate" (22 March 2019 *The Conversation*). "Specified authorities" must comply with the legal obligation and so s 36 requires local authorities to ensure that a panel of persons is appointed and tasked with the responsibility of assessing the extent to which individuals are vulnerable to being drawn into terrorism and developing action plans with measures to address radicalisation. Compliance is overseen by the Home Office (s 32), which may issue a mandatory order should any authority fail in its duty (s 33). Despite assurances provided in s 31 to protect freedom of speech, speech is drastically limited under this act (see Chapter 3). And some speech is considered of itself an indicator of radicalisation or extremism.

Racialised stereotyping feeds suspicion turning the innocent into suspects and creating and manufacturing the "Muslim menace" of whom Said (ed) (2003: xvi) and Gheorghiu (2018) spoke. It seems that few lessons have been learned from the mistakes of the racial profiling of black communities in policing and in the operation of criminal justice (Blom-Cooper and Drabble 1982; MacPherson 1999). In February 2019 police use of "predictive analytics" was instituted as part of police practice to identify potential perpetrators of crime bringing the "Pre-Cogs" into service and lending scientific respectability to a deeply flawed and unreliable methodology. Kundnani (2015: 12) had already noted the way in which the FBI had developed a taxonomy and identified the characteristics and influences which they thought indicated those likely to become terrorists, setting down a set of "pre-radicalisation indicators". These indicators were no more than bigoted ignorance and stupidity, and included growing a beard, wearing traditional Islamic clothing and increased activity with a Muslim group.

In the UK similar suspect methodology and pseudo-scientific terrorist profiling gibberish caricatured who is likely to be radicalised and what the radicalised look like. "Contest" set out to identify social, and psychological factors that might propel a person into terrorism listing, a sense of injustice, a sense of personal alienation and community disadvantage, and an exposure to radical ideas. By 2009, "Contest 2" extended the net of supposed indicators of potential extremism shaped, by apparently new thinking which reflected the concern played by "vulnerability" in radicalisation. "Contest 2" thinking reflected a much more nuanced consideration of sociological, geopolitical and personal factors, including "lack of ties" to the UK community, a crisis in identity, a feeling of not being accepted, and alienation and anomie. Perhaps here was envisaged an individual being acted upon more than being propelled. By 2010, the term "violent extremism" within this "Prevent" strategy was abandoned as being too broad, and the term "radicalisation" appeared. Whilst "extremism" was retained it was defined to include whatever was deemed to be "a vocal and active opposition to fundamental British values", this of course trespassed on freedom of speech. (This definition was successfully challenged in 2019, in the Butt decision, below.) To support this "Prevent agenda" the newly titled "Channel programme" was instituted in 2011.

The presumption that lack of ties, and not being accepted since it is characterises many migrant and diasporic communities, who have a great sense of connection with their own communities but not necessarily with UK communities, as a possible factor in radicalisation and extremism is problematic and overdetermined. A sense of not being accepted is common to all minority communities. Africans, Caribbean's, Indians,

South Asians, Arabs, etc. and the racism they have directly experienced or witnessed compounds their sense of exclusion, otherness and outsiderness. The "Contest" strategy is also underpinned by blame, sensed in the wording: "communities who cannot or will not participate in civic society are more likely to be vulnerable to radicalisation by all kinds of terrorist groups" (Martin 2014: 67; Richards 2017). The "phantasm of community belonging" set out by Benedict Anderson in his *Imagined Communities* (2016) seems now to be proscribed and ordered as the panacea. But as Bikhu Parekh reminds us, if some cultures wish to live within their own communities, we should respect them for that (Parekh 2000). Forced living together and forcing others to live like "us" is the new multiculturalism. The Joint Partly Dissenting Opinion of Judges Nussberger And Jäderblom in *SAS v France* Application Number: 43835/1 (2014) discussed in Chapter 7 upholds the right to be an outsider. The dissenting judgments espouse this view. "[8] Furthermore, it can hardly be argued that an individual has a right (sic duty) to enter contact with other people, in public places, against their will. Whilst communication is admittedly essential for life in society, the right to respect for private life also comprises the right not to communicate and not to enter into contact with others in public places—the right to be an outsider".

From the outset, the "Prevent" programme, especially its silencing of dissent and critical thinking, and its targeting of, especially Muslim communities prompted the University and College Union (UCU) in 2015 to boycott the implementation of the "Prevent" initiative. The UCU said "Prevent" would, force its members to "spy on learners" and be involved in the "racist labelling of students" principally Muslims, and contested the "fundamental British values" jingle as vague and smacking of British colonialism and cultural supremacism. There is some evidence for this. The National Police Chiefs' Council (NPCC) recorded that 1800 children had been referred to the "de radicalisation" "Channel" programme from 2012 to 2016. In 2015–2016, 7631 people were referred to the "Prevent" counter-extremism programme, and 7318 in 2017/18. There is concern about what behaviour or person might trigger a referral, growing a beard, wearing Islamic dress, carrying a prayer book or prayer beads perhaps? Such ignorance, racism and bigotry about what kind of person is likely to become a terrorist is informed by the very Orientalist tropes and anti-Muslim prejudice that Said (1997) had discoursed (see Chapter 2) and have become part of the cultural fabric (see Chapter 3). Gearson and Rosemont (2015) reported that in one case a child found himself under investigation having misspelt "terraced" house, writing instead in his schoolbook that he lived in a "terrorist" house. In another case, a teenage boy who raised money for a charity for Palestinian children and wore a "Free Palestine" badge at his school (Challney High School for Boys, Luton) and was in possession of a leaflet advocating Palestinian rights by the pressure group "Friends of al-Aqsa", was placed under investigation, although he had previously sought and been granted permission from the school to fundraise for children affected by the Israeli occupation. James Fitzgerald also recounts how airport officials called the police after finding three academic books on terrorism in his luggage as he was about to travel to a conference in the US (38).

"Prevent" sought to shut down speech and especially criminalised the dissentient and critical speech of Muslim communities. On 8 March 2019, the Court of Appeal ruled in *R v Butt v Secretary of State for the Home Department* [2019] EWCA Civ 256, that the Prevent programme had gone a step too far. The Court found that paragraph 11 of the "Prevent duty guidance issued to higher education institutions", unlawful, by holding that "extremist views" included views that "actively oppose fundamental British values". The Court found that it had sabotaged s 31 of the Act which defended freedom of speech. The racialised labelling of any Muslim critique as not merely dissent but a sign of radicalisation is particularly chilling. Tania Saeed (2019) explores the specific implication of this presumption for the student. Her research in 2011–2012 examined responses of 40 Muslim female University students who self-censored for fear of being labelled extremist. Guest et al.'s (2017: 6) research recommended "that universities re-affirm their existing strengths in critical thinking to encourage open debate about all forms of ideology—political and religious—especially when relevant to current systems of national and international governance" (see also Scott-Baumann et al. 2020).

Local authorities in implementing their Prevent duty policed the boundaries of speech, opinion and conduct of families for whom they were responsible. Local authorities suspicious of the views and opinions of some Muslim families made applications in local authority care proceedings to remove children into local authority care where a parent or older sibling, in their opinion, might be "radicalised". Courts in private law proceedings regarding custody applications also heard allegations of radicalisation where parental responsibility and contact were being considered (see *Re A and B (Children: Restrictions on Parental Responsibility: Radicalisation and Extremism)* [2016]). The court in its wardship jurisdiction also heard applications where radicalisation was considered to be a factor. This says Ahdash (2018: 403) has been identified as a distinct new facet of child protection. Ahdash's research found during her interviews with solicitors and barristers that they "expressed both surprise and unease at how readily the family judges in the radicalisation cases have accepted allegations of harm based on radicalisation and extremism and their willingness to assess and even make findings regarding the religious and political beliefs of parents" (404). However, Lord Justice Munby when President of the family court called for caution following several cases where local authorities in exercising their jurisdiction of making applications to take children into care, had "overreacted" and identified as "suspect" Muslim families those who for example had expressed a humanitarian concern about the plight of Palestinians, opposed the occupation of "occupied territories" in Israel, opposed the West's WOT or expressed a concern for the treatment of Muslim subjects in detention, and in consequence were judged by the local authority to be eschewing traditional British values. Such suspiciousness was evidenced in the case of *Tower Hamlets London Borough v B* [2016] where the court was asked to consider making a care order in respect of children whom the local authority alleged had been "radicalised". The expert report, by Silke and Brown, outlined the problem of overreaction. "[6] There is no single root cause of radicalisation. More than 200 different factors have been identified by research which could play a role in the radicalisation process. Not all factors feature in every case, and there is often very considerable variation". The court did not make an order. In the case of *A Local Authority v A Mother and Others* [2017] the local authority alleged radicalisation of the children. However later, it conceded error, and made an application to withdraw the original application on the basis that they had wrongly instigated an investigation. The court said:

> [67] It is easy to assume that a straight line can, without more, be drawn between a parent who is said to hold extremist views, or a parent who is said to be involved in terror related activity and the suffering of significant harm or the risk of significant harm to that parent's child or children. However, the evidence in this case demonstrates that the position is more complex than that and one that falls to be considered carefully on a

case-by-case basis considering the evidence in a given set of proceedings. (Judgment of McDonald J.)

Ahdash's conclusion cannot be challenged "The ways in which the judges in the radicalisation cases articulate or struggle to articulate, the harm of radicalisation and extremism reflects the influence of these recent changes in the UK's counter-terrorist landscape on the family courts" (406).

Conclusion—a Justified Sense of Muslim Hurt!

Official statistics on the prosecution of suspects for "terrorist related offences" under the Terrorism Act 2000 for the year 2019 reported 268 arrests and 90 persons charged for terrorism offences (Allen and Kirk-Wade 2020) in 2014–2015, there were 299 arrests, of these 118 persons were charged with an offence, of which 85% were "terrorist related" offences. 12% of offences in 2014–2015 related to 35 women. This is a very small number considering the vaguely drafted legislation which enables suspects like Samina Malik to be prosecuted for her till receipt scribblings. Many of these cases involve minor offences and circumstances which as Cornford (2020) has suggested seeming to entrap people in the legal machinery who ought not to be there. Whilst the Muslim community are concerned that terrorism legislation at the point of charging disproportionally impacts on them, David Anderson's review in 2011 concluded on the evidence available at the time, that it did not. His report found that between 1 September 2001 and 31 August 2012, 2297 persons were arrested for terrorism-related offences of which 46% were self-declared Muslims and 54% of "different religions, no religion or unknown", and that there was no difference in treatment of these two groups. Of course, the "unknown" category may well have included many Muslims who through fear of racialised prosecution may well have kept their religious identity to themselves. Grouping these responses together in this way camouflages the real disproportionately and effect of policing, prosecution and the law. It is a significant omission that since 2011 there appears to be no proper analysis of the religion of terrorist suspects, or arrestees.

Differential treatment of Muslims is systemic throughout the whole of the criminal justice system from the crafting of offences through to surveillance, prosecution, to the trial process and sentencing, as has already been demonstrated here. The "surveillance creep" is all encompassing as can be seen in the governmental infiltration, for example, in Muslim women's groups and for example the funding of the "Super Sisters" website aimed at British Muslim women and funded by the UK anti-extremism programme which was found to be attempting to shape Muslim women's attitudes. Funded by the Home Office, Sabah Ismail, social media manager for Super Sisters, said: "In my naivety, I thought that through this 'opportunity' at Super Sisters, I really could help to make real change, pushing forward a different narrative from Musnationalism women themselves, showing that we are empowered and multi-faceted ... I realise now that with the Home Office funding the project at the root, there was no way I could do this, regardless of the content I was pushing out" (*The Guardian*, 15 September 2019).

Being Muslim and having an opinion, dissenting on UK foreign policy decisions for example the war in Iraq, the selling of arms to Saudi Arabia, holding a view on the plight of the Palestinians, can place a Muslim under suspicion. Given the proliferation of counter-terrorism legislation, its impact on Muslim communities, fear of being targeted in a jurisdiction where there is calcified and systemic Islamophobia and the over-surveillance of Muslim communities is all very real placing Muslims in fear (see Fussey 2013). As Breen-Smyth points out there is no such thing as a "suspect community" it being a phantasm in the imagined fears of its non-members (230), "existing in public suspiciousness created by a discourse focused on security, insecurity, terrorism, and threat, and reproduced by media and security practitioners and political actors" (231).

"Prevent" and its corollaries limit and crush free expression where academic debate in institutions of learning is subject to policing. Liberty in evidence to the House of Commons House of Lords Joint Committee on Human Rights Legislative Scrutiny: Counter-Terrorism and Border Security Bill had already maintained that much of the activity criminalised is "not terrorism per se; but protected free expression". Liberty expressed concern about the "stifling of" academic debate and the chilling effect legislation would have on preventing core speech, and in evidence to the Joint Committee, "Reporters without Borders" highlighted restrictions on press freedom to express legitimate concerns, for example, around a new proscription or a proscribed group.

The old law is now being pushed aside by new law and an executive bent on denying "core political speech" and opinion and particularly denying representation to potentially political (Muslim) actors whilst labelling the forms of political self-assertion unacceptable. Meanwhile, we are being watched. It seems a far cry from Hannah Arendt's plea for "freedom to think otherwise" (1958). We live in a state where as Cornel West reminds us in his lecture "Speaking Truth to Power" (2018) "Frank speech will get you in trouble". This is the effect of the discursive, these are the material effects of Islamophobia and anti-Muslim racism, call it what you will. This is the effect of counter-terror measures on law and on justice. In the strivings to protect, safeguard and securitise we have yielded too much. The justice system is broken for Muslim communities under constant suspicion and surveillance and it is broken for us all. As Strawson said 9/11 had "turned law to ground zero" (cited in Banakar 2010: 211).

References

Ahdash, F. 2018. The Interaction Between Family Law and Counter-Terrorism: A Critical Examination of Radicalisation Cases in Family Courts. *Child and Family Law Quarterly* 30 (4): 389–413.

A Local Authority v A Mother and Others [2017] EWHC 1515. https://www. familylawweek.co.uk/site.aspx?i=ed178398. Accessed 11 November.

A and others v Secretary of State for the Home Department [2004] 2 AC 68. https://publications.parliament.uk/pa/ld200405/ldjudgmt/jd041216/ a&oth-1.htm. Accessed 11 November.

A and others v Secretary of State for the Home Department (No 2) [2005] UKHL 71. https://publications.parliament.uk/pa/ld200506/ldjudgmt/jd0 51208/aand-1.htm. Accessed 11 November.

A and others v United Kingdom [No 2] (App. No. 3455/05) [2009] All ER (D) 203. https://hudoc.echr.coe.int/app/conversion/pdf/?library=ECHR& id=002...PDFfile. Accessed 11 November.

Abu Rideh v Secretary of State for the Home Department [2007] EWHC 804. https://www.casemine.com/judgement/uk/5a8ff7d760d03e7 f57eb26af. Accessed 11 November.

Anderson, B. 2016 [1983]. *Imagined Communities: Reflections on the Origin and Spread of Nationalism*. London: Verso.

Anderson, D. 2016. *Report of the Bulk Powers Review Independent Reviewer of Terrorism Legislation*, August 2016. Cm 9326 Crown Copyright. https://terrorismlegislationreviewer.independent.gov.uk/wp-content/ uploads/2016/08/Bulk-Powers-Review-final-report.pdf. Accessed 8 August 2020.

Allen, G., and E. Kirk-Wade. 2020. *Terrorism in Great Britain: Statistics.* House of Commons Briefing Paper Number CBP-7613. https://researchbrie fings.files.parliament.uk/documents/CBP-7613/CBP-7613.pdf. Accessed 8 August 2020.

Arendt, H. 1958. *The Human Condition.* Chicago: University of Chicago Press.

Banakar, R. (ed.). 2010. *Rights in Context: Law and Justice in Late Modern Society.* London: Ashgate.

Bingham, T. 2011. *The Rule of Law.* London: Penguin.

Big Brother Watch & Ors v United Kingdom [2018] (Application No 58170/13). https://www.europarl.europa.eu/meetdocs/2009_2014/documents/libe/dv/bbw_org_ep_ck_v_uk_/bbw_org_ep_ck_v_uk_en.pdf. Accessed 11 November.

Blom-Cooper, L., and R. Drabble. 1982. Police Perception of Crime: Brixton and the Operational Response. *British Journal of Criminology* 22 (2): 1.

Bowring, B. 2010. 'Terrorist Lists' and Procedural Human Rights: A Collision Between UN Law, EU Law and Strasbourg Law? In *Rights in Context: Law and Justice in Late Modern Society*, ed. R. Banakar, 231–252. London: Ashgate.

Breen-Smyth, M. 2014. Theorising the "Suspect Community": Counterterrorism, Security Practices and the Public Imagination. *Critical Studies on Terrorism* 7 (2): 223–240.

Césaire, A. 2000 [1955]. *Discourse on Colonialism.* New York: Monthly Review Press.

Cochrane, F. 2013. Not so Extraordinary: The Democratisation of UK Counterinsurgency Strategy. *Critical Studies on Terrorism* 6 (1): 29–49.

Cornford, A. 2020. Terrorist Precursor Offences: Evaluating the Law in Practice. *Criminal Law Review* 8: 663–685.

Counter-Terrorism and Sentencing Bill 21 September 2020 HL Second Reading. https://hansard.parliament.uk/Lords/2020-09-21/debates/A62 2E717-DE61-4496-A0DB-5EE2FF47A3FB/Counter-TerrorismAndSenten cingBill. Accessed 9 November 2020.

Covert Human Intelligence Sources (Criminal Conduct) Bill 5 October 2020 Vol. 681. https://hansard.parliament.uk/Commons/2020-10-05/debates/ DF29B1ED-6BB3-414A-A65E-53CD4BAB694A/CovertHumanIntelligen ceSources(CriminalConduct)Bill. Accessed 9 November 2020.

D v Secretary of State for the Home Department [2014] EWHC 3820. https://www.bailii.org/ew/cases/EWHC/Admin/2014/3820.html. Accessed 9 November 2020.

Debrix, F., and A.D. Barder. 2009. Nothing to Fear but Fear: Governmentality and the Biopolitical Production of Terror. *International Political Sociology* 3 (4): 398–413.

D'souza-Lodhi, A. 2019. Hijabi-(R)evolution. In *It's Not About the Burqa*, ed. M. Khan, 115–126. London: Picador.

Elliott, M. 2006. United Kingdom: Detention Without Trial and the 'War on Terror'. *International Journal of Constitutional Law* 4 (3): 553–566.

Ericson, R.V. 2007. *Crime in an Insecure World*. Cambridge: Polity.

Foucault, M. 2000 [1978]. Security, Territory, and Population. In *Michel Foucault Power Essential Works of Foucault 1954–1984*, vol. 3, ed. J.D. Faubion. London: Penguin.

Foucault, M. (ed.). 1980 [1977]. *Power and Knowledge Selected Interviews and Writings 1972–1977*, ed. C. Gordon. New York: Pantheon, The Harvester Press.

Fussey, P. 2013. Contested Typologies of UK Counterterrorist Surveillance: The Rise and Fall of Project Champion. *Critical Studies on Terrorism* 6 (3): 351–370.

Gearty, C. 2017. Is The Human Rights Era Drawing to a Close? *European Human Rights Law Review* 1361–1526.

Gearson, J. and H. Rosemont. 2015. CONTEST as Strategy: Reassessing Britain's Counterterrorism Approach. *Studies in Conflict and Terrorism* 38 (12): 1038–1064.

Ghani, H., and I. Nagdee. 2019. Islamophobia in UK Universities. In *The Routledge International Handbook on Islamophobia*, ed. I. Zempi and I. Awan, Ch 14. London: Routledge.

Hage, G. 2017. *Is Racism and Environmental Threat?* Cambridge: Polity.

Guest, M., A. Scott-Baumann, S. Cheruvallil-Contractor, S. Naguib, A. Phoenix, Y. Lee, and T. Al-Baghal. 2017. *Islam and Muslims on UK University Campuses: Perceptions and Challenges*. https://www.soas.ac.uk/representing islamoncampus/publications/file148310.pdf. Accessed 9 November 2020.

Gheorghiu, O.C. 2018. *British and American Representations of 9/11*. New York: Springer.

Greer, S. 2018. Terrorism and Counter-Terrorism in the UK: From Northern Irish Troubles to Global Islamist Jihad. In *Counter-Terrorism, Constitutionalism and Miscarriages of Justice: A Festschrift for Professor Clive Walker*, ed. G. Lennon, C. King, and C. McCartney, 45–62. Oxford: Hart.

Hall, S. 1992. New Ethnicities. In *'Race', Culture and Difference*, ed. J. Donald and A. Rattansi, 252–259. London: Sage.

Haggerty, K.D. and R.V. Ericson. 2000. The Surveillant Assemblage. *British Journal of Sociology* 51 (4): 605–622. https://www.uio.no/studier/emner/matnat/ifi/INF3700/v17/bakgrunnsnotat/the_surveillant_assemblage.pdf. Accessed 8 August 2020.

Hargreaves, J. 2018. Police Stop and Search Within British Muslim Communities: Evidence from the Crime Survey 2011. *British Journal of Criminology* 58 (6): 1281–1302.

Higgins, R. 1997. The General International Law of Terrorism. In *Terrorism and International Law*, ed. R. Higgins and M. Flory, 13–30. London: Routledge.

Home Office. 2019. *Proscribed Terrorist Groups or Organisations*. https://www.gov.uk/government/publications/proscribed-terror-groups-or-organisations-2. Accessed 8 August 2020.

Human Rights Watch. Briefing Paper. 2004. *Neither Just nor Effective Indefinite Detention Without Trial in The United Kingdom Under Part 4 of the Anti-Terrorism, Crime and Security Act 2001*. https://www.hrw.org/legacy/backgrounder/eca/uk/4.htm. Accessed 8 August 2020.

Jackson, R. 2004. *Writing the War on Terrorism Language, Politics, and Counterterrorism*. Manchester: Manchester University Press.

Jackson, J. 2018. The Use of Special Advocates in Countering Terrorism, Human Rights, Best Practice and Procedural Tradition. In *Counter-Terrorism, Constitutionalism and Miscarriages of Justice: A Festschrift for Professor Clive Walker*, ed. G. Lennon, C. King, and C. McCartney. Oxford: Hart.

Jarvis, L., and T. Legrand. 2018. The Proscription or Listing of Terrorist Organisations: Understanding, Assessment, and International Comparisons. *Terrorism and Political Violence* 30 (2): 199–215.

Jarvis, L., and T. Legrand. 2020. *Banning Them Securing Us*. Manchester: Manchester University Press.

Judge, I. 2015. *The Safest Shield, Lectures, Speeches and Essays*. London: Hart.

Kafka, F. 1994 [1925]. *The Trial*. London: Penguin Classics.

Kentridge, S. 2014. *Free Country*. London: Hart.

Kundnani, A. 2015. *The Muslims Are Coming! Islamophobia, Extremism, and the Domestic War on Terror*. London: Verso.

Kurdistan Workers' Party (PKK) v Council of the European Union (15 November 2018) ECLI:EU: T:2018:788 Judgment of the General Court, Third Chamber, Extended Composition, 15 November 2018. In Case T-316/14. http://curia.europa.eu/juris/liste.jsf?num=T-316/14. Accessed 9 November 2020.

Kurdistan Workers' Party PKK v (2019/939 IC/Folio: 555 Court of Appeal of Brussels) see https://ekurd.net/pkk-not-terrorist-organization-2020-01-29; https://www.brusselstimes.com/belgium/92787/belgian-government-defies-ruling-of-its-supreme-court-on-pkk/. Accessed 9 November 2020.

Lammy, D. 2017. *The Lammy Review an Independent Review into the Treatment of, and Outcomes for, Black, Asian, and Minority Ethnic Individuals in the Criminal Justice System*. https://www.gov.uk/government/publications/lammy-review-final-report. Accessed 9 November 2020.

Lennon, G., C. King, and C. McCartney (eds.). 2018. *Counter-Terrorism, Constitutionalism and Miscarriages of Justice: A Festschrift for Professor Clive Walker*. Oxford: Hart.

Liberty's Report Stage Briefing. 2018. On the Counter Terrorism and Border Security Bill. https://www.libertyhumanrights.org.uk/issue/terrorism-off ences-briefings-and-reports/4/. Accessed 1 August 2020; https://www.lib ertyhumanrights.org.uk/wp-content/uploads/2020/02/Libertys-Report-Stage-Briefing-on-the-Counter-Terrorism-and-Border-Security-Bill-Sep-2018. pdf. Accessed 1 August 2020.

MacPherson Report. 1999. *Report of the Stephen Lawrence Inquiry.* By Sir William MacPherson of Cluny. Cm. 4262. London: HMSO.

Martin, T. 2014. Governing an Unknowable Future: The Politics of Britain's Prevent Policy. *Critical Studies on Terrorism* 7 (1): 62–78.

McCulloch, J., and S. Pickering. 2009. Pre-Crime and Counter-Terrorism: Imag-ining Future Crime in the 'War on Terror'. *British Journal of Criminology* 49 (5): 628–645.

Muller, M. 2008. Terrorism, Proscription, and the Right to Resist in the Age of Conflict. *The Denning Law Journal* 20: 111–131.

Mythen, G., and S. Walklate. 2006. Criminology and Terrorism: Which Thesis? Risk Society or Governmentality? *The British Journal of Criminology* 46 (3): 379–398.

Ní Aoláin, F. 2018. Lawyers, Military Commissions, and the Rule of Law in Democratic States. In *Counter-terrorism, Constitutionalism and Miscarriages of Justice: A Festschrift for Professor Clive Walker*, ed. G. Lennon, C. King, and C. McCartney, 117–134. Oxford: Hart.

Orwell, G. 1989 [1949]. *Nineteen Eighty-Four.* London: Penguin.

Pantazis, C., and S. Pemberton. 2009. From the 'Old' to the 'New' Suspect Community Examining the Impacts of Recent UK Counter-Terrorist Legisla-tion. *British Journal of Criminology* 49 (5): 646–666.

Parekh, B. 2000. *Rethinking Multiculturalism: Cultural Diversity and Political Theory.* Harvard: Harvard University Press.

Privacy and Security: A Modern and Transparent Legal Framework. 2015. Intelli-gence and Security Committee of Parliament HC 1075. https://regmedia.co. uk/2016/02/08/privacy_and_security_isc_report.pdf. Accessed 9 November 2020.

PWR and others v Director of Public Prosecutions [2020] EWHC 798. https:// www.thetimes.co.uk/article/strict-liability-for-shows-of-support-for-terrorists-qsj3w2bt0. Accessed 9 November 2020.

R v Choudary (Anjem) and another (No 2) [2016] EWCA Crim 61. https:// www.casemine.com/judgement/uk/5a8ff71d60d03e7f57ea7b0f. Accessed 9 November 2020.

Re A and B (Children: Restrictions on Parental Responsibility: Radicalisation and Extremism) [2016] 2 FLR 977. https://www.familylawhub.co.uk/def ault.aspx?i=ce5293. Accessed 9 November 2020.

R v F [2007] EWCA Crim 243. https://www.casemine.com/judgement/uk/ 5a8ff71660d03e7f57ea759b. Accessed 9 November 2020.

R v Faraz [2013] 1 WLR 261. https://www.bailii.org/ew/cases/EWCA/ Crim/2012/2820.html. Accessed 9 November 2020.

R v K [2008] 2 WLR 1026. https://www.bailii.org/ew/cases/EWCA/Crim/ 2008/185.html. Accessed 9 November 2020.

R v Khan (Runa) [2015] EWCA Crim 1341. Thompson Reuters WESTLAW Edge UK. Accessed 9 November 2020.

R (Khan) v Secretary of State for Justice [2020] 1 WLR 3932. https://www.bai lii.org/ew/cases/EWHC/Admin/2020/2084.html. Accessed 9 November 2020.

R v Lane and another [2018] 1 WLR 3647. https://www.bailii.org/uk/cases/ UKSC/2018/36.html. Accessed 9 November 2020.

R v Butt v Secretary of State for the Home Department [2019] EWCA Civ 256. https://www.judiciary.uk/wp-content/uploads/2019/03/r-butt-v-sshd-judgment.pdf. Accessed 9 November 2020.

R v Malik [2008] EWCA Crim 1450. Thompson Reuters WESTLAW Edge UK. Accessed 9 November 2020.

R (on the application of National Council for Civil Liberties (Liberty) v Secretary of State for the Home Department and another (National Union of Journalists intervening) [2019] EWHC 2057). https://www.judiciary.uk/wp-content/ uploads/2019/07/Liberty-judgment-Press-Summary-Draft-2.pdf. Accessed 9 November 2020.

Richards, J. 2017. *Extremism, Radicalization and Security.* New York and London: Palgrave.

Richardson, M. 2016. Surveillance Publics After Edward Snowden. *Contemporary Publics* 163–180.

Rose, J. 2011. 'Imponderables in Thin Air': Zionism as Psychoanalysis. In *The Jacqueline Rose Reader,* ed. J. Clemens and B. Naparstek, 188–241. Durham and London: Duke University Press.

Saeed, T. 2019. Islamophobia and the Muslim Student. In *The Routledge International Handbook on Islamophobia,* ed. I. Zempi and I. Awan, Ch 14. London: Routledge.

Said, E. 1997. *Covering Islam.* London: Vintage.

Said, E. (ed.). 2003. *Orientalism.* London. Penguin.

Scott-Baumann, et al. 2020. *Islam on Campus: Contested Identities and the Cultures of Higher Education in Britain.* Oxford: Oxford University Press.

Secretary of State for the Home Department v LG and others [2017] (EWHC 1529). https://www.casemine.com/judgement/uk/5b2897fb2c94 e06b9e19e9b3. Accessed 11 November 2020.

Secretary of State for the Home Department v MB; Secretary of State for the Home Department v AF [2007] UKHL 46. https://publications.parliament.uk/pa/ld200607/ldjudgmt/jd071031/home-1.htm. Accessed 11 November 2020.

SIAC Report. 2004–2005. *The Operation of the Special Immigration Appeals Commission (SIAC) and the Use of Special Advocates.* House of Commons Constitutional Affairs Committee: Seventh Report of Session 2004–05 HC 323-I 3 April 2005 House of Commons London: The Stationery Office Limited. https://publications.parliament.uk/pa/cm2 00405/cmselect/cmconst/323/323i.pdf. Accessed 8 August 2020.

Strossen, N. 2018. *Hate: Why We Should Resist It with Free Speech, Not Censorship.* Oxford: OUP.

Thompson, E. P. 1980. *Writing by Candlelight.* London: Merlin.

Tower Hamlets London Borough v B [2016] EWHC 1707. https://www.casemine.com/judgement/uk/5a8ff7bc60d03e7f57eb1ab8. Accessed 25 October 2020.

Walker, C. 2018. Living with Counter-Terrorism Laws and Their Discontents. In *Counter-Terrorism, Constitutionalism and Miscarriages of Justice: A Festschrift for Professor Clive Walker,* ed. G. Lennon, C. King, and C. McCartney, 307–325. Oxford: Hart.

Walsh, D. 2018. Beyond the Ordinary: Criminal Law and Terrorism. In *Counter-Terrorism, Constitutionalism and Miscarriages of Justice: A Festschrift for Professor Clive Walker,* ed. G. Lennon, C. King, and C. McCartney. Oxford: Hart.

West, C. 2018. Cornel West: "Speaking Truth to Power", March 2. https://www.youtube.com/watch?v=-Bc6TRjptKI. Accessed 25 October 2020.

Zempi, I., and I. Awan (eds.). 2019. *The Routledge International Handbook on Islamophobia.* London: Routledge.

CHAPTER 6

US Counter-Terror Law and the "Chronicles of Torture"

INTRODUCTION

What marks out the US is not only its "War on Terror" (WOT) on other countries, the proliferation of counter-terror law and the enactment of Executive orders which authorised the banishment and exclusion of Muslim men, women and children from its dominion, but an exceptional ideology that sanctioned the collective punishment of Arab and Muslim men who were the victims of state torture and sexual sadism carried out by the US military on detainees held in Guantánamo Bay and Abu Ghraib. So terrible, that Lord Falconer, as did many, denounced this retribution as a "shocking affront to the principles of democracy" and accused the US of "deliberately seeking to put detainees beyond the rule of law in Guantánamo Bay". So shocking, that in Guantánamo within the first month two detainees and two prison guards committed suicide. The Senate Select Intelligence Committee (SSIC) Senate Committee Report on Torture (SCRT) (2014, p. 3 of 499) received evidence that following the so-called "'enhanced interrogation' techniques against the detainee Al-Nashiri; the Chief Interrogator threatened 'to quit' because additional techniques might 'push [Al-Nashiri] over the edge psychologically'". Not everyone caught up in this behemoth were complicit or willing. Tara McKelvey (2018) interviewed Jeremy Sivits who years later says, "I hated myself for the Abu Ghraib abuse". As Frantz Fanon (2008 [1952]) discovered in

© The Author(s), under exclusive license to Springer Nature Switzerland AG 2021
S. S. M. Edwards, *The Political Appropriation of the Muslim Body*, https://doi.org/10.1007/978-3-030-68896-7_6

the French occupation of Algeria, colonial struggles inflicted psychiatric damage on both the colonisers and the colonised.

The US contended that securitisation and the nation's safety justified the suspension of human rights and the introduction of a programme of counter-terror measures outside the "Rule of Law" (ROL). Throughout this reign of terror, a psychological profile of US state-authorised perpetrators emerged as men who believed that Muslim detainees did not deserve human rights protections or fair treatment, or to be treated like human beings but deserved to be tortured. Torture had become the national character and US exceptionalism was marked by lawlessness, the use of detention without charge or trial, the routinised use of torture, supported by the complicity of politicians and the public who endorsed it. Susan Sontag understood the depths of psychological corruption and, when writing on the Abu Ghraib photographs, said: "The photographs are us". This is what the US had become.

In this chapter I begin, first, with a consideration of US state power, what it is and what it has become. Second, I set out the framework of US counter-terror law following 9/11. Third, and it is here that US exceptionalism emerges with audacity, I document the unlawful detention and torture of Muslim detainees in Guantánamo where Orientalised tropes of the Arab and Muslim "Other" as barbaric and dangerous were appropriated (see Said 1978). Fourth, I consider how this exceptionalism is also demonstrated in the sexual abuse and sadism perpetrated by US military officers both men and women, on Muslim prisoners held in Abu Ghraib, Iraq, including the creation and distribution of the permanent photographic record of their abuse. State orchestrated ideology and propaganda in support of these crimes relied on "states of denial" (Cohen 2001), which were rehearsed at official and public level and also pleaded by officers who were called to account for their conduct before Military Tribunals. The US state and its torture lawyers justified such cruelty with utilitarian claims that "torture saved lives", and, through a series of cases brought before the Supreme Court, I consider the resolve of an independent judiciary, acting as "the safest shield", who ruled detention without trial and torture, unlawful. Finally, I reflect on the impact such acts of state terrorism have had on all Muslims, men and women, the US Muslim community, the UK Muslim community, Muslim majority countries and right-thinking people everywhere. As Hensman (2003: 31) writes: "I don't even have to be an Arab or a Muslim to feel grief and fury at the cruelty and injustice of it all".

CREEPING "EXECUTIVISATION" AND THE "IMPERIAL GRAND STRATEGY"

Torture and sexual sadism was not, as some would have preferred to concede, the conduct of a handful of psychopaths who otherwise might have met their fate in the US criminal injustice system by lethal injection, nor does such conduct arise in a vacuum, but was conduct condoned and authorised by US state and executive power. Executive power, has stealthily, dominated decision-making in the US, especially but not exclusively, since 9/11. Foucault's construct of "governmentality", developed in his thesis in "Security, Territory, and Population" 1977–1978 (Faubion 2000: 201–222), (and discussed elsewhere in this book) provides some assistance in understanding the hegemonic potential of state power. The omnipotence of this power was apparent long before 9/11. In 1973, Arthur Schlesinger, in his book *The Imperial Presidency*, documented a US presidency "out of control", well exceeding its constitutional limits (see Tiefer 1983; Ignatieff 2003, 2005). This "Imperial Grand strategy" already in sway took advantage of 9/11 which served as the pretext for dispensing with international law, its norms and institutions, and releasing the US from any restraint, facilitating US incursions into other countries, in its so-called international WOT (Chapter 4), which led to the development of barbarism in its treatment of foreign nationals, including, kidnapping, "forcible rendition", and the legalisation of indefinite detention and torture. The President and executive contumaciously disregarded human rights norms turning their own conduct into a virtue and expression of strength, hypermasculinity and patriotism. Both Bush and Blair spoke in fist fighting metaphors of: "Taking gloves off" regarding the internment of suspected terrorist/"enemy combatants" under US control, in Guantánamo and in Iraq and Afghanistan. The US presidency considered international law, irrelevant and said so.

Bush to "Trumpism"—Executive Branch Unilateralism

Following 9/11, the United Nations Security Council provided a global framework for preventing, detecting and prosecuting terrorism, and the Security Council Resolution (1368) called on all states to: "work together urgently to bring to justice the perpetrators, organizers and sponsors" of the attacks (3), and "to prevent and suppress terrorist acts including by increased cooperation and full implementation of the relevant international anti-terrorist conventions and Security Council resolutions" (5). The US regarded this resolution, however, as a green light for its own imperial ambitions bolstering the Presidential executive mandate to use its already existing "emergency powers". Such a precedent for executive decision-making in "times of emergency" or "war" had already been established in World War II in the German saboteur's case (*Ex parte Quirin*, 317 US 1 (1942)). In this case, eight Nazi spies who had entered the US, were tried by military tribunal following President Roosevelt's Executive Proclamation 2561 of 1942, which established a military tribunal to prosecute the German spies outside domestic criminal law. Although upheld as lawful by the US Supreme Court, Justice Robert H. Jackson expressed concern regarding the scope of the President's constitutional war powers and considered the setting up of the Tribunal outside domestic criminal law, a mistake. The case was to set a precedent for trial by military commission of any future "unlawful combatant" against the US.

The US, in deeming the terrorist acts of 9/11 as a "war on and against the United States", provided a veneer of legality to its own arbitrary and global WOT. Considering the US reading and interpretation of "state of emergency" Bingham (2010: 137) identifies three differences between the US and the UK responses. First, the President of the US declared a WOT (137) which the UK had not done, albeit that Prime Minister Blair did nothing to oppose US action in Afghanistan and Iraq and in fact "shoulder to shoulder" with the US, supported it. Second, by a resolution adopted on 18 September 2001, US congress authorised the President to: "use all necessary and appropriate force against those nations, organizations, or persons he determined planned, authorised, committed or aided terror attacks". This was followed on 13 November 2001 by a presidential military order (Military Order November 13) authorising trials of suspects by military tribunal, including the detention, treatment and trial of certain non-citizens. The UK, by contrast, continued to use the criminal courts to try terrorist suspects, albeit that some men were unlawfully detained for a period and some trials were held in secret. Sir Ken Macdonald, setting out the difference said: "the fight against terrorism on the streets of Britain is not a war. It is the prevention of crime". The third area of difference relates to the US practice of "rendition". As Bingham points out, this was a new and novel expression to describe the kidnapping of a person in one country to stand trial in another (139) (This was not practised in the UK). The US endorsed the use of torture as necessary in the fight against terrorism, whereas the UK rejected the use of torture recognising information gained from it as useless (albeit the UK government was nevertheless prepared, in certain cases, to rely on evidence obtained from torture exacted in countries outside the UK). Both countries, Bingham observed, shared similarities including, the introduction of counter-terrorism legislation (143), stringent provisions against non-nationals, detention without charge (145), erosion of a fair hearing (150), increased surveillance (152) and the joint invasion of Iraq (158).

On 13 November 2001, President Bush declared a state of emergency and introducing a series of legal provisions through a raft of executive orders, (126 in all) displayed a stunning disregard for international human rights norms. Bush gave the Military Commissions exclusive jurisdiction over persons considered to be connected to Al-Qaeda, or Osama Bin Laden, or otherwise terrorist suspects who were captured by the US in Afghanistan by the Afghan Northern Alliance and Pakistani forces, thereby emasculating criminal law and international law norms. Critics of this expanding reach of executive power said such measures were devised to provide US Military Tribunals with immunity and to circumvent the Federal prohibition on torture. The original draft of the President's Executive Order, authorising Military Tribunals, reveals the reach of this, and his power and the usurping of criminal law norms:

> Under President Bush's November 13th Military Order on military commissions, any foreign national designated by the President as a suspected terrorist or as aiding terrorists could potentially be arrested, tried, convicted and even executed without a public trial, without adequate access to counsel, without the presumption of innocence or even proof of guilt beyond reasonable doubt, and without the right to judicial appeal. ... 'Given the danger to the safety of the United States and the nature of international terrorism, and to the extent provided by and under this order, I find consistent with the Section 836 of title 10, United States Code, that it is not practicable to apply in military commissions under this order the principles of law and the rules of evidence generally recognized in the trial of criminal cases in the United States district courts'. (Section 1(f))

John Ashcroft, US Attorney General for the Justice Department, demonstrating the audacity of President Bush's new Military Order, suspended all legal safeguards for suspects and said: "it [is] fundamental that if you hold someone as an enemy combatant, obviously you hold them without access to family members and without access to counsel" (Chomsky 2004: 26). Judicial resistance to this contumacious flouting of human rights and criminal justice by judges unwilling to be constrained, prompted further government drafting. For example, when the Supreme Court in *Hamdan v Rumsfeld* [2006] ruled that the Combatant Status Review Tribunals were unconstitutional, asserting: "[3] The military commission at issue is not expressly authorized by any congressional Act" violating the Geneva Conventions and the Uniform Code of Military Justice (Bingham 2010: 152), Congress responded by approving the Military Commissions Act 2006, (extended further in the Military Commissions Act 2009), authorising trial by military commission for violations of the law of war, and for other purposes. The 2006 Act gave statutory force to the executive practices that had preceded it, including removal of the right of habeas corpus, later challenged in *Boumediene v Bush* [2008] (below).

Sands (2006: 212–214) in *Lawless World*, asks how was it that the US could show such flagrant disregard for international law, and how could President Bush act as a law unto himself? Professor Mark Tushnet (2005) in response identifies what he calls "executive branch unilateralism" as responsible for the numerous contumacious breaches of international law norms. Barak-Erez (2009) includes amongst these breaches, the infamous torture memos, the use of torture itself, the trials by Military Commissions (discussed later), which the Supreme Court ruled as unconstitutional, and all of these brutish acts committed in the absence of congressional approval. Here again, Foucault's conjectures on the might of sovereign power "to take life or to let live" (*The History of Sexuality* 1978: 136) is constituted in US executive authorisation of the use of torture, where punishment and cruelty per se are used as weapons of war by "the sovereign", and in which, as we shall see later, some of the sovereign's subjects delight.

COUNTER-TERROR "LAW" LESSNESS—VIOLATING DUE PROCESS AND INTERNATIONAL NORMS

How to Be a Patriot

The literal meaning of the word "patriot" is to be a good and loyal and virtuous citizen. It is a word that is "performative" it invokes a swathe of emotions and sentiments, and a sense of national identity and pride.

As Edward Snowden's (2018) disclosures revealed, the Patriot Acts were certainly not virtuous, they contributed nothing to good deeds but much to public, police and prosecutorial hysteria, discrimination and bigotry, and sanctioned xenophobia. President Bush said: "New thinking was required". Blair similarly called for "New thinking on law of war" (Poole 179). The Patriot Act and its "patriotic" measures were supported by a propaganda offensive outlawing dissent, critical inquiry and counter-discourse, with the chiming chant: "You are either with us or with the terrorists" creating a Manichean world in which differences and shades of opinion were written out, demonising, essentialising and denouncing anyone with a different view as an outlaw and traitor to "our values". State and executive power was exercised in the name of a Christian God and nationalism, where peace, humanity and "saving others" was appropriated. The darker side of patriotism paints an exclusionary vista founded on male pride and hubris, characterised by men showing other men their force and strength through military might. Martha Nussbaum had already in 1994 said: "I believe... that this emphasis on patriotic pride is both morally dangerous and, ultimately, subversive of some of the worthy goals patriotism sets out to serve — for example, the goal of national unity in devotion to worthy moral ideals of justice and equality". Patriotism with its nationalist fervour demonstrated its xenophobic face and 9/11 became the catalyst and justification for war mongering, a global endeavour of force and might, unleashing a belief in the rightness and necessity of suspending due process and human rights norms and a different treatment of foreign nationals and of Muslims per se. The eponymously titled Patriot Act of 2001, and 2006 singled out Muslims individually, and as a group, for special mistreatment, including increased surveillance, inspection, registration, airport profiling, monitoring, increased criminal process oversight, disproportionate police surveillance, investigation and detention (Mégret 2009; Wong 2006: 164–165). Under the Patriot Act, state powers were widened, extending electronic surveillance and intelligence gathering, including police powers of surveillance, monitoring of political groups, political dissidents and advocacy groups. Immediately after 2001, the Attorney General, under instructions from the President, issued this warning:

> Let the terrorists among us be warned ... If you overstay your visa, even by one day, we will arrest you. If you violate a local law, you will be put in jail and kept in custody if possible. We will use every available statute. We

will seek every prosecutorial advantage. We will use all our weapons within the law and under the Constitution to protect life and enhance security for America". (cited in Wong: 173, see also Bricmont 2007)

Bush demonstrating his disregard for internationally agreed norms said: "Terrorism is what our leaders declare it to be" (Chomsky 2004: 110). This had consequences. The head of information technology at a London firm of solicitors was detained in the US simply because he was Muslim (Wong: 169). Muslim lawyers were being subjected to increased surveillance including phone tapping, and Muslims were being randomly questioned about what they thought about terror attacks (168). As Bourke (2007: 373) observes, "the supposed threat posed by 'Arab' – a synonym, albeit inaccurate for 'Muslim': - was a virulent one. After the attack on the Twin Tower a thousand people thought to be 'Arab' were assaulted and at least six murdered". The Office of the Inspector General, in its report entitled *The September 11 Detainees* (2003: 134) reported deportations and hearings based on secret evidence without charge and detentions. This surveillance strategy was further strengthened in the "Terrorism Information Awareness Program" of 2003 and the Domestic Security and Enhancement Act (2003) which provided for the rescinding of citizenship if "material" was provided to a proscribed organisation (this was a more draconian punishment than that under UK law where the penalty is a community order up to nine year's custody for proscribed organisation membership (see Terrorism Act 2000, s 11, Chapter 5). The Patriot Act 2006, reauthorised some provisions originally contained within the 2001 Act, including the so-called "sunset provisions" which had limited the duration of certain security operations and extended these provisions for further indefinite periods. The Patriot Acts of 2001 and 2011 expanded the powers of federal security agencies, including the National Security Agency, (NSA) requiring telecommunications agencies to hand over metadata. The Patriot Sunset Extension Act 2011 extended earlier provisions on roving wiretapping, and surveillance on individuals and business records and introduced increased border security. The extent of this intrusion into privacy and wiretapping, which Edward Snowden exposed were all said to be necessary in winning the WOT and saving lives. The Act set out to deter and punish terrorist acts in the US and also created a new definition of domestic terrorism including conduct "dangerous to human life that are a violation of the criminal laws of the United States or of any State" intended to "intimidate or coerce a civilian population", or "influence the policy of a government by intimidation or coercion" or are undertaken "to affect the conduct of a government by mass destruction, assassination, or kidnapping" whilst in the jurisdiction of the US. This vague and wide definition created concerns over its potential reach into other jurisdictions facilitated by the nebulous phrase of "other purposes" and "any State". Bussone (2011: 88) dubbed the Patriot Act 2011 a "tempest among the structures of freedom". There was some resistance. Madeleine Albright, the US Secretary of State, in a speech to the University of World Economy and Diplomacy at Tashkent Uzbekistan on 17 April 2000, recognised:

> One of the most dangerous temptations for a government facing violent threats is to respond in heavy-handed ways that violate the rights of innocent citizens. Terrorism is a criminal act and should be treated accordingly – and that means applying the law fairly and consistently…the best way to defeat terrorist threats is to increase law enforcement capabilities while at the same time promoting democracy and human rights. (quoted in Bingham 2010: 133)

The Demise of Criminal Justice—The Rise of Military Commissions

The most egregious demonstration of US contempt for the ROL and human rights norms was the handing over of unlawful combatant/detainees to Military Commissions, their indefinite detention and the arbitrary, repeated and prolonged use of torture. Amnesty International, *USA: Human dignity denied: Torture and accountability in the 'war on terror'* (2004) identified this terror to include the denial of habeas corpus; the use of incommunicado and secret detention; a pattern of official commentary on the presumed guilt of detainees; the sanctioning of harsh interrogation techniques in the pursuit of 'intelligence'; the blurring of the lines between powers of detention and interrogation; the setting up of military commissions which could admit coerced evidence; and a selective approach to international human rights and humanitarian law obligations (8). Whereas Military Commissions were originally established to oversee crimes of war in the battlefield, under Executive Order, they were now authorised to usurp the criminal courts where suspects, were "enemy combatants" who then fell into a legal abyss devoid of due process norms and safeguards otherwise afforded criminal suspects. The US's evasion of international law was skillfully machinated as Camp X,

Guantánamo Bay, was situated outside US territory on land leased in Cuba and said to be outside international law's geographical boundary. The US deftly argued that the "enemy combatants" had no enforceable human rights protections (Sands 2006: 211). In addition, the designation of criminal suspects as "unlawful enemy combatants" led President Bush to determine that the Geneva Convention protections, including the four treaties and three additional protocols that establish the standards of international law for humanitarian treatment in war, established in 1949, including protection of sick, those wounded in conflict and civilians and prisoners, simply did not apply. Vice President, Dick Cheney added his retributive zeal and said: "they don't deserve to be treated as Prisoners of War" (Robertson 2012: 501). Robertson along with many other human rights advocates argued that irrespective of what they were called or what label was applied, they were entitled to a fair process and a fair trial. President Bush however continued on his own lawless trajectory declaring that if what was being done was consistent with American law then it was consistent with international law, choosing to ignore the principle that where a conflict exists between domestic and international law, then international law prevails.

The setting up of Military Commissions, outside criminal law norms, outside the criminal court process and outside criminal justice itself, and the institutionalised use of torture have no comparator in UK law, procedure or practice. The Military Commissions are merely an extension of the President's sovereign power (Robertson 2012: 504). This US practice persisted without interference by the courts, at least (and in part only) until the cases of *Hamdan v Rumsfeld* [2006] and *Boumediene v Bush* [2008]. In the UK, whilst judges and human rights lawyers and some politicians condemned this unmitigated assault on the ROL and international justice norms, the UK executive fell conspicuously silent. Lord Steyn (2003) speaking for the judges, in his lecture "*Guantanamo Bay: The Legal Black Hole*" said the Military Commissions were "kangaroo courts" and:

> The most powerful democracy is detaining hundreds of suspected foot soldiers of the Taliban in a legal black hole at the United States naval base at Guantánamo Bay, where they await trial on capital charges by military tribunals…Judicial branches of government, although charged with the duty of standing between the government and individuals, are often

too deferential to the executive in time of peace. How then would the same judges act in a time of crisis?

REWRITING TORTURE BESPOKED FOR MUSLIM MEN

Shepherds, Bakers, Farmers, Taxi Drivers and Journalists

This sovereign power exceptionalism if not directly, then indirectly, autho-rised inconceivable acts of torture, or to put it another way, the US Military considered that they had the President's approval for what they were doing, and the President did nothing to disavow them of this belief. Muslim prisoners held at Guantánamo had been captured in Afghanistan and in other US military bases, and were forcibly arrested and kidnapped by "forcible rendition", taken to Cuba and interned in the "new Gulags" (Sands 2006: 254). Labelled as "unlawful enemy combat-ants" and "battlefield detainees", the US won popular support for this unlawful practice by engaging in a propaganda offensive with an orches-trated press campaign which instilled panic and fear into the public mind about terror attacks and threats committed by Muslims, and in this process racialised all Muslims who became suspects such that men with beards and women with headscarves created suspicion and alarm. As Abel (2018: 104, 107) observes: "Indefinite detention without trial of nearly 800 men at Guantánamo (GB) was the most prominent and constant US violation of the rule of law after 9/11". Their detention was kept out of the public eye for three and a half years.

Who were these unlawful enemy combatants, these allegedly Al-Qaeda, and Taliban foot soldiers? They were shepherds, bakers, farmers. They were taxi drivers. They were humanitarian aid workers (see Al Odah who was one of the litigants in *Boumediene v Bush* [2008] discussed later). They were journalists. Sami Al Haj, imprisoned for six years, was a cameraman for Al Jazeera (Abel 2018: 128). One presumed unlawful enemy combatant was a boy of 15 years of age, another, a man of 90 years (Robertson 2012: 636). They were all Muslim. Department of Defence "intelligence" about them was fantastical. Of Zahir Shah, a farmer, one of the detained men, the Pentagon claimed he had a rocket launcher in his house. Shah replied: "The only thing I did in Afghanistan was farming. We grew wheat, corn, vegetables and watermelons" (*New York Times*, 3 April 2006, "US reveals the identities of detainees"). Robertson reports that only six, out of 779 detainees held at Guantánamo were convicted of any crimes (Robertson: 636). It was also well known that men were detained in Guantánamo despite the US authorities knowing that they had no connection with Al-Qaeda or the Taliban, or any group, or posed any security risk whatever. One such case was the detainee Ronald Fiddler, a British convert to Islam (*The Guardian*, 25 April 2011).

Objectification and Dehumanisation

Securing public and political compliance for state brutality in Guantánamo also depended on neutralising the state acts of torture by presenting such unlawful conduct as necessary for security and national safety and gaining vital intelligence and by creating and promulgating a discourse that represented Muslim detainees as highly dangerous and evil (see Chapters 2 and 3, and Carlson and Weber (eds) 2007). Part of securing popular consent for this brutality also required divesting the "enemy combatants" of any humanity, personhood, identity or individuality. On arrival at Guantánamo there was shackling, and numerous degradation ceremonies, including removal of personal clothing, being dressed identically in fluorescent orange, numbered, stripped of any name, made to kneel, mouths covered with blue masks and kept naked in cells, forced to wear a "diaper" and denied toilet facilities. Numerous other indignities were devised all intended to render the person a non-person. Cohen (2001: 83) forensically documents dehumanisation as a typical feature of such strategies integral to making atrocities possible. The Senate Select Intelligence Committee (SSIC) Senate Committee Report on Torture (SCRT), also reported and condemned the practices of "ghost detainees", those detainees who had no number and therefore were not accounted for and could be easily disappeared. It said, "the Department of Defense did not believe an adequate articulation of military necessity or national security reasons warranting nondisclosure existed" [and that] "DoD is tired of 'taking hits' for CIA 'ghost detainees'", [and that] "the US government ...should not be in the position of causing people to 'disappear'" (p. 121 of 499, p. 442 nb 2478) (see also Poole 2006: 187). The model of creating a non-person is also noted by Vulliamy (1994, 2012) who writing on the genocide of Bosnian Muslims said that this pattern of dehumanisation used against the Bosnian Muslims was not untypical.

The appropriation of language also played its part in the official denials by US government officials. The torture camp was called

GTMO/"Gitmo". Now, how could a place with a name like "Gitmo" oversee such horror? Jonathan Glover (2012) records extensively the deliberate use of euphemism to camouflage the reality of torture regimes. Denial also makes this torture possible. Cohen utilises the work of Sykes and Matza's (1957) theory of excuses of everyday criminal conduct, to explore the neutralisation tactics utilised by perpetrators to disavow monstrous conduct. Such excuses include a denial of responsibility, a denial of harm, a denial of the rights of the victim, a condemnation of the condemners and an appeal to higher loyalties. Importantly, Sykes and Matza found that such neutralisations serve as justifications which precede the conduct, and facilitate and enable the conduct by releasing the perpetrator from any moral bind which might operate as a restraint. (Schutz 1967) describes the preceding motive as an "in order to" motive). Cohen, utilising this framework, provides as one example, the plight of Palestinians and their treatment, in unravelling this process of denial, normalisation, knowing/not knowing, lies and self-deception, collusion and cover up and the cultural stock of rhetorical devices which he says are "embedded in popular culture, banal language codes and state-encouraged legitimations". All these expressions of subterfuge came to characterise the treatment of Muslims held in GTMO "Gitmo" on the coast of Guantánamo Bay in Cuba.

"Interrogation"—Dying Is Not Permitted

Dick Cheney, former Vice President of the US, a grandmaster of subterfuge denied the reality of the conditions under which the Guantánamo detainees were held. He said: "They are living in the tropics. They're well fed, they've got everything they could possibly want" (Abel 2018: 114). Donald Rumsfeld with similar duplicity wrote a note on a memo of an Executive order authorising the use of "stress positions" (a euphemism for physical abuse), "I stand for 8-10 h a day why is standing limited to 4 h?" (Poole 169). The SSIC, SCRT (p. 69 of 499), noted in the case of Al-Rashiri that "in a standing stress position", "his hands were affixed over his head for two and a half days". Sleep deprivation for hours on end was instead referred to as "sleep management".

This theft of meaning through a veneer of pretence and subterfuge led military and executive officials to dispense with the word "torture", and deploy instead, the euphemism "interrogation", and substitute for "extreme torture" the euphemism of "coercive interrogation". Randall

Schmidt when tasked with conducting an inquiry into FBI reports of inhumane treatment said he found none but did find the long-term effect of this so-called "interrogation" "degrading and abusive" especially where detainees were subjected to continuous interrogation, for 18–20 h each day and for weeks and months on end (*Schmidt Report* 2005). This contumacious linguistic rebranding authorised the most extreme methods of cruelty, flagrantly outside international law. George Steiner recognises the "illocutionary and performative force" of language, and when writing on the holocaust, said: "Something of the lies and sadism settle in the marrow of language" (1967: 150–151). Cohen, in other contexts, identified what he calls "banal language codes" which encouraged the legitimation of torture (77). Amnesty International in its 2004 Report, *USA: Human dignity denied: Torture and accountability in the "war on terror"*, recognised the danger: "Euphemizing human rights violations threatens to promote tolerance of them" (3). This manipulation of language is also found in the statute itself where the Military Commissions Act 2006 utilises the term "coercion" and "coerced testimonies" as bland pretences for what is torture (Viterbo 2014: 301) (see Part iii Military Commission Rules of Evidence Section I General Provision 2015).

Assistant Attorney General, Jay Bybee, (Head of the Office of Legal Counsel of the US Department of Justice), was one of the torture revisionists, who signed what became known as the "Bybee memos", otherwise the "Torture memos" of 2002. Advising the President and the CIA, the memos stated that certain torture methods could be used notwithstanding the prohibitions in international human rights law and the Convention against Torture and Other Cruel, Inhuman or Degrading Treatment or Punishment (UNCAT) (1984). As Poole (167) points out the US entered a reservation to the Convention saying that it would only be bound by its own definition of torture, which as US exceptionalism and Bush had demonstrated meant, "It's what I say it is!". John Yoo, as Deputy Assistant Attorney General, was its drafter, redefining torture specifically for use on Muslim detainees in Guantánamo, Bagram and Iraq, by simply striking through and deleting the word "torture" from the text (Poole 2006: 4). Rebranded as "coercive interrogation", only those acts considered by the US authorities as "extreme", which involved "serious physical injury, such as organ failure, impairment of bodily function, or death... prolonged mental harm" now fell within torture's definition and, in defining "prolonged mental harm", the memo stated, that such harm must last for "months or even years". Along with this official authorisation and with the inuring and desensitisation of the interrogators (the subject of Cohen's atrocity triangle, 2001: 90), as Pfiffner (2014) observed, cruelty without restraint escalated. The US Department of Justice Interrogation memo, 1 August 2002, held that any challenge to the definition of torture under 18 U.S. Code (US Criminal Code), could be barred as it would represent an "unconstitutional infringement of the President's authority to conduct war"; and that "under the current circumstances, necessity or self-defence may justify interrogation methods that might violate... (s 2340A)". Of course, this had little at all to do with war or self-defence and everything to do with authorising gratuitous torture. Donald Rumsfeld (US Secretary of Defence 2001–2006) in continuing this mission authorised "Special Interrogation Plans" for detainees in Guantánamo. Mohammed al-Qahtani was harshly "interrogated" for over 50 days, and Mohamedou Slahi, was subjected to a mock execution at sea, solitary confinement, beatings, sexual humiliation and "environmental manipulation" (another euphemism for sensory violence) which included exposure to heat, to cold, to induced hypothermia and to sound. Yet even when detainees were murdered, and therefore the level of abuse inflicted had met the US's own defined threshold of torture, there were no prosecutions of officers and no Military Commissions (Luban 2007: 176). This perverted legal doctrine of calling torture, "interrogation" and declaring it necessary, said Alfred McCoy (2007: 47) laid the groundwork for legal impunity and undermined the "monumental achievement" of the Geneva Convention (1949) and Torture Convention (1951) (see also Robertson 2012: 632, 639).

What of the doctors who had signed the Hippocratic oath? Dr. David Tornberg, Deputy Assistant Secretary of Defense for Health Affairs, came to their aid and provided them with any absolution they might have needed when he said: ".... when a physician assists in interrogation he is not functioning as a physician and the obligations of the Hippocratic Oath to uphold ethical standards, do not apply, maintaining the confidentiality of patient can be eschewed when doctors go to war". The responsibility of the torture doctors then was to keep prisoners alive, not out of love or humanity but to ensure that death was avoided, and consequently avert the possibility that US conduct might be described as "torture" as defined in the Bybee memo. Hitchens (2015: 160) wrote: "the nasty fact must be faced: torture regimes have always been able to find doctors to advise on torture", and as Wilcox pithily observed: "dying is not permitted!"

(2011). Adnan Farhan Abdul Latif, a tortured detainee, wrote to his lawyer one day in 2012, before he took his own life. "To die is better than to live" (Abel 2018: 126).

How was this unprecedented cruelty justified to US citizens—the general public? First, it was hidden and kept secret. Vulliamy also talks of the "conspiracy of silence" as a typical shield in referring to Omarska and the torture, killing and raping of Bosnian Muslim men and women in the Bosnian conflict in 1992–1994 (Vulliamy 2012: 43, 56, 161). When the truth of the atrocities seeped out state justification relied on the propaganda machine where the state and the media, demonised, vilified and degraded Muslim men and women everywhere and the male Muslim "enemy combatants" in particular. It was said of them that they were different, not like any other men, not like ordinary prisoners, and that they did not "cooperate". After all, "Atrocities are easier to commit if respect for the victims can be neutralized, for this reason, humiliation handed out by those with power can be ominous" (Glover: 36, 17). This is what Cohen calls the "simultaneity of literal denial and ideological justification" (82).

Gregg Bloche explained that: "By late 2002, growing frustration with the slow pace of intelligence production at Guantánamo led to calls from commanders for innovative tactics. Major General Geoffrey Miller, who took command of Guantánamo in late 2002, approved the creation of a 'Behavioural Science Consultation Team' (BSCT, pronounced 'Biscuit') to develop new strategies". What could a programme pronounced "Biscuit" do that was harmful? It seems inconceivable that anyone could truly consider that such cruelty could lead to producing any information that would secure America's safety or assist in America's self-defence. Muslim suspects from anywhere were simply grotesquely punished for 9/11 and retribution poured down in every way possible. The architects of BSCT were two psychologists, Mitchell and Jensen (discussed in detail later), whom the CIA contracted to develop, operate and assess its interrogation operations, neither psychologist had any experience as an interrogator, no specialised knowledge of Al-Qaeda, no background in counter-terrorism, and no relevant cultural or linguistic expertise (*The Guardian* News, 22 April 2016, "CIA Torture Report").

One tries to imagine how this scheme worked and the minds, thinking and personalities of these men who conceived and dreamt up the torture, these orchestrators, planners, architects and drafters who penned it to paper, and then the perpetrators who skin to skin carried out the torture.

In this list was Bybee and Yoo; military officers, executive officials and the caring professions, the psychologists and doctors, all together thinking up more and more extreme and sadistic methods of torture. But perhaps it is not too hard to imagine as being possible, since US pilots killing innocent civilians in Iraq demonstrated the potential for a warped mentality. For example, the lead helicopter, using the name "Crazyhorse", in a raid on a civilian target when looking for insurgents, in Bagdad in July 2007, opens fire.

'Hahaha. I hit 'em,' shouts one of the American crew. Another responds: 'Oh yeah, look at those dead bastards'. (*The Guardian*, 5 April 2010, https://www.theguardian.com/world/2010/apr/05/wikileaks-us-army-iraqIraq-attack)

There was culpable neutrality, but not from all. Jack Goldsmith (who went on to write The *Terror Presidency* 2007) when legal adviser to the General Counsel of the Department of Defense, objected. He was soon silenced for his dissident unpatriotic speech and forced to resign.

Festivals of Cruelty—Keeping the Body Killing the Soul

Truth has its way of seeping out. By 2003, the secrecy of the torture programme began to fracture and the Bybee memo leaked into the public domain together with the testimonies from 18 Guantánamo prisoners who were released in 2003, including the "Tipton Three" (from Tipton in the UK) who wrote an account of their interrogation and abuse in Afghanistan and Guantánamo and of being "stripped, beaten, deprived of sleep, placed in stress positions, threatened with death, and shown videos of prisoners sodomising each other" (Abel: 107). (See also Michael Winterbottom's documentary on *The Tipton Three* BBC 4, 2006.) Such testimony was soon followed by the Abu Ghraib revelations in April 2004 (see below). In 2004, in a United Nations Press Release (17 June 2004) Secretary General, Kofi Annan, said he was sickened and shocked by the torture memos and reminded the US, and all nation states, of the Convention against torture and its application in all territories under their jurisdiction and control, stating: "Nor is torture permissible when it is called something else. Euphemisms cannot be used to bypass legal obligations". Diane Feinstein, Chairwoman of the Senate Select Intelligence

Committee (SSIC) in the Senate Committee Report on Torture (SCRT), said of the CIA's practices: "CIA personnel, aided by two outside contractors, decided to initiate a program of indefinite secret detention and the use of brutal interrogation" (Feinstein foreword p. 2 of 6, v).

Mounting international pressure forced the withdrawal of the Bybee memos and the definition and meaning of torture "as death or near death" was again rewritten, this time becoming the Levin memos, with an allegedly lighter touch where torture was now conceded at a lower threshold of brutality (watch it carefully as you might well miss it!). Torture was rescripted, this time as constituting: "severe physical pain ... a condition of some extended duration or persistence as well as intensity". This modification was forced upon the US military following Joe Darby (a former US Army Reservist), and at enormous personal expense to himself, blowing hard on the moral whistle on what had happened in Abu Ghraib. "It violated everything I personally believed in and all I'd been taught about the rules of war". Darby rose above the erosion of moral identity about which Glover speaks (2012: 35 [2002]). He provided two CD-ROMs of photographs to Special Agent Tyler Pieron of the US Army Criminal Investigation Command, at Abu Ghraib. Darby, for this act of moral courage, was reviled, threatened and called a traitor, such that he and his family had to be taken into protective custody. In an interview, he said of Abu Ghraib:

> The abuse started earlier than anybody realizes. Nobody has ever said that publicly, but there were things going on before our unit even got there. The day we arrived, back in October of 2003, we were getting a tour of the compound and we saw like fifteen prisoners sitting in their cells in women's underwear. This was day one; nobody from our unit had ever set foot in the prison. We asked the MPs in charge—the Seventy-second, out of Las Vegas—why the prisoners were wearing panties. They told us that it was a corrective action, that these guys had been mortaring the compound. So probably the MPs decided to mess with these guys. ... After we took over, it basically just escalated. (Hylton 2006)

The extent of the sadism perpetrated upon detainees in Guantánamo, Abu Ghraib and Bagram raises questions again about the state of mind of interrogators and the minds of commanding officers who had knowledge of, and approved, these abuses. Methods of torture or, as the US preferred, methods of interrogation and coercive interrogation (Luban 2006: 51, 71) included beatings, where in some cases, detainees were beaten to death. "Physical privation", a euphemism appropriated to neutralise the extent of the cruelty of this method, led to the death from hypothermia, otherwise "environmental manipulation or management" in 2002, of Gul Rahman. He was held in a secret prison in Kabul, Afghanistan, kept naked, except for a diaper in a cell on a concrete floor in freezing conditions, during which time he was further subjected to cold showers (see below the civil case, and noted in the SSIC, SCRT 2014, "Findings and conclusions" p. 10 of 19, xiv). Other methods of torture included near suffocation, euphemistically called "wet towelling" or "waterboarding", which involved holding the victim down whilst pouring water over the nose and mouth so as to fill the mouth and lungs with water and induce suffocation and choking (Eisenman 2007a: 135). Denial of injury (Sykes and Matza 1957; Cohen 2001) was an evasive disavowal appropriated by the perpetrators. Poole (171) points out how the commander of the "interrogation teams" at Guantánamo, Lt. Col Jerald Phifer, said that suffocation was a "misperception" and that the detainees were not really suffocating or drowning at all, they just "thought" they were. The SSIC, SCRT findings reported the case of Abu Zubaydah, who after waterboarding and near drowning, his torso was left in involuntary spasm, bubbles were rising from his open mouth and he was totally unresponsive. On this occasion his abusers recognised this as real and not as a misperception ("Findings and conclusions" p. 3 of 19[4] xii, and p. 495 of 499). Abu Zubaydah regained consciousness only after a "xyphoid thrust". The records of two of these "sessions" were also missing. Other forms of torture, "walling" (slamming detainees up against the wall) were used, together with blindfolding, hooding, sleep deprivation, being kept in a pitch black room and subjected to loud noise, stress positions, including standing for several hours ("Findings and conclusions" p. 3 of 19, xii) (see also Viterbo: 290, Del Rosso 2015: xii). These forms of torture were authorised in an Executive order by President Bush and written into the US Army's Field Manual No 34-52. Authorisation for further "stress" methods was sought in 2002 by Phifer entitled, "Request for approval of Counter-Resistance strategies". Poole (2006: 169) points out that one of these so-called "stress" positions resulted in the death of a prisoner. Manadel al-Jamadi, a detainee in Abu Ghraib, was shackled with his wrists tied behind his back and suspended. He died within half an hour (Hersh 2004). The CIA autopsy report recorded: "According to investigating agents, during interrogation of the detainee, a hood made of synthetic material was placed over the head and neck of the detainee. He died whilst detained at Abu Ghraib prison in Iraq. Cause of death: Blunt force injuries complicated by compromised respiration. Manner of Death: Homicide" (ACLU *The Torture Database* (*Final Report of the Independent Panel to Review DoD Detention Operations) DOD/ACLU-RDI-5146 No ME 03-504*). Known as Palestinian hanging torture, such a method was also routinely used by the French in Algeria (see Guido Pontecorvo's 1966 film *The Battle of Algiers*). Following the murder of Manadel al-Jamadi, ten navy personnel were put on trial, nine were found guilty and received a non-judicial penalty and the tenth was acquitted (Eisenman 2007a: 124). The SSIC, SCRT ("Findings and conclusions" p. 14 of 19 [17] xxiii) found that:

> The CIA rarely reprimanded or held personnel accountable for serious and significant violations, inappropriate activities, and systemic and individual management failures. CIA managers who were aware of failings and short-comings in the program but did not intervene, or who failed to provide proper leadership and management, were also not held to account.

Manadel al-Jamadi's dead body is on the www for his family and the world to see as US army officers' grin over his dead body. The abuse lives on forever. There is no property in the dignity of the murdered dead!

The captors invented more and more ways to wreak their sadism, hardly likely to produce intelligence to reduce any security risk or in self-defence, as 18 U.S. Code (Criminal Code s 2340A) (cited above) claimed was its purpose. What kind of interrogation technique is "rectal feeding and rehydration,"? and what possible answers to questions could such a method of violence possibly elicit, asks Iglesias (2014b). The SSIC, SCRT findings detailed how: "Abd al-Rahim al-Nashiri was placed in a forward-facing position ... with head lower than torso at which point the enema began. An officer described the procedure as regarding the rectal tube, if you place it and open up the IV tubing, the flow will self-regulate, and sloshing up the large intestines ... [what] I infer is that you get a tube up as far as you can, then open the IV wide. No need to squeeze the bag – let gravity do the work". An officer also recorded: "We used the largest Ewald [sic] tube we had" (reported in *The Guardian*, 9 December 2014). *The Guardian* report stated: "The 'lunch tray' for one detainee, which contained hummus, pasta with sauce, nuts and raisins, was 'pureed' and rectally infused". The SCRT recorded: "One detainee whose rectal examination was conducted with 'excessive force' was later diagnosed with chronic haemorrhoids, anal fissures and rectal prolapse". This was on any assessment an act of violent instrumental rape.

Invisible violence, leaving no physical mark was also part of the interrogator's torture strategy for concealing and denying that abuse had happened. In June 2006, Gordon England, the US Deputy Secretary of Defense, said that if nothing can be seen on the body of the detainee, it is possible to assert that nothing ever happened (McLagan and McKee 2012: 252). Viterbo documents what he calls "distal" methods (292) where violence and torture is perpetrated in secret: "if it can't be proved it can be refuted" (286, 294). One interrogator told the detainee, Riduan Isamuddin, that he would never go to court, because: "we can never let the world know what I have done to you" (see SSIC, SCRT, Findings p. 4 of 19). Shaker Aamer, a UK detainee, imprisoned in 2001 and released on 30 October 2015, said that his captors told him that since he would never get out, he could not tell the world what had happened. Aamer was detained because it was alleged that he had led a Taliban unit and was an associate of Osama Bin Laden. He denied this as fantastical. Strategies of interrogation focused, in Aamer's case, on destroying his mind and his normative and metaphysical world, including targeting his religious beliefs and telling him that his family would be threatened and harmed. In 2002, the US Secretary of Defense approved, what Bellaby (2016) describes as "torture lite" which included methods which focused on metaphysical techniques designed to destroy a person's semblance of self and their sanity including "Category II (8) 'Removal of all comfort items' (including religious items) ... (11) Forced grooming (shaving of facial hair) ...Category III ... (1) for example. Dabashi (2011: 2) understands the metaphysical destruction, he writes, "The Quran has been flushed down the toilet and used as target practice in American torture chambers". This also included convincing the detainee "that death or severely painful consequences are imminent for him and/or his family" (Janis et al. 2008: 205). CIA officers threatened at least three detainees with harm to their families including threats to sexually abuse the mother of a detainee, to cut [a detainee's] mother's throat and to harm the children of a detainee (SSIC, SCRT, "Findings and conclusions" p. 4 of 19, xiii). Aamer describes how the interrogator said that his five-year-old daughter would be sexually assaulted. They said: "If you don't start talking, we will rape your daughter and you will hear her crying 'daddy, daddy'" (reported in *The Independent*, 14 December 2015). The chief interrogator of the detainee Khalid Sheikh said, such methods were devised to obtain "total control over the detainee" (SSIC, SCRT 448 of 449, see also Laughland 2015). As Cover (1986) notes in his essay, *Violence and the Law*, torture is used to destroy the victim's normative world, to destroy what the victim values (1603) and to assert the superiority and power of the captor over the captured.

Other psychological techniques as Bellaby (2014: 144) observes were designed to create: "… a paradoxical dependency upon the torturer: the victim is brought to believe that his fate is entirely within the hands of the torturer … the victim must realise that he is completely at the mercy of the torturer. As a result of this asymmetric relationship, the victim starts to feel obliged to the torturer both as his punisher and saviour…. And to break the individual's will and force him to turn against himself". Reminiscent of the end of life for Joseph K in Kafka's *The Trial*, who, at the point of being brutally murdered, realises too that in fact he was expected to kill himself. "K. now knew it would be his duty to take the knife as it passed from hand to hand above him and thrust it into himself. But he did not do it…" These "interrogation" techniques used in Guantánamo were also "standard operating procedure" (SOP) outside Guantánamo (Sands 2006: 254). A report detailing torture at Rusafa, Iraq, reported in the *New York Times*, 27 April 2010, revealed: "…at least 505 cases of torture were documented in Iraqi prisons in 2009, according to a report released by the state department in March". Human Rights Watch (2010) reported that: "Detainees in a secret Baghdad detention facility were hung upside-down, deprived of air, kicked, whipped, beaten, given electric shocks, and sodomized". Lisa Hijjar reporting, in *The Nation* (19 June 2018) on five Guantánamo detainees on trial in Military Commissions tribunals for their alleged roles in the 9/11 terrorist attacks, found that the defendants were tortured in CIA "black sites" before transfer to Guantánamo in 2006. In her report she details the abuse of Mustafa al-Hawsawi who was accused of being one of the financiers behind the 9/11 attack. Al-Hawsawi, said his counsel, was unable to attend all the hearing because of the sodomisation and repeated rape to which he was subjected whilst in detention. His counsel explained his absence. "In October 2016, he underwent rectal surgery, but he still suffers in ways that, as learned counsel Ruiz has explained, force him to constantly choose between eating and defecating painfully, or fasting". Poole (2006) documents the case of two prisoners detained in the US base in Bagram, Afghanistan, who died after "trauma" to the legs following the "repetitive administration of legitimate force" (yet another euphemism in the neutralisation armoury). The coroner described the injuries somewhat differently, comparing them to being run over by a bus. The official investigation into the circumstances of one of the deaths is again a demonstration of the normalisation and the banality of denial (I am applying Hannah Arendt's (2011 [1963]) concept of "banality" here). "No one blow could be determined to have caused the death.... It is reasonable to conclude at the time that repetitive administration of *legitimate force* resulted in all the injuries we saw" (cited in Poole 163).

That such cruelties also function as entertainment is widely documented (Vulliamy 1994: 253; Glover 33). Poole (164–165) reports that in 2002 in Bagram, Specialist Jones, a military policeman, testified how using cruelty entertained the military in the case of a man who when beaten cried out to God. "It became a kind of running joke, and people kept on showing up to give this detainee a common peroneal strike just to hear him scream out 'Allah'". This "entertainment" went on over a 24-hour period. He died. His torturers—"interrogators" concluded later that he was not involved in any way with terrorism and was in fact "an innocent taxi driver".

The US repeatedly held fast to the specious claim that such methods of torture they called "interrogation" were justified because of the potential to reveal intelligence and to prevent the ticking bomb (see Ramsey 2006). Such a presumption runs contrary to everything that is known about confessional evidence obtained under duress (Robertson 2012: 33). As Gudjonsson (2012), whose work has been internationally recognised since the 1980s, and Gudjonsson and Pearse (2011) found, suspects who want the violence and coercion to stop will say anything at all to effect this result. Was there a ticking bomb? Could these shepherds, bakers, farmers, taxi drivers and journalists have known anything to prevent the ticking bomb? Yet, even in the face of all the evidence and revelations, CIA officials, torture lawyers and President Bush, claimed and continued to claim that countless lives have been saved and "our Homeland is more secure" (Timm 2014; Poole 2006: 186). This preposterous lie lives on and "Republican candidates for the presidency in 2011 and 2012 agreed that the use of "enhanced interrogation techniques" and "extreme interrogation techniques" (EITs), particularly waterboarding, was necessary in order to protect the US (Timm: 127; Lightcap and Pfiffner 2014). Such justifications were further embellished by appropriating human rights and the ROL claiming that such measures protected others from terrorism (Bricmont) such that torture became rewritten as an act of altruism to save us all, which the linguistic turn transformed. The US positioned themselves, as Luban (42) argues, as kindly torturers and not as tyrants. Yet, as David Iglesias, a former prosecutor said, no terror plot was stopped due to abusive interrogations (Iglesias 2014a) producing only false knowledge (Wilcox 2015: 64, 113) and false positives (Leo and Ofshe 1998). The SSIC, SCIT released only 525 of its 6700 pages, the full report remaining classified. The investigators concluded that there was no correlation between the success of counter-terrorism and the so-called interrogation techniques used ("Findings and conclusions" p. 10 of 19, xix) (see also Harris 2014), and held that any claim made regarding torture's success was inaccurate ("Findings and conclusions" p. 5 of 19, xiv) asserting:

We cannot again allow history to be forgotten and grievous past mistakes to be repeated. ("Findings and conclusions" p. 3 of 6, xii)

Protections for criminal suspects evolved in English common law and shared across common law jurisdictions were simply ripped up where Muslims were deemed "enemy combatants" and international human rights protections set aside. The US returned to the medievalism of the Star Chamber. International condemnation was mixed. As Bingham had stated, some in the UK were ambivalent. Jack Straw MP, echoing the culpable neutrality of the international community said: "I am not going to second guess the decisions they make" (Abel 127). Archbishop Desmond Tutu, criticised the US, UK and the allies for their complicity (127). But there was more to come.

THE GENDERING OF SEXUAL SADISM

Abu Ghraib prison is located 20 miles to the west of Baghdad. It was opened in the 1950s as a maximum-security prison. By the 1980s, it was used by Saddam Hussein until its closure in 2002, and from 2000 to 2006 used by the US coalition forces as a detention facility (Baghdad Central Correctional Facility). Those detained in the prison included, civilians randomly picked up, those involved in a range of criminal offences, and those detained in connection with alleged crimes against the coalition. Most detainees, as noted by the CIA report, were held for criminal violations including thefts, assault, etc. It was here that a particularly exaggerated and perverse use of sexual violence, sadism, humiliation, decimation of human dignity was used as part of a wider tactic of torture committed by US army officers against Iraqi detainees. The details became known following publication by CBS news, in April 2004, of "the" photographs. The US military and President Bush's administration responded immediately, and in distancing itself, claimed the abuse to be nothing more than the doings of a few rogue soldiers. But this sexual abuse did not go on in the desert, unseen, unheard, it went on under the supervision of the US military, its senior commanders and supervisors and with their knowledge and complicity.

On the Night Shift

James Schlesinger, who served as Chairman to the inquiry on DoD *Detention Operations* in the *Final Report of the Independent Panel to Review DoD Detention Operations* (2004: 5) said: "The events of October through to December 2003 on the night shift of Tier 1 at Abu Ghraib prison were acts of brutality and purposeless sadism". These "acts" were perpetrated on Iraqi Muslim male prisoners, who were stripped naked, piled up on top of one another in a human pyramid, sexually abused in many ways, terrorised by dogs and tortured. Naked prisoners were forced to masturbate, and to enact so-called "homoerotic acts" on one another (I consider the appropriateness of this description as "homo-erotic", below). Male and female officers who perpetrated these abuses took trophy photographs of the humiliation of their captees. One of the photographs shows an officer holding the end of a leash, which is tied as a noose around the neck of a prisoner, whose wrists and ankles are bound, and naked except for a diaper, and lying on the floor, he is forced to crawl. The permanency of the photograph disseminated glob-ally repeats the abuse and lives forever on the www. The male and female US army officers responsible, when court martialed, said in their defence that they "lacked training", and that their superiors "had knowledge" of what they were doing and approved of their conduct (Del Rosso: 14). Schlesinger reported: "(9) On September 14, 2003 LTG Sanchez signed a memorandum authorizing a dozen techniques beyond Field Manual 34-52 - five beyond those approved for Guantánamo". One of the many photographs circulated on the www is of the face and naked body of the tortured and dead Manadel al-Jamadi (note his face is not hidden or pixe-lated and his dignity not protected, for there is no property in the dead) with officers Charles Graner and Sabrina Harman smiling triumphantly, as if they had captured a trophy deer. This said the *Los Angeles Times* was one of the most indelible images yet made public (*LA Times* "Death of Prisoner Detailed in Testimony", 18 May 2004). To neutralise these acts and excuse the US soldiers, Rush Limbaugh (an American radio talk show host and conservative political commentator) said, that this was: "Horseplay by soldiers blowing off steam" "having a good time!"

> You know, if you look at, if you, really, if you look at these pictures, I mean, I don't know if it's just me, but it looks just like anything you'd see Madonna, or Britney Spears do on stage. Maybe I'm.... yeah.... And get an NEA grant for something like this. I mean, this is something that you can see on stage at Lincoln Center from an NEA grant, maybe on Sex in the City, the movie. I mean, I don't, it's just me. (Wildau and Seifter 2004, cited in Del Rosso 2015)

Some acts of sadism and cruelty were specifically designed to psychologically humiliate, and such tactics had originally been authorised in the Bybee/Levin/Phifer memos for use in all places of detention under US control. These methods included, removing prisoner's clothing, keeping prisoners naked, dressing prisoners in women's underpants, forcing them to wear diapers and using dogs to terrorise. Together with the extreme acts of sexual sadism Schlesinger conceded in his report: "There was a sadism on the night shift at Abu Ghraib, sadism that was certainly not authorized .... It was a kind of 'Animal House' on the night shift" (cited in Del Rosso: 92).

These acts of sexual sadism perpetrated on Muslim men happened after the International Criminal Court Tribunal for Yugoslavia judgment in *Prosecutor v Furundžija* 1998 (Case IT-95-17/1-tq, Judgment, 10 Dec 1998.1998 Musema Jan 27 2000) and after the judgment in *Kunarac, Vuković and Kovač* [2002] that sexual sadism, sexual slavery and sexual abuse of Muslim women in Bosnia, where women were raped and murdered as part of a deliberate strategy to humiliate and break Muslim women and men and their communities, was a war crime. The abuse at Abu Ghraib happened after the judgment in Jean-Paul Akayesu 1998 (*Prosecutor v Jean-Paul Akayesu* [1998] where the International Criminal Tribunal for Rwanda (ICCR) found that women were raped and murdered and where the court defined sexual violence, sexual sadism and rape as:

...any act of a sexual nature which is committed on a person under circumstances which are coercive. Sexual violence is not limited to physical invasion of the human body and may include acts which do not involve penetration or even physical contact ... coercive circumstances need not be evidenced by a show of physical force. Threats, intimidation, extortion and other forms of duress which prey on fear or desperation may constitute coercion, and coercion may be inherent in certain circumstances, such as armed conflict or the military presence of Interahamwe among refugee Tutsi women at the bureau communal.' ([688]).

The details of these killings and acts of sexual abuse became global public knowledge reported in the media for several years and certainly some of the older officers at Abu Ghraib would have been aware of these international cases decided only a few years prior to their own abusive conduct in Abu Ghraib. The ICC Tribunals rejected the soldiers' claim that they were only following orders. In Abu Ghraib prison in the winter of 2003 were perpetrators and army superiors oblivious to these international cases and the judgments?

The Camera as an Instrument of Torture

There was first the sexual abuse and sadism, and the violence and other acts of torture. Then the double victimisation in the photograph being taken of the abuse and circulated amongst those in the prison. Then the triple abuse, a few years later, in the permanent photographic record memoralising the abuse on the www and with the capacity to haunt and shame ad infinitum. The photographic record itself and the acts perpetrated in the photographic record invoked responses from many writers. Judith Butler (2007: 956) considered the photographs showed evidence of war crimes.

...the photographs taken within the Abu Ghraib prison showed brutality, humiliation, rape, murder, and in that sense, they were clear representational evidence of war crimes. These pictorial records of the abuse have functioned in many ways, including as evidence in legal proceedings against those who are pictured as engaging in acts of torture and humiliation. They have also become iconic for the way that the US government, in alliance with Britain, has spurned the Geneva Conventions, particularly the protocols governing the fair treatment of prisoners of war. ...there was a systematic mistreatment of prisoners in Iraq, paralleling a systematic mistreatment at Guantánamo (2) Only later did it become clear that the protocols devised for Guantánamo were explicitly used by the personnel at Abu Ghraib, and that both sets of protocols were indifferent to the Geneva Accords.

Sontag speaks of the shock of the photograph and that it cannot fail to unite people of good will, and that it is a means making "real" (or more real) matters that the privileged and the merely safe might prefer to ignore (2003: 6). Her writings on war photography have become a lens through which we can consider the photographs of Abu Ghraib, and in *On Photography* (1997) Sontag recognised, the camera's predatory power.

At Abu Ghraib, the camera was such a predatory weapon, the act of taking and making, the act of showing and distributing and the effect long after in the permanency and global reach of the image constitutes the totality of the abuse. Donald Rumsfeld, as Secretary of Defence, one of the architects of the torture programme (albeit action against him was dismissed *Arkan Mohammed Ali* Et Al., *Appellants v. Donald H. Rumsfeld, Individually,* Et Al., *Appellees Consolidated with 07-5185, 07-5186, 07-5187* (2011)), also conceded the predatory power of the camera. He said:

> It is the photographs that gives one the vivid realization of what actually took place. Words don't do it. The words that there were abuses, that it was cruel, that it was inhumane – all of which is true - that it was blatant, you read that and it's one thing. You see the photographs and you get a sense of it and you cannot help but be outraged. (see ACLU *The Torture Database* UCLA DoD memo-052528)

He was outraged but hiding behind technicalities in an interview on *Online NewsHour*, he said: "I'm not a lawyer. My impression is that what has been charged thus far is abuse, which I believe technically is different from torture" (cited in Dauenhauer 2009).

The capacity of the photographic record to prospectively perpetuate harm was also recognised: "The photograph is a kind of promise that the event will continue, is that very continuation of the event, producing an equivocation at the level of the temporality of the event; did those actions happen then; do they continue to happen? Does the photograph continue the event in the present?" (Butler 2007). Moreover, the suffering of the victims and those with connections to them individually and the affront to a wider Muslim conscience was exacerbated in knowledge of the victors' pleasure in the photographs. This was not documentary photography. Nor was it photography to show the horror and pity of war. Nor were the photographs taken from a moral standpoint in order to shock the conscience of the world into action. The compelling motive of these photographs occupied none of these realms, instead the motive of both photographer and abuser were welded into one, delighting in the abuse, the power, the victory and the degradation of the Muslim subject and in the absolute power of the perpetrator to demonstrate what they could do and the extent of depravity they could compel. This was the face of ultimate Nietzschean sadistic power in a love of cruelty, and in what in general terms Glover has identified as "a festival of cruelty" (35). The permanent predatory and continuous power of the pornographic photograph was recognised by Andrea Dworkin, who, when speaking of pornography said, "the photographs live on forever" and of the photographer she says. "He can pimp her forever"! (Omnibus interview 1991) The living record of the Abu Ghraib photographs is not merely a historical record of a war crime, the living record allows the abuse to continue and to live on, abusing the individual subject and the corporeal Arab and Muslim body in perpetuity.

Sontag in her last publication before her death, an article in the *New York Times*, "Regarding the Torture of Others" 23 May 2004, and indicting the US, said of the Abu Ghraib photographs and the US's collective responsibility: "These photos are us, the nature of policies prosecuted by ... [the Bush] administration and the hierarchies deployed to carry them out...".

Constituting the Subject of Sexual Abuse—To Be Abused "Like A Woman"

These photographs functioned as pornography where men were sexually abused as women, where male power used by male officers and masculinised power used by female officers sexualised and degraded the male Muslim subject. David Levi Strauss (2005) (photographer and cultural critic) did not agree with, talk show, Rush Limbaugh's assessment that the photographs were merely pictures of army personnel "blowing off steam" (see above). Levi Strauss, when he first saw the photographs, said he did not know what he was looking at because he hadn't seen anything like that before and couldn't make sense of them. This was no doubt because what was a war crime was being pornographised at the point of its commission.

Pornographic scenarios of violence and humiliation had been turned upside down in several ways. At Abu Ghraib, the perpetrators of this sexual humiliation and assault were not only men, but also women. The victims were men and not women. In the methods of abuse and relations of power the male and female perpetrators behaved as heteronormative men abusing women. The victim's humiliation and shame was intensified in being abused and subjugated not as heteronormative men but as women and in some scenarios, as homosexual. Both male and female officers in the masculinist mode of domination forced the Muslim prisoners to sexually abuse one another and enact homosexual abuse. Luban (2007) points out, that it is unlikely that officers had specific instructions to do what they did. "Humiliate", was the instruction. There was no written order to pile naked prisoners on top of each other in simulated sexual positions. There was no written order to force nude prisoners to masturbate. There was no written order to place women's underwear over the faces and heads of bound prisoners. Were those who demanded and orchestrated these indignities sexual sadists, or were they ordinary soldiers?

Levi Strauss, familiar with photographic images of females being insulted, abjected and degraded by men, so redolent in the staple scenarios both enacted and real in pornographic representation, and in real abuses against women in war crimes, did not know what to make of the photographs of Arab Muslim men victimised in real scenarios of abjection, sexual degradation and abuse where the binaries of gender were inverted. Glover documents the gendered sexual element in torture in war and civil war and observes that the captors and perpetrators are always men, and men and women their victims. Glover (34) documents the layering of cruelty, indignity with humiliation and ridicule: "Typical are the cruelties and humiliations inflicted on Brazilian women tortured under the military regime, who described being paraded naked, having their nipples repeatedly pinched, being genitally violated with bits of wood, and being made to work naked whilst being subjected to a barrage of obscenities and jokes". Vulliamy (2011: 56, 253) documents the extent of mass rape as a weapon of war in Bosnia. But at Abu Ghraib this special "festival of cruelty" was different turning the binarism of sexual sadism and harm of correspondence of perpetrator and victim on its head, where abuse was conceived and contrived to do maximum injury to men by abusing them as women. On sexual sadism, war and pornography, Dworkin wrote there is nothing that the pornographers have not weaved scenarios around in humiliating and abusing women (1997, 1989: 233–235). George Steiner in "Night Words" (1976: 76) had also recognised as Dworkin (1989: 145) puts it, the assimilation of concentration camp [values] into present erotic sensibility.

Male victims in fear of their lives were ordered, arranged, positioned and styled, by their abusers, to enact sexually degrading and humiliating pornographic scenarios for their captors and the camera, including scenarios where male prisoners were forced to perform sexual abuses on other male prisoners.

Sexual sadism was committed by both the perpetrator of the abuse, and the photographer who filmed it. Joanna Bourke writing on Abu Ghraib in "Torture as pornography" (2004) said that the abusers seemed oblivious. "The people taking the photographs exult in the genitals of their victims. There is no moral confusion here: the photographers don't even seem aware that they are recording a war crime. There is no suggestion that they are documenting anything particularly morally skewed. For the person behind the camera, the aesthetic of pornography protects them from blame".

Whilst there was no specific memo of authorisation, no Bybee memo, no Levin memo, no Phifer memo, some of the tactics deployed which juxtaposed insult with preciously held religious values did in fact mimic the torture methodology approved by the Secretary of Defense Rumsfeld in 2002 "Category II (8), ... stripping prisoners naked and placing them in diapers". At Abu Ghraib, sexual elements redolent in the pornographic imagery of coercion and rape were added. As Eisenman points out, what had been described as "forced homoeroticism" was compelled and photographed (2007a: 134). Butler notes the deliberate desecration of Muslim sensitivities. "The US soldiers exploit the Muslim prohibition against nudity, homosexuality, and masturbation in order to tear down the cultural fabric that keeps the integrity of these persons intact. But the US soldiers have their own erotic shame and fear, one that is mixed with aggression in some very distinct ways" (Butler 2007: 963). I am unable to agree that what was demanded of male prisoners one to another was in fact "forced homoeroticism". Homoeroticism presumes consent of the parties involved. What Muslim detainees were forced to perform, one on another, was a prelude to oral rape between two men. Neither do I agree that the insult, abuse and humiliation in forcing a man to masturbate is culturally or religiously specific in its potential to offend. The cultural impact is over-orientalised. This would have insulted any man! However what magnifies the harm for the Muslim prisoner is in his knowledge of the perpetrator's intent, and the intent of the perpetrators lay in their efforts to imply that their victims were homosexual (which was intended to insult) and would under any conditions enjoy and want oral sex with another man. The harm is magnified in the knowledge that they are being abused precisely like this because they are Muslims and that the scenarios of abuse are created around what the captors consider are most likely to offend (see Eisenman 2007a: 133).

The insult to them was in their feminisation (Gronnvoll 2007: 390; Das 2008) and as Khalili (2010) explains this feminisation was further enforced by white, Western female army officers further reinforcing the racial and sexual hierarchies. Drawing on Butler's *Gender Trouble*, Kaufman-Osborn (2005) explores the multiple ways in which specifically gendered practices, can be detached from the bodies they conventionally regulate and used to humiliate and degrade through the performativity of the acts themselves, which characterised the abuse at Abu Ghraib.

The impact of the abuse on Muslim detainees was exacerbated by US triumphalism, photographs of smiling, gleeful US soldiers, thumbs up, gloating over the dead body of Manadel al-Jamadi and celebrating the unlimited possibilities of what they could do. Said recognised the centrality of US triumphalism to power and submission in "The Arab Portrayed" (1968) where at Princeton University's tenth reunion after the June "Arab – Israeli" war, the students were to dress in Arab costume, and to process with their hands above their head "in a gesture of abject defeat" (Said 1968: 1) (see here Chapter 2). "Triumphalism" is the signature of the victor. Meir Pa'il (a colonel in the Israel Defense Forces) described how at Deir Yassin surviving men were: "loaded into freight trucks and led in a victory parade like a Roman triumph and then executed" (Palumbo 1987: 52).

Court Martials, Denials and Refutations Neutralising Sexual Abuse

There were eleven court martials, including amongst them Staff Sergeant Ivan Frederick, US Army Reserve Charles Graner, US Army Reserve Sabrina Harman and US Army Reserve Lynddie England. These officers on the night watch were charged with offences of dereliction of duty, maltreatment, aggravated assault and battery. The legal language and charges against them are presented in flat factual narrations, which fail to capture the harm, insult, repugnance and specificity of their criminal conduct. Major General Geoffrey Miller's testimony on the general conditions at Abu Ghraib reveals precisely how language functioned to neutralise and camouflage the acts and the perpetrator's intention.

> During the period 1 October 2003 through 4 January 2004 the following interrogation techniques among others were employed at Abu Ghraib by Military Intelligence personnel. They were: -Sleep deprivation -Dietary manipulation -Stress positions -Change of scenery -Environmental manipulation -Sensory deprivation Upon my taking command these techniques were terminated and more congenial passive intelligence gathering techniques were employed. I have found these passive techniques are more effective in gathering intelligence. I am of the opinion that keeping detainee's nude for long periods and handcuffing detainees to cells while nude are violations of the Geneva Conventions. (*The Torture Data Base*, Court-Martial Record: Staff Sergeant Ivan L. Frederick, II (Volume 5 of 8) ACLU-RDI 1756: 4).

During 2003, a report by Major General Taguba had already identified the euphemistically called "institutional failures" (see Bartone 2010) including details of conduct which the tribunal found were "sadistic, blatant, and wanton criminal abuses":

> Breaking chemical lights and pouring the phosphoric liquid on detainees; pouring cold water on naked detainees; beating detainees with a broom handle and a chair; threatening male detainees with rape; allowing a military police guard to stitch the wound of a detainee who was injured after being slammed against the wall in his cell; sodomizing a detainee with a chemical light and perhaps a broom stick, and using military working dogs to frighten and intimidate detainees with threats of attack, and in one instance actually biting a detainee.

Both Miller's testimony and Taguba's report demonstrated that the abuse was not committed by a "few rogue soldiers" as the Bush administration preferred to assert but was instead institutionalised practice. The testimonies of the officers who were bystander/witnesses revealed the widespread knowledge and condonation by superior officers of these methods of abuse. In giving evidence bystander/witnesses said that when they questioned the perpetrators about the conduct towards the prisoners, the officers replied: "We know what we're doing". Some officers reported the incidents to platoon leaders and senior officers. The defendants made excuses for their conduct by appealing to the inuring conditions, and their lawyers spoke of desensitisation and the blunting of natural responses resulting in a moral blindness, calling it the "Abu Ghraib effect". The "Abu Ghraib effect" did not affect all. Other officers in giving evidence said that they challenged the perpetrators, asking rhetorically: "haven't you gone over the line?"

Frederick, Graner, Harman and England, all mitigated their behaviour by appealing to well established "techniques of neutralisation" (Sykes and Matza 1957) denying responsibility, injury, the worth of the victim and appealed to higher loyalties. Houge (2016) has made an important study of sexual abuse in recent war crimes trials, including the Abu Ghraib Court Martials, noting the appropriation by those charged of these excusatory narratives. Frederick, Graner, Harman and England also pleaded "obedience", in that they were following orders and lacked training. Cohen (2001) in drawing on Sykes and Matza's excusatory narratives analyses their deployment by perpetrators in many instances of genocide and mass murder, especially in the Nazi treatment of the Jews, noting the iteration of the excuse of blind obedience (89). The Abu Ghraib officers in their pleadings said that no harm was done. They condemned and exceptionalised their victims, they claimed that their prisoners had no worth and were dangerous hardened men echoing the same justificatory accounts given by officers accounting for the torture strategy used on Muslim men at Guantánamo, and also found in the excuses made by British army officers responsible for the killing of Baha Mousa (see Chapter 4). They also appealed to higher loyalties, stating they were acting to protect others. Of the "trophy" photographs they took of their conduct, they accepted that they were to be shared amongst officers and their families and to be shown to the prisoners to cause further shame and humiliation (Eisenman 2007b: 34).

Ivan Frederick, (ACLU *The Torture Database* DoD-041209, see Court-Martial Record: Staff Sergeant Ivan L. Frederick, II (Volume 1 of 8) was a "trained" correctional officer and a former prison officer in civilian life (see Frederick 2004). The ten charges against him included conspiracy with Specialist Roman Krol, Charles Graner, Specialist Armin J. Cruz, Sabrina Harman and others to abuse detainees, including forcing the nudity of detainees, forcing detainees to balance naked in a human pyramid, ordering the detainees to masturbate in front of other detainees and soldiers, placing one in a position so that the detainee's face was directly in front of the genitals of another detainee to simulate fellatio, creating mock executions and physical abuse. Physical abuse charges against him included, being charged with striking a prisoner with force "likely to cause death or grievous bodily harm", this near-death assault, at trial was reduced to a mere assault. He was also charged with photographing the detainees during some of these acts. In his defence, he denied responsibility. He said he had asked his superiors, on several occasions, if his treatment of the prisoners was acceptable, and he said that they had said that what he was doing was "acceptable" and encouraged him "to continue with these tactics". His defence counsel tried to establish that although he was described as a "trained" officer, who had undergone some training having served in other similar situations, he actually lacked training. It was however acceded that he lacked leadership. Cross-examined on the defence's argument that he lacked training, the prosecutor, Captain Michael Holly asked rhetorically: "How much training do you need to know that it's wrong to force a man to masturbate? You don't need training. A 5-year-old knows that that's wrong" (*The Guardian*, 24 October 2004) (see also Houge 2016: 432). One of the bystander officers in giving evidence reported: "I returned later because someone wanted me to get SSG Frederick for something. I went down to tier 1, and when I looked down the corridor, I saw two naked detainees, one masturbating to another kneeling with his mouth open. I thought I should just get out of there. I didn't think it was right, as it seemed like the wrong thing to do. I saw SSG Frederick walking towards me, and he said, "Look what these animals do when you leave them alone for two seconds. I heard PFC England shout out, 'he's getting hard'" (Frederick 2004, Vol 6 Court-Martial Record 1757: 48). Frederick was also charged with the mock execution, involving participating and allowing the placing of wires on the detainee's hands whilst he stood on a *Meals Ready to Eat* box with his head covered, and allowing the detainee to be told he would be electrocuted if he fell off of the box, and allowing the detainee to be photographed (Frederick 2004, Vol 1 Court-Martial Record: 17). Frederick pleaded guilty to all charges and following a plea bargain and mitigation, his counsel in mitigation pleaded that what he had done was an "aberration" and that he had "atoned by providing full co-operation." (It should be noted that offering a guilty plea to charges in exchange for a reduction in sentence does not amount to atonement nor does providing information on the conduct of other soldiers to save himself). His defence counsel argued that the stressful environment, "made the violence inevitable" (cited in Houge 2016: 431). He was sentenced to eight years imprisonment and released on parole after serving only three.

Considering the role of Charles Graner, a corporal in the military police, with extensive experience as a correctional officer, he was also charged with placing naked detainees in a human pyramid, photographing and being photographed with the pyramid of naked detainees, ordering detainees to strip, to masturbate in front of other detainees and soldiers and forcing detainees to simulate fellatio and photographing the detainees during these acts. There were also additional charges of violent assault. In one of these photographs taken, Lynddie England is smirking and holding a leash wrapped around the neck of a detainee to look as if she is dragging the detainee out of his cell. In another, Graner, is posing in the photograph with England behind the pyramid of naked detainees. Graner in his defence said he was complying with a general command climate requiring the humiliation of detainees. Continually in denial and subterfuge, he said that the act of putting a tether round the neck of a naked detainee, as if a dog, and making him crawl was "a creative thing to do" and retorted "it could have been a lot worse" (cited in Houge: 429). His defence counsel said, "a tether is a valid tool". Of the naked human pyramid, he said "cheerleaders all over America do this". His continuing disdain for the prisoners is evident when in his evidence he is reported to have said: "In Texas we'd lasso them and drag them out of there" (*BBC News*, 11 January 2005, "Abu Ghraib Troops 'did not abuse'"). Graner said that the detainees were "unworthy", dangerous and hardened terrorists who had to be controlled and that he had assumed that all Iraqi's were terrorists. (It is worth being reminded that the majority of men in Abu Ghraib were either civilians caught up in the fighting or ordinary criminals, see Chapter 3.) Found guilty he was sentenced to 10 years imprisonment. He appealed in *United States, Appellee v Charles Graner* Jr [2010] on the grounds that the trial court had wrongly limited the testimony of a defence witness. "The military judge refused to allow Mr. Archambault to testify concerning the appropriateness of the leash (or tether) around the neck and stacking techniques. The military judge concluded that such testimony was irrelevant" (14). The appeals court agreed. He was released on parole after serving six and a half years of his sentence.

Women Like Men Degrading Men, Like Men Degrading Women

In Abu Ghraib sexual assault on male prisoners was perpetrated by women (notably Specialists Lynddie England, Meghan Ambuhl and Sabrina Harman) adding a further dimension to this abuse (Holland 2009; Houge 2016). Susan Sontag prior to the Abu Ghraib revelations had already published what was to be her last book, *Regarding the Pain of Others* (2003), in which she explored the impact of war photography recognising, as did Virginia Woolf, that war is a man's game, and the killing machine has a gender (5). Bush on 8 February 2004 had after all declared "I am a war President" (*BBC News*). Christina Lamb (2020) cites Virginia Woolf (1938) who wrote "War makes beasts of men" but in Abu Ghraib, war made beasts of women too.

Elizabeth Goldberg recognises that most difficult to comprehend and to witness was the spectacle of young women engaged in the torture and abuse of male detainees (2007: 113). It was the women behaving like male sexual abusers that was the most shocking and their abuse of men as men abuse women. Meghan Ambuhl, the least culpable who did not participate in the abuse of detainees, was originally charged with Article 81 (conspiracy to commit maltreatment), Article 92 (dereliction of duty), Article 93 (maltreatment) and Article 134 (indecent acts). She later pleaded guilty to dereliction of duty in that she failed to report the activities of Military Police and Military Intelligence personnel at Abu Ghraib Prison. She was sentenced to forfeiture of half a months' pay for one month and reduction to the category of a *"Private"* (ACLU *The Torture database* Court-Martial: Specialist Megan Ambuhl [Record of Proceeding Vol. III of III] Oct. 1, 2000 DOA ACLU-RDI 2064). In her defence she said she was following orders that female soldiers were told to ridicule naked detainees: "They wanted me to be in the shower [and] point to male genitals and laugh".

Of all the women involved, Lynddie England, was cast as the "she devil". It was England's involvement especially, that shocked. Goldberg (2007: 112) said that she was the most puzzling. She was found guilty of one count of conspiracy, four counts of maltreating detainees and one count of committing an indecent act. It was she who had held the leash round the prisoner's neck, was in the photographs, and also took the photographs. The photographs of the prisoner on a leash were, she said, taken for amusement, although Graner had originally said in his defense that he was going to use the photographs as a training aid (*Irish Examiner*, 22 September 2005). England claimed that she was not responsible that her superior officers knew what was happening and did not intervene. "Everyone in the company from the commander down [knew what was going on] The pictures were shown to anyone who wanted to see them. Cpl. [Charles] Graner told me he showed them to his platoon sergeant and platoon leader" (Serrano 2004). England told investigators that guards forced detainees to crawl on their hands and knees on broken glass, threw a Nerf football at handcuffed prisoners and forced male detainees to wear women's "maxi pads" (Serrano). Mitigation advanced on her behalf was that she was acting under duress of Graner, with whom she was having a relationship. Her counsel said that she was a victim of military misogyny, and lacked training and preparation for the conditions in Iraq. She said: "I was used by Private Charles Graner. I didn't realise it at the time". Sentenced to three years imprisonment, she appealed against her sentence (see *United States, v Private First Class Lynndie R. England* [2005]. One of the grounds of appeal was that she was following senior orders of Graner, was coerced by him, and as his girlfriend acted under his direction. These arguments of duress and coercion had some measure of success in reducing sentence.

The lack of training excuse was also appropriated in Sabrina Harman's defence where her counsel said she had been put in an invidious position and that it was a "[s]hame on the army for putting an untrained junior specialist in a position where she has to challenge her (…) leadership to do the right thing" (cited in Houge 2016: 432). Of the man standing on the box, the prosecution said, "he was trembling and shaking" whilst the defence described it as a "joking type of thing" (Poole 172). Ehrenreich (2005) wrote: "Here, in these photos from Abu Ghraib, you have everything that the Islamic fundamentalists believe characterizes Western culture, all nicely arranged in one hideous image - imperial arrogance, sexual depravity … and gender equality" (170). Joseph and Sharma (xii) ask whether women's role in war is an anomaly, why England did not bring to bear a softer side? (Khalili 2011). Was she trying to demonstrate she could do the same? Was she a victim of misogyny and patriarchal structures in the military?

Abu Ghraib was said by many to be an isolated incident (Del Rosso 2015: 74). Yet, following Joe Darby's disclosures the Australian media published another five-dozen photographs of abuse some of which were even more gratuitous including a photograph of a naked man smeared in faeces, hanging upside down from a top bunk. He was abused and called "shitboy" (Eisenman 2007b: 26). In June 2004, the CID report compiled by Special Agent James E Seigmund, was the subject of an article by Suzanne Goldenberg for *The Guardian* (17 February 2006) which reported on a further 1325 images of suspected detainee abuse, 93 video films of the same, 600 images of adult pornography, 546 suspected dead Iraqi prisoners, 29 images of simulated sex acts, 37 images of dogs abusing prisoners (Abel 2018: 88) which provides further corroboration that this treatment was not limited to a few rogue soldiers. Atwan (2015: 39) reporting on a UK-run facility near Basra, in 2010, noted that 200 ex-detainees described how they were starved, sexually abused by women soldiers, given electric shocks, forced to kneel and deprived of sleep.

JUDGES FOR HUMAN RIGHTS V STATE TERRORISM AND THE TORTURE LAWYERS

Torture and abuse at Guantánamo, Bagram, Abu Ghraib Iraq, demonstrates US state brutality and contempt for international human rights norms, and has prompted the question how was torture legitimised in a supposedly democratic state with all its safeguards? (Luban 2006: 51, 71). Alfred McCoy refers to a long history in which "psychological torture has emerged as a clandestine facet of American foreign policy" (cited in Dauenhauer 2015: 14). Sands in *Lawless Worlds* (146) is baffled: "It is deeply disturbing that lawyers in the service of government could so advise" such that "the war on terrorism has led many lawyers astray" (206). Goldberg (88–94) documents how some of the country's best lawyers believed that torture was a necessary evil. Here, one is reminded of Alan Dershowitz. Luban (2006: 51, 71) wonders how "torture lawyers" could create a "torture culture" of acceptance and complicity. The former Chief Prosecutor of the Military Commission's at Guantánamo Bay, Mike Davis, acknowledged that prisoners had fallen between legal conventions and rules and a banal situation had arisen where "if it isn't named as torture then it isn't torture" (Vulliamy 2011).

BRINGING HUMAN RIGHTS ON

The Supreme Court, in a series of momentous decisions, reaffirmed again, and again, the moral values underpinning the ROL and demonstrated the independence of a judiciary determined to uphold human rights norms, and to stand up to executive power in its denial of habeas corpus for those detained in Guantánamo. The case of *Rasul v Bush* [2004], and other petitioners including *Al Odah*, was brought by Rasul and Asif Iqbal (of the Tipton Three) and David Hicks an Australian citizen, said to be with the Taliban, and 12 Kuwaiti nationals who were engaged in humanitarian work in the region. They were seized by villagers in Afghanistan in exchange for money and handed over to US forces and taken to Guantánamo. The US Supreme Court, by a majority of 6 to 3, ruled that foreign nationals held in Guantánamo could petition Federal courts for a writ of habeas corpus to review the legality of their detention. Justice Breyer for the majority ruled: "It seems rather contrary to an idea of a constitution with three branches that the executive would be free to do whatever they want, without a check". Justice Scalia in a dissenting judgment said of his fellow justices, that theirs was "judicial adventurism of the worst sort", and of the law in general terms that it was "an expendable luxury".

On the same day, the case of *Hamdi v Rumsfeld* [2004] was heard. Unlike litigants in the Rasul case, and Al Odah cases. Hamdi was born in the US, he said he went to the region as a relief worker where he was captured by the Afghan Northern Alliance and taken to Guantánamo. As he had joint US and Saudi citizenship he was transferred out of Guantánamo to another prison. Six of the nine justices of the Court agreed that the executive branch does not have the power to hold a US citizen indefinitely without basic due process protections enforceable through judicial review. Justice O'Connor wrote a plurality opinion representing the Court's judgment, which was joined by Chief Justice Rehnquist and Justices Breyer and Kennedy (143, 156) and ruled that detainees who are US citizens must have the rights of due process and as such his detention violated the right to a fair trial and the Geneva Convention. The Bush administration quickly responded to the judgment and created the Combat Status Review Tribunals (CSRT's), where detainees regardless of nationality were denied legal representation. Further challenges by Guantánamo detainees followed. In *Boumediene v Bush* [2008] a writ of habeas corpus was brought. Justice Kennedy delivered the 5–4 majority opinion and held that the prisoners had a right to the writ of *habeas corpus* under the US Constitution, that the Military Commissions Act 2006 was an unconstitutional suspension of that right, and that the CSRT's were an inadequate substitute for habeas corpus, and ordered the release of Boumediene and five others. Again, Justice Scalia dissented. As de Londras (2008, 2010) notes, in all these cases, the US Supreme Court demonstrates its resolute determinedness to stand firm against the limitless power of the executive which had become a dangerous branch of the law.

Such challenges continue and in 2016 a civil lawsuit was brought by the American Civil Liberties Union (ACLU) on behalf of Salim and Ben-Soud, and the family of Gul Rahman (*Salim v Mitchell* [2017]) against the psychologists, James Mitchell and Bruce Jessen, architects of the CIA's "enhanced interrogation" programme "BSCT". Suleiman Abdullah Salim was a Tanzanian fisherman, Mohamed Ahmed Ben-Soud, a Libyan, who was living in exile from Muammar Gaddafi's regime, and Gul Rahman, an Afghan refugee, (who froze to death whilst being detained and interrogated under CIA control). Mitchell and Jessen refused to concede that they committed acts of torture, but as evidenced by the settlement, acknowledged that they had worked with the CIA to develop a programme that contemplated the use of specific "coercive methods" to interrogate detainees. It is alleged that Jessen interrogated Rahman for more than 48 h, using what was euphemistically called the "enhanced interrogation technique" known as the "facial slap". He said that he had assessed Rahman and believed he could endure more "environmental deprivations". Two unauthorised techniques were used on Rahman including a "hard take-down", a euphemism for being dragged from his cell, stripped of clothing, hands taped, hood put on his head, forced to run up and down a hallway and if stumbled was dragged and slapped and punched in the stomach. Rahman died. In March 2005, after his death, Mitchell and Jessen set up their own company to provide "qualified interrogators, and detainee security officers for CIA detention sites, and curriculum development and training services" for the torture programme. They were paid from $72 to $81 million dollars (Gosztoler 2017). Legal action continues, and in 2019, three detainees Suhail Najim Abdullah Al Shimari, Asa'ad Hamza Hanfoosh Zuba'e and Salah Hasan Nusaif Al-Ejaili, brought an action against CACI Premier Technology, which supplied the army with civilian interrogators. Salah Al-Ejaili, an Al Jazeera journalistic, held for 48 days before being released, was kept naked, suffered sexual humiliation, threats, hooding, sensory and sleep deprivation and was kept in a state of anticipated fear hearing other prisoners being abused.

The symbol of the American ROL is no longer represented by Lady Justice Justitia, holding the scales of Justice, judging with reason and rationality, subservient to justice, holding high and protecting the ROL above all else, seeing no gender, no religion, no ethnicity, no colour, because she dispenses law and justice impartially. The symbol of America's deliverance of the ROL is an image of a man, hooded, covered in a shroud, standing on a box with electrical cords attached to his fingers, a torture to which Ali Shallal al-Qaisi (see below) and others were subjected:

> Then [the guard] brought a box of food and he made me stand on it, and he started punishing me. Then a tall black soldier came and put electrical wires on my fingers and toes and on my penis, and I had a bag over my head. Then he was saying 'which switch is on for electricity'? (Statement of Abdou Hussain Saad Faleh, Iraqi detainee, Abu Ghraib prison, obtained by *The Washington Post* 16 January 2004)

The hooded man on the box is a real man, an Arab man, a Muslim man. In Abu Ghraib and in Guantánamo, the US acted outside the law and outside international law, in what Vulliamy (2011) describes as the "law free zone". Guantánamo stood outside the Geneva Convention, outside the Torture Convention, outside criminal law protections, outside the protection of the US constitution. Those detained were denied legal representation, denied access to a court or tribunal, held without charge and where the safeguards of international law were suspended. The US claimed that the prisoners were members of Al-Qaeda and in another piece of their twisted logic said that as Al-Qaeda was a foreign terrorist organisation which without a "state personality" could not therefore be a party to the Geneva Convention neither could its members be treated as part of a state. As Tiefenbrun points out confusion arose over whether terrorists' acts were criminal acts or acts of war (2010: 90). The US government chose to define the actions of the criminals/terrorists who perpetrated 9/11 as acts of war, such that those detained were involved in acts of war. As Senator Reed, in opening the case in *United States v Graner* [2010] said:

> Let me begin by stating the obvious. For the next 50 years in the Islamic world and many other parts of the world, the image of the United States will be that of an American dragging a prostrate naked Iraqi across the floor on a leash. This is unfair to the honor and the courage of our soldiers, but unfortunately, I think it's become a fact. This is a disaster. (ACLU *The Torture Database* ACLU-RDI 2294 p. 105, DOD-052523)

CONCLUSION—"IT NEVER REALLY LEFT ME"—SEARED INTO THE MUSLIM PSYCHE

The US, together with the entire world, is rightly concerned about Islamic terrorism. There is no doubt of the threat it poses, the fear is strikes and the devastation it inflicts, but as has been said time and time again, fighting fire with fire is not the answer, nor torturing, nor sadism, nor sexual abuse, nor unlawful detention, nor summary "justice", nor the US's glorification and triumphalism in such victories on Muslims per se. All the worlds Catholics were not scorned and collectively persecuted for acts of violence and bombings on UK soil by the IRA. The treatment of the Guantánamo, Abu Ghraib and Bagram detainees provides a chilling testimony to institutionalised US state terrorism and to what Alfred McCoy calls a "clandestine facet of American foreign policy". Cohen (2001: x) asks the question "what do we do with the knowledge of the suffering of others"? His answer is poignantly rhetorical "normalisation and denial" (xi) and by way of illustration cites the life and death of a Palestinian, Abed al-Samad Harizat, who, on 22 April 1995, died after "interrogation", by Israel defence forces, who shook him to death causing a brain haemorrhage. Israel was condemned for torture by shaking (*BMJ* 1995: 311, 1323). Cohen says with reference to Israel and with dismay that "after twenty years of military occupation, daily humiliation, unprovoked killings even liberals do not react" (xii). The US claimed all of this WOT was executed to make the world a safer place. It has not done so. On the contrary it has fuelled and mobilised support for Islamic terrorism and as Hensman writes provided terrorism with recruits (31). A Pentagon spokesman recognised the impact of the pictures of abuse and their effects and said that the release of the additional images of abuse "could only further inflame and possibly incite unnecessary violence in the world" (Goldenberg 2006). As Rumney (2013) observes: "the use of torture, along with other contributory factors, may *inter alia* boost support for terrorist groups, fuel anger and a desire for revenge amongst recruits to the terrorist cause". Outrage, indignation and fear was, and still is, felt by Muslim communities across the world. Sir David Omand, the former Security, and Intelligence Co-ordinator in the UK's Cabinet Office noted that the invasion of Iraq would likely increase the threat of terrorism in the United Kingdom. Perhaps we should consider too how a sense of victimhood that can fan the worst flames. Ed Vulliamy (1994: xxvii) identifies the fervent ethnic Serbian nationalism, fascism and racism and

Serbian identity, emerging out of a cult of victimhood rooted in Ottoman rule and ancestral defeat 600 years ago.

US terror has harmed Muslim men who are still incarcerated. It has harmed, Muslim detainees, their families and friends and communities, who have been released and survived. It has harmed all Muslims, Muslim men and women, those with Muslim connections and right-thinking non-Muslims. Poole (173) reports that in 2003 alone in Guantánamo there were 350 incidents of self-harm reported and 120 "hanging gestures", a euphemism for attempted suicide. As for the impact on Muslim prisoners, the Al Jazeera journalist Salah al-Ejaili, said: "It never really left me". Enhanced interrogation techniques and extended isolation has led to psychological and behavioral issues, hallucinations, paranoia, insomnia, attempts at self-harm and self-mutilation and to long-term PTSD.

Ali Shallal al-Qaisi, the hooded man standing on a box said in a video posted on Twitter: "It crushed our psyches". What had he done? He said, "I wasn't a military commander or a government official. I was just a resident of Baghdad, where I grew up, and just like any other Iraqi I was against the US invasion and I spoke out against it". Al-Qaisi said he was just the owner of a football pitch where the occupying forces used to dump bodies and al-Qaisi complained. (*The New Arab*, 27 November 2015).

Alisdair Soussi (2019) reports on Chris Bartlett, a photographer, who went to Iraq to try and restore some humanity to the victims of Abu Ghraib, and since the camera and the photographs were instruments of torture, Bartlett wanted to use the camera and the photograph to bring humanity back and rehabilitate. Bartlett's photographs are remarkable and moving, they exude a stillness but also a quiet agency and ownership. The look is now returned by those Iraqi former prisoners, but not of defiance, or of victory, or of power, or of triumphalism, or of masculine might, or of a tortured survival, but of a harmony, peace, grace and eloquence and supreme dignity, that the camera and the photograph has restored.

But for Muslim men and women who see fellow Muslims tortured as a collective punishment of all Muslims for those that commit act of Islamic terrorism it promotes a sense of victimisation within Muslim communities and out-group reinforcement. Matthews says: "[r]epression ... appear[s] to have ... the effect of reinforcing a sense of self as a member of an out-group, leading to identification with victims of harsh repression"

(Matthews quoted in Rumney 2015: 23). Atwan says of the maltreatment in Abu Ghraib: "All of this feeds into men's psyche in Iraq". As for counter-terror legislation in the US, Wong writes:

> As time passes, the unintended consequences of the Act and related anti-terrorism measures have mushroomed, resulting in ramifications that are increasingly felt throughout American society. Foreign students have been deterred from coming to the United States. Librarians have started to concern themselves with government monitoring activities. Neither of these examples, however, compare to the impact felt by Muslims in the U.S., the group most affected. (164)

The impact on Muslim women is no less, if not more, as wives, mothers and sisters, who feel the insult against their communities and reflect and remember. No one who is aware of the horrors perpetrated against Muslims in US detention can fail to ask what impact this has had on Muslim self and on identity. Muslim identity post 9/11 emerges shaped by this context. Joanna Bourke asserts, "Instead of recognizing that Western imperialism and support for oppressive regimes in the Shah's Iran, Numeri's Sudan, Lebanon and Palestine has alienated millions of people all over the Muslim world, America and its allies depicted 'this' enemy as an irrational, monolithic beast, epitomized by the names of the 'popes of Islam'.... Islam was extremism" (Bourke 2006: 373). And, "Yes", identity post 9/11 shapes counter-narratives and subversive speech, and resistance, and outrage and "Yes", a return to the safety of one's faith as a "Self-verifying symbol of ... Muslim identity" (Richards: 49), And "Yes", for some a visible symbol of one's Muslimness that has been so decimated may mean a reclaiming of Islamic identity through dress. Choosing to wear the headscarf/hijab or the face covering/niqab cannot be cleaved from a consciousness which holds in the continuous present how Muslims, and Muslim men especially, have been insulted and tortured, and knowing too that Donald Trump when President said he would bring back these very cruelties (see Fullerton 2017). Contrary to all the evidence, Trump continues to believe that waterboarding works and that he should retain it: "I have spoken with people at the highest level of intelligence and I asked them the question 'Does it work? Does torture work?' and the answer was 'Yes, absolutely.'" (26 January 2017 BBC news) And back again we go back to the future.

We are left then as we began with the ticking bomb of US executive power, its rampant lawlessness, violence and racism. Can Muslim men and women expect it to be any different under President Biden?

Abel, R. 2018. *Law's Wars: The Fate of the Rule of Law in the US 'War on Terror'.* Cambridge: Cambridge University Press.
ACLU. *The Torture Database.* https://www.thetorturedatabase.org/search/apa chesolr_search. Accessed 7 August 2020.
Ambuhl (Megan) ACLU. *The Torture Database.* Court-Martial: Specialist Megan Ambuhl (Record of Proceeding Vol. III of III) Oct. 1, 2000 | DOA | ACLU-RDI 2064).
Amnesty Report. 2004. *USA: Human Dignity Denied: Torture and Accountability in the 'War on Terror'.* https://www.amnesty.org/download/Docume nts/92000/amr511452004en.pdf. Accessed 7 August 2020.
Arendt, H. 2011 [1963]. *Eichmann in Jerusalem on the Banality of Evil.* London: Penguin.
Arkan Mohammed Ali Et Al., Appellants v. Donald H. Rumsfeld, Individually, Et Al., Appellees Consolidated with 07-5185, 07-5186, 07-5187 (2011).
Atwan, A.B. 2015. *Islamic State the Digital Caliphate.* London: Saqi Books.
Barak-Erez, D. 2009. Terrorism Law Between the Executive and Legislative Models. *The American Journal of Comparative Law* 57 (4): 877–896.
Bartone, P. 2010. Preventing Prisoner Abuse: Leadership Lessons of Abu Ghraib. *Ethics and Behavior* 20 (2): 161–173.
Bellaby, R. 2014. *The Ethics of Intelligence: A New Framework.* London: Routledge.
Bellaby, R. 2016. Torture-Lite: An Ethical Middle-Ground? *International Journal of Applied Philosophy* 29 (2): 177–190.
Bingham, T. 2010. *The Rule of Law.* London: Penguin.
Bloche, G.M., and J.H. Marks. 2005. Doctors, and Interrogators at Guantánamo Bay. *New England Journal of Medicine* 352 (3–6): 188.
Boumediene et al v Bush. 2008. (Certiorari to The United States Court of Appeals for The District of Columbia Circuit No. 06-1195) 553 US 723. https://www.supremecourt.gov/opinions/07pdf/06-1195.pdf. Accessed 12 November 2020.
Bourke, J. 2004. Torture as Pornography. *The Guardian,* May 7.
Bourke, J. 2006. *Fear a Cultural History.* London: Virago.
Bourke, J. 2007. *Fear: A Cultural History.* London: Virago.
Bricmont, B. 2007. *Humanitarian Imperialism: Using Human Rights to Sell War.* New York: Monthly Review Press.

British Medical Journal. 1995. News "Israel Condemned for Torture by Shaking" 311: 1323.

Bussone, A. 2011. Security for Liberty: Ten Years After 9/11 Why Americans Should Care About the Extension of the Patriot Act and Its Civil Liberties Implications. *The Florida Coastal Law Review* 85: 87–88.

Butler, J. 2007. Torture and the Ethics of Photography. *Environment and Planning D: Society and Space.* 25: 951–966.

Carlson, J.A., and E. Weber (eds.). 2007. *Speaking About Torture.* New York: Fordham University Press.

Chomsky, N. 2004. *Hegemony or Survival: America's Quest for Global Dominance.* London: Penguin.

Cohen, S. 2001. *States of Denial.* London: Polity.

Court-Martial Record: Staff Sergeant Ivan L. Frederick, II (Volume 5 of 8) ACLU-RDI 1756. https://www.thetorturedatabase.org/search/apachesolr_search/frederick. Accessed 12 November 2020.

Cover, R.M. 1986. Violence and the Word. *Yale Law Journal* 95 (8): 1601–1630.

Dabashi, H. 2011. *Brown Skin, White Masks (The Islamic Mediterranean).* London: Pluto.

Das, V. 2008. Violence, Gender, and Subjectivity. *Annual Review of Anthropology* 37: 283–299.

Dauenhauer, K. 2009. Do the Photos Tell it All? Representing Torture in the Images from Abu Ghraib. vol 10 COPAS vol 10 https://copas.uni-regensburg.de/article/view/116/140. Accessed 7 August 2020.

Dauenhauer, K. 2015. *The Shadow of Torture: Debating US Transgressions in Military Intervention.* Berlin: Peter Land GmbH.

De Londras, F. 2008. Guantánamo Bay: Towards Legality? *Modern Law Review* 71 (1): 36–58.

De Londras, F. 2010. Controlling the Executive in Times of Terrorism: Competing Perspectives on Effective Oversight Mechanisms. *Oxford Journal of Legal Studies* 30 (1): 19.

Del Rosso, J. 2015. *Talking About Torture: How Political Discourse Shapes the Debate.* New York, NY: Columbia University Press.

Dworkin, A. 1989. *Pornography: Men Possessing Women.* London and New York: Penguin.

Dworkin, A. 1991. *Against Pornography: The Feminism of Andrea Dworkin.* October 25, 1991, Omnibus, Producer David Evans, https://www.youtube.com/watch?v=L9j7-zZks08. Accessed 12 June 2020.

Dworkin, A. 1997. *Life and Death.* Glencoe: The Free Press.

Ehrenreich, B. 2005. Feminism's Assumptions Upended Abu Ghraib and the Politics of Torture. *South Central Review* 24 (1), On Torture (Spring, 2007): 170–173.

Eisenman, S.F. 2007a. Waterboarding: Political and Sacred Torture. In *Speaking About Torture*, ed. J.A. Carlson and E. Weber, 129–139. New York: Fordham University Press.

Eisenman, S.F. 2007b. *Abu Ghraib Effect*. London: Reaktion Books.

Fanon, F. 2008 [1952]. *Black Skin, White Masks*. New York: Grove Press.

Faubion, J.D. (ed.). 2000. *Michel Foucault Power Essential Works 1954–1984 Volume 3*. New York: Penguin.

Foucault, M. 1978. *The History of Sexuality*. New York: Pantheon.

Frederick Ivan L II. (ACLU *The Torture Database*) DoD-041209, Court-Martial Record: Staff Sergeant Ivan L. Frederick, II (Volume 1 of 8) May 20, 2004 | DOA | OJAG | ACLU-RDI 1752.

Fullerton, M. 2017. Trump, Turmoil, and Terrorism: The US Immigration and Refugee Ban, Presidents—Above the Law? *International Journal of Refugee Law* 29 (2): 327–338.

Glover, J. 2012 [1999]. *Humanity a Moral History of the 20th century*, 2nd. ed. New Haven and London: Yale University Press.

Goldberg, E.S. 2007. *Beyond Terror*. New Brunswick, New Jersey, and London: Rutgers University Press.

Goldenberg, S. 2006. Abu Ghraib Leaked Report Reveals Full Extent of Abuse. 17 February https://www.theguardian.com/world/2006/feb/17/iraq.suzannegoldenberg. Accessed 7 August 2020.

Goldsmith, J. 2007. *The Terror Presidency*. W. W. Norton and Company; Reprint edition (2009).

Gosztoler. 2017. Survivors Win Confidential Settlement Against CIA Torture Psychologists. *Shadowproof*. August 17. https://shadowproof.com/2017/08/17/cia-torture-psychologists-settlement/ Accessed 7 August 2020.

Greenberg, K.J. 2007. *The Torture Debate in America*. Cambridge: Cambridge University Press.

Gronnvoll, M. 2007. Gender Invisibility at Abu Ghraib. *Rhetoric and Public Affairs* 10 (3): 371–398.

Gudjonsson, G.H. 2011–2012. False Confessions and Correcting Injustices. *New England Law Review* 46: 689.

Gudjonsson, G. H., and J. Pearse. 2011. Suspect Interviews and False Confessions. *Current Directions in Psychological Science* 20 (1): 33–37.

Hamdan v Rumsfeld [2006] 165. L. Ed 2nd 723. https://h2o.law.harvard.edu/cases/1228. Accessed 12 November 2020.

Hamdi v Rumsfeld [2004] 542 U.S. 507. https://supreme.justia.com/cases/federal/us/542/507/. Accessed 12 November 2020.

Harris, Shane. 2014. "The Most Gruesome Moments in the CIA 'Torture Report.'" *The Daily Beast*. September 12. http://www.thedailybeast.com/articles/2014/12/09/the-most-gruesome-moments-in-the-cia-torture-report.html. Accessed 12 November 2020.

Hensman, R. 2003. The Only Alternative to Global Terror. In *Terror Counter-Terror Women Speak Out*, ed. A. Joseph and K. Sharma. London and New York: Zed.

Hersh, S.M. 2004. Torture at Abu Ghraib. *The New Yorker*, May 10.

Hijjar, L. 2018. How Government Secrecy on Torture Has Stymied the 9/11 Terror Prosecution. *The Nation*, June 19.

Hitchens, C. 2015. *And Yet... Essays*. New York: Simon and Schuster.

Holland, H. 2009. The Enigmatic Lynndie England: Gendered Explanations for the Crisis at Abu Ghraib. *Communication and Critical/Cultural Studies* 6 (3): 246–264.

Houge, A.B. 2016. Re-presentations of Defendant Perpetrators in Sexual War Violence Cases Before International and Military Criminal Courts. *British Journal of Criminology* 56 (3): 419–437.

Human Rights Watch. 2010. Iraq: Detainees Describe Torture in Secret Jail. April 27. http://www.hrw.org/en/news/2010/04/27/iraq-detainees-describe-torture-secret-jail. Accessed 7 August 2020.

Hylton, W. 2006. Prisoner of Conscience. *GQ*. August 1. https://www.gq.com/story/joe-darby-abu-ghraib. Accessed 7 August 2020.

Iglesias, D. 2014a. Why Torture Is a Complete Failure. December 16. *Christianity Today*. http://www.christianitytoday.com/ct/2014/december-web-only/christian-response-to-senate-torture-report. Accessed 7 August 2020.

Iglesias, D. 2014b. Shock and Anal Probe: Reading Between the Redactions in the CIA Torture Report. *The Guardian*. December 9.

Ignatieff, M. 2003. The American Empire, The Burden. *New York Times*. January 5. https://www.nytimes.com/2003/01/05/magazine/the-american-empire-the-burden.html. Accessed 7 August 2020.

Ignatieff, M. 2005. *American Exceptionalism and Human Rights*. Princeton: Princeton University Press.

Investigation into FBI Allegations of Detainee Abuse at Guantanamo Bay, Cuba Detention Facility. 2005. https://www.globalsecurity.org/security/library/report/2005/d20050714report.pdf. Accessed 11 November 2020.

Janis, M.W., R.S. Kay, and A.W. Bradley. 2008. *European Human Rights Law*. Oxford: Oxford University Press.

Kafka, F. 1925. The Project Gutenberg EBook of *the Trial*, by Franz Kafka. Translated by David Wyllie, 2003.

Kaufman-Osborn, T. 2005. Gender Trouble at Abu Ghraib? *Politics and Gender* 1 (4): 597–619.

Khalili, L. 2011. Gendered Practices of Counterinsurgency. *Review of International Studies* 37 (4): 1471–1491.

Kunarac, Vuković and Kovač [2002] https://www.icty.org/x/cases/kunarac/acjug/en/kun-aj020612e.pdf. Accessed 11 November 2020.

Lamb, C. 2020. *Our Bodies Their Battlefield*. London: William Collins.

Laughland, O. 2015. How the CIA Tortured Its Detainees. *The Guardian*. 20 May 2015. http://www.theguardian.com/us-news/2014/dec/09/cia-tor ture-methods-waterboarding-sleep-deprivation. Accessed 11 November 2020.

Leo, R., and R. Ofshe. 1997–1998. Consequences of False Confessions: Depri vations of Liberty and Miscarriages of Justice in the Age of Psychological Interrogation. *Journal of Criminal Law & Criminology* 88 (2): 429–496.

Levi Strauss, D. 2005. Inconvenient Evidence: The Effects of Abu Ghraib. https://brooklynrail.org/2005/01/express/inconvenient-evidence. Accessed 11 November 2020.

Lightcap, T., and J.P. Pfiffner (eds.). 2014. *Examining Torture: Empirical Studies of State Repression*. New York: Palgrave Macmillan.

Luban, D. 2006. Liberalism, Torture, and the Ticking Bomb. In *The Torture Debates in America*, ed. K.J. Greenberg, 35–83. Cambridge: Cambridge University Press.

Luban, D. 2007. The Torture Lawyers of Washington. In *Legal Ethics and Human Dignity*, ed. D. Luban, 162–206. Cambridge: Cambridge University Press.

McCoy, Alfred W. 2007. In the Minotaur's' Labyrinth: Psychological Torture, Public Forgetting, and the Contested History. In *Speaking About Torture*, ed. J.A. Carlson and E. Weber. New York: Fordham University Press.

McKelvey, T. 2018. I Hated Myself for Abu Ghraib Abuse. https://www.bbc. co.uk/news/44031774. Accessed 12 November 2020.

McLagan, M., and Y. McKee. 2012. *Sensible Politics: The Visual Culture of Nongovernmental Activism*. New York: Zone Books.

Mégret, F. 2009. From 'Savages' to 'Unlawful Combatants': A Post-Colonial Look at International Humanitarian Law's 'Other'. In *International Law and Its 'Others'*, ed. A. Orford, 265–317. Cambridge: Cambridge University Press.

Military Commission Rules of Evidence Section I General Provision. 2015. https://jsc.defense.gov/Portals/99/Documents/MREsRemoved412e.pdf. Accessed 7 August 2020.

Military Order of November 13. 2001. *Detention, Treatment and Trial of Certain Non- Citizens in the War Against Terrorism* 66 Fed.Reg. 57831. https://fas.org/irp/offdocs/eo/mo-111301.htm. Accessed 7 August 2020.

Nussbaum. M. 1994. Patriotism and Cosmopolitanism. *Boston Review*. October/November. http://www.bostonreview.net/archives/BR19.5/nus sbaum.php. Accessed 7 August 2020.

Office of the Inspector Gen., I, U.S. Dep't of Justice, *The September 11 Detainees: A Review of the Treatment of Aliens Held on Immigration Charges in Connection with the Investigation of the September 11 Attacks*. 2003. https://www.globalsecurity.org/security/library/report/2003/9-11_ detainees_doj-oig_0306_ch4.htm. Accessed 11 November 2020.

Palumbo, M. 1987. *The Palestinian Catastrophe*. London New York: Quartet.

Pfiffner, S. 2014. The Efficacy of Coercive Interrogation. In *Examining Torture: Empirical Studies of State Repression*, ed. T. Lightcap and S. Pfiffner, 127–158. New York: Palgrave Macmillan.

Pontecorvo, G. 1966. *The Battle of Algiers*. Director: Gillo Pontecorvo.

Poole, S. 2006. *Unspeak*. London: Little Brown.

Prosecutor v Furundžija [1998] (Case IT-95-17/1-tq, Judgement, 10 Dec 1998). https://www.icty.org/x/cases/furundzija/tjug/en/fur-tj9812 10e.pdf. Accessed 7 August 2020.

Prosecutor v Jean-Paul Akayesu [1998] Judgment, ICTR-96-4-T, September 2. https://unictr.irmct.org/sites/unictr.org/files/case-documents/ictr-96-4/ trial-judgements/en/980902.pdf. Accessed 7 August 2020.

Ramsey, M. 2006. Can the Torture of Terrorist Suspects Be Justified? *The International Journal of Human Rights* 10 (2): 103–119. https://doi.org/10. 1080/13642980600608384. Accessed 7 August 2020.

Rasul v Bush 542 U.S. 466 [2004]. https://supreme.justia.com/cases/federal/ us/542/466/. Accessed 7 August 2020.

Richards, J. 2015. *Extremism, Radicalization and Security: An Identity Theory Approach*. New York and London: Palgrave Macmillan.

Robertson, G. 2012. *Crimes Against Humanity*, 4th ed. London: Penguin Books.

Rumney, P.N.S. 2013. Making Things Worse? Interrogational Torture as a Counterterrorism Strategy. *Contemporary Issues in Law* 12 (4) CIL: 339–372.

Rumney, P.N.S. 2015. *Torturing Terrorists: Exploring the Limits of Law, Human Rights, and Academic*. London: Routledge.

Saad Faleh, A. H. 2004. Statement of Abdou Hussain Saad Faleh, obtained by *The Washington Post*. http://media.washingtonpost.com/wp-srv/world/ iraq/abughraib/18170.pdf. Accessed 12 November 2020.

Said, E. 1970/1968. The Arab Portrayed. In ed. L. Abu-Lughod. *The Arab-Israeli Confrontation of June 1967*, 1–9. Evanston: Northwestern University Press.

Said, E. 1978. *Orientalism*. London: Penguin.

Salim v Mitchell [2017]. https://www.aclu.org/cases/salim-v-mitchell-lawsuit-against-psychologists-behind-cia-torture-program. Accessed 11 November 2020.

Sands, P. 2006. *Lawless World*. London: Penguin.

Schlesinger, A. 1973. *The Imperial Presidency*. Houghton Mifflin Company; Book Club Edition.

Schlesinger, J. 2004. *Final Report of the Independent Panel to Review DoD Detention Operations*. August. https://www.loc.gov/item/2006475632/. Accessed 7 August 2020.

Schmidt Report. 2005. *FBI Schmidt Report on Guantanamo Military Interrogations*. 2005 Army Regulation 15-6: Final Report. https://www.prisonlegaln

ews.org/media/publications/fbi_schmidt_report_on_guantanamo_military_i nterrogations_2005.pdf. Accessed 7 August 2020.

Schutz, A. 1967. *The Phenomenology of the Social World.* London: Heinemann.

Senate Committee on Torture. 2014. *Report of The Senate Select Committee on Intelligence Committee Study of The Central Intelligence Agency's Detention and Interrogation Program Together with Foreword by Chairman Feinstein and Additional and Minority Views,* December 9. Report 113/288 https://www.intelligence.senate.gov/sites/def ault/files/publications/CRPT-113srpt288.pdf. Accessed 11 November 2020. Also at https://www.aclu.org/files/assets/SSCIStudyCIAsDetentionInterrog ationProgramES.pdf. Accessed 11 November 2020.

Serrano, R. 2004. Death of Prisoner Detailed in Testimony. *Los Angeles Times,* May 18.

Snowden, E. 2018. *Permanent Record.* London and New York: Macmillan.

Sontag, S. 1997. *On Photography.* London: Penguin.

Sontag, S. 2003. *Regarding the Pain of Others.* London: Penguin.

Sontag, S. 2004. Regarding the Torture of Others. *New York Times,* May 23.

Soussi, A. 2019. 15 Years Later: Abu Ghraib and the Faces of Torture in Iraq. *The National News Arts and Culture.* 28 April. https://www.thenationaln ews.com/arts-culture/15-years-later-abu-ghraib-and-the-faces-of-torture-in- iraq-1.854512. Accessed 12 November 2020.

Steiner, G. 1976 [1967]. *Language and Silence.* London: Faber and Faber.

Steyn, J. 2003. Guantánamo Bay: The Legal Black Hole. Twenty-Seventh F.A. Mann Lecture: 25 November. *International and Comparative Law Quarterly* 53, 1 January 2004, 1–15. http://www.rcpbml.org.uk/wdie-03/d03- 119.htm. Accessed 7 August 2020.

Sykes, G.M., and M. Matza. 1957. Techniques of Neutralization: A Theory of Delinquency. *American Sociological Review* 22 (6): 664–670.

Tiefenbrun, S. 2010. *Decoding International Law: Semiotics and the Humanities.* Oxford: Oxford University Press.

Tiefer, C. 1983. The Constitutionality of Independent Officers as Checks on Abuses of Executive Power. *Boston University Law Review* 63: 59.

The New Arab. 27 November 2015. https://english.alaraby.co.uk/english/fea tures/2015/11/27/inside-abu-ghraib-meeting-ali-shallal-al-qaisi.

The Tipton Three BBC 4, 2006 "The Road to Guantanamo" Film directed by Michael Winterbottom and Mat Whitecross. (see also https://en.wikipe dia.org/wiki/Tipton_Three#:~:text=The%20Tipton%20Three%20is%20the% 20collective%20name%20given,estimated%20that%20Shafiq%20Rasul%20was% 20born%20in%201977.) Accessed 15 November 2020.

Timm, T. 2014. Stop Believing the Lies: America Tortured More That 'Some Folks'– And Covered It Up. *The Guardian.* December 9.

Tushnet, M.V. 2005. Controlling Executive Power in the War on Terrorism. Georgetown University Law Center. *Harvard Law Review* 118: 2673–2682.

United States, Appellee v Charles. Graner Jr., Specialist U.S. Army, Appellant No. 09-0432 Crim. App. No. 20050054 United States Court of Appeals for the Armed Forces Argued May 3, 2010 Decided June 25, 2010. https://www.armfor.uscourts.gov/newcaaf/opinions/2009SepTerm/09-0432.pdf. Accessed 12 November 2020.

United States, v Private First Class Lynndie R. England. 20051170 United States Army Court of Criminal Appeals https://www.law.upenn.edu/live/files/5865-a-us-v-englandpdf. Accessed 12 November 2020.

United Nations Press Release. 2004. Prohibition of Torture 'absolute', Binding on All States, in All Circumstances. 17 June SG/SM/9373 OBV/428, https://www.un.org/press/en/2004/sgsm9373.doc.htm. Accessed 7 August 2020.

Viterbo, H. 2014. Seeing Torture Anew: A Transnational Reconceptualization of State Torture and Visual Evidence. *Stanford Journal of International Law* 50 (2): 281–317.

Vulliamy, E. 1994. *Seasons in Hell*. London: St Martin's Press.

Vulliamy, E. 2011. Former US Chief Prosecutor Condemns 'Law-Free Zone' of Guantánamo". *The Guardian*, October 30. http://www.theguardian.com/world/2011/oct/30/guantanamo-morris-davis. Accessed 15 November 2020.

Vulliamy, E. 2012. *The War is Dead Long Live the War*. London Vintage.

Wilcox, L.B. 2011. Dying Is Not Permitted: Sovereignty, Biopower, and Force-Feeding at Guantánamo Bay. In *Global Re-visions: Torture: Power, Democracy, and the Human Body*, ed. S. Biswas and Z. Zalloua, 101–128. Washington: University of Washington Press.

Wilcox, L.B. 2015. *Bodies of Violence: Theorizing Embodied Subjects in International Relations*. Oxford: Oxford University Press.

Wildau, G., and A. Seifter. 2004. Limbaugh on Torture of Iraqis: U.S. Guards Were 'Having a Good Time,' 'blow[ing] some steam off'". 5 May https://www.mediamatters.org/rush-limbaugh/limbaugh-torture-iraqis-us-guards-were-having-good-time-blowing-some-steam. Accessed 7 August 2020.

Wong, K.C. 2006. The USA Patriot Act: A Policy of Alienation. *Michigan Journal of Race and Law* 12 (1): 161–202.

CHAPTER 7

Discipline and Punish: Muslim Women's Body and the "Covering" Laws

INTRODUCTION

9/11 especially, was a catalyst that legitimated the discipline, control and punishment of Muslim men, Muslim women, Muslim countries, and Muslim communities. The West's "War on Terror" (WOT) was a collective punishment for the terrorist atrocities of Al-Qaeda, ISIS, and Islamic terrorism. At the heart of appropriating Muslim women lay a dualism, on the one hand, the West's mission of "saving Muslim women" from Muslim men and religious dictat in Muslim majority countries (Abu-Lughod 2013; Khan 2020) whilst on the other, the domestic proscribing the Muslim female body and dress, and divesting Muslim women "metaphysically" of a core element of their identity.

The "metaphysical" world of Muslim women is under attack in countries across Europe and in the US, Canada and Australia, and elsewhere, where institutional practices and the law has been enlisted to command this. Fanon's (1965: 37) essay "Algeria Unveiled" documents the French colonialist's strategy to strike at the metaphysical heart of Algerian society by forcibly unveiling Algerian women. Fanon in observing the tyranny of the colonialist understood that not only men but women were "equally victims of the same tyranny" (120). This tyranny today enlists the law along with other coercive and discriminatory social practices and propaganda strategies including all the ideological state apparatuses of which Althusser spoke in general terms (considered in Chapter 3) to affect

© The Author(s), under exclusive license to Springer Nature Switzerland AG 2021
S. S. M. Edwards, *The Political Appropriation of the Muslim Body*, https://doi.org/10.1007/978-3-030-68896-7_7

this purpose. Nation states appropriate the substantive norms of gender equality which Farris has called "femonationalism" (2017), human rights and the Rule of Law (ROL) all masquerading under the banner of "secularism" to impel the control of Muslim communities through regulating women's body.

In official discourse on what is often referred to as "covering" the Muslim woman is objectified and reified and made an object, spoken of as the "hijab'd" or "niqab'd" woman, through iterative "performances" in words, language, acts, gestures and through state regulatory practices (Butler 1988, 1996) and the garment that covers is anthropomorphised. Her headscarf (hijab) and face veil (niqab) has been simultaneously the object of fascination, repulsion, prejudice and xenophobia (Grace 2004). Melanie Phillips has made the silk, polyester and cotton headscarf and the face veil something of a personal brooding echoing a more general social and public fixation. Phillips describes what Muslim women wear as "central to discussions in public life" (2006: 32). Muslim women are constituted and defined by others, in and by official discourse, as both the oppressed woman to be "saved", and as Hussein (2019) points out, the suspect terrorist. Both these stigmatising representations have provided the raison d'être for Western intervention in Muslim majority countries and foreign policy and legal regulation (see Chapter 4) albeit that there is no such homogenised identity. Women who perceive themselves as Muslim may have parents of Muslim faith, or one parent of Muslim faith, they may have converted to the faith, they may practice their religion or not, "Muslims, like other people, include in their ranks orthodox believers, practising individuals, non-practising skeptics, secular and laic members" (Moghissi and Ghorashi 2010: 1).

When the subject of Muslim women's body and her dress is discussed, Muslim women are invariably excluded (Scott 2007; Benhabib 2002; Brems 2014) whilst governments, political figures, the media and mainstream feminism consider themselves to be the standard bearers and key interlocutors of the meaning of "her" bodily appearance (see Chapters 1 and 2). Brems when conducting research on the face veil in Europe, in Belgium, the Netherlands, Denmark, France and the UK, observed: "One of the most remarkable aspects pertaining to these bans and debates is the fact that they proceed on the basis of assumptions about women wearing the face veil, that lack any basis in knowledge" (2014: 22). Her findings reiterated (as had earlier feminist scholarship) the polysemicity of face covering which stands in sharp contradistinction to state and public declarations of its meaning. Nonetheless, empirical research remains fragmented. The online discussion run by *The Telegraph*, in 2014, following the experience of a 16-year-old student at Camden School for Girls in North London, who wanting to wear the face veil/niqab to school was refused, revealed a multiplicity reasons for wearing the niqab, from faith to fashion, identity, choice and force, confirming the findings of Hoodfar (1997), Zempi and Chakraborti (2014), Hussein (2019), Ahmed, L. (2011) and Ahmed, A. (2020: 65).

The marginalisation of Muslim women's voice is symptomatic of the general widespread erasure of Muslim women's accounts from public discourse. Fanon's (1952) observations on the silencing of the African voice, who in the field of vision of European racism is excised and erased, provides an instructive parallel. Hall, in his commentary on Fanon, explains: "...in the colonised, colonial relationship there is no recognition going on, that is why Fanon is concerned that racism depersonalises, it is a denial of recognition. It is the master saying, 'I do not see you at all'" (in Julien 1996 at 3.32–3.50 minutes). As for the Muslim woman, especially those wearing the niqab, she too is denied recognition and stripped of agency, as racialised Oriental tropes continue to define her. Khan (2020: 105) beratingly says: "White Feminism (which is still the mainstream) centres the agenda and needs of white, straight, middle-class, cis, able bodied women while making claims that it speaks on behalf of all women". Little wonder that resistance to a recent Belgium Constitutional Court ruling on June 4, 2020 (see Francisco Ferrer Brussels University, below) which held that if a University wished to ban the headscarf it would not be unconstitutional to do so, was met with protest. The protesters banners spoke to their agency and resistance: "Take your hands off my headscarf", and "Get off my body".

Fanon spoke of the importance of social context and materiality to an understanding of what he observed as the "historic dynamism of the veil" (1965: 63). This dynamism is subject to historical, political, economic, social and cultural and local articulations and has been considered by feminist scholars, El Guindi (2003), Grace (2004), Saadawi (1980), Khan (2020), Almila and Inglis (2019) and Hussein (2019). "Covering" in these several ways is central to identity, belonging and being as Brems (2014), Almila and Inglis (2019), Zempi and Chakraborti (2014) amongst others have discovered, symbolising a myriad of complex meanings including amongst others, an adherence to the precepts of a particular interpretation of Islamic faith, an expression of identity, culture, a resistance to Western-imposed definitions, a reaction to the sexualisation of women, a public statement and expression of solidarity with a group constantly maligned and stigmatised and subjected to Western aggression and Western occupation in Arab/Muslim countries (see Chapter 3), and with those who are surveilled and targeted by repressive counter-terrorism laws in UK, Europe, the US and Australia (see Chapters 5 and 6). It may symbolise empathy with Muslim men tortured in Guantánamo and Abu Ghraib, Iraq (see Chapter 6) or resistance to the West's "War on Terror", or the occupation of Palestine (see Chapter 4), or a reaction to the use of Western law to restrict women's freedom in civic and public spaces, as in Europe, or a response to the gendered and racialised deprivations. "Covering," especially with the face veil and long dress/jilbab/gelabaya, may also be rebellion against the sexualised commercialisation of the Western female body (Khan 2020). Notwithstanding, the West argues that explanations are to be found in social, family and faith pressures, denying that Muslim women have agency (Abu-Lughod 39; Ahmed 2020). Khan's (2020) book of essays, *It's not about the burqa*, shouts agency from every page.

It is acknowledged, that women in some Muslim majority countries have less power to determine what they wear, how they look or the appearance of their body, (see Almila and Inglis 2019), and that for some Muslim women diaspora in Western countries in some communities where religious conservatism and fundamentalism has taken root their power to determine their body is compromised (Moghissi and Ghorashi 2010). It is also recognised that some women of the Muslim faith, who once wore a symbol of their religious faith, have now removed any outwardly visible sign of identity in order to protect themselves from assault on the street (Zempi and Chakraborti 2014) (see Chapter 3). What is certain then is that there is no homogenous reading.

The "9/11 syndrome" (Joseph and Sharma 2003), Brexit, far-right nationalism and spiralling Islamophobia, and gendered Islamophobia (see Chapter 3) has centred Muslim women as the target of racism online and on the streets, where repressive laws of Western governments, who as part of their domestic WOT, have regulated Islamic dress, in schools and public places. In France and Belgium (see for example Easat-Daas 2019) the face veil is criminalised, and such act of covering a breach of the law carrying a sentence of imprisonment. Here, criminalisation of the Muslim woman's body is bolstered by pseudo-altruistic, equality and security justifications. Political rhetoric is characteristically uniform, confecting a paternalistic concern of protecting women's rights to equality and where stripping a woman of her dress is said to be "saving her" (see Abu-Lughod 2013). This same entreaty runs through the West's justification for its territorial ambitions in the WOT and lawless invasion of non-Western countries, notably Afghanistan and Iraq (see Chapters 3, 5 and 8). President Bush and Prime Minister Blair appropriated the equality norms of women's liberation, to serve as a: "handmaid to colonialism…. this theft of feminist rhetoric is not new, particularly if its function is national expansion" (Viner 2002). Such paternalistic fawnings couched in equality rhetoric, have receded in recent years as public, political and media narratives make way for a new and upcoming rhetoric which suffuses her dress and body coverings with a text of social and political dissent, an unwillingness to integrate, a display of anti-Western values and, in some cases, evidence of radicalisation and support for terrorist sympathies (see Chapters 2 and 3). These insinuations are appropriated by official and legal others such that her dress and body has become, in an Althusserian sense, overdetermined. These presumptions drive legislative purpose where, her dress, headscarf (hijab), face veil (niqab), full body covering/burqa, jilbab/gelabaya (long dress or tunic) and more recently her "burkini" (covering the body in beach/swimming attire) have become anthropomorphised as a racial marker (Kundnani 2015: 11).

Since law functions, on the one hand, as an arm of the state and expression of state interest and protector of community interest (see Chapter 4) and on the other, protects the right to freedom of expression and religious belief of individuals and groups, both are locked in contest, with both appropriating human rights discourse and protections to serve their respective positions. COVID-19 has injected its own irony into this face veil restriction since this covering considered by others to be an emblem of the oppression of women or of Islamic extremism, has now been transformed into a saviour and protector provided of course that it is worn for public health reasons and resembles a surgical mask. For those European countries, for example, France and Belgium, which have criminalised the niqab/face veil as part of "securitisation" measures, an exemption is now made where wearing a mask provided that it doesn't look like a niqab is now compulsory so as to prevent any risk of contagion by COVID-19 where the fine for covering the face for religious purposes is 165 euros, whilst the fine for not covering the face where public health and Covid measures have deemed it a necessity is 135 euros.

In this chapter I interrogate first, the law's function and question whether it has any legitimacy in regulating body covering and consider through a number of case examples the use of law to discipline, and, in some cases, to erase a group. Second, in focusing on Islamic dress I examine the appropriation of law in reviewing the civil law restrictions (education and employment) placed on Muslim women and girls who wear the headscarf, face veil and long dress/jilbab, in France, Belgium, Turkey and the UK, in schools and Universities, and the use of employment law to instate a "corporate image" which erases the headscarf and potentially the female Muslim woman from the workplace. Third, through an analysis of selected legal decisions, I examine the exceptional use of the criminal law, in some European countries, which criminalise the face covering/niqab. Finally, I consider the efforts in France through imposition of local bye-laws (albeit enacted momentarily) in some of France's coastal towns to strip Muslim women and divest them of most of their outer bodily garments in promoting a model of women's freedom which seems to be epitomised by a state of semi nudity. Stripping women repeats the colonisers strategy, bent on public humiliation and shaming to bring about punishment and metaphysical destruction of a group whether women of the Maghreb in Algeria in the 1950' and 1960s, or in Cannes in 2016.

THE LAW AND THE PHYSICAL, METAPHYSICAL AND CORPOREAL BODY

De Certeau (1984: 139) writes,

> There is no law that is not inscribed on bodies. Every law has a hold on the body....From birth to mourning after death, law 'takes hold of' bodies in order to make them its text [and] 140...articulates them in the juridical corpus....The power of the law is written on the backs of its subjects.

Why has the law "taken hold" of Muslim women's bodies? and why has their dress and wardrobe become of such concern to the state to the extent that "her" dress is a matter of legal regulation and interference? Since the function of the criminal law is to prohibit criminal conduct, civil law to regulate civic matters, employment and education law, to regulate matters in the workplace and in places of education, how is what a particular group of women wear a matter for law's interference? John Stuart Mill writing in 1869 (2016) (see Chapter 3) on the function of criminal law, said: "the only purpose for which power can be rightfully exercised over any member of a civilized community, against his will, is to prevent harm to others" a binding principle accepted across all systems of Anglo-American jurisprudence. Joel Feinberg (1984 [1990]), in *Harmless Wrongdoing*, engages with Mill's "liberalism thesis" and agrees that legal moralism may legitimately prohibit certain actions on the ground that they are immoral, but any kind of "free-floating evil" (he gives examples of exploitation and coercion) is not sufficient (173). Hart's counter claim to Mill's harm principle, regards legal intervention as legitimate when protecting a moral order and in regulation of private behaviour. Emile Durkheim, in *The Division of Labour in Society* ([1898], 1964) who, influenced Hart, had identified the maintenance of social soli-darity and social integration as an integral part of the law's function. Since the face veil/niqab is criminalised in all public spaces in France and Belgium, and in some other European countries, then, in consid-ering Mill's thesis surely, we need to name the harm and provide the evidence of the harm her dress causes, and in considering Hart's coun-terpoint thesis, to identify any moral order necessity that drives the law. These questions present compelling and cogent challenges to the legiti-macy of law's proscription of Muslim women's dress. Political and legal justifications for prohibition are littered with loquacious chattering's of preservation of a particular "way of life", and the need for harmony and "social cohesion". Feinberg (1984 [1990]: 52) makes the point that: "...a neighbourhood can be harmonious and attractive for anyone to live in even though it contains Liberal and Fundamentalist Protestant, Roman and Greek Catholics, Reform and Orthodox Jews, Moslems, Buddhists, atheists, and indifferents". Not all seem to agree.

Since the body, as Elizabeth Grosz explains is "a surface on which social law, morality, and values are inscribed" (1995: 33) law has always had a role in controlling and regulating sexual conduct and desire (see Foucault 1978; Smart 1989; Butler 1999), variously proscribing heteronormativity, regulating homosexuality and transgenderism in public and private, posi-tioning and constructing, ordering and disciplining the body (Foucault 1978; Crossley 2001). Visual representations of the body, for example, and what has been defined as "erotic", "pornographic" and "obscene" have been historically regulated and reconceptualised. For example porno-graphic representation, redefined as harm and as an equality and dignity violation (MacKinnon 1993) is found in recent UK legislation prohibiting visual representations of rape and "extreme pornographic images" (s 63 Criminal Justice and Immigration Act 2008, s 16 Criminal Justice and

Courts Act 2015). Many feminist scholars question why some consider that women's rights in European modernity can only be delivered by a state of undress (Saadawi 1997; McRobbie 2013: 96). The fashion industry has joined the debate in contesting the freedom and equality of a clothed body having built its empire on profit and baring female flesh it is not difficult to see why. In the face of criticism Remona Aly proclaims: "If I want to buy a burkini I bloody well will!" (*The Guardian* 31 March 2016). Hart states in general terms that legal interference is necessary when the thing in question is so organically connected with the central core (1984: 11). This seems also to be Phillips view. As Hussein, Bloul and Poynting (2019: 266) point out "Hardline- anti-Muslim writers including Bat Ye'or, Orlana Fallaci, Melanie Phillips and Ayaan Hirsi Ali have contributed to this 'Eurabia' discourse [establishing].... A genre of dystopian literature forecasting a new Dark Age in which Europe is reduced to a state or servitude by Muslim immigrants from its former colonies". Muslim women's wardrobe is certainly the "G spot" of the body politic!

Undress to Destroy—Instances of Ethnic Erasure

Legal prohibitions, throughout history, have arranged body styles, configured clothing, bodily adornment, including hair braids and corn weaves, as part of a strategy to enforce the dominant power relationships of class, status, gender, race, ethnicity, and religion. So, whilst the regulation of Muslim women's dress takes on an exceptional form in the modern era, other historical moments have regulated body styles of less powerful and marginalised groups. Body covering for the Scots in the seventeenth century, the American zootsuiters of the 1940s, and Algerian face veiled women in the 1950s and 1960s are such moments where body coverings constituted for the wearer the core of identity and personhood and destroying this essence of authenticity vital in the victor's strategy of domination and ethnic erasure. The Disarming Act 1746, or "dress act" was enacted by the English Monarchs to preserve their hegemony by coercing the assimilation and submission of the Scots and to establish civic control over Scotland and its highlands by criminalising the dress traditionally worn by Highlanders (Caffentzis 2005). "Any persons within Scotland, whether man or boy (excepting officers and soldiers in his majesty's service), who should wear the plaid, philibeg, trews, shoulder belts, or any part of the Highland garb,..... should, without the alternative of a fine, be imprisoned for the first conviction for six months, without bail, and on the second conviction be transported for seven years" (repealed in 1782). The City of Los Angeles in 1943, made wearing long jackets and baggy trousers (referred to as "zoot suits" and commonly worn by Mexican Americans) a criminal offence punishable with imprisonment. In June 1943, riots broke out between American servicemen and "zoot suiters" who were physically assaulted, and their clothes ripped from their backs. Such attacks were part of a wider programme of repression and exclusion following the earlier deportation by the US of 2 million people of Mexican descent of whom 1.2 million were US citizens. Del Olmo (2000) points out that the act of wearing the "zoot suit" originally a mark of identity became transformed into an emblem of resistance by disadvantaged migrants. Disrobing the powerless to disarm, assimilate and conquer, was a vital weapon of France's colonial occupation of Algeria until 1960s, where forcible removal of women's dress was part of a strategy to psychologically and metaphysically destroy. The occupiers recognised: "If we want to destroy the structure of Algeria, its capacity for resistance, we must first of all conquer the women" (Fanon 1965: 14). Targeting women to defeat the group was also a strategy used by the Serbs in the genocide of Bosnian Muslims. The trial Chamber of the International Criminal Tribunal for the former Yugoslavia (ICTY) in *Kunarac, Kovač and Vuković* (2002), heard that Muslim women were kept in detention centres, repeatedly raped, specifically targeted and specifically impregnated. The rapes were one of the many ways in which Serbs could assert their superiority and victory over the Muslims.

In Algeria, as in Abu Ghraib (see Chapter 6), the photograph was one of the weapons of war in its capacity to cause immediate and repeated insult in its permanent record of abuse. The camera invaded Muslim women's modesty and personhood, forcing unveiling, photographing and recording that moment of undress, exacting maximum humiliation on Algerian society. Fanon wrote: "Every veil that fell, ... every face that offered itself to the bold and impatient glance of the occupier, was a negative expression of the fact that Algeria was beginning to deny herself and was accepting the rape of the colonizer" (1965: 43). Marc Garanger (1960, 2002) stationed in Algeria was instructed by the French military to take ID photographs of Algerians living in internment camps under military supervision. Garanger's photographs of unveiled women are not a testimony to their liberation from Maghreb's male patriarchy, as the French propaganda promoted (Perego 2015), but memoralise the injustice of the French coloniser's metaphysical abuse of women and violation of their customs and religion. Fred Ritchin (2008) describes the photographs as "visual rape", where: "public humiliation formed part of a collective punishment". It was, as MacMaster (2012) understood, part of "revolutionary warfare" to defeat the National Liberation Front by penetrating the Muslim family. Women, as unwilling subjects marked their resistance in reversing the coloniser's possessive gaze and returned their look down the camera's lens. The pictures disturb and looking on them invokes a sense of one's own complicity. There is a danger of being a mere spectator. David Levi Strauss in "Photography and Belief" is interested in the power of the photograph both as an accurate record and as a vehicle to construct identity (2003: 74). The purpose of the photograph in Algeria was to desecrate cherished identities and create and impose an identity of submission and humiliation. Whilst many women are visibly seen to be broken, ashamed, abjected and despairing, in some of the photographs they return a look of defiance and resistance. Marc Garanger, who himself was also an unwilling subject, wrote: "For twenty-four months I never stopped, sure that one day I would be able to testify, to tell stories with their images" (see Garanger, *Photography Algerian*, Eileraas 2003; Estrin 2010; Du Preeze 2008).

EUROPE'S "SECULAR FUNDAMENTALISM" AND VIOLATION OF MUSLIM WOMEN'S BODIES

The Right to Religious Manifestation

So, what exactly is the function and legitimacy of laws that prohibit the wearing of the headscarf/hijab, long dress/gelabaya or jilbab, face veil/niqab and more recently the burkini in countries in Western Europe? and how do legal prohibitions on Muslim women's dress in secular societies co-exist with human rights obligations in international and domestic law which protect freedom of choice and personal and religious autonomy? Why has the headscarf and other items of Muslim women's clothing been regarded as: "an icon of intolerable difference" (Scott 2007: 5), and why has clothing style been appropriated by others as the barometer of freedom, secularism and modernity?

The right to a dress in a particular way is protected in law and rarely has it been subject to regulation (excepting states of undress and public nudity). Covering the head with a headscarf or part of one's face, when that act of covering carries a religious significance, is a protected right under the European Convention of Human Rights (ECHR). The right to religious freedom (Article 9), though not an absolute right is balanced against the "rights of others". Article 3 may also be engaged since it provides protection from torture and inhuman or degrading treatment or punishment such that any dress prohibition that may demand the removal of a particular article of clothing, may impact on the dignity of the wearer. Article 8 may also be engaged since this right protects a person's privacy and family life. Article 10, (discussed in Chapter 3) protects freedom of speech, in this regard, dress is a symbolic and visual expression of opinion and speech. Article 11, which protects the right to assembly, may also be engaged since, for example, prohibiting a woman from wearing an Islamic face covering in public interferes with her freedom to access public spaces and services. Article 14 protects against discrimination on the grounds of sex, race, colour, language, religion, political or other opinion, national or social origin, association with a national minority, property, birth, or other status in respect of any of the rights in the Convention. All these rights are potentially engaged where European countries impose prohibitions on Muslim women's dress.

Eurocentric/"Secular Racism"—The Headscarf Question

Widely recognised by Hall (1996), Said (1997), Hussein (2019), Eltahawy (2015), Meer and Modood (2019), "Muslim" is imagined and essentialised, as if a racial category. Across Europe, notably France, Belgium and Turkey, Islamic dress in some form is prohibited. Wearing the headscarf/hijab is prohibited in state schools in France and Belgium, and (until 2012) in Universities in Turkey, and, in places of work, for example, in France and Belgium (see "corporate image" cases below). The UK has no such limitations. Highly politicised, there has been an increasing public and governmental mood across Europe against religious symbolism and especially all kinds of Islamic symbolism (see Waldron 2012: 76, 77; Almila and Inglis 2019: 9; Fornerod 2019: 53, Chapter 3). France and Turkey provide two, amongst several other instances of country regulation, though their histories and cultures could not be more diverse. The French prohibition on the headscarf derives from its history of struggle for liberation from the control of the Catholic Church. Turkey, by contrast, once part of the Ottoman Empire from 1600 to

1923 and subject to Islamic influence, is characterised by its strivings to "modernise" (by this it is meant, to free itself from a particular interpretation of Islamic and political influence) which is reflected in the prohibition of the headscarf (until 2012).

Since 2004, France has regulated the headscarf in schools resulting in legal challenges which have invoked, albeit unsuccessfully, the protection afforded by Article 9. In 2016, the headscarf prohibition, was extended into the workplace when the European Court of Justice (ECJ) upheld the right of two employers to ban the headscarf, if certain conditions prevailed (see below), thereby giving permission to other employers if they so wished to do likewise.

Fornerod's (2019) incisive essay sets out the background and justification for the headscarf prohibition, said to be found in France's doctrine of secularism or laïcité, established in 1905 by the Act of the Law of Separation of the Churches and the State (loi du 9 décembre 1905 concernant la séparation des Églises et de l'État). Article I asserts that the Republic ensures liberty of conscience and guarantees the free exercise of religion, under restrictions prescribed by the interest in public order, whilst Article 2 asserts that the republic does not recognise, remunerate or subsidise any religious denomination (McGoldrick 2006: 36). Such a contradictory law has led to many contesting the meaning of laïcité and its application. McGoldrick (38) identifies three possible interpretations. First, laïcité, he points out, has been taken to require the exclusion of religion from public life and public spaces including civic and educational spaces. Second, laïcité, means, for some, a suppression of religion, and a third, a counter interpretation is that it ensures positive protection for religious freedom. Fornerod (54) explores how there has been an attempt to balance such restrictions by distinguishing between the private and public spheres. "As a rule, the principles of laïcité applies to people involved in the carrying out of public service activities... Religious neutrality, however, does not impose upon the users of public service activities. In this regard, pupils in public schools' exception to the rule". "Laïcité", some argue has a darker side. Scott considers that the headscarf affair is in fact part of the history of French racism (2007: 41). "Racism was the subtext of the headscarf controversy, but secularism was its explicit justification" (90). Since 12% of the population are Muslim and given France's colonialist occupation of Algeria from 1830 to 1962 and the appropriation of women's bodies and dress in that conquest, that the recent legislative prohibitions are racist is a reasonable conclusion to draw (see Valfort 2017).

The headscarf affair "l'affaire du foulard" (Benhabib 2002: 97; Bouteldja 2005, 2014) epitomises the fragility of maintaining a balance between respecting freedom of conscience and religion and protecting a public sphere of laïcité devoid of symbols (Fornerod). In 1989, Fatima, Leila and Samira, who were excluded, from Gabriel Havez un Criel College, for wearing a headscarf at school, mounted a legal challenge invoking their human rights' protections. The Education Minister, Lionel Jospin, sought an opinion from the French court, the Conseil d'État (avis no 346.893 du 27 November 1989) (see McGoldrick 2006: 60 fnb 200). The court, in an ambiguous opinion advised: "the wearing of signs by which they intend to demonstrate their belonging to a religion is not in itself incompatible with the principle of secularism ....[and] Freedom does not permit students to display signs of religious belonging ... worn individually or collectively, or by their ostentatious or campaigning/protesting nature, would constitute an act of pressure, provocation, proselytism or propaganda..." (70). Jospin responding unhelpfully said it would be for the Principal of the school to make a case-by-case ruling, and this is exactly what schools did. Not surprisingly other challenges followed, when, in 2003, the Levy sisters, (whose father was an agnostic and of Jewish background and their mother a non-practising Muslim of Algerian origin), were suspended for wearing a headscarf to school. In حجابى هويتى "Hijab is my identity" they set out their story. In 2003 Nadjet Abdallah, a civil servant, who challenged the ban also had her appeal dismissed (*Agence France Presse*, 13 July 2003).

President Chirac, in July 2003, established the Stasi committee (*Committee of Reflection on the Application of the Principle of Secularity in the Republic*) to consider the principle of laïcité, freedom of thought and freedom from religion in relation to the headscarf. The Stasi findings did indeed find evidence of "race hatred" (Stasi Report 2004: 83). Notwithstanding, the French parliament in March 2004 following the Senate (276–20) and National Assembly votes (494–36), passed a law banning the headscarf in schools. Prime Minister Raffarin articulating the "official" state understanding of the headscarf's meaning said: "De facto they [headscarves] are taking on political significance and can no longer be regarded exclusively as personal signs of religious belonging" (*BBC News* 3 February 2004 "French PM defends headscarf ban"), adding that prohibition would protect women "from fundamentalist pressures".

The ban extended to teachers, civil servants and hospital workers. From thereon, in public and political discourse, the headscarf was deemed a threat, an expression of defiance, of resistance and potentially terrorist sympathy. Feminist commentators, Benhabib (2002: 95), Malik (2014, 2018) and McRobbie (2013) contended, as did many others, that these legal prohibitions were expressions of racism and hostility against Muslims fuelled by postcolonial guilt, fear and nationalism (Scott 2007: 98) where the "headscarf ... figured as an important political emblem" (99).

Headscarf bans continue to be contested and the Constitutional Court of Belgium on June 4, 2020 in *Francisco Ferrer Brussels* university (la Haute École Francisco Ferrer) ruled that the prohibition of religious symbols, including the headscarf, in higher education would not constitute a violation of the right to human dignity or the right of religious freedom and allowed the college to impose a ban. This led to 12 Universities, to make public statements that they would not be imposing such a ban. The Free University of Brussels tweeted stating: "Equality and inclusion are central to VUB. Diversity is a fact, at our university as well. So, let it be clear that every student is welcome with us regardless of gender, origin, or social status. With or without headscarf". Mass public demonstrations, #TouchePasAMesEtudes ("Don't touch my studies") and #HijabisFightBack, followed. Such dress bans reflect the increasing lurch to the right as far-right nationalistic tendencies further embed their popularist politics into the social, political and legal fabric drumming out diversity and inclusion. The impact of these anti-Muslim women measures further emboldened anti-immigration tendencies of the far-right as well as liberals across Europe (see Chapter 3) and intensified feelings of Muslim exclusion and no doubt provoked Islamic extremism.

France's Corporate "Woman Slaughter"

By 2016, this exclusion (Scott) (some would say laïcité), extended beyond the school and University and civic employment into private commercial workplaces. Ironically, at a moment when female gender stereotyping for women in business is under gender equality scrutiny (Heilman 2012), and where masculinist tropes of female "professionalism" which elide gender and dress in promoting a sexualised and particular feminised "corporate image" are challenged and contested (see Avery and Crain 2007), we witness a femonationalistic fashioning of the corporate image by excluding Muslim women's headscarf. This move is justified through fawnings of allegiance to a "neutral" corporate image, which by precluding the wearing of a headscarf targets Muslim women and finds legal endorsement in the decision of the European Court of Justice (ECJ) in the cases of *Achbita and anor v G4s Secure Solutions NV* and *Bougnaoui and ADDH v Micropole SA* (2016). The court ruled that employers are entitled to prohibit employees from: "wearing any political, philosophical or religious sign" which includes headscarves. Ms. Archbita, a receptionist employed by G4s in Belgium and who wore a headscarf, was dismissed for so doing. Since the EU, Employment Equality Directive 2000/78/EC, protects against direct discrimination, for example where a person is treated less favourably on grounds of religion, Ms. Archbita challenged this decision. (An exemption is only permitted where there is a genuine occupational requirement or else occupational activities, and indirect discrimination protects against discrimination where there is a neutral requirement which impacts disproportionately.) She commenced employment with G4s in 2006 and informed her employer that she would be wearing a headscarf. G4s had a written policy, at that time, stating that religious insignia was not permitted, and subsequently dismissed her. The court held that G4s decision to dismiss was lawful and that there was no direct discrimination against her based on religion (Article 2[2] [a] of the Directive), although it said that it may constitute indirect discrimination based on religion under Article 2(2) (b). So, in short, if a company publicises a policy albeit it may be ethnocentric and anti-Muslim, as G4's clearly was, then such a prohibition is lawful. The second case involved Ms. Bourgnaoiu, a design engineer with Micropole, who refused to remove her headscarf when visiting a client company. The client company had apparently made a complaint about being "embarrassed" about a woman in a headscarf. Embarrassed? Micropole responded by dismissing her in 2008. However, Micropole did not have a written policy prohibiting articles of faith, and in this case the employer's defence was rejected. The ECJ found that promoting a "neutral image" (in these cases, an anti-Muslim image) is a legitimate aim, but only if such a rule is in place, thereby opening the door to gendered anti-Muslim racism and xenophobia. No one has yet tested whether wearing a head covering on fashion grounds would be so prohibited. Bribosia and Rorive (2016) write: "Behind Mrs Achbita and Mrs Bougnaoui cases lies the access to employment of thousands of Muslim women. A crucial question in countries with significant employment discrimination rate". This is the dark revengeance of so-called neutrality where corporate branding is the new veneer behind which corporate racism lurks (Bribosia and Rorive 2016; Flake 2014; Cloots 2018). There is evidence too that this anti-Muslim verve has extended its creep to Muslim mothers, who wearing headscarves when helping in a voluntary capacity in schools are being told to remove them (*The Guardian* 16 October 2019 "French government resists calls for school trip headscarf ban"). In this sense, the French colonisers efforts to decimate the culture of the Maghreb in Algeria as part of the colonising project, repeats itself, as Muslim women are being erased, bit by bit, piece by piece, from French public life.

Anti-Muslim corporate branding is found beyond France and Belgium's borders, Ruby (2019: 50) documents several cases in the US. The Supreme Court case of Abercrombie and Fitch (*Equal Employment Opportunity Commission v Abercrombie & Fitch Inc* 2015) where Samantha Elauf who wore a black headscarf was denied a sales job in 2008 at an Abercrombie Kids store in Tulsa, Oklahoma. "because her head scarf conflicted with the company's dress code". However, the court found in her favour, Justice Alito concuring with the judgment that said "...Abercrombie rejected Elauf because of a practice that Abercrombie knew was religious. It is undisputed that Abercrombie rejected Elauf because she wore a headscarf, and there is ample evidence in the summary judgment record to prove that Abercrombie knew that Elauf is a Muslim and that she wore the scarf for a religious reason" [9].

Turkey's Political Appropriation of the Headscarf

Turkey, until 2013, banned the headscarf in schools and Universities (Atasoy 2006, 2019; McGoldrick 2006: 137). Atasoy locates the complex changes in regulating woman dress in the context of a process of liberalisation since the 1930s where the headscarf prohibition demonstrates efforts to excise conservative Islam's historical bind. Turkey, unlike France, is 90% Muslim and its history of Islamic dress prohibition and relaxation underscores its politicisation. Attempts to modernise and reform by Kemal Atatürk led to the Education Services (Merger) Act 1924 and the Dress (Regulations) Act 1934, which prohibited religious attire including the headscarf/hijab. Bleiberg (2005: 133) more pointedly identified this move as Atatürk's "scorched earth campaign against religious power". Dress restrictions since, have waxed and waned, reflecting political and nationalist struggles (Atasoy 2019). In 1993, Ms Karaduman (*Karaduman v Turkey* [1993]) who was refused a certificate of graduation from the University of Ankara (the University requiring a photograph of her without a headscarf, which she was not willing to remove), brought a case before the then European Commission of Human Rights alleging breaches of Articles 9 and 14 of the Convention. The Commission in interpreting Article 9, determined that "respect for the rights and freedoms of others" trumped her right, which it said was influenced by the growth of "certain religious fundamentalist currents" [7]. In 1998, Turkey's ban on Islamists further emboldened the existing restrictions on religious clothing provoking further legal challenges before the domestic and international courts, and especially from University students (Vakulenko 2007; Saktanber and Çorbacioğlu 2008). In 2005, Ms. Şahin (*Şahin v Turkey* [2005]), a University student, who was denied access to University lectures, brought a claim before the European Court of Human Rights (ECtHR). The ECtHR upheld the Turkish Constitutional Court ruling prohibiting University students from attending University lectures wearing a headscarf. The court whilst accepting that the headscarf ban interfered with her right to freedom of religion, held that it pursued a legitimate aim and was "necessary in a democratic society". The ECtHR added a panoply of further reasons in support of its ruling, appropriating gender equality ([98]) and the "threat to republican values". The court in overdetermining its meaning described the headscarf as an "active symbol" which represented extremist political movements (Bleiberg: 148). Judge Tulkans in her dissenting judgment articulated quite different concerns:

I end by noting that all these issues must also be considered in the light of the observations set out in the annual activity report published in June 2005 of the European Commission against Racism and Intolerance (ECRI), which expresses concern about the climate of hostility existing against persons who are or are believed to be Muslim, and considers that the situation requires attention and action in the future. Above all, the message that needs to be repeated is that the best means of preventing and combating fanaticism and extremism is to uphold human rights. ([20])

The ban on the headscarf, the subject of struggle between the President and the Constitutional Court, was finally lifted on 1 October 2013 as part of the so-called "democratisation process", amending Article 5 of the dress code regulation.

State Sovereignty

Whilst international human rights were developed to protect individual rights and to allow challenge to state sovereignty, the rulings of the ECtHR a least over Muslim women's dress, demonstrate not a fierce defence of those rights but a deference to the power of the state. This is the truth of the balancing act of which Fornerod speaks. The interpretation and application of Article 9, for example, has done little to protect the religious freedom of Muslim women. The "margin of appreciation", which allows individual states considerable room to manoeuvre when interpreting Convention rights, Geoffrey Robertson (2012) has described as a "cowards' cloak". What these cases demonstrate is that the state can enforce Muslim dress laws largely unfettered. For instance, in *Şahin*, the courts reasoned, somewhat compliantly, that: "the national authorities are in principle better placed than an international court to evaluate local needs and conditions [and] the role of the Convention machinery is essentially subsidiary" [100]. Criticism of the decrepitude of the ECtHR led the UK House of Lords to remark, somewhat restrainedly, in (*R [on the application of Begum [by her litigation friend, Rahman]] v Headteacher and Governors of Denbigh High School* 2006), that "Strasbourg jurisprudence" is "limited". A position which seems to remain unchanged. Scott (2007: ciii, ix) considered the ECtHR, ruling in upholding the Turkish ban on headscarves in public buildings as "a victory for Ankara's secularists", pointing out that the decision was fuelled by fear and nationalism. What the court determines as "necessary in a democratic society" is as slippery and multifaceted as the "Rule of Law" (ROL), as Waldron (2012) and Shklar's (1998) discovered (see Chapter 4) allowing for lip service to be paid to democratic principles and rights whilst, in practice, pandering to the inconstant nature of state power and interest.

With the rise in right-wing nationalism and popularism, countries in Europe are decidedly anti-immigrant and anti-Muslim (see Chapter 3) and headscarf bans are the racist mood of this racist moment. In Germany, by 2019, following a 2003 Constitutional Court ruling restrictions on religious dress are permissible if explicitly laid down in law. Half of Germany's 16 states (Länder)- Baden-Württemberg, Bavaria, Berlin, Bremen, Hesse, Lower Saxony, North Rhine-Westphalia, and Saarland have laws prohibiting public school teachers and other civil servants from wearing the headscarf. Muslim women who wear the headscarf find difficulty in securing employment (*TRT World*, 23 July 2019 "Hijab-wearing women struggle to find work in Germany") and there is a feeling that women who wear headscarves need not bother applying (*Foreign policy* 12 July 2019 "Women with Headscarves Need Not Apply in Germany"). This racialisation of dress is washing over Europe.

UK—Anti-Muslim Dress Narratives

In the UK, whilst there is no legal restriction on wearing the headscarf/hijab in schools or in the workplace, negative commentary and invective profiling of women who chose to do so, is invidious. Kelvin Mackenzie, former editor of *The Sun* newspaper, in an article headlined: "Why did Channel 4 have a presenter in a hijab fronting coverage of Muslim terror in Nice?" (July 18, 2016) said that the UK presenter, Fatima Manji, who wears a headscarf, should not have presented Channel Four's coverage of the 2016 Nice terrorist attacks. Fatima Manji complained to the Independent Press Standards Organisation (IPSO) contending that *The Sun* breached Clause 1 (Accuracy), Clause 3 (Harassment) and Clause 12 (Discrimination) of the Editors' Code of Practice. The IPSO ruling did not uphold her complaint finding instead:

[19] While the columnist's opinions were undoubtedly offensive to the complainant, and to others, these were views he had been entitled to express. The article did not include a prejudicial or pejorative reference to the complainant on the grounds of her religion. Accordingly, it was not a breach of Clause 12. ... [21]. the columnist's view that Islam is 'clearly a violent religion' was a statement of his opinion. This view, however extreme or offensive to many, did not raise a breach of Clause 1. The suggestion that the complainant was a 'pawn in this TV news game' was clearly conjecture and underlined that the author's criticism was directed at Channel 4 and not at the individual newsreader. There was no breach of Clause 1. (IPSO ruling 05935-16 *Manji v The Sun*)

So, it would appear racial insult is a matter of opinion, conjecture and protected speech (see Chapter 3).

In the Shabina Begum case, the House of Lords considered whether a school's prohibition on a Muslim girl who wished to wear a jilbab/gelabaya (long dress) at school should be upheld (*R [on the application of Begum] v Headteacher and Governors of Denbigh High School*

[2006]). The court decided, based on promoting the values of "pluralism", that the long dress interfered with the rights of others, those others, being girls in the school who may have felt under pressure to dress similarly. As I argued elsewhere (Edwards 2007: 17; 2011): "It is an interesting logic and an interesting fear (manufactured rather than natural) that the jilbab contains the exclusive potential to influence and convert in a way that is not considered relevant to discussions of the wearing of the headscarf or indeed the shalwa kameeze". This decision attracted diverse responses. Malik (2010) in her judgment in this case (as part of the "feminist judgment project") agrees with the outcome but rejects restricting dress by appealing to reasons of national security or gender equality and says: "there is no evidence that Shabina Begum adopted the jilbab as anything other than an autonomous choice" (342) and argues for a recognition of Begum's autonomy and of her right to choose. Whilst Patel (2016) considers that Begum was under the influence of her brother, and conservative Islamic pressures. More recently a Muslim estate agent filed a case before and Employment Tribunal after her former employer allegedly told to remove her black headscarf because the garment had "terrorist affiliations" (*The Independent* 11 July 2017).

EUROPE—CRIMING THE NIQAB

The face veil/niqab, the most contested and regulated of garments, worn by a very few Muslim women throughout Europe, has taken the law, Mill would certainly have argued, beyond the borders of its legitimacy in using the criminal law to compel dress choice. European countries, notably France, Belgium, the Netherlands, Denmark, Italy and Switzerland, have criminalised women who wear the face veil in public. In the Machbour case (Mme M) (Conseil d'État, 27 juin 2008, Mme Machbour, no. 286798) Mme M's was not welcome on French soil and her application for French nationality was rejected on the basis of her choice of niqab and long cloak, which were garments considered incompatible with French values (Vakulenko 2007). Amiraux and Koussens (2016: 126) cite from the judgment of the court: "It seems that Mrs. Machbour has not embraced the values of the Republic, in particular those relating to the equality of the sexes".

In France and Belgium, since 2011, wearing a face covering for religious purposes in a public place, is a criminal offence (Malik 2014;

Fadil 2014; Edwards 2014) and failure to comply with the prohibition is punishable by a fine, attendance at a citizenship course and/or imprisonment. Muslim women are the primary target. Barras writes:

> The burqa in a couple of weeks had become the antonym, par excellence, of Frenchness, laïcité and the universal values it conveyed. This debate caught the attention of the French President, Nicolas Sarkozy, who in June 2009 in a speech to the French Parliament on the economic crisis, included a paragraph on French laïcité. Indeed, he stated that the burqa was not a religious sign, but a sign of enslavement and that it was not welcomed on French secular soil. (2010: 230)

Those who defied the ban and wore a face veil, as did Hind Ahmas and Najate Nit Ali, were prosecuted. Ahmas, when stopped by police, was willing to confirm her identity by lowering her face veil but refused to remove it altogether. She was brought before the Tribunal de Grande Instance, the Court of First instance for civil and criminal matters and sentenced to a 15-day citizenship course. She appealed, but her conviction was upheld by the higher court.

In 2015, in the case of *SAS v France* (2015) a 24-year-old French citizen originally from Pakistan, and a (Sunni) Muslim mounted a challenge in the ECtHR to the 2010 statute (in force 2011). She said that wearing a face veil was a mark of women's emancipation, self-assertion and allowed her to participate in society. She said that Article 3, the right to be free from degrading treatment, Article 8, the right to a private and family life, Article 9, the right to religious belief, Article 10, the right to freedom of expression and Article 11, the right to freedom of assembly taken separately, and together with Article 14, the right to be free from discrimination, all protected her right to wear the face veil. The ECtHR upheld the French ban concluding that the objective of ensuring "living together" was overriding and trumped any individual rights the applicant had. However, recognising that there had been an interference with her rights, the court ruled that such interference was legitimate conceding that: "Pluralism, tolerance and broadmindedness are hallmarks of a 'democratic society' [128]". The court was influenced by this relatively new concept of "living together". It considered the "travaux preparatoires", that is background documentation, in interpreting the law, including a report from a cross party Parliamentary commission, *The wearing of the full-face veil on national territory*, which concluded that

the full-face veil "represented a denial of fraternity, constituting the nega-
tion of contact with others and a flagrant infringement of the French
principle of 'living together' (*le 'vivre ensemble'*)" [15]. The court also
considered the explanatory memorandum to the bill which stated: "The
voluntary and systematic concealment of the face is problematic because it
is quite simply incompatible with the fundamental requirements of 'living
together' in French society" [25]. Already by 2012, when the Constitutional Court dismissed the original application in this case, it had said that
the legislative history pursued three aims, public safety, gender equality
and a "certain conception of 'living together'" [(B.21) 42]. Drawing on
this background the case for the government in *SAS* was presented in this
way: "The effect of concealing one's face in public places is to break the
social tie and to manifest a refusal of the principle of 'living together' (*le
'vivre ensemble'*)" [82]. It was also of significance that the Belgian government, acting as third-party intervenor, referred to two challenges that had
been dismissed in the Belgium Constitutional Court in 2012 (the original applications of *Samia Belkacemi, and Yamina Oussar* 2012) on the
grounds that the face veil posed a safety issue, was an obstacle to the right
of women to equality and dignity, and, more fundamentally, undermined
the very essence of the principle of "living together" [87]. The court in
SAS concluded:

> The Court is therefore able to accept that the barrier raised against others
> by a veil concealing the face is perceived by the respondent State as
> breaching the right of others to live in a space of socialisation which makes
> living together easier... in view of the flexibility of the notion of 'living
> together' and the resulting risk of abuse, the Court must engage in a
> careful examination of the necessity of the impugned limitation [122,142].
> ... the Court finds that the impugned ban can be regarded as justified in
> its principle solely in so far as it seeks to guarantee the conditions of 'living
> together' [151]. ...and the ban imposed by the Law of 11 October 2010
> can be regarded as proportionate to the aim pursued, namely the preserva-
> tion of the conditions of 'living together' as an element of the 'protection
> of the rights and freedoms of others'. [157]

The judges who dissented, contended that the concept of "living
together" did not fall directly under any of the rights and freedoms
guaranteed within the Convention [5, 10, 25].

Furthermore, it can hardly be argued that an individual has a right to enter into contact with other people, in public places, against their will. While communication is admittedly essential for life in society, the right to respect for private life also comprises the right not to communicate and not to enter into contact with others in public places – the right to be an outsider. [8]

Whilst the concept of "living together" is discussed in a document *Living Together* (2009) published by the Council of Europe (see Lange), and in the Belgium judgment of 2012, this concept was in its infancy. Importantly, the President of the UK Supreme Court, Baroness Hale, said: "The concept of 'living together' relied upon by France was not a fundamental right – France had not established a connection between any fundamental rights of others and the ability to see a veiled woman's face in public" (Hale 2019: 10). As Hunter-Henin (2015) observes, the court, was concerned about using such a malleable notion as "living together" as a justification for restricting Convention rights (albeit that it did just that) and accepted that the French law may have "upset" some sections of the Muslim community and that the ban may promote Islamophobia ([148]). As for women who wear the face veil, and those who want to do so they have said that it allows them to participate when they would otherwise have been unable (Brems 2014; Berry 2018).

Further challenges followed and in 2017 Samia Belkacemi/(Belcacemi), a Belgian national, and Yamina Oussar, a Moroccan national (*Belcacemi and Oussar v Belgium* [2017]), and Fouzia Dakir a Belgian national (*Dakir v Belgium* [2017]), challenged the Belgium face veil ban in the ECtHR. The court found that the bans were necessary to ensure the functioning of a democratic society and found no violation of Article 8 or Article 9 and asserted that "covering ones face is a practice incompatible with the modalities of social communication, and the establishment of human relations indispensable for life in society" (*Belkacemi and Oussar*, [53]; *Dakir*, [56]). This "necessary to ensure function" test takes the precept of "living together" relied upon in the French case of *SAS* to an even higher threshold.

Other European countries have introduced similar bans. Switzerland implemented a ban in 2016 and a Danish ban came into force on 1 August 2018. There has been a partial ban in Italy's Lombardy region, since 2015. In Germany, since 2016, there has also been a partial ban. In 2017, Austria banned face veils whilst driving. In the Netherlands, since

26 June 2018, there has been a ban in schools and on public transport and accessing services i.e., in hospitals, albeit with several exceptions. In June 2018, the parliament of Norway passed a bill banning face covering in educational institutions as well as daycare centres. In Spain, several parts of Catalonia have laws against face veils. In Luxembourg, Prime Minister Xavier Bettel, was more measured and said he wanted: "to settle this problem with a calm mind. We must not fall into populism and, above all, we have to avoid amalgams".

Other practices adhered to by a small section of the Muslim community are also controlled and condemned through citizenship refusal. Refusing to shake hands at a citizenship ceremony is a ground for refusal of citizenship (*New York Times* 21 April 2018, "No Handshake, No Citizenship, French Court Tells Algerian Woman"), since it is considered to indicate, a sign of a lack of assimilation. However, Social Democratic Mayors in Denmark called for abolition of the handshake requirement as it targeted Muslims (*The Local* Denmark, 12 September 2019). Covid-19 has seen off the handshake and the Western ritual is no longer enforced for public health reasons, Denmark suspending the handshake in April 2020.

UK FACE VEIL

Whilst the face veil has not been the subject of criminal law regulation in the UK, local authorities have been allowed to decide in respect of teachers in schools. In 2007 Aishah Azmi, was suspended on full pay after staff at Headfield Church of England Junior School in Dewsbury, West Yorkshire, said pupils found it hard to understand her. An employment tribunal in Leeds dismissed three of her claims of discrimination and harassment but awarded her £1,000 for "injury to feelings" (see *Azmi v Kirklees MBC* [2007] *BBC News*, 20 January 2007, "Veil row woman challenges sacking"). The position today for schoolteachers is that schools can decide (*The Guardian*, 19 January 2016, "Schools can decide whether to ban full-face veils, says Morgan"). School pupils however have been prohibited from wearing a face covering, as was decided in *R (on the application of X) v The Head teacher of Y School and another* [2007] (see *BBC News*, 12 February 2007, "School head explains niqab ban"). Efforts by politicians, bringing private bills, and far-right campaigns pressing for regulation have failed. In 2013, Phillip Hollobone MP first presented the Face Coverings (Prohibition) Bill as a Private Member's Bill, heard on 28 February 2014 (Hollobone 2013). This was his case. "There is growing concern among my constituents, and indeed throughout the country, about the increasing number of people who are going about in public places covering their faces. It is causing alarm and distress to many people in our country. I have received numerous letters and e-mails, not only from my constituents but from people the length and breadth of the land who fear that the nation is heading in the wrong direction. (Col 569)". The Bill met with resounding opposition. Philip Davies MP, responded. "Does my hon. Friend really want to live in a country where we have the Government telling people what they can and cannot wear, because that is the bit that makes me very nervous about our having that kind of authoritarian state" (Col 570). Lyn Brown MP said: "The Bill is about singling out Muslim women, telling them how to dress, and threatening them with arrest if they do not comply. In spite of the general wording of this Bill, it is clear that it is designed to target Muslim women who wear the burqa or the niqab, both of which cover the face, as a means of religious or cultural expression" (Col 590).

Other Western democracies have also sought to criminalise the face veil/niqab. By 2017, Quebec, Canada had drafted Bill 62 which proposed to ban the face veil/niqab in public place making it illegal to provide or receive government services wearing niqabs and prohibiting them on university campuses or in public places. In November 2017 an application for a stay of a judicial review from the *National Council of Canadian Muslims (NCCM) and Marie-Michelle Lacoste, and Corporation of the Canadian Civil Liberties Association (CCLA) v the Attorney General of Quebec* was filed in the Superior Court to suspend Bill 62. Superior Court Justice Marc-André Blanchard extended the suspension of face veil proposals but in June 2019 the ban was imposed pending constitutional challenge and some teachers, lawyers, police officers and others in the public sphere were banned from wearing religious symbols at work including the Islamic headscarf, kippahs worn by Jewish men, and turbans worn by Sikhs. Now called "the Laciety Act" Bill 21 on November 2, 2020 the Quebec court commenced a hearing challenging the Bill brought by the National Council of Canadian Muslims (NCCM), the Canadian Civil Liberties Association (CCLA) and Ichrak Nourel Hakit.

In concluding this section of the discussion, the impact of such a ban in some countries in Europe is to exclude Muslim women and erase them from the public sphere. Those who defy the ban are forcibly removed from public transport, from the streets, refused hospital treatment and have their face coverings removed by any street vigilante and their safety compromised. The bans may appear neutral, but their impact is not. The legislative history and political context demonstrate the racialisation and Orientalisation of a Muslims as a targeted group. The fears of the campaigning group "ARTICLE 19" that the ban would confine women in the home, exclude them from public life and expose Muslim women to physical violence and verbal attacks has been borne out (Chapter 3). The problem is stated by Burchardt et al. (2019):

> .... justificatory repertoires have become increasingly standardized as burqa controversies are transposed from locally embedded political fields to transnationally structured judicial fields. We suggest that this standardization of justificatory repertoires in the long run facilitates the rapid spread of burqa bans across Europe.

The imposition of these laws makes disingenuous claims to human rights norms, of liberty and equality (see Juss 2015). Yet these laws are the very antithesis, forcing removal of a headscarf in schools, criminalising the face covering on the streets, and forcing the Western style of greeting—the handshake—in a desire to exclude those particular groups who are forced to yield.

STRIPPING FOR SECULARISM—STATE TERRORISM

Banning Muslim women from wearing items of Islamic clothing is one strategy of outlawing and terrorising a group, physically stripping Muslim women in public in the name of freedom and secularism demonstrates the violence of state terrorism. Like the French military who forcibly removed Muslim women's face veils during the occupation of Algeria and the US military who forcibly stripped Muslim men in Guantánamo and Abu Ghraib, during the summer of 2016, following local council official dictat, police in France, as part of "metaphysical" violence and collective punishment for Islamic terrorism, stripped Muslim women. On 14 July 2016, on the Promenade des Anglais, Nice, a truck was driven into crowds of people celebrating Bastille Day, killing 86 people, and injuring 458. Mohamed Lahouaiej-Bouhlel, a 31-year-old Tunisian man, with mental health problems and diagnosed as psychotic, was responsible, although ISIS claimed responsibility. France responded and local bye-law ordinances in 30 resorts across the French Riviera introduced "burkini" bans, prohibiting full body swimming costumes and clothing ensembles of tunics, leggings and headscarfs enforcing a state of semi nudity on French beaches. On 28th July 2016, the local council of Villeneuve-Loubet set legal precedent and anyone breaching the bye-law would be subject on a first offence to a written warning and on a subsequent offence to a fine of 38 euros. Justifying the ordinance, Cannes Mayor, David Lisnard explained that swimwear: "ostentatiously exhibiting religious affiliation, while France and its religious sites are currently the targets of terrorist attacks, could pose a risk to public order". In other words, covering the body (in a way which has become anthropomorphised), and in a way that has become read as a Muslim female signature on a public beach could lead to disorder. The Mayor, rather than preventing attacks against Muslims by imposing conditions on attackers or putative attackers, imposed a clothing curfew on putative female Muslim victims the sight of whose clothed bodies might lead to public disorder. This was a salient reminder of the masculinism of laws that have historically required women to self-curfew and stay indoors and refrain from night travel in order to protect themselves from male violence or otherwise if assaulted then run the risk of being deemed contributory negligent. On 13 August 2016, the ordinance was challenged when the Ligue des droits de l'homme (Human Rights League) and Patrice Spinosi, and M. B. and D, (represented by Sefen Guez of the Collective Against Islamophobia in France [CCIF]) filed an application before the Administrative Tribunal of Nice, requesting the judge to order the suspension of the bans (4.3 of Article 4 of the Order of 5 August 2016 of the Mayor of the Municipality of Villeneuve-Loubet).

On 16 August 2016, a French woman wearing a long-sleeved blouse, a headscarf and leggings, sitting on the beach of the Promenade d'Anglais, was approached by four police officers, carrying guns, who demanded that she remove her "illegal" headscarf, blouse and leggings. This spectacular undressing was photographed and published in *The Guardian* on 23 August, and film footage of the incident uploaded on Youtube (see "French Politicians defend Burqa Ban"). As far as is known no one intervened, no feminist, no French woman, no French man, none came to her aid, otherwise seen to be bystander spectators as this scene unfolded. Similar incidents on other beaches were reported. On 16 August (*BBC News* 23 August 2016 "Muslim Frenchwoman fined for veil on Cannes beach") another woman calling herself Siam was fined 11 euros on the Place de la Bocca Beach, for wearing what police said, "amounted to a burkini". Wearing a headscarf, long-sleeved blouse, and leggings she said: "I wasn't intending on bathing, just dipping my feet in the water". She said that police asked her whether she was aware of the order in force that beach users had to wear "proper dresses" and that she could remain on the beach if she rearranged her scarf as a headband. She refused and was fined. In Cannes, a mother of two was fined for wearing a similar ensemble and issued with a ticket which detailed her dereliction of appropriate beach attire which mandated "an outfit respecting good morals and secularism". Several further videos were uploaded on Twitter showing officers patrolling beaches and waiting for women wearing a burkini (full body swimsuit and head covering or similar) to come out of the water.

"Looking Like an Islamist"

So, what exactly is the meaning of "good morals and secularism"? The French Prime Minister, Manuel Valls said the beach clothing worn by women represented an "enslavement of women. ...the translation of a political project... a counter society....an archaic vision of a woman's position in society". Nice's Deputy Mayor, Rudi Saille drumming up further a "moral panic" (ala Cohen 1980) said that wearing the burkini was a "provocation" and "the feeling of the people is very important when you go to a place if you see an Islamist, or something looking like Islamist on the beach, on the streets you don't feel safe" (*BBC News* 24 August 2016 and *BBC News Hour* "Nice Deputy Mayor: Burkini is an 'Islamist provocation'"). On 22 August 2016, the presiding judge refused to overturn the Cannes Burkini Ban, citing as his reason the French constitution, laïcité, and national security. On appeal to the Conseil d'Etat in Paris on 26 August, the court quashed the order:

> [5] Although the mayor is given responsibility by the provisions cited in point 4 for maintaining order in the municipality, he must reconcile the fulfilment of his duties with the respect of the freedoms guaranteed by the laws. ... It is not the mayor's responsibility to take other considerations into account and any restrictions that he makes to freedoms must be justified by proven risks of a threat to public order...The emotion and concerns arising from the terrorist attacks, notably the one perpetrated in Nice on July 14, cannot suffice to justify in law the contested prohibition measure.

Following this ruling on 29 August, Manuel Valls bit back, commenting on Eugène Delacroix's 1830 painting "Liberty Leading the People". "Marianne has a naked breast because she is feeding the people! She is not veiled, because she is free! That is the republic!" Ange-Pierre Vivon, the mayor of Sisco, the French Mediterranean island of Corsica, said he would not lift the ban following the ruling (Valls 2019 in *Le Monde*). On 30 August, the United Nations Human Rights Office (OHCHGR) in a press statement called on the authorities in all the French towns and resorts that had adopted similar bans to take note of the Conseil d'Etat's ruling. Quite rightly, Rupert Colville, a spokesperson for the Office of the UN High Commissioner for Human Rights (OHCHR) told reporters in Geneva that, public order concerns should be addressed by targeting those who incite hatred or react violently, and not by targeting women who simply want to walk on the beach or go for a swim in clothing they feel comfortable wearing. # *wearwhatyou want*, and Alliance Citoyenne rights report that women in burkinis in public swimming pools are still being banned (https://www.aljazeera.com/news/2019/6/27/pools-in-france-close-after-women-defy-burkini-ban).

The burkini, however, had been around long before this French retributive restriction, and had already had its own polysemic history and political appropriation elsewhere. First introduced in 2005 in Australia, Aheda Zanetti, a Lebanese Australian, designed a form of swimwear that would be modest and would meet the needs of Muslim women who wished to cover and allow their participation in lifeguard and related sporting activities (Hussein et al. 2019: 265; Pfister 2010). The burkini bears a striking resemblance to a wetsuit for diving. Mecca Laalaa, the first Australian female lifeguard when wearing the burkini/wetsuit pleaded "...just because I choose to have a particular style of clothing doesn't make me any different, I am just as Aussie as anyone else" (Fitzpatrick 2009). The burkini's fluidity, polysemicity and changing symbolic meaning and significance is driven by wider events in the French context (the Bastille Day Massacre) and is clearly illustrated, since in 2007 Laalaa and the burkini was featured as "The Heart of the Nation" to showcase Australia's multicultural inclusion. Significantly, eleven years later the same newspaper "was outraged that the Australian Department of Foreign Affairs and Trade (DFAT) had provided sponsorship for the 'Faith, Fashion: Muslim Style in Australia' exhibition (in which Laalaa was a prominent feature)" (Hussein 2019: 88; Hussein et al. 2019: 265). In the US, Conan O'Brien, NBC presenter, introduced the September 16 2007 edition with this remark; "This week, a new swimsuit for Muslim women was introduced called the 'burkini', which is a stylish water-safe burqa meant for swimming. The manufacturer says it's perfect for the Muslim woman who loves to swim, but hates being stoned to death"!

(Fitzpatrick 2009: 8). Marks and Spencer as well as other clothing outlets announced that they would be stocking burkini's in their UK stores. A furore followed. Yves Saint Laurent's, Pierre Bergé, said:

> Creators should have nothing to do with Islamic fashion. Designers are there to make women more beautiful, to give them their freedom, not to collaborate with this dictatorship which imposes this abominable thing by which we hide women and make them live a hidden life.

As Catherine Shakdam, Director of Programs for the Shafaqna Institute for Middle Eastern Studies in the UK, has said, it is: "Absolutely ridiculous that we have to take off our clothes This time we have to take off our clothes to please society to express our republican values or prove to France that we are so democratic". Sheryl Garratt agrees (*The Guardian*, 24 August 2016, "What it really means when we criminalise clothes"), "it seems, it is our civic and moral duty to display as much bare flesh as possible while sunbathing".

CONCLUSION—THE METAPHYSICAL DECIMATION OF THE MUSLIM FEMALE BODY

Mill contends that the only lawful purpose for criminal law intervention is to prevent harm to oneself or others. Justifications for the face covering ban have been framed around national security and the liberation of women. However, the "saving women" rhetoric has now taken second place as a justification for legal coercion yielding to the discourse that: "wearing the veil [headscarf] is a kind of aggression" or an "affront to French values" (President Sarkozy). In recent years justifications have been more openly hostile as society has become inured to anti-Muslim speech whilst the rise of far-right political parties and popularist movements across Europe, who have called for de Islamisation and banning the face veil have become more centrist. Open hostility is condoned coming from the right of centre as demonstrated by the electoral success of far-right political parties such as Front Nationale (Erk 2005). As Moors (2014: 61–62) points out, in the Netherlands, Gert Wilders banning campaign was, so he said speciously, motivated by the desire to free women from oppression. The far-right Vlaams Belang party campaign of 2013, in Belgium, betrays the real sinister motive behind many such altruistic claims (see Chapter 3). In Holland, since 27 June 2018, a face veil applied on public transport, in hospitals and Government buildings. Senator Marjolein Faber-Van de Klashorst (PVV right-wing popularist) called this: "a historical day because this is the first step to de-Islamize the Netherlands". She said: "This is the first step, and the next step is to close all the mosques in the Netherlands". Where the face veil ban has been resisted, women have been subject to the might of the law. In the Mirail neighbourhood of Toulouse in April 2018, a woman wearing a face veil was arrested because she refused to show her face. Her resistance resulted in a charge of "rebellion, outrage and violence on a custodian person holding public authority". Five nights of riots followed resulting in 23 arrests, 76 burned cars and 200 police mobilised (*The Independent* 24 October 2019, "France's niqab ban violates human rights by leaving Muslim women 'confined at home', UN panel rules").

The impact of this is to exclude women who wear the face veil from public spaces, from access to public services and to keep them imprisoned in their own homes, a concern of the United Nations Human Rights Committee (see Giroux 2002). France and Belgium, as other countries in Europe, have become inhospitable places for Muslim women who wish to wear the face covering on the street and in public spaces. Little surprise then that women have made applications for asylum in the UK, though hardly more hospitable! Inhospitable too, for women who wish to wear the headscarf in the workplace, as in some places a corporate masculinist and ethnocentric anti-Muslim dictat disallows it.

Public animosity to Muslim women in speech, rhetoric and abuse (see Chapters 2 and 3) has influenced and shaped the law and infected its neutrality, undermining equality. Politically fluid notions of "social cohesion" have forced assimilation and empowered a sovereign hegemony over diversity in what Martha Nussbaum (2010b) (if I can borrow her thesis from another sphere) calls "projective disgust" which is the reaction of people on the pretext of self-protection. Far-right popularism, as well as liberal politicians through the media have driven this agenda characterised by hate invective, exclusion, notions of "in group" and "out group", nationalism and preserving the "we" which leaks into the mainstream and into laws and judicial reasoning. The treatment of women who wear the face veil or burkini, especially, but also the headscarf find the law is misappropriated to exact a collective punishment on them for Islamic terrorism. The local bye-laws and criminalisation are part of the wider panoply of the domestic WOT through a counter-identity law which defines all Muslims as suspect communities (see Chapter 4).

Women who wear the headscarf/hijab and face veil/niqab burkini, jilbab, long cloak are subjected to discipline and control of their bodies. Theirs is the body of the modern condemned (Foucault 1977: 3). No scaffold, no torture, but a very public condemnation and degradation ceremony (Goffman 1963). The assault on the female Muslim body in this way is an assault on the corporeal Muslim body as a whole and as Fanon (1965: 38) observed, this was the very strategy of the French colonialist, conquering women and their bodies was the route to destroying Algeria. As Kundnani (2007: 139) perceptively points out, in so far as the West is concerned, "Renunciation of one's identity becomes a prerequisite of emancipation".

"Her" resistance is also a metaphysical resistance. Fanon explored the face veil and its metaphysical dynamic through the psychoanalytical concept of "the gaze" developed by Sartre in *Being and Nothingness*. The power of seeing but not being seen. Women who wear the face veil see but cannot be seen. The one who cannot see and scrutinise the other is disempowered and frustrated. The veiled woman will not submit. The West's gaze responds and tries to fix the identity of the Muslim female subject (borrowing again from Nussbaum's concept) in "projective disgust". The face veiled woman returns the power of "the look" and defies. Muslim women's decision to dress is a "performative" demonstration of resistance against right-wing patriarchs and liberal feminists, and what Farris has called "femonationalism", a term she uses to describe the way in which equality and feminist themes have been appropriated by nationalist and neo-liberals in anti-Islam campaigns (4, 115). As Hussein (2019: 133) identifies, with reference to the face covering: "...as the panic over burqa's illustrates this invisibility is widely regarded as a dangerous subversive power that allows women to escape male surveillance and authority".

Let those governments who appropriate the law and secularity and equality agendas to do their political anti-Muslim purpose against women of the Muslim faith and Muslim communities, heed the growing movement as Mona Eltahawy proclaims in her TEDxEuston presentation *My Body belongs to me* (2016) "My body is mine; it does not belong to the state ...."

As I move into the final chapter I take up Eltahawy continuation of this expression of agency "........it does not belong to the mosque, it does not belong to the church, it does not belong to my family it belongs to me".

REFERENCES

Abu-Lughod, L. 2013. *Do Muslim Women Need Saving?*. Cambridge, MA: Harvard University Press.

Achbita and anor v G4s Secure Solutions N. 2017. (Case C-157/15). http://curia.europa.eu/juris/document/document.jsf?text=&docid=188852&pageIndex=0&doclang=en&mode=req&dir=&occ=first&part=1&cid=132173. Accessed 13 November 2020.

Ahmed, L. 2011. *A Quiet Revolution: The Veil's Resurgence from the Middle East to America*. Yale: Yale University Press.

Ahmed, A. 2020. The Clothes of My Faith. In *Its Not About the Burqa*, ed. M. Khan, 65–77. London: Picador.

Almila, A., and D. Inglis (eds.). 2019. *The Routledge International Handbook to Veils and Veiling Practices*. New York and London: Routledge.

Amiraux, V., and D. Koussens. 2016. From Law to Narratives: Unveiling Contemporary French Secularism. In *Multireligious Society: Dealing with Religious Diversity in Theory and Practice*, ed. F. Gonzalez and G. D'Amato. London: Routledge.

Atasoy, Y. 2006. Governing Women's Morality: A Study of Islamic Veiling in Canada. *European Journal of Cultural Studies* 9 (2): 203–221.

Atasoy, Y. 2019. Neoliberalization and Homo Islam Economicus: The Politics of Women's Veiling in Turkey. In *The Routledge International Handbook to Veils and Veiling Practices*, vol. 2, ed. A. Almila and D. Inglis, 9–41. New York and London: Routledge.

Avery, D., and M. Crain. 2007. Branded: Corporate Image, Sexual Stereotyping, and the New Face of Capitalism. *Duke Journal of Gender Law and Policy* 14: 13–124.

Azmi v Kirklees MBC, Employment Appeal Tribunal. 2007. IRLR 434. https://www.bailii.org/uk/cases/UKEAT/2007/0009_07_3003.html. Accessed 13 November 2020.

Barras, A. 2010. Contemporary Laïcité: Setting the Terms of a New Social Contract? The Slow Exclusion of Women Wearing Headscarves. *Totalitarian Movements and Political Religions* 11 (2): 229–248.

BBC News Hour. 2016. "Nice Deputy Mayor: Burkini is an 'Islamist provocation'". https://www.bbc.co.uk/programmes/p045r4hc. Accessed 10 August 2020.

Belcacemi and Oussar v Belgium. 2017. ECHR 655. https://hudoc.echr.coe.int/eng#{%22itemid%22:[%22001-175141%22]}. Accessed 13 November 2020.

Benhabib, S. 2002. *The Claims of Culture Equality and Diversity in the Global Era*. Princeton: Princeton University Press.

Berry, S. 2018. Aligning Interculturalism with International Human Rights Law: 'Living Together' Without Assimilation. *Human Rights Law Review* 18 (3): 441–471.

Bleiberg, B. 2005. Unveiling the Real Issue: Evaluating the European Court of Human Rights' Decision to Enforce the Turkish Headscarf Ban in *Leyla Sahin v Turkey*. *Cornell Law Review* 91 (1): 129–169. https://scholarship.law.cornell.edu/cgi/viewcontent.cgi?referer=https://search.yahoo.com/&htt psredir=1&article=3012&context=clr. Accessed 10 August 2020.

Bougnaoui and ADDH v Micropole SA. 2016. (Case C-188/15). https://eur-lex.europa.eu/legal-content/EN/TXT/?uri=CELEX%3A62015CJ0188. Accessed 13 November 2020.

Bouteldja, N. 2005. The Reality of l'affaire du foulard. *The Guardian*, February 25.

Bouteldja, N. 2014. France v England. In *The Experiences of Face Veil Wearers in Europe and the Law*, ed. E. Brems, 115–160. Cambridge: Cambridge University Press.

Brems, E. (ed.). 2014. *The Experiences of Face Veil Wearers in Europe and the Law*. Cambridge: Cambridge University Press.

Bribosia, E., and I. Rorive. 2016. ECJ Headscarf Series (4): The Dark Side of Neutrality. https://strasbourgobservers.com/2016/09/14/ecj-headscarf-series-4-the-dark-side-of-neutrality/. Accessed 10 August 2020.

Burchardt, M., Z. Yanasmayan, and M. Koenig. 2019. The Judicial Politics of Burqa Bans in Belgium and Spain—Socio-Legal Field Dynamics and the Standardization of Justificatory Repertoires. *Law and Social Inquiry* 4 (4): 333–358.

Butler, J. 1988. Performative Acts and Gender Constitution: An Essay in Phenomenology and Feminist Theory. *Theatre Journal* 40 (4): 519–531, reprinted in Arnot, M. and M. Mac an Ghiall (eds.). 2006. *Reader in Gender and Education*, 61–70. London: Routledge.

Butler, J. 1996. Gender as Performance. In *Interview with Intellectuals: A Critical Sense*, ed. Peter Osborne, 109–125. London: Routledge.

Butler, J. 2006 [1999]. *Gender Trouble*. London: Routledge.

Butler, J., J. Habermas, C. Taylor, and C. West. 2011. *The Power of Religion in the Public Sphere*. New York Chichester, West Sussex: Columbia University Press.

Caffentzis, C.G. 2005. Civilizing the Highlands: Hume, Money and the Annexing Act. *Historical Reflections/Réflexions Historiques* 31 (1): 169–194, Money in the Enlightenment.

Cloots, E. 2018. Safe Harbour or Open Sea for Corporate Headscarf Bans? *Achbita* and *Bougnaoui (2018)* 55. *Common Market Law Review* (2): 589–624.

Cohen, S. 1980. *Folk Devils and Moral Panics*. London: Routledge Classics.

Cover, R. 1985–1986. Violence and the Word. Yale Law School, Yale Law School Legal Scholarship Repository, Faculty Scholarship Series. 95 *Yale L.J.* 1601.

Crossley, N. 2001. *The Social Body: Habit, Identity, and Desire*. London: Sage.

Dakir v Belgium. 2017. ECHR 656. https://strasbourgobservers.com/cat egory/cases/dakir-v-belgium/. Accessed 13 November 2020.

De Certeau, M. 1984. *The Practice of Everyday Life.* Berkeley: University of California Press.

Del Olmo, F. 2000. L.A.'s Latinos to the Chandlers: Que se Vayan. *Los Angeles Times,* March 19.

Du Preeze, A. 2008. Through the Empire's Eyes: Engaging the Gaze. *Religion and Theology* 15: 427–466.

Durkheim, E. 1964 [1898]. The *Division of Labour in Society.* Glencoe: Free Press.

Easat-Daas, A. 2019. The Gendered Dimension of Islamophobia in Belgium. In *The Routledge International Handbook on Islamophobia,* ed. I. Zempi and I. Awan. London: Routledge. Ch. 10.

Edwards, S.S.M. 2007. Imagining Islam ...of Meaning and Metaphor Symbolising the Jilbab, R (on the Application of Begum) v Head Teacher and Governors of Denbigh High School. *Child and Family Law Quarterly* 19 (2): 247–268.

Edwards, S.S.M. 2011. Defacing Muslim Women—Dialectical Meanings of Dress in the Body Politic. In *Rights in Context Law and Justice in Late Modern Society,* ed. R. Banakar. London: Routledge.

Edwards, S.S.M. 2014. "Case Commentary: No Burqas We're French! The Wide Margin of Appreciation and The ECtHR Burqa Ruling *SAS v France*" (application no 43835/11) Unreported, July 1, 2014 (ECtHR) Grand Chamber. *Denning Law Journal* 26: 246–260.

Eileraas, K. 2003. Reframing the Colonial Gaze: Photography, Ownership, and Feminist Resistance. *MLN* 118 (4): 807–840, French Issue.

El Guindi, F. 2003. *Veil: Modesty, Privacy and Resistance.* London: Bloomsbury.

Eltahawy, M. 2015. *Headscarves and Hymens.* Farrar, Straus and Giroux: Macmillan.

Eltahawy, M. 2016. "My Body Is Mine" Ted X Talk. https://www.youtube.com/watch?v=PZmb30fsF54. Accessed 10 August 2020.

Equal Employment Opportunity Commission v Abercrombie & Fitch Inc 135 S.Ct. 2028. 2015. (Sup Ct (US). https://www.supremecourt.gov/opinions/14pdf/14-86_p86b.pdf. Accessed 13 November 2020.

Equal Employment Opportunity Commission v Abercrombie & Fitch Inc 575 U.S. 2015.

Erk, J. 2005. From Vlaams Blok to Vlaams Belang: The Belgian Far-Right Renames Itself. *West European Politics.* 28 (3): 493–502.

Estrin, J. 2010. Unwilling Subjects in the Algerian War. *New York Times,* May 14.

Fadil, N. 2014. Asserting State Sovereignty: The Face Veil Ban in Belgium. In *The Experiences of Face Veil Wearers in Europe and the Law*, ed. E. Brems, 251–262. Cambridge: Cambridge University Press.

Fanon, F. 1965. Algerian Unveiled. In *Studies in Dying Colonialism*. New York: Monthly Review Press.

Fanon, F. 2008 [1952]. *Black Skin White Masks* 2007 (ed). Grove Press/Atlantic Monthly Press.

Farris, S. 2017. *In the Name of Women's Rights: The Rise of Femonationalism*. Durham: Duke University Press.

Feinberg, J. 1984 [1990]. *Harmless Wrongdoing the Moral Limits of the Criminal Law*, vol. 4. Oxford: Oxford University Press.

Fitzpatrick, S. 2009. Covering Muslim Women at the Beach: Media Representations of the Burkini. UCLA: Center for the Study of Women. https://eschol arship.org/uc/item/9d0860x7. Accessed 10 August 2020.

Flake, D.F. 2014. Image Is Everything: Corporate Branding and Religious Accommodation in the Workplace. *U. Pa. L. Rev*, 163: 699–754.

Fornerod, A. 2019. Wearing a Veil in the Context of laïcité. In *The Routledge International Handbook to Veils and Veiling Practices*, ed. A. Almila and D. Inglis. New York and London: Routledge.

Foucault, M. 1977. *Discipline and Punish*. London: Penguin.

Foucault, M. 1978. *The History of Sexuality*. New York: Pantheon.

Francisco Ferrer Brussels university Belgium Constitutional Court ruling on June 4, 2020 (no. 2020–081). https://www.const-court.be/public/f/2020/2020-081f.pdf. Accessed 10 September 2020.

Garanger, M. 1960. *Garanger Photography Algerian*. http://www.gagdaily.com/educative/1361-women-unveiled-marc-garangers-contested-portraits-of-1960s-. Accessed 13 November 2020.

Garanger, M. 2002. *Femmes algériennes 1960*. Atlantica: Atlantica Edition.

Giroux, H. 2002. *Public Spaces, Private Lives: Democracy Beyond 9/11*. London: Rowman and Littlefield.

GITMO Interrogation techniques. 2004. https://www.esd.whs.mil/Por tals/54/Documents/FOID/Reading%20Room/Detainne_Related/07-F-2406_doc_2.pdf. Accessed 13 November 2020.

Goffman, E. 1963. *Stigma Notes on the Management of Spoiled Identity*. London: Penguin.

Grace, D. 2004. *The Woman in the Muslin Mask: Veiling and Identity in Post-Colonial Literature*. London: Pluto.

Grosz, E. (ed.). 1995. *Sexy Bodies: The Strange Carnalities of Feminism*. London: Routledge.

Hale, B. 2019. "Religious Dress". Woolf Institute, Cambridge Lady Hale, President of the Supreme Court, 28 February. https://www.supremecourt.uk/docs/speech-190228.pdf. Accessed 13 November 2020.

Hall, S. 1996. New Ethnicities. In *Critical Dialogues in Cultural Studies*, ed. D. Morley and K.H. Chen, 441–450. New York: Routledge.

Hart, H.L.A. 1984. Social Solidarity and the Enforcement of Morality. In *Essays in Jurisprudence and Philosophy*, ed. H.L.A. Hart. Oxford: Oxford University Press.

Heilman, M. 2012. Gender Stereotypes and Workplace Bias. *Research in Organizational Behavior* 32: 113–135.

Hollobone, P. 2013. Face Covering Bill (2013). https://services.parliament.uk/bills/2013-14/facecoveringsprohibition.html. Accessed 8 November 2020.

Hoodfar, H. 1997. The Veil in Their Minds and on Our Heads: Veiling Practices and Muslim Women. In *Post-Contemporary Interventions The Politics of Culture in the Shadow of Capital*, ed. D. Lloyd and L. Lowe. Durham, NC: Duke University Press.

Hunter-Henin, M. 2015. Living Together in an Age of Religious Diversity: Lessons from Baby Loup and SAS. *Oxford Journal of Law and Religion* 4 (11): 94118.

Hussein, S. 2019 [2016]. *From Victims to Suspects*. Yale: Yale University Press.

Hussein, S., S. Bloul, and S. Poynting. 2019. Diasporas and Dystopias on the Beach: Burkini Wards in France and Australia. In *The Routledge International Handbook on Islamophobia*, ed. I. Zempi and I. Awan, 263–274. London: Routledge.

Joseph, A., and K. Sharma. 2003. *Terror Counter-Terror Women Speak Out*. London and New York: Zed.

Julien, I. 1996. *Frantz Fanon: Black Skin, White Masks*. Film Directed by Isaac Julien, Video Pal Format. San Franscisco. CA California Newsreel 1996. https://www.youtube.com/watch?v=tQhwK0QM1gA. Accessed 13 November 2020.

Juss, S.J. 2015. Burqa-Bashing and the Charlie Hebdo Cartoons. *King's Law Journal* 26 (1): 27–43.

Karaduman v Turkey. 1993. app. no.16278/90. https://www.strasbourgconsortium.org/common/document.view.php?DocumentID=4237. Accessed 13 November 2020.

Khan, M. 2020. Feminism Needs to Die. In *It's Not About the Burqa*, ed. M. Khan, 105–114. London: Picador.

Kingston and Richmond Area Health Authority v Kaur (Tajwinder). 1981. I.C.R. 631 [1981] IRLR 337. Thompson Reuters Westlaw Edge UK.

Kunarac, Vuković and Kovač. 2002. https://www.icty.org/x/cases/kunarac/acjug/en/kun-aj020612e.pdf. Accessed 11 November 2020.

Kundnani, A. 2007. *The End of Tolerance*. London: Pluto.

Kundnani, A. (ed.). 2014, 2015. *The Muslims are Coming: Islamophobia, Extremism, and the Domestic War on Terror*. London: Verso.

Lachiri v Belgium. 2018. ECHR 727. https://www.bailii.org/eu/cases/ECHR/2018/727.html. Accessed 13 November.

Lange, Y. (ed). (2009). *Living Together* (Council of Europe) Media and Information Society Division, Directorate General of Human Rights and Legal Affairs.

MacKinnon, C. 1993. *Only Words*. Harvard: Harvard University Press.

MacMaster, N. 2012. *Burning the Veil: The Algerian War and the 'Emancipation' of Muslim Women 1954–62*. Manchester: Manchester University Press.

Malik, M. 2010. R (Begum) v Governors of Denbigh High School. In *Feminist judgments: From theory to practice*, eds., E. Rackley, C. McGlynn, and R.C. Hunter. Oxford: Hart.

Malik, M. 2014. The Return of a Persecuting Society? Criminalizing Facial Veils in Europe. In *The Experiences of Face Veil Wearers in Europe and the Law*, ed. E. Brems, 232–250. Cambridge: Cambridge University Press.

Malik, M. 2018. Freedom's Fascists: Hate Speech and the New European Far Right. *The Immanent Frame SSRC*. https://tif.ssrc.org/2018/12/21/freedoms-fascists-hate-speech-and-the-new-european-far-right/. Accessed 2 November 2020.

Mandla (Sewa Singh) And another Appellants and Dowell Lee And Others Respondents [House of Lords]. 1983. 2 AC 548. https://www.casemine.com/judgement/uk/5a8ff8c960d03e7f57ecd6d7. Accessed 12 November 2020.

McGoldrick, D. 2006. *Human Rights and Religion—The Islamic Headscarf Debate in Europe*. Oxford: Hart.

McRobbie, A. 2013. Unveiling France's Border Strategies: Gender and the Politics of the Headscarf Ban. In *Current Perspectives in Feminist Media Studies*, ed. L. McLaughlin and C. Carter. London: Routledge.

Meer, N., and T. Modood. 2019. The Racialisation of Muslims. In *The Routledge International Handbook of Islamophobia*, 18–31. London: Routledge.

Mill, J.S. 1869, 2016. *On Liberty*. CreateSpace Independent Publishing Platform.

Moghissi, H., and H. Ghorashi. 2010. *Muslim Diaspora in the West*. London: Ashgate.

Moors, A. 2014. Face Veiling in the Netherlands: Public Debates are Women's Narratives. In *The Experiences of Face Veil Wearers in Europe and the Law*, ed. E. Brems, 19–41. Cambridge: Cambridge University Press.

National Council of Canadian Muslims (NCCM) and Marie-Michelle Lacoste, and Corporation of the Canadian Civil Liberties Association (CCLA) v the Attorney General of Quebec. 2017. https://www.nccm.ca/nccm-and-ccla-launch-legal-challenge-against-quebecs-bill-62/. Accessed 12 November 2020.

Nussbaum, M. 2010a. "Veiled Threats?" *The New York Times*, July 11. https://opinionator.blogs.nytimes.com/2010/07/11/veiled-threats/. Accessed 8 August 2020.

Nussbaum, M. 2010b. *From Disgust to Humanity: Sexual Orientation and Constitutional Law*. USA: OUP.

Patel, P. 2016. No Place for Women: Harmful Practices, Religion and State Responses. In *Women, Law and Culture, Conformity, Contradiction, and Conflict*, ed. J. Scutt, 181–204. Palgrave: Macmillan.

Perego, E. 2015. The Veil or a Brother's Life: French Manipulations of Muslim Women's Images During the Algerian War 1954–62. *The Journal of North African Studies* 20 (3): 1–25.

Phillips, M. 2006. *Londonistan*. New York: Encounter Books.

R (on the application of Begum [by her litigation friend, Rahman]) v Headteacher and Governors of Denbigh High School. 2006. UKHL. https://publications.par liament.uk/pa/ld200506/ldjudgmt/jd060322/begum-1.htm. Accessed 13 November.

R (on the application of X) v The Head teacher of Y School and another. 2007. EWHC 298 (Admin). Thompson Reuters Westlaw Edge UK. Accessed 13 November.

R v D (R). 2014. 1 LRC 629. (*The Queen v. D [R]*, 2013). https://www.jud iciary.uk/wp-content/uploads/JCO/Documents/Judgments/The+Queen+-v-+D+(R).pdf. Accessed 13 November. See also https://www.iclr.co.uk/blog/commentary/further-reflections-on-the-niqab-ruling/. Accessed 13 November.

R v NS. 2012. 3 SCR 726. https://www.canlii.org/en/ca/scc/doc/2012/201 2scc72/2012scc72.html?resultIndex=1. Accessed 13 November.

Ritchin, F. 2008. *After Photography*. New York: W. W. Norton.

Robertson. 2012. *Crimes Against Humanity*. London: Penguin.

Ruby, T. 2019. Discourses of Veiling and the Precarity of Choice Representations in the Post-9/11 US. In *The Routledge International Handbook to Veils and Veiling Practices*, ed. A. Almila and D. Inglis. New York and London: Routledge.

Saadawi, N. 1980. *The Hidden Face of Eve*. London: Zed.

Saadawi, N. 1997. *The Nawal Saadawi Reader*. London: Zed Press.

Şahin v Turkey. 2005. Application no. 44774/98, 41 EHRR 8. https://www.bailii.org/eu/cases/ECHR/2004/299.html. Accessed 13 November.

Said, E. 1997. *Covering Islam*. New York: Vintage.

Saktanber, A., and G. Çorbacioğlu. 2008. Veiling and Headscarf-Skepticism in Turkey. *Social Politics: International Studies in Gender, State and Society*. 15 (4): 514–538.

Samia Belkacemi, and Yamina Oussar. 2012. (see *Judgment number: 145/2012 Belgian Constitutional Court*. https://www.const-court.be/en/common/home.html. Accessed 20 August 2020.

SAS v France. 2014. *Application no. 43835/11*. https://www.bailii.org/eu/cases/ECHR/2014/695.html. Accessed 13 November.

Scott, J.W. 2007. *The Politics of the Veil*. Princeton: Princeton University Press.

Shklar, J.N. 1998. *Political Thought and Political Thinkers (edited by S. Kaufmann)*. Chicago: University of Chicago Press.

Singh v Lyons Maid Ltd. 1975. IRLR 3285 Thompson Reuters Westlaw Edge UK.

Smart, C. 1989. *Feminism and the Power of Law*. London: Routledge.

Stasi Report. 2004. (*Committee of Reflection on the Application of the Principle of Secularity in the Republic*), 1 Dec. Robert O'Brien Bernard Stasi.

Strauss, D.Levi. 2003. *Between the Eyes Essays on Photography and Politics*. New York: Aperture Foundation.

Vakulenko, A. 2007. Islamic Headscarves and the European Convention on Human Rights: An Intersectional Perspective. *Social and Legal Studies*, 16: 183–199.

Valfort, M. 2017. "LGBTI in OECD Countries: A Review", OECD Social, Employment and Migration Working Papers 198, OECD Publishing.

Valls, M. 2019. in Le Monde. https://www.lemonde.fr/societe/article/2016/08/26/le-conseil-d-etat-suspend-l-arrete-anti-burkini-de-villeneuve-loubet_4988472_3224.html. Accessed 2 November 2020.

Viner, K. 2002. Feminism as Imperialism. *The Guardian*, September 21.

Waldron, J. 2012. *The Harm in Hate Speech*. Harvard: Harvard University Press.

You Tube "French Politicians Defend Burqa Ban" CNN. https://www.youtube.com/watch?v=PUn1XyrOEqg. Accessed 2 November 2020.

Zempi, I., and N. Chakraborti. 2014. *Islamophobia, Victimisation, and the Veil*. London: Palgrave Macmillan.

CHAPTER 8

Western Complicity in Non-Western Mandated "Covering"

Introduction

Muslim women's bodies have been a site of political contest, appropriated by governments and political parties for their own ends, by statesmen to justify war and territorial ambition, by right-wing nationalism and popularist movements, by religious factions, by fundamentalist and conservative movements, by communities, and by families, but always by others. Abu-Lughod (2013: 9) says: "I am not alone in raising doubts about the images of Muslim women we are offered in the West. Nor am I the only one to question the connection between these images and the prevailing politics of violence". This final chapter explores this dualism, on the one hand, of political and Islamic forces that have appropriated her body, and on the other, Western representations to save "her" reminiscent of French Algeria of the 1950s and 1960s, and more recently the experience in Afghanistan and Iraq.

Throughout this work, I have, documented the West's presentation and treatment in discursive practices and material effects of the "Othering" of Muslim men, and Muslim women, prior to, and since 9/11, and explored the function of Orientalist ideologies in shaping so-called "knowledge" and the "regime of truth" about Muslim peoples. In this discourse Muslim women have been objectified and fetishised to be saved and liberated from the barbaric Muslim male, and freed if necessary by

© The Author(s), under exclusive license to Springer Nature Switzerland AG 2021
S. S. M. Edwards, *The Political Appropriation of the Muslim Body*, https://doi.org/10.1007/978-3-030-68896-7_8

brute force from religiosity, and if suspected of terrorist sympathies, then to be doubly victimised, disciplined, punished and denied a right of return (see Shamima Begum in Chapter 2).

I have documented the appropriation of the "saving Muslim women" rhetoric by neo-liberals in what Farris calls "femonationalism" to describe the co-option of the discourse of human rights and equality norms as a pretext to legitimate Western foreign policy incursions and territorial ambitions elsewhere, whilst acting as a smokescreen for US and Western empire building in the War on Terror (WOT) (see Al-Ali and Pratt 2013: 7, and Chapter 4). I have demonstrated how male imperialists, including statesmen, politicians and neo-liberals, together with Islamophobes and racists, debase Muslim women, their religion and mock their bodies, using freedom of speech arguments to protect such insult (Zempi and Chakraborti 2014) (see Chapter 3). I document where, hating Muslims has become for some so elided with patriotism that it has been remodeled into a patriotic virtue and for some a matter of personal pride. Polly Toynbee writing in *The Independent* (23 October 1997), speaking of all Muslims said: "I am an Islamophobe, and proud of it". I have documented the domestic WOT, considering the UK experience, describing how Muslim men and Muslim women are the primary targets of counter-terrorism legislation, of enhanced policing and over-surveillance, and subject to profiling as "suspect terrorist communities" (Pantazis and Pemberton 2009) (see Chapter 5). In focusing on the US brand of summary justice, in (Chapter 6), I have detailed the state condonation and use of torture against Muslim men in Guantánamo Bay and Abu Ghraib, and in other places of detention under US military control, in a collective retribution against all Muslims for the terrorist attacks by Al-Qaeda and ISIS. In Chapter 7, I explored further acts of state violence evidenced in the discipline and control of Muslim women, yet another facet of the use of law in the domestic WOT, where, as an expression of the collective punishment of the Muslim community, the exceptional enactment of dress laws perpetrate an assault on the corporeal body of the Muslim community as a whole. This repeated, all-pervasive treatment, condoned at every level of the ideological and state apparatus of one group based on faith becomes impossible to ignore for what it is—anti-Muslim, racialised and Islamophobic. To quote Edward Said once again: "Malicious generalisations about Islam have become the last acceptable form of denigration of foreign culture in the West; what is said about the Muslim mind, or character, or religion, or culture as a whole cannot now be said in mainstream discussions about Africans, Jews, other Orientals, or Asians" (2007: xii).

In this final chapter I consider first the enduring problem of "double colonialism" in non-Western countries and its impact especially on Muslim women. Second, I examine through three country case examples the way in which the West uses the position of women in these countries to its political advantage. My purpose is to demonstrate how the West has appropriated the situation of women in Iran and Afghanistan (as just two examples) in order to exploit the binaristic trope of the civilized West and uncivilised East for a broader political purpose. What is striking is the West's selective condemnation of particular Middle Eastern countries, whilst simultaneously ignoring the human rights abuses and the suborned position of women in Saudi Arabia (my third country example) where here the political rhetoric of statesmen and women talk up this "special relationship", although a rescinding is suggested under President Biden. Third, I explore the ongoing problem of the essentialism of Muslim women, this time not from neo-liberals or right-wing tendencies but within certain strands of feminism itself. Fourth, I return to my overriding thesis which has preoccupied this work and make a plea to end this calcified racism against men and women which is directed against them on the basis of a particular religious belief.

Duplicity: the Bane of "Double Colonialism"

First, a word on the complexity and experience of "double colonialism", the backdrop to my three country case studies. It is well recognised that patriarchy to varying degrees characterises every society, and patriarchy's elision with religious ideology and political forces is certainly not peculiar to Muslim communities. However, Africa, Asia and the Middle East have historically been subjected not only to patriarchal oppression from within their own communities, but also to colonial and postcolonial manipulation from the West, a force which has at times colluded with this oppression, whilst at other times contested it, but always acting in the service of imperialist objectives. This tendency has been referred to as "double colonialism" (McLeod 2000: 175). Bhaba (1994) and Spivak (1998) identify the precise configuration of this experience for the South Asian experience, Saadawi (1997), Ahmed (1992), Al-Ali and Pratt (2013) and Abu-Lughod (2013), examine the specific configuration in Middle Eastern society, particularly as these twin forces have shaped nationalist struggles against Western colonisation. In these liberation struggles women have stood alongside men and been promised equality with men, yet, when independence has been wrested women were often driven back into the private sphere and "retraditionalised".

Rana Kabbani's (1994) *Imperial Fictions, Europe's Myths of the Orient*, for example, demonstrates how, despite nationalism's gains, patriarchy continued to determine woman's lives and opportunities in the public and private worlds, where women living in societies under Muslim law, found family and personal status prescribed and restrictions placed on their social interaction within and outside the home, including their body appearance and dress.

"Double colonialism" continues to have a resonance in the current era, as Western, and especially US foreign policy interventions in the Middle East, adopt a messianic evangelical stance appropriating the agenda of "saving women" aka "Operation Freedom" whilst pressing their "Imperial Grand strategy", in Afghanistan, Saudi Arabia, Iran, and elsewhere (Chomsky 2011 [2003]: 11) either confronting or colluding with these regimes. In this matter, the US and the West has been duplicitous, since this "saving women" has been twinned with a military and economic expansionist agenda which whilst claiming to defeat religious fundamentalism, when it suited, has served to embolden, the very forces that suborn women. Atwan in identifying the real motive in "Operation Freedom", writes: "The West has played a dangerous game in its attempts to exploit radical Islam in serving the interests of their own foreign policy in the region including divide and rule and oil security" (2015: 184, 186, 198), and as a means to counter Arab nationalism (189). Citing John Pilger's findings Atwan writes: "More than 1000, 000 Islamic militants were trained in Pakistan between 1986-1992, in camps overseen by the CIA and MI6, with the SAS training future al-Qaeda and Taliban fighters in bomb making and other black arts. Their leaders were trained at a CIA camp in Virginia" (189–190). US President Bush and former President Trump together with UK former Prime Minister's Blair and May, and now Prime Minister Johnson, are selective in their country condemnation, forging political alliances and "friendships", particularly with Saudi Arabia, and in this particular case, lending support to a regime which has decimated human rights and women's freedoms. Atwan (193) suggests security is one of the motives to explain this selective ablepsia: "The West continues to behave as if Saudi Arabia can deliver the world from the menace of extremism. Yet the kingdom has spent $50 billion promoting Wahhabism around the world, and most of the funding for al-Qa'ida amounting to billions of dollars-still comes from private individuals and organisations in Saudi Arabia".

The UK and the West peddles its "saving women" rhetoric whilst governments continue to sell arms to those regimes which are most oppressive to women (see Chapter 4). On 7 July 2020, the UK government announced it would resume selling arms to the Saudi-led coalition currently bombing Yemen satisfied that a review had been conducted which concluded that any abuses were "isolated incidents" which could be ignored and thereby lift the embargo on existing licenses. Liz Truss, the International Trade Secretary said: "The undertaking that my predecessor gave to the court – that we would not grant any new licenses for the export of arms or military equipment to Saudi Arabia for possible use in Yemen falls away" (*The Independent*, 7 July 2020). This is in contravention of a Court of Appeal ruling in 2019 which declared the sales, illegal, *R (on the Application of Campaign Against Arms Trade) v Secretary of State for International Trade and Others* [2019] (see Chapter 4). On the 27 October, the Campaign Against the Arms Trade (CAAT) issued proceedings for judicial review to challenge the government action in renewing sales. "Double colonialism" takes on a very specific configuration in those societies which operate a cruel translation of patriarchy and where politico-religious regimes have taken control and where Islamic fundamentalist forces and the West through a new guise of neo-colonialism, seek to exercise influence and forge unconscionable alliances to further their interest (Adib-Moghaddam 2013). In resisting Western imperialistic influence, some regimes in Middle Eastern majority Muslim countries have responded by demanding a retrenchment of women's rights (Al-Ali and Pratt 2013: 13) and in this way creating a vicious circle, which then triggers Western appropriation of women's subornation providing it with an opportunity, to position itself as "savior" and so "civilized", once again occupying the moral high ground.

Western Exploitation of Theocratic Regimes

It is important to be reminded that Muslim majority countries governed by Muslim law demonstrate different configurations of theocratic and political power and religious fundamentalism. Religious fundamentalism in some form is also a feature of Christian, Jewish and other faithed communities and societies, which also demand gender conformity and share common features of ultraconservative practices which oppress women (Sahgal and Yuval-Davis 1992). As Saadawi (1997: 93) wrote: "All fundamentalists - whether Christian, Jewish, or otherwise are partners in an attempt to breed division, strife, racism and sexism". We only have to be reminded of the Christian Right's influence in the US, and in Europe, where for example there is unrest regarding restrictions on abortion (Poland 31 October 2020), and in the US, Trump's Executive Order, 13798 (2017) appropriated the ideas of free speech and religious liberty to empower right-wing conservatives and religious organisations who opposed same-sex marriage, transgender identity, and pre-marital sex. Trump's proposed ban on transgender persons from the US Military (see *Jane Doe v Trump* 2017) under Trump was a ban the US was still, seeking to defend.

"Fundamentalism" in general terms, describes modern political movements that use religion to gain or consolidate power and oppress women. As the network "Women living Under Muslim law" (WLUML) and "transnational" and "third wave feminists" have emphasised, there is no single homogenous Muslim world, nor single experience of women living under Muslim laws since: "religious dictates are not timeless truths but, like all cultural practices, expressions of particular historical and social conditions and power relationships" (Reilly 2009: 143). This is important, since of course some countries governed by Muslim laws are not governed by fundamentalism, and covering with a headscarf/face veil/cloak/long dress/gelabaya is not a state enforced practice, nor is dissent from a particular practice of covering punishable. There is no monolithic identity or Muslim "ummah", or community of believers, either (Richards 2017: 128). However, these power relationships whatever their configurations, do share a preoccupation with the control of women's sexuality, their rights, personhood, individuality, bodies, their status and family relationships (Eltahawy 2015: 11).

Women living in all societies under Muslim law may certainly have less rights and freedoms and remain to varying degrees outside international human rights norms and protections. So for example the Convention on the Elimination of All Forms of Discrimination against Women (CEDAW), introduced in 1979, to mainstream women's rights into the human rights framework, has no mandate to protect women in countries that have not signed the treaty. Iran (Shia Muslim) and Sudan (Sunni Muslim), for example, have yet to ratify CEDAW. However, it is an irony, and an example of hypocrisy, that the US for all its "saving women" and "we are so civilized" rhetoric, is also yet to ratify this Treaty. Then, there are countries that have ratified the Treaty, but have entered reservations contending that the Treaty promotes a Western and imperialist agenda and interferes with their sovereignty (Reilly 2009). Adoption of the treaty is: "hampered by the phenomenon of general reservations, which usually take the form of a reference to the reserving state's constitutional law or to dicta of the Sharia" (Schabas 1997: 111). So, for women in many societies under Muslim law, family life and relationships, for example, the custodianship of children, fall outside the protection of the United Nations Protection on Human Rights (UNDHR) (1948) or CEDAW (1979). In Morocco, Egypt, Tunisia, Algeria, Palestine, Saudi Arabia, Kuwait, UAE, Jordan, Yemen, Afghanistan, Iran and Lebanon, the father is the "natural" custodian, and typically, a male child remains with the mother until he is seven years of age when custody becomes the father's automatic right. In some countries a mother's short custodianship can also be removed through her remarriage or her "conduct" (which is subject to a wide discretion) (see Welchman 2016; Edwards 2014).

Where societies are governed by religious conservatism or fundamentalism then the Islamic doctrines of Wahhabism and Salafism emanating from Saudi Arabia, or else a particular interpretation of Shi'ism as developed by the ruling religious clergy in, for example, Iran, is important to consider. Wahhabism is a branch of Islamic thought that derives from a Sunni interpretation of Islam. It has a wide reach beyond Saudi Arabia influencing for example the Taliban in Afghanistan and is an ideology that has been exported throughout the Middle East by the Saudi establishment, assisted by the expansion of extremist mosques, schools and Universities (Atwan: 161, 196). Strict adherence to Wahhabism prohibits mixing of the sexes, and particular forms of personal expression, and requires strict personal observance of shaving, prohibition of alcohol, etc. There is no room for other interpretations, such that Wahhabism treats those of the Shia and Sufi branches of Islam as non-Muslims. Derived from the teachings of Abd'al Wahhab (1703–1792), Wahhabist teachings impress that women should be suborned, remain within the family and the private domain, and keep their bodies covered. Wahhabism is followed by the Taliban in Afghanistan and is also a significant force in Syria and Iraq, and dissent is rooted out, as for example, in the brutal assassination in October 2018 of the journalist Jamal Khashoggi, a critic both of Wahhabism and of the Saudi regime. In this, Atwan (2015: 196) points out: "the House of Saud and Islamic State claim to follow the 'true path' of Islam i.e. Wahhabism". Cockburn (2015) and Atwan (2015) regard Wahhabism as a serious threat to world order as well as to women, and consider that its recent emergence is as a direct response to Western intervention in Iraq 2003 and Syria 2011 (Cockburn: ix).

A further concern is that Wahhabism/Salafism is spreading into diasporic communities across Europe. Phillips in *Londonistan* (2006) may on this be right that "London is a home to the largest collection of Islamist activists since the terrorist production line was established in Afghanistan" (3). What is also significant is that both Phillips and Curtis although from very different positions on the political spectrum, have argued that British authorities have allowed extremist activity to continue with impunity and even less challenged the oppression of women, except in Afghanistan and against insurgent forces in Iraq where condemnation and intervention worked to their territorial aspirations in the region. Whilst the UK's silence on Saudi Arabia suggest incoherence, Alibhai-Brown (2015: 20) points to the oil rich reward as the more obvious explanation: "the British state seems to be aiding and abetting Islamicist obscurantism and ideological reach. The government wants to keep the Saudis and Qataris-both nations home to Wahhabism and Salafism – as 'allies' in the 'War on Terror'.… Their oil and wealth have captured our political classes". Atwan (2015) and Curtis (2018) agree. The primacy of UK economic self-interest is evident in the recent trade agreements on export arms licensing (see Chapter 4). Atwan (192) reporting on this long lasting collusion cites as evidence Margaret Thatcher's remarks when Prime Minister, at a Chatham House meeting in 1994, when she said: "The Kingdom of Saudi Arabia is a strong force for moderation and stability on the world stage".

Afghanistan: Western Exploitation of Women's Oppression, and the Burqa "Chadari"

For all the feigned concern voiced by Western governments about women's oppression in Afghanistan, the West's complicity in supporting the insurgent Taliban whilst pleading for the lives of women is a demonstration of its hypocrisy. The USSR invaded Afghanistan 1979–1989, and the US, to defeat the Soviet forces and retain power and hegemony in the region, provided military aid and weapons to some Afghan tribes. In this way the US supported and emboldened fundamentalism (Deobandism—a revivalist movement within Hanafi/Salafi Islam), and a force the US naively thought they could control, later creating the Taliban. In this, the US was supported by Saudi Arabia and Pakistan (and Osama

Bin Laden, whom the US killed) and the mujahedeen of Afghanistan, who received Western aid from the UK, Pakistan, China, Saudi Arabia and Egypt (Monagan 2016: 30). As Hirschkind and Mahmood (2002) report: "It is striking that even among many of those who came to acknowledge the US involvement in the civil war in Afghanistan, the neat circuit of women's oppression, Taliban evil, and Islamic fundamentalism remained largely unchallenged…. Overall, the US funneled more than $3 billion to the mujahedeen, with an equal if not greater amount coming from Saudi Arabia, one of the staunchest US allies" (342). Financial and military support from Saudi Arabia and the US (united in their "special relationship") to Afghan tribes and the Taliban, enabled religious schools of Salafism/Wahhabism to take further root. Following 9/11, the Taliban had three quarters of the country under its control. On 13 August 1997, Saudi Arabia, the United Arab Emirates and Pakistan recognised the legitimacy of the Taliban government, thereby impliedly endorsing its oppression of women, disregard of Islamic laws of inheritance, denying women the right to property, withholding consent to marriage, and excluding women from public life, from work, from political involvement and from public spaces (Telesetsky 1998). Under Taliban rule women are hidden in what is called the "burqa-chadari", a full body and head covering of ten yards of fabric with an embroidered mesh eye piece to allow women just enough vision to see the path in front of them. This is not a body wrapping of choice, but proof of men's absolute power over women, enforcing a non-person status. Such a denegation (to use Spivak's term) is demanded and part of a broader strategy of dehumanisation.

I set out in Chapter 6 how, the US military divested Muslim men of any individuality or personhood in Guantánamo Bay and in Abu Ghraib, so too, women in Afghanistan under the Taliban are stripped of dignity, objectified, robbed of individuality, where identical attire reduces them to mere objects, things, and releases the perpetrator from the moral bind to treat them humanely. As Emcke (2019: xv) maintains, invisibility is part of the wider pattern into which hatred can be poured. Women's resistance to this Talibanist political-religious patriarchy leads to punishment and death. Amnesty International (2017–2018) reported an increase in cases of gender-based violence against women, especially in areas under Taliban control, including beatings, killings and acid attacks. The United Nations Assistance Mission in Afghanistan (UNAMA) found that armed groups tried to restrict girls' access to education and threatened forced closure of girls' schools in some villages in Farah province.

Women are being stoned to death for having sex outside marriage and a woman was shot dead for trying to escape domestic abuse. When men kill women, they have claimed extenuating circumstances, blaming women's transgressions, and claiming that such killings are justified as "honour killings" (see Cooney 2019; Gill et al. 2014) (see also IWPR's *Promoting Human Rights and Good Governance in Afghanistan* initiative, funded by the European Union Delegation to Afghanistan). As Cooney (2019), Gill et al. (2014) and others recognise, this treatment of women by the Taliban was used by the US as a pretext to invade Afghanistan (see Chapter 4). President Bush then went on to claim the invasion as a humanitarian victory for the "civilized" US declaring that America had liberated Afghan women. Laura Bush demonstrated the visible face of imperial feminism or femonationalism and claimed: "Because of our recent military gains in much of Afghanistan, women are no longer imprisoned in their homes... The fight against terrorism is also a fight for the rights and dignity of women" (Brodsky 2011: 113). Repeating this mantra, Bush in his speech in 2004 on the "State of the Nation", said: "we liberated people... We freed people... these girls.... Our action in Afghanistan fulfilled a word... we keep our word" (Brodsky: 118). Hussein (2019: 3) points out that President Trump's promise to withdraw troops from Afghanistan, was soon reversed, the justification for this change of heart similarly framed around "saving women" from oppression and enforced dress codes. At the same time as the "saving women" rhetoric is iterated, it is reported that Afghan women have been at the receiving end of rape and murder by US troops (RAWA, 2 December 2012). This is the "double colonialism" that determines women's lives. As for the current situation in 2020, the US is withdrawing from Afghanistan and leaving the Taliban in power. Babb (2020) reports that Stephen Lynch, the chairman of the US Subcommittee on National Security, has said of the peace deal negotiated between the US and the Taliban, that it does nothing to protect the rights of Afghan women and girls.

Western Exploitation: Iran—Khomeinist Shi'ism, and the Hijab

It also suits the political and strategic purpose of the US and UK governments to vocalise the human rights abuses of women in Iran governed by Shia Khomeinist fundamentalism, where women are required to cover, at the least, their heads with a headscarf. Khomeinist fundamentalism is a complex product of resistance to Western imperialism, a rejection of Reza Shah's attempts to modernise Iran, and the rise of a religious ideology, where Shi'ite clergy, marginalised under the Shah's regime, have regained power and influence and where Shi'ism represents, for many, a return to the sacred texts (see Arjomand 1998; Mohsen 1994; Abrahamian 1983, 1993; Bakhash 1985; Bayat 1983; Keddie 1993). The West's wax and wane of diplomatic relations with Iran has also been shaped by Iran's support for the Palestinians, and the threat Iran poses to the hegemony of Saudi Arabia (the UK's "friend"). The West, especially the US and UK, has long pinned its colours to a mast of anti-Iranian, pro-Israel/anti-Palestinian stance, and support for Saudi Arabia.

Iran's history, straddling the twin forces of modernity and traditionalism, has been characterised where over the past eighty years by veiling, unveiling, and re-veiling of women's bodies which has been read as a barometer of these conflicted positions (see Shirazi 2019; Sedghi 2007). Moghadam (2011: 141–142) explains: "The unveiled, publicly visible woman was the product of Western attacks on indigenous culture, and the growing number of educated and employed women frightened and offended men of certain social groups, who came to regard the modern woman as the manifestation of Westernization and imperialist culture and a threat to their own manhood". On 8 January 1936, Reza Shah, in a series of dress reform laws intended to mark the modernising of Iran (El Guindi 1999), banned all types of veiling of women including the religious clothing of men. Following the defeat of Shah Pahlavi in 1978, the headscarf was reintroduced as compulsory, asserting the power of the mullahs, of Islamic statism and rejection of Western imperialism. Since 1978, a series of laws have been introduced which have restricted women's lives within the private and public sphere, including dress code requirements. Iran has also entered reservations to CEDAW enabling implementation of its personal and family status laws without outside interference. As Graves (1996) writes: "Iran signs conventions entering reservations whilst at the same time detaining hundreds of women in Iran for wearing lipstick or allowing their hair to be seen in public".

Since 2005 there has been a reversion to Iran's post-revolution position on laws regarding dress, significantly article 196 of the 2005 "Law on Promoting the Culture of Chastity and Modesty", has led to Universities and places of work imposing stricter dress codes on female students and employees. Amnesty International's report of 2012 found that this has led some universities to threaten students who do not comply with the dress code with a ban on completing their studies (see also Report of the Secretary-General 2011). There are further restrictions, and the male guardianship system prohibits single women from travel abroad without the permission of their guardian (Kokabisaghi 2018). Masih Alinijad, who started a "Facebook" campaign of "No" to the headscarf was forced to flee the country for fear of imprisonment. Repression continues and on 16 January 22, 2019, Reza Khandan and Farhad Meysami were sentenced to six years imprisonment for offences of "assembly and collusion against national security", "propaganda against the state" and protesting the headscarf/hijab laws.

Nasrin Sotoudeh, a human rights lawyer representing women who have been refusing to wear the hijab, has been sentenced to an additional 33 years in prison and has had 148 lashes added to her existing sentence, after her March 2019 appeal to the Chief Justice Ebrahim Raisi, failed (Centre for Human Rights 2020). In November 2020 following hunger strike she was temporarily released and then ordered back to jail (https://www.aljazeera.com/news/2020/12/2/nasrin-sotoudeh-iranian-human-rights-lawyer-to-go-back-to-jail). The International Bar Association are amongst many human rights bodies calling for her release, and on 4 December hosted a seminar to discuss human rights in Iran, and the persecution of lawyers, and to launch the film "Nasrin" in which she says, "As long as it (hijab) is in their hands they can decide our lives" (Nasrin 2020). Persecution of the unveiled continues. The West's political and diplomatic condemnation of Iran is further served by highlighting such oppressive laws as these but in this the West manipulates the predicament of the forcibly head scarfed woman to their own advantage pointing to Iran as uncivilized and unstable, with a nuclear potential posing a threat to the entire world.

Saudi Arabia: Wahhabism, and the "Abaya"

My third country case is Saudi Arabia, where, like the Taliban in Afghanistan, the doctrine of Wahhabism is pre-eminent. Women are subordinated in family, personal and public life, there is gender segregation on public transport, parks, beaches and women are forced to cover in abayas (long black robes) and head coverings. In this case, the US and the UK, have remained silent over human rights abuses and its treatment of women, as economic interest including protecting lucrative arms contracts (discussed in Chapter 4) and securing a military advantage and foothold in the region are key objectives. Together, with Saudi Arabia's internal patriarchal control, Western self-interest provides the modern configuration of "double colonialism". Saudi Arabia is extolled as an ally of the West and the "special relationship" is lyricised by US and UK government politicians. Philip Hammond MP, when Secretary of State for Foreign and Commonwealth Affairs, July 2014–July 2016, said the UK would "support the Saudis in every practical way short of engaging in combat" (49). This has included support for Saudi action in Yemen (see Hall 2019). In this regard the Saudi-led coalition has some very unlikely bedfellows (which speak for the complicity of the West) including UK, USA, UAE, Qatar, Bahrain, Kuwait, Jordan, Egypt, Morocco, Senegal and Sudan, Malaysia, Djibouti, and Pakistan who joined the coalition later (expelling Qatar in June 2017). Western government's muteness over Saudi Arabia's human rights record, and the influence of Saudi preachers has left Islamic fundamentalism and extremism, to develop unchecked, which Cockburn says Saudi Arabia funds (2015: 7, 57) accusing the UK of "fantastical" complicity (*Belfast Telegraph*, 15 January 2015, "Saudi Arabia's history of hypocrisy we choose to ignore"). Atwan (2015: 200–201) agrees and says: "The safe and secure exploitation of Saudi Arabia's oil by Western companies requires a stable, friendly and compliant regime. While the US has flown the banner of democracy and freedom over most of its adventures in the Middle East (including the invasions of Afghanistan and Iraq, and more recent interventions in Libya and Syria), it consistently turns a blind eye to the absence of these prerogatives in Saudi Arabia". However, Hilary Clinton, when US Secretary of State in 2009, in a private document revealed by WikiLeaks could not have been clearer when she stated that donors in Saudi Arabia constituted the most significant source of funding of Sunni terrorist groups worldwide (see also Wilson 2017). Whilst the West's relative economic powerlessness may twist its own wrist of complicity there is some, albeit short lived, evidence of moral integrity at least from Europe. On 14 February 2019, the European Union declared its intention to put Saudi Arabia on its blacklist for money laundering and terrorist financing. Saudi Arabia responded threatening to severe all economic ties with the EU. Following "negotiations" the EU proposal was withdrawn. Significantly, the US led WOT à la "Operation Freedom" never targeted Saudi Arabia, albeit that 15 of the 19, 9/11 hijackers came from the region. Nor did it target Pakistan, which played a significant role in supporting the Taliban, in Afghanistan. As Cockburn (2015: 4) points out: "without the involvement of these two countries in Afghanistan, 9/11 was unlikely to have happened". The United Nations Human Rights Council (UNHRC) is bolder and has condemned Saudi

Arabia's record on human rights, signed by 28 member states. Yet only a year after the Khashoggi extrajudicial execution on 2 October 2019, the US rekindled its trade links.

Few speak about women's suborned position (see Gill 2019), or a dress code that requires covering from head to toe. As to Saudi Arabia's human rights record, the country abstained from the UNDHR in 1948 because it conflicted with its version of Sharia law and whilst it ratified the Convention on the Rights of the Child in 1996, it entered reservations: "with respect to all such articles as conflict with the provisions of Islamic law". Regarding CEDAW, Saudi Arabia also entered reservations. Western criticism and freedom of speech comes at an extremely high price and criticism of Saudi Arabia's treatment of women has, in some cases, ended trade relationships (see for example, ATV's "The Death of a Princess" 1980, White and Ganley 2005, Hansard Parliamentary Debates 1980). Further criticism of Saudi Arabia followed and in 2000 Amnesty International called on the United Nations to break the "wall of silence" surrounding human rights abuses and the position of women in a day conference on "Saudi Arabia: A State of Secrecy" held in London (which I attended). During the session on "Women's Rights" (not attended by any Saudi women unsurprisingly), a self-proclaimed male professor of Sociology from Saudi Arabia spoke trying to reassure the participants that his empirical study on women drivers had found that 75% of women who were questioned did not want to drive cars. I asked what had happened to the other 25% of respondents. He retorted: "How would you know about what women in Saudi Arabia want, you have never been there". I had indeed "Been there"! On a field trip in the 1980s I experienced first-hand the banishment of women from public places, their forced invisibility and exclusion. I was unable to buy food from any cafe or restaurant or to find shelter from the 45 degrees heat, or to rest, as shopping mall signs forbade women to sit in the malls. Since then the change that has been reported from Saudi Arabia itself, is window dressing.

Atwan (2015: 199) reports that Saudi Arabia has no written constitution, no elected Parliament, no judicial system, no political parties, very few civil rights, and with an education system that focuses largely on Wahhabism. The World Economic Forum's 2016 Global Gender Gap Report ranked Saudi Arabia, 141 out of 144 countries for gender parity. Some morsels of autonomy have been won. In August 2019, it was hailed as a victory for women's rights that women could apply for a passport and travel alone without being accompanied by a "male guardian" (*International Policy Digest*, 20 October 2019). Amnesty International remains unconvinced, and reports that these reforms lack interpretation and are cosmetic. This title of male "guardian" functions only to control. Aziza Al-Yousef, Samar Badawi with others, led the campaign "I am my own guardian" to challenge the system which requires women to seek permission for everything they do including travel, marriage, and even the permission of their abuser to be treated in hospital when he has physically abused her. The male guardianship system means that women have no access to their passport, or legal documents (see Tonnessen 2016). In 2016, Al-Yousef delivered a petition to the Shura Council, signed by 14,500 calling for an end to male guardianship, Loujain al-Haithloul, Iman al-Nafjan, Al-Yousef and Ruqayyaa al-Mhareb who have campaigned for women to have a presence in public places, including the right to drive, to meet freely in public, to participate in public education, in leisure, and in employment, have been held in prison since May 2018, they, and ten other women, accused of the crime of speaking to the media have been described by the public prosecutor as engaging in: "coordinated activity to undermine the security, stability and social harmony of the kingdom". On March 28, 2019, whilst Amnesty International announced their release it added that charges against them had not in fact been dropped. Amnesty reported that eight of the 13 women activists were temporarily released in 2019, although al-Hathloul, Badawi, Nassima al-Sada and two other women's rights activists remain in prison (Harwood 2020). Unlike the UKs public, political, and diplomatic or military action elsewhere, none of this in Saudi Arabia has provoked any official criticism, even less diplomatic action. On the contrary, Former Prime Minister Theresa May, as other politicians, have said that the UK must leave Saudi Arabia to sort out its own affairs. Under President Biden the tide might be so slightly turning.

Continuing Essentialism and Feminism

The experience of women living in these countries is exploited by the West, not to save, but to press its power and to use women's position as a lever to secure advantage and as an ideological tool to position its own moral superiority. On this moral superiority I turn to address the problem of essentialism, which I have already addressed in Chapters 2 and 3, but here, I address it within some strands of feminism itself. Susan Okin's (1999) "Is Multiculturalism Bad for Women?" claims to speak from a feminist position. It is a text which has had enormous influence within feminism and grapples with the issue of multiculturalism and women's rights and the rights of minorities and asks what should be done when the claims of minority cultures or religions clash with the norm of gender equality. These are profoundly serious questions and certainly relevant given the need to challenge conservative practices within all religious communities. Of course, she is right when she says some practices within conservative communities limit the capacity of women and girls for equality and dignity. She is right when she says this needs to be tackled. But she also essentialises the position of women within minorities as if "culture" is fixed and treats the very worst examples of their oppression as if habituated and more commonplace practice. Her "what is to be done" proposal and solution, is chilling in that she calls for cultural "extinction".

> In the case of a more patriarchal minority culture, no argument can be made based on self-respect or freedom that the female members of the culture have a clear interest in its preservation. Indeed, they might be much better off if the culture into which they were born were either to become extinct (so that its members would become integrated into the less sexist surrounding culture) or, preferably, to be encouraged to alter itself so as to reinforce the equality of women .... (Okin: 2–3)

Saadawi has tackled what she considers as the moral superiority of some feminist academics who she says have excluded Arab female academics. Citing the Wellesley Conference, she writes: "Third World women were invited where mostly US scholars; were interpreting for us our condition, our culture, our religion, and our experiences" (146). Accad (1990) similarly recounts this problem within feminist academia. This moral superiority reflects the core of Said's case as he describes the gaze of the West on "the Other"—the Middle East. In this instance we see it materialise in feminist practice and politics. Saadawi remains concerned: "Liberate yourself before you liberate me! This is the problem. I had to quarrel with American feminists – Gloria Steinem, Robin Morgan – because I noticed that many of them were oppressed by their husbands, and then they came here to liberate me!" (Cooke interview, *The Guardian*, 11 October 2015). As to covering, Saadawi doubts that Western feminism's drive to uncover is always about a concern with her freedom.

   More recently the use of feminist politics in the broadest sense to press a position which is anti-Muslim women is evident in the activism of "Femen" who style themselves as "feminist." In a reductionist interpretation of Islam they have appropriated nudity calling for a "Topless

Jihad" with the logo, "Bare breasts against Islamism!" targeting religious institutions and mosques across several European countries, reifying and fetishising Muslim dress symbols in a way that reiterates Oriental tropes and stereotypes. Bim Adewunmi (2013) regards Femen's demonstration as yet another expression of Islamophobia. Adewunmi says they seem to be saying: "Your bodies are your own – do with them what you will. Except you over there in the headscarf. You should be topless". There is also the presumption that baring the breast is indisputably liberating. This underscores Saadawi's (1997) criticism that Western imperialist feminists have for too long defined the terms of the debate. Such posturing provides an example of Farris's "femonationalism" (2017).

On an international level this moral superiority is also a structuring feature of relationships between third world and Western women and their participation in global issues. Radhikha Coomaraswamy, UN Special Rapporteur on violence against women 1994–2003, has sought to change this: "As Special Rapporteur I sought to develop the argument that women's rights must be asserted in a manner which allows women to be full participants in the communities they choose" (2005: xiii). The privileging of a white socialist feminist discourse within feminism is what Adrienne Rich has called "white solipsism to the exclusion of 'black' and other subjectivities". It is what Al-Ali and Pratt (9) have identified as the latent racism of the British women's movement towards women in third world countries, a challenge voiced by Valerie Amos and Pratibha Parmar (1984) who had already asked why "White Eurocentric and Western feminism" [had] "positioned itself as the only legitimate feminism in current political practice?"

Since the Amos and Parmar question, "Third wave feminism" (see Patel 1997), and "transnational feminism" has emerged giving "Othered" women the space and the platform to speak from their subject position, and to engage for themselves both with the issues facing Muslim women in diasporic communities and as second-generation Muslims, as well as women's struggle in countries governed by religious fundamentalism. Women Against Fundamentalism (WAF), is a consortium of women's groups forging a global alliance, challenge Islamophobia and racism and the essentialising of Muslim communities and the marginalisation of women's issues together with resisting religious fundamentalism and conservatism in non-Western countries and in secular societies (see Dhaliwal and Yuval Davis 2014; Hélie-Lucas 2011: 20; Sahgal 1990; Sahgal and Yuval-Davis 1992; Patel 2011; Hélie-Lucas 2011; Bennoune

2011: 11; Sahgal 2011: 112). WAF has joined forces with women's movements, in Afghanistan, Saudi Arabia, Iran (Rajavi 2013) Egypt (Saadawi 1997; Eltahawy 2015) and elsewhere. These feminist movements share several broad objectives including, a rejection of colonialism, imperialism and neo-liberalism, and building on the scholarship of Said (2007), Saadawi (1997), Benhabib (2004), Bhaba (1994), Spivak (1998) and others (see Chapter 2), challenge the over-deterministic and essentialised representation of Muslim women (and men) and their treatment as a racial category within the West (Hall 1996, 2012). Their scholarship and activism is built on an understanding of the importance of adopting an intersectional consideration of the cross-cutting of race, religion, and gender and other dimensions in shaping Muslim women's disparate experience in diasporic communities together with a critique of mainstream feminism's uniform depiction of Muslim women as victims without agency (Carby 1997: 50; Eric-Udorie 2018; Eddo-Lodge 2018; Khan 2020).

However, there is also a fracturing within some segments of these groups demonstrated in recent debates, for example, concerning the proposed definition by the All-Party Parliamentary Group on British Muslims of the term "Islamophobia" and its general adoption, which has been resisted by the political right and some segments of the feminist left (see Chapter 1). The concern from some segments of the feminist left is that conceding such a term might "privilege [Muslim] victimhood" and also prohibit criticism of the conservative elements within their communities. What is urgently needed is a feminism that considers all women, setting "intersectionality" at the heart of the action and critique, and a feminism that responds to the multiple layeredness of women's experience, as it is affected by race, ethnicity, class, colour, sexuality, gender, religion and other relevant dimensions. As Spivak, in 1988, pleaded,—let the "subaltern" speak! and Carby (1997: 50) demanded,—let her be heard! The writings and activism of Eddo-Lodge (2018) Mariam Khan (2020) and Eric-Udorie (2018) are testimonies to a call to action from marginalised voices, engaging in a trenchant critique of mainstream feminism, tired of being "talked about", "Othered" and subjected to a barrage of "white feminisms" superiority, condescension and misunderstandings. "Why do you wear the hijab?" (Khan 2020: 110) "You can't be a feminist if you are a Muslim!" (108). Little wonder that Khan says, "feminism as we know it needs to die" (113). Eric-Udorie echoes this sentiment: "Organise with us but let us be the authority on our own experience. Don't speak for us we can speak for ourselves" (2018).

CONCLUSION: STILL ORIENTALISED AND APPROPRIATED

The problem of religious fundamentalism and conservatism in Muslim majority countries is very real and so too is the influence of conservatism within second generation or diasporic communities in the West. But these forces have been appropriated by the West to deflect attention away from the inexorable reality and omnipresence of Islamophobia and anti-Muslim racism within societies in the West including the UK and US. So, what needs to be done? This extraordinary essentialism of Muslims and Muslim communities needs to be challenged. Muslim identities, like any, are diverse, different and polymorphic. There are those who consider themselves Muslims, some of whom follow one of the several branches of the faith of Islam and some who follow none. Some are on the left, some on the right of politics, living across continents, regions, localities, each with quite different histories, and different racial and ethnic backgrounds, and nationalities. Then there are the children of a Muslim parent, some who follow one of the several recognised branches of the faith of Islam and some who do not. Some are heterosexual, some are not, some are some homosexual, bisexual, transgendered, all of whom are much like any other community of any other people. There are also Muslims who actively reject the faith "Ex Muslims against Islam". There has also been a return to the faith by many, Marieme Hélie-Lucas (2011: 55) the Algerian sociologist and feminist asks, how is it when mothers and grandmothers were either never veiled or took off their veils do, we now find their daughters and granddaughters veiling? Some of the diaspora, as Al-Ali and Pratt (2013) point out have been created by war and conflict and Western interference. Part of this essentialising manifests in movements to ban women's Islamic dress that come both from right-wing and anti-Muslim forces as well as from those who desire to free women from patriarchy and religious fundamentalism and conservatism. WAF, who favor such legal intervention regard dress freedom (not to wear the headscarf, etc.) as a central aspect of women's rights and call for headscarf and niqab bans alongside those of the far-right of the political spectrum (see Emcke 2019, 66, 74, 98, 101, 123). The indelible reality is that some women want to cover. If they say they do, who is to say otherwise and who is to say that every woman who covers is oppressed or lives in a state of false consciousness? Who is to say that wearing faithed symbols cannot carry meanings other than oppression? (Holt and Jawad 2013).

Especially since 9/11, "covering" in all its forms requires a contextual reading. Hall's commentary on Fanon's writing on the face veil is prescient:

> ... a real insight of Fanon's in that you cannot abstract a cultural sign from its context and that no cultural sign is fixed in its meaning. So, you can't say just because the veil has functioned in the relation between men and women in Islamic societies in this way in the past that it is going to be the same for evermore and always will be. It goes back to some of the interest in 'the look' in what he had written about in *Black Skin and White Masks* [1952], at what is veiled and what is revealed. Women sometimes in the armed struggle appropriated the veil as a way of taking arms from one place to another and delivering explosives. And that was because they could depend on the reactionary reading of the French and they could say a dependent woman is never brave enough to commit that act. So, in a sense they could turn the veil against its meaning return the look in the opposite way. (see Julien 1996 at 39.51 mins)

So, it remains today, that a cultural sign cannot be abstracted from its meaning, and meaning and signification shift in time, place, cultural, religious and political context, and local articulation intersects with gender, sexual orientation, class, creed, etc. It may be the flag of religious conservatism or the emblem of subjugation and oppression, or piety, or culture or fashion, it may be the voice of agency or of political resistance. "... the act of wearing the hijab is far from simple. It is burdened with meanings: oppressed woman, pure woman, conservative woman, strong woman, asexual woman, uptight woman, liberated woman" (Eltahawy 2015: 35, 2016).

Why do others so object? or to return to Phillip's fixation, why is it that what Muslim women wear is so "central to discussions in public life"? (2006: 32), why be troubled about a length of cotton or polyester fabric worn on the head, the headscarf was after all the high fashion, haute couture, of the sixties worn with aplomb by Bridgette Bardot, Jackie Kennedy Princess Grace and today by the Her Majesty the Queen. Why be troubled by the face veil now being re fashioned as part of the bridal ensemble. The core of the objection lies in its assumed meaning and what the Western Occident considers that meaning at any one time to be in its reiteration of orientalist tropes (Said 1978). Such meanings have been "subject to disarrangement and 'symbolic theft'" (McClintock 1995: 67) where Western-imposed denotation continues to Orientalise and essentialise the Muslim female subject inscribing her body and her clothing with a signification, political, cultural and social, "from the social space of the viewer" (Young 2003: 89). Reified, the Muslim female subject becomes the dress, and is objectified as "the hijabi" and "the niqabi". Muslim dress becomes a sign (Yeğenoğlu 1999) but not Hall's floating signifier, since polysemicity is denied in a rigid binarism of imposed meaning either of suppression or terrorist sympathy (Chapter 2). In one moment it is a symbol of subornation and in another a standard bearer of assertion, of power and a visible sign of resistance to Western imperialism, its war on terror and its decadence (Brems 2014; Zempi and Chakraborti 2014). Or is it that the West use its laws to discipline and control because she asserts the right to be different and go against the grain?

Her reasons for covering her head or face are forged historically and presently from the experience of racism, of colonialism, a reaction and protest to the WOT, to foreign policy, to Western supremacy, bearing witness to the accounts of state sanctioned US sadism and treatment of Muslim men in Guantánamo, and Abu Ghraib (Chapter 6) and a resistance to the over-surveillance and targeting of all Muslims under counter-terror laws. Dress may be a strident and visible statement of solidarity with Muslim men and an affirmation of Muslim "identity," however problematic, or an assertion of opposition to the tsunami of hostility Muslims experience at every level of the state ideological and repressive apparatus and from far-right nationalist and popularist groups and from communities and from individuals and groups on line and on the street. Dress choice may be a protest against Western laws that specifically target and prohibit Muslim women's dress or an assertive statement of contest against the seeping creep of counter-terrorism legislation specifically targeting Muslim communities (Chapter 5). There is no one answer, except to say the influence of religious conservatism or religious fundamentalism or patriarchy is but one part of the explanation. Abu-Lughod (2013: 40) in reflecting on this complexity, argues, it is no good simply employing a reductive interpretation of veiling as a sign of women's unfreedom but the concern is that women should simply be free to determine this question for themselves.

The main purpose of this work has been to document and expose the essentialised and malign representations of Muslim men and women at every level of the state apparatus, ideological, cultural and from within popular culture and discourse and to expose the appropriation of these tropes in the service of the state's wider military and political objectives. In this assault men and women of the Muslim faith have been reduced to a singular identity subjected to a disproportionate impact of counter-terror laws and been collectively punished for Islamic terrorism through physical torture in Guantánamo Bay and Abu Ghraib and metaphysical erasure of identity which has especially targeted women's appearance whilst speciously claiming to free her. The rule of law and freedom of speech and gender equality rhetoric has been employed to drive this agenda. The position of women in theocratic regimes is also exploited to demonise Islam everywhere. It is necessary to expose the West's hypocrisy in its selective appropriation of women's subjugation elsewhere as a means of securing a foothold in other regions in pursuit of economic, political and military advantage.

We have a moral responsibility not to take others space, but we also have a responsibility to speak. And in this context the scourge of Islamophobia and anti-Muslim racism must be challenged called out and contested by all right-thinking people. Whether one is Muslim or not, then to apply the analogy Rose's (2013) used in another context, this problem must appropriate us all. This Western racism against Muslims appropriated the late Stuart Hall, and the late Edward Said, and Noam Chomsky, although none of them were Muslim. It is a central concern for Lila Abu-Lughod, Shakira Hussein and many others, it is a racism which must be challenged and contested, in activism, protest, speech and in the written word.

REFERENCES

Abrahamian, E. 1983. *Iran Between Two Revolutions*. Cambridge: Cambridge University Press.

Abrahamian, E. 1993. History Used and Abused. In *Khomeinism: Essays on the Islamic Republic*. Berkeley, CA: University of California Press.

Abu-Lughod, L. 2013. *Do Muslim Women Need Saving?* Harvard: Harvard University Press.

Accad, E. 1990. *Sexuality and War*. New York: New York University Press.

Adewunmi, B. 2013. The Inconsistency of Femen's Imperialist 'One Size Fits All' Attitude. *The New Statesman*, April 5.

Adib-Moghaddam, A. 2013. *On the Arab Revolts and the Iranian Revolution: Power and Resistance Today*. London: Bloomsbury.

Ahmed, L. 1992. *Women and Gender in Islam*. London: Yale University Press.

Al-Ali, N., and N. Pratt. 2013. *Women and War in the Middle East*. London: Zed Press.

Alibhai-Brown, Y. 2015. *Refusing the Veil*. London: Biteback Books.

Amnesty International Report. 2012. We Are Ordered to Crush You. https://www.amnesty.org/en/documents/MDE13/002/2012/en/.

Amnesty International. 2020. Iran: Activist Sentenced to 24 Years in Prison 18 May 2020. #WalkingUnveiled. https://www.amnesty.org.uk/resources/iran-activist-sentenced-24-years-prison-0. Accessed 7 August 2020.

Amos, V., and P. Parmar. 1984. Challenging Imperial Feminism. *Feminist Review.* 17 (1): 3–19.

Atwan, A.B. 2015. *Islamic State the Digital Caliphate.* London: Saqi Books.

Arjomand, A. 1998. *From Turban to Crown; The Islamic Revolution in Iran.* Oxford and New York: Oxford University Press.

Babb, C. 2020. Are Afghan Women Being Overlooked Under Peace Deal? VOA News, July 23. https://www.voanews.com/south-central-asia/are-afghan-women-being-overlooked-under-peace-deal. Accessed 13 November 2020.

Bakhash, S. 1985. *The Reign of the Ayatollahs.* London: Basic Books.

Bayat, M. 1983. The Iranian Revolution of 1978–79: Fundamentalist or Modern? *Middle East Journal* 37 (1, Winter): 30–42.

Benhabib, S. 2004. *The Rights of Others.* Cambridge: Cambridge University Press.

Bennoune, K. 2011. The Law of the Republic Versus the 'Law of Brothers': A Story of France's Law Banning Religious Symbols in Public. In *The Struggle for Secularism in Europe and North America: Women From Migrant Descent Facing the Rise of Fundamentalism,* ed. M. Hélie-Lucas, 11–42. London: WLUML.

Bhaba, H. 2004 [1994]. *The Location of Culture.* London: Routledge.

Brems, E. 2014. *The Experiences of Face Veil Wearers in Europe and the Law.* Cambridge: Cambridge University Press.

Brodsky, A. 2011. Violence Against Afghan Women, Tradition, Religion, Conflict and War. In *Gender and Violence in the Middle East,* ed. M. Moha Ennui and F. Sadiqi, 115–137. London: Routledge.

Carby, H.V. 1997. White Woman Listen! Black Feminism and the Boundaries of Sisterhood. In *Black British Feminism: A Reader,* ed. H. Mirza, 45–53. London: Routledge.

Centre for Human Rights. 2020. *Nasrin Sotoudeh: "If We're Going to Die, Let Us Be by Our Families' Sides",* March 17. https://www.iranhumanrights.org/2020/03/coronavirus-nasrin-sotoudeh-if-were-going-to-die-let-us-be-by-our-families-sides/. Accessed 7 August 2020.

Chomsky, N. (ed.). 2011 [2003]. *Power and Terror Talks and Interviews.* New York: Seven Stories Press, U.S.

Cockburn, P. 2015. *The Rise of Islamic State.* London: Verso.

Cooke, Rachel. 2015. Nawal El Saadawi: 'Do You Feel You Are Liberated? I Feel I Am Not.' *Guardian,* October 11. https://www.theguardian.com/books/2015/oct/11/nawal-el-saadawi-interview-do-you-feel-you-are-liberated-not.

Coomaraswamy, R. 2005. Preface: Violence Against Women and 'Crimes of Honour'. In *Honour Crimes: Paradigms and Violence Against Women,* ed.

L. Welchman, S. Hossain, and L. Welchman. London and New York: Zed Books.

Cooney, M. 2019. *Execution by Family: A Theory of Honor Violence.* London: Routledge.

Curtis, M. 2018. *Secret Affairs Britain's Collusion with Radical Islam.* London: Serpent's Tail.

Dhaliwal, S., and N. Yuval Davis (eds.). 2014. *Women Against Fundamentalism: Stories of Dissent and Solidarity.* London: Lawrence and Wishart.

Doe v Trump [2017]. (1:17-cv-01597-CKK). https://law.justia.com/cases/fed eral/district-courts/district-of-columbia/dcdce/1:2017cv01597/188597/160/. Accessed 15 November 2020.

Eddo-Lodge, R. 2018. *Why I Am No Longer Talking to White People About Race.* London and New York: Bloomsbury.

Edwards, S.S.M. 2014. The Claims of Culture: The Occident and the Orient in Child Custody. In *The 1980 Hague Abduction Convention: Comparative Aspects*, ed. R. Rains, 326–358. London: Wildy, Simmonds and Hill Publishing.

El Guindi, F. 1999. *Veil: Modesty, Privacy and Resistance.* Oxford and New York: Berg Publishers Bloomsbury Academic.

Eltahawy, M. 2015. *Headscarves and Hymens: Why the Middle East Needs a Sexual Revolution.* London: Weidenfeld and Nicolson.

Eltahawy, M. 2016. My Body Belongs to Me. TEDxEuston, January 27. https://www.youtube.com/watch?v=PZmb30fsF54. Accessed 7 August 2020.

Emcke, C. 2019. *Against Hate.* London: Polity Press.

Eric-Udorie, J. (ed.). 2018. *Can We All Be Feminists?* London: Virago.

Fanon, F. 1952. *Black Skin, White Masks.* Paris: Grove Press.

Farris, S. 2017. *In the Name of Women's Rights: The Rise of Femonationalism.* Durham: Duke University Press.

Gill, A., C. Strange, and K. Roberts. 2014. *Honour Killing and Violence.* Palgrave: Macmillan.

Gill, A. 2019. Saudi Arabia's Grim Discrimination Against Women Is Exposed by Rahaf Mohammed al-Qunun's Startling Bravery, January 7. https://www.independent.co.uk/voices/save-rahaf-mohammed-al-qunun-saudi-arabia-women-forced-marriage-thailand-a8715996.html.

Graves, A.E. 1996. Women in Iran: Obstacles to Human Rights and Possible Solutions. *Journal of Gender and the Law* 5 (1): 57–92.

Hall, S. 1996. New Ethnicities. In *Critical Dialogues in Cultural Studies*, ed. D. Morley and K.H. Chen, 441–450. New York: Routledge.

Hall, S. (ed.). 2012 [1979]. *Representation: Cultural Representations and Signifying Practices.* London: Sage.

Hall, R. 2019. Yemen War: UK-Backed Bombing Campaign Has Killed More Than 8,000 Civilians. *The Independent*, March 26.

Hansard Parliamentary Debates. 1980. https://hansard.parliament.uk/Lords/1980-04-24/debates/fde1fc1d-d9c6-43d0-86e0-131e93ce1dcb/SaudiArabia. Accessed 7 August 2020.

Harwood, A. 2020. Exclusive: Sister of Jailed Saudi Activist Loujain al-Hathloul Speaks Out After Trial Postponed by Coronavirus. *The New Arab*, March 24. https://english.alaraby.co.uk/english/indepth/2020/3/24/exclusive-loujain-al-hathlouls-sister-speaks-out-after-trial-postponed. Accessed 7 August 2020.

Hélie-Lucas, M. 2011. How Fundamentalism and Its Values and Programme Have Entered the UN. In *The Struggle for Secularism in Europe and North America: Women from Migrant Descent Facing the Rise of Fundamentalism*, ed. M. Hélie-Lucas, 275–281. London: WLUML.

Hirschkind, C. and S. Mamood. 2002. Feminism, the Taliban, and Politics of Counter-Insurgency. *Anthropological Quarterly* 75 (2, Spring): 339–354.

Holt, M., and H. Jawad. 2013. *Women, Islam, and Resistance in the Arab World*. Colorado: Lynne Reiner Publishers.

Hussein, S. 2015 [2019]. *From Victims to Suspects: Muslim Women Since 9/11*. Sydney: UNSW Press.

Julien, I. 1996. *Fanon: Black Skin, White Mask*/Directed by Isaac Julien (Video Pal Format). https://www.youtube.com/watch?v=tQhwK0QM1Ga. Accessed 7 August 2020.

Kabbani, R. 1994. *Imperial Fictions: Europe's Myths of the Orient*. London: Pandora.

Keddie, N. 1993. Iranian Revolutions in Comparative Perspective. In *The Modern Middle East*, ed. A. Hourani, P. Khoury, and M. Wilson. Berkeley, CA: University of California Press.

Khan, M. (ed). 2020. It's not about the Burqa. London: Pan Macmillan.

Kokabisaghi, F. 2018. The Role of the Male Guardian in Women's Access to Health Services in Iran. *International Journal of Law, Policy and the Family* 32 (2): 230–249.

McClintock, A. 1995. *Imperial Leather*. London: Routledge.

McLeod, J. 2000. *Beginning PostColonialism*. Manchester: Manchester University Press.

Moghadam, V. 2011. Religious-Based Violence Against Women, and Feminist Responses; Iran, Afghanistan, and Algeria. In *Gender and Violence in the Middle East*, ed. M. Ennji and F. Sadiqi, 141–152. London: Routledge.

Mohsen, M.M. 1994. *The Making of Iran's Islamic Revolution: From Monarchy to Islamic Republic*. New York: Westview Press.

Monagan, S. 2016. *On War and Women: Operation Enduring Freedom's Impact on the Lives of Afghan Women*. Lulu.com.

Okin, S.M. 1999. Is Multiculturalism Bad for Women? In *Is Multiculturalism Bad for Women*, ed. J. Cohen, M. Howard, M.C. Nussbaum. Princeton: Princeton University Press.

Pantazis, C., and S. Pemberton. 2009. From the 'Old' to the 'New' Suspect Community Examining the Impacts of Recent UK Counter-Terrorist Legislation. *British Journal of Criminology* 49 (5): 646–666.

Patel, P. 1997. Third Wave Feminism and Black Women's Activism. In *Black British Feminism: A Reader*, ed. H. Mirza, 255–268. London: Routledge.

Patel, P. 2011. Cohesion, Multi-Faithism and Erosion of Secular Spaces in the UK: Implications for the Human Rights of Minority Women. In *The Struggle for Secularism in Europe and North America: Women from Migrant Descent Facing the Rise of Fundamentalism*, ed. M. Hélie-Lucas, 127. London: WLUML.

Phillips, M. 2006. *Londonistan: How Britain Is Creating a Terror State Within*. London: Encounter Books.

R (on the application of Campaign against Arms Trade) v Secretary of State for International Trade and others [2019] EWCA Civ 1020. https://www.jud iciary.uk/publications/campaign-against-the-arms-trade-v-the-secretary-of-state-for-international-trade-and-others/. Accessed 13 November 2020.

Rajavi, M. 2013. *Women Against Fundamentalism*. Berkeley, CA: Seven Locks Press.

RAWA. 2012, December 2. http://rawa.org/temp/runews/2012/12/26/us-special-forces-accused-of-raping-afghan-women-during-raid.html. Accessed 13 November 2020.

Reilly, N. 2009. *Women's Human Rights*. London: Polity.

Report of the Secretary-General. 2011. *The Situation of Human Rights in the Islamic Republic of Iran*. United Nations General Assembly Sixty-Sixth Session Item 69 (c) of the Provisional Agenda* Promotion and Protection of Human Rights: Human Rights Situations and Reports of Special Rapporteurs and Representatives, September 2011.

Richards, J. 2017. *Extremism, Radicalization and Security*. London: Palgrave Macmillan.

Rose, J. (2013). *Jacqueline Rose on Zionism, Freud, Sylvia Plath and more*. Melbourne Writers Festival 2013 in a series of events from the London Review of Books. https://www.youtube.com/watch?v=D-qyuEBL0-o. Accessed 11 November 2020.

Saadawi, N. 1997. *The Nawal Saadawi Reader*. London: Zed Press.

Sahgal, G. 1990. Fundamentalism and the Multi-Culturalist Fallacy. In *Against the Grain*. Southall: Southall Black Sisters.

Sahgal, G. 2011. The Question Asked About Satan; Doubt, Dissent, and Discrimination in 21st-Century Britain. In *The Struggle for Secularism in*

Europe and North America: Women from Migrant Descent Facing the Rise of Fundamentalism, ed. M. Hélie-Lucas, 109–126. London: WLUML.

Sahgal, G., and N. Yuval-Davis (eds.). 1992. *Refusing Holy Orders: Women and Fundamentalism in Britain*. London: Virago.

Said, E. 1978. *Orientalism*. London: Penguin.

Said, E. 2007 [1997]. *Covering Islam*. London: Vintage.

Schabas, W. 1997. Reservations to the Convention on the Elimination of All Forms of Discrimination: Against Women and the Convention on the Rights of the Child. *William and Mary Journal of Women and the Law* 3: 79. http://scholarship.law.wm.edu/wmjowl/vol3/iss1/4. Accessed 7 August 2020.

Sedghi, H. 2007. *Women and Politics in Iran: Veiling, Unveiling, and Reveiling*. Cambridge: Cambridge University Press.

Shirazi, F. 2019. Iran's Compulsory Hijab: From Politics and Religious Authority to Fashion Shows. In *The Routledge International Handbook to Veils and Veiling Practices*, ed. A. Almila and D. Inglis, 97–113. New York and London: Routledge.

Spivak, G. 1988. Can the Subaltern Speak? In *Marxism and the Interpretation of Culture*, ed. C. Nelson and L. Grossberg, 271–313. Illinois: University of Illinois Press.

Spivak, G. 2006 [1998]. *In Other Worlds*. London: Routledge.

Telesetsky, A. 1998. In the Shadows and Behind the Veil: Women in Afghanistan Under the Taliban Rule. *Berkeley Women's Law Journal* 13: 293–305.

Tonnessen, L. 2016. *Women's Activism in Saudi Arabia: Male Guardianship and Sexual Violence*. Bergen: Chr. Michelsen Institute.

Welchman, L. 2016. A Historiography of Islamic Family Law. In *The Oxford Handbook of Islamic Law*, ed. M. Emon and R. Ahmed. Oxford: Oxford University Press.

White, T. and G. Ganley. 2005. The Death of a Princess Controversy. https://www.pbs.org/wgbh/pages/frontline/shows/princess/reflect/harvard.html. Accessed 7 August 2020.

Wilson, T. 2017. *Foreign Funded Islamist Extremism in the UK*. Centre for the Response to Radicalisation and Terrorism, Research Paper No. 9.

Yeğenoğlu, M. 1999. *Colonial Fantasies: Towards a Feminist Reading*. Cambridge: Cambridge University Press.

Young, R. 2003. *Postcolonialism*. Oxford: Oxford University Press.

Zempi, I., and N. Chakraborti. 2014. *Islamophobia, Victimisation, and the Veil*. London: Palgrave Macmillan.

Index

© The Editor(s) (if applicable) and The Author(s), under exclusive license to Springer Nature Switzerland AG 2021
S. S. M. Edwards, *The Political Appropriation of the Muslim Body*, https://doi.org/10.1007/978-3-030-68896-7